Heritage Eaters

HERITAGE EATERS

Insects & Fungi in Heritage Collections

MARY-LOU FLORIAN

Published by James & James (Science Publishers) Ltd,
8–12 Camden High Street, London NW1 0JH, UK

First published 1997
Moved to print on demand 2002

A catalogue record for this book is available from the British Library

ISBN 1 873936 49 4

Printed in the UK by Antony Rowe Ltd (Eastbourne)

Contents

This book is dedicated to our heritage objects.
Like ourselves they too are dust and unto dust they will return.
However, I hope this book will help slow down the process.

For my grandchildren, Molley, Joey and Katelyn

1

Introduction

THE COLLECTION FRENZY

The 19th-century enthusiasm for collecting heritage objects, both cultural and natural history items, has left us many problems. Never before have such large numbers of objects been brought together to be preserved – forever.

Objects of curiosity from around the world were collected first, then artifacts from archaeological excavations, and nowadays objects of our own natural and cultural heritage. The collecting phenomenon has been driven by our inherent curiosity, our quest for knowledge of the world, our cultural aesthetic values and our need to connect personally with our past.

Our first collections from the ancient world, archaeological objects, were mostly inorganic in nature and were not at risk from biodeterioration by insects and fungi. Once objects made from organic materials were stored in large collections, difficulties emerged. With manuscripts, documents and books stored in monasteries and libraries, biodeterioration problems became rampant. Now, the greatest threat is to natural history specimens collected to record today's biodiversity.

We are no longer satisfied with just looking at objects. We want heritage buildings and sites saved and often the objects in them used, or at least their use demonstrated, as in eco-museums. Keeping items in storage and on display involves certain types of problem, but objects used in open areas present others.

How can large collections, which are so vulnerable to insect and fungal deterioration, be protected, not only in storage and on display, but also in use?

The compelling answer to biodeterioration problems in heritage collections is prevention.

PROTECTION FROM INSECT AND FUNGAL HERITAGE EATERS: THE PREVENTIVE APPROACH

Cosmopolitan nature of insect and fungal pests

In reviewing the literature, one sees that there are only a few common insect pests found in museums, or in our homes. The species are cosmopolitan, occurring in museums all over the globe. There are some specific species in each environment, but the genera are represented worldwide. The insect species are those which seem to have become dependent on people and their life style, living in their environments and off their food materials. They often take advantage of the human habit of storing food, as well as heritage objects.

A summary from around the world of the fungi found on heritage objects also reveals many species in common. Four genera (*Alternaria*, *Aspergillus*, *Cladosporium* and *Penicillium*) are found on all objects and in the air worldwide. This supports a common origin for the fungi contaminating heritage objects: coming from airborne conidia during fabrication or during use. They are rarely substrate specific.

Prevention and eradication methods are cosmopolitan

The methods of prevention and eradication used against all the insect species are basically the same. When we encounter a clothes moth infestation, the eradication and prevention methods are the same no matter whether it is *Tineola bisselliella*, the webbing clothes moth, *Tinea pellionella*, the case-making moth or *Trichophaga tapetzella*, the tapestry moth. Our methods against *Anthrenus verbasci*, the varied carpet beetle, *Dermestes lardarius*, the larder beetle, *Attagenus megatoma*, the black carpet beetle, or *Anthrenus scrophulariae*, the common carpet beetle, are as for the moths.

The control of fungal problems is also the same all over the world. Fungi need a special environment for growth. A preventive approach identifies such an environment, whether a microenvironment like a drawer, or a macroenvironment like a whole room, and controls it to prevent fungal development.

Identification of the species

We are rightly interested in the identification of the heritage-eating insects and fungi and carefully document this information, but usually the identification comes after the treatment.

A permanent record of the activity of problem insects will be revealed if new species have presented themselves or if previously documented species have disappeared, increased, etc. Entomologists are interested in distribution of species in nature: we are interested in the distribution of insect pests inside a building.

Fungi may present a health hazard, so, in some cases where there is a massive infestation, species identification should be documented. Professional advice should be sought in these cases: the health of yourself, staff and the public should never be compromised.

Materials of heritage objects

We are striving together to protect our heritage objects, no matter whether they are documents (ancient parchment, palm leaf or paper), woollen textiles, wooden sculptures or insect collections. Heritage objects are unique to the cultures in which they were created but fundamentally they all have the same materials and potential pests. These objects share, besides their attacking insects and fungi, the materials constituting them, primarily proteins, fats and cellulose, which are as cosmopolitan as the organisms consuming them. Biodeterioration of heritage objects is a universal problem with common parameters.

The microenvironment

It is essential, but on its own not enough, to control the temperature and moisture in the air of a room. This is a macroenvironment. Insects and fungi are always in little microenvironments (unless, for example, there has been a disaster and everything is wet). It is these microenvironments we are looking for in inspecting entire collections or a few drawers. It is the moisture and nutrient content of the material that is critical for the survival of insects and fungi. So, besides controlling the macroenvironment, we must find and solve the problems of the microenvironments.

Control methods

It is interesting to look at the historical development of the pest control measures. The earliest methods of protection were isolation and individual protection of objects, which were stored in special containers, such as cedar chests, sometimes using natural pesticides in the form of, for example, aromatic plants or woods.

Grain was first stored in airtight buried chambers or underground silos. The insects and fungi present soon consumed the oxygen. The resultant anoxic environment prevented any further biodeterioration.

The burial chambers in pyramids, in which precious funerary objects were preserved, may also have been oxygen-free. Today, anoxic environments developed by controlling the amounts of the atmospheric gases in airtight containers are being tested for eradication andcontrol of infestations of heritage objects.

When the technology of synthetic pesticides, insecticides and fungicides developed, they were hailed as the panacea to all biodeterioration problems and widely used. We all, however, know the story of DDT, and it is important to understand the abnormal reverence we gave these substances. They certainly killed the pests, but we never considered the hazard to the object, to ourselves or to the environment. Methods are changing, because of our growing awareness of the influence of the chemicals at these separate levels. We are using methods that are 'environmentally friendly' and are not health hazards, but we have not thoroughly researched their influence on heritage objects' materials. New methods of control must be questioned and full answers obtained before they are brought into use.

TECHNOLOGY TRANSFER

We are always searching for methods, such as biological control, that will cause populations of insects to disappear. We look to the stored food, forestry and agriculture industries and their development of such techniques. 'Because it works for the orchards and warehouses, it must work for us', is the attitude to this technology transfer.

The main difference with our situation is that we have to eliminate every last one of the insects causing damage to our objects, whereas in other areas all they strive for is a reduction in the insect pest population, never hoping or aiming for complete eradication.

Using pheromones is an example of jumping on a technology bandwagon. These chemicals are of great value in forestry and agriculture but can also cause many problems, as they do in food storage. They attract insects that prey on the target insect and can also bring in the target species from other territories. Using pheromones for control in our field would require much more knowledge and assurance.

Time

Another driving force in our control activities is time. We all want a quick fix: methods of prevention and eradication that do not take too long.

An integrated insect pest control programme involves time and dedication. We must get beyond 'mass treatment syndrome' and realize that the object for which we have taken ethical responsibility often needs personal attention. Sometimes, for example, large numbers of objects can be treated together for eradication of active insect infestation but then the follow-up cleaning of all the insect remains requires dedication to each individual item. This is essential because it is the only way, at a later date, to tell if the treatment was successful or if the object has become infested once again.

Time is also required to assess the storage site in which an insect infestation has been found. It must be determined why the infestation occurred, where the insects came from, why there is a habitat for them there and how to prevent reinfestation. Time is needed to undertake inspections and monitor collections on a continuous basis.

Prevention is essential. Initially it takes a lot of personal time to eradicate infestations, survey storage areas and design methods of prevention but, once it is done, a preventive regime is easy to maintain and is not so time-consuming. Even in the tropics, where massive infestations may occur, preventive measures can solve the problem, as long as all the basic work is done to reach the stage of implementing the prevention programme.

Ethical responsibility to heritage objects

An owner or other person caring for heritage objects has an ethical responsibility to be sure that any treatment undertaken on an object will not destroy its aesthetic or physical integrity, cause any permanent deterioration or compromise its research potential. Conservators, who usually undertake treatments such as cleaning and freezing, are professionally bound by their code of ethics. For collection managers and curators there are also codes of ethics and elements in job descriptions explaining this ethical responsibility. Heritage objects cannot be used for treatment research. It is not acceptable to expose them to treatments (including those available commercially or proved in other fields), before these have been thoroughly researched, to ensure that they can cause no harm. A Victorian dancing slipper is not the same as a new shoe.

Countering mind-sets

Objectivity is important in presenting information. An obstacle to achieving this is unawareness of entrenched mind-sets, which, unexamined, can cause fundamental problems. Most museum pest control publications, for example, have full biological details and wonderful illustrations of the adult insect but nothing on the larva, the heritage-eating machine. This is the result of a mind-set. Another example is found with environmental monitoring. We do an excellent job of monitoring the air, but must realize that it is in the microenvironment, which includes the material of the object and its moisture content, that the problem lies. In discussing fungal problems, we consider the environment that is conducive to the vegetative growth of the fungus, but tend to overlook the germination of the conidia that initiates infestations and it is this we should be concerned about – another mind-set. A final example is our cultural need to identify emotionally with the heritage items in our care, but we thus fail to treat them as compositions of organic materials. In facing, as we must, the challenges posed by their materials, in no way do we forget the preciousness of the objects and our ethical responsibility towards them.

THIS BOOK'S CONTRIBUTION

The book's subject is the problems that insect and fungi pests present to those keeping heritage objects in a variety of storage areas – museums, historic buildings and homes – and its goal is to provide the information necessary to solve these problems. Because each collection, with its environment, is unique, standard procedures cannot be recommended. A broad understanding of all the parameters – the heritage eaters, material of the heritage object, environment of the storage area, extent of the infestation, nature of the collection and staff availability – is needed to design treatments and preventive procedures that will ensure the objects have the protection they require. Readers are encouraged to develop procedures for their specific problems.

The book is arranged within its major sections on insect and fungal heritage eaters into discrete units, or chapters, each of which stands alone with its own references.

Following the introduction is a review of pertinent information on environmental parameters and their influence on the insects and fungi. The emphasis is on the moisture in the materials of heritage objects, because of its major contribution to the support of the organisms.

An introduction to insect classification and life cycle patterns related to the insect species commonly encountered in infestations of heritage objects illustrates the taxonomic relationships of this small group of insects.

The physiology of insects is a gigantic topic. This book is not intended to be a biology text book, thus only two aspects of physiology are discussed as separate units, the tracheal and exoskeleton system. These two are reviewed because of their importance in reference to eradication methods which directly influence these life-dependent systems. The two systems are the most vulnerable to damage and are the most important systems for survival because they maintain necessary oxygen and body water.

Chapters on the egg, larva and pupa of the beetle and moth, review their structure, identification, physiology and biology which is pertinent to identification of and understanding prevention and eradication of insect problems.

The nymphs and their adults are presented separately because, unlike the beetles and moths, they do not have larval and pupal stages. They live separately from where they feed and their presence indicates building environmental problems. Termites are not discussed in detail in this book. The fact that the city of Palermo in Sicily is built on a termite colony illustrates the enormity of the problem. Termites are essentially a building problem but free-standing objects that are infested are included in the discussion on wood beetle damage.

Information on adult beetles and moths is presented in reference to monitoring methods, because it is this life stage which is captured in the monitoring traps. Information on the monitoring methods is discussed in reference to the physiological responses, light wave sensitivity and pheromone production of the target adults. The pros and cons and suggestions of use are presented.

A chapter on the insect infestation presents information on how to inspect heritage objects in order to find the infestation. Procedures for enclosing and moving the infestation so as to prevent its spreading and eradication treatments are suggested. Analyses of evidence of insect activity is presented to assist in identifying the causative insect.

A thorough review of eradication methods' (temperature extremes, anoxic environments and others) influence on the insect and the heritage object material is presented. This information is essential because the treatments are interventive treatments.

Information on how to establish an integrated insect pest control programme, a preventive programme, is presented. The programme can be designed for a chest of drawers or a museum storage area. The approach is the same but specific procedures must be developed for each unique space. The reader is encouraged to develop procedures for their specific problem. An example of a programme is presented as well as the real-life difficulties often encountered when establishing a preventive programme.

The first chapter on the fungi gives a simple description of their life cycle. The cosmopolitan nature of the conidial fungi which produce the surface growth on heritage objects is illustrated. The importance of the conidia is emphasised, in reference to causing fungal spots or infestations. The physiology of the breaking of the dormancy of the conidia, activation, is discussed in reference to the potential activation by conservation treatments as well as by moisture or inherent chemicals in the material.

The environmental factors, their influence on the moisture in materials and the state and availability of the water to the conidia and vegetative growth of a fungal colony is reviewed.

A new approach to analysis of fungal infestations is presented in the chapter on the manifestation of the fungal growth and its relationship to the methods of containment. The fungal infestation is also looked at in reference to what is actually present in the infestation: the fungal structures as well as their chemical make up and the metabolic products of vegetative growth.

Eradication methods are discussed in reference to their success and their effect on the organisms and the materials of the heritage object.

Suggestions of removal of fungal infestations or collection recovery, pros and cons of degree of success, influence on the organism and materials of the object and health hazards is outlined. The importance of preparedness in the event of disasters which result in extensive fungal infestations is emphasised.

Again the goal of the book is to give the reader the information and the encouragement to pursue information which is required to undertake logical eradication and preventive measures against the heritage eaters, insect and fungal pests.

PREVENTION FOR THE FUTURE

The information in this book provides just a taste of the state of current knowledge. We know a great deal, but there remains much to be discovered. In the future treatment and storage methods for heritage objects may change radically but, in the meantime, prevention is the key to protecting heritage objects from biodeterioration.

2

Environmental Parameters: their Relevance in Fungal and Insect Activity

The purpose of this chapter is to introduce the basic concepts relating to environmental parameters – radiation, light and temperature; the water in air and relative humidity (RH); the water in materials and equilibrium moisture content (EMC) of materials; interactions between RH and EMC and dust, and to emphasize the relevant aspects influencing fungal and insect activity.

2.1 MACROENVIRONMENTS AND MICROENVIRONMENTS

The environment in a room is a macroenvironment, of which the ambient air is the major component. We usually monitor the temperature and RH of the ambient air in rooms and feel complacent. But there are many microenvironments or local areas, around, in and on heritage objects, such as drawers, boxes, bottom shelves, the lowest piece of paper in a pile, in which the environmental parameters vary from the ambient macroenvironment. The importance of microenvironments is often overlooked but they have a major influence on the behaviour and life cycle of insect and fungal pests, as well as on the organic materials of the objects. Nearly all insect and fungal activity in museums and in homes occurs in microenvironments. Only when there is a major macroenvironmental breakdown or disaster, or when an initial infestation is neglected, is a whole room or large area involved.

2.2 RADIATION EFFECTS

2.2.1 The light of light

Light in our homes and museums comes from the sun and from light bulbs. Light is made up of high-energy radiation consisting of photons, which move in a wave. Photons have different wavelengths (Table 2.1). Brill (1980) showed the size relationship of this radiation and conversion factors for other units of length (Table 2.2). The shorter the wavelength, the stronger the energy of the photon. We can see only wavelengths of 400–700nm, the visible light, but our bodies respond to the

Table 2.1. Molecular events induced by various wavelengths of radiation (Brill, 1980).

Wavelength	Frequency (Hz)	Region name	Response of atoms and molecules
(3×10^8)–(3×10^5)m	1–10^3	Power	None
(3×10^5)–300m	10^3–10^6	Audio	None
300–3m	10^6–10^8	Radiowave	Molecular translations, nuclear reorientations
3–10^{-4}m	10^8–(3×10^{12})	Microwave	Molecular rotations, electron reorientations
10^5–700nm	(3×10^{12})–(4×10^{14})	Infrared	Molecular vibrations and direct heat effects
700–400nm	(4×10^{14})–(7×10^{14})	Visible	Low-energy electronic transitions in valence shell
400–10nm	(7×10^{14})–(3×10^{16})	Ultraviolet	High-energy electronic transitions in valence shell
10–0.03nm	(3×10^{16})–10^{19}	X-ray	Electronic transitions in the inner shell, diffraction by atoms
0.03–(3×10^{-4})nm	10^{19}–10^{23}	Gamma-ray	Nuclear transitions

Table 2.2. Conversion factors for units of length (after Brill, 1980).*

Multiply number of → by to obtain number of ↓	Angstroms (A°)	Nanometres (ηm, mμ)	Micrometres (μ, μm)	Millimetres (mm)	Centimetres (cm)	Metres (m)
Angstroms (A°)	1	10	10^4	10^7	10^8	10^{10}
Nanometres (ηm, mμ)	10^{-1}	1	10^3	10^6	10^7	10^9
Micrometres (μ, μm)	10^{-4}	10^{-3}	1	10^3	10^4	10^6
Millimetres (mm)	10^{-7}	10^{-6}	10^{-3}	1	10	10^3
Centimetres (cm)	10^{-8}	10^{-7}	10^{-4}	0.1	1	10^2
Metres (m)	10^{-10}	10^{-9}	10^{-6}	10^{-3}	10^{-2}	1

* Note that micrometres (μm) are sometimes referred to as microns (μ) and nanometres (ηm) as millimicrons (mμ).

high-energy, short ultraviolet waves (below 400nm) and the low-energy, long infrared heat waves (above 700nm). We are aware of the damage from ultraviolet rays and infrared heat waves, but any light can cause deterioration to the materials of heritage objects (Brill, 1980).

Photons that hit the surfaces of objects may be reflected or absorbed, depending on the surface colour. If absorbed, the photons hit molecules of the material and change the electronic state of these molecules. If the photon is released from the molecules and the energy converted to heat, there is no light damage, i.e. no fading of colours. If the photon is not released as heat and it remains in the material in the form of high-energy radicals, these react with oxygen and water and cause the formation of peroxides, which cause colours to fade and initiate the destructive chemical reactions of photo-oxidation.

Lighting in museums is most important in display and work areas, where heritage objects are exposed to the light for long periods of time. In these cases the light intensity, the heat (infrared rays) and the ultraviolet rays the light emits should be measured and controlled (Michalski, 1989).

For further information, see Brill (1980), Michalski (1987) and Thomson (1986).

2.2.2 Temperature

Temperature is the degree of hotness or coldness, as measured on the centigrade or Fahrenheit scales. The centigrade (Celsius) thermometer is divided into 100 units between the freezing point (0°C) and the boiling point (100°C) of water. The Fahrenheit thermometer reading of 32°F corresponds to 0°C and 212°F to 100°C.

Differences in temperature are a result of the presence of different amounts of heat. Heat is the result of infrared heat radiation or rays (Table 2.1) emitted from a light source such as burning fuel, an incandescent light or the sun.

An increase in heat causes an increase in the rate of movement of molecules, which is expressed mainly as an increase in the rate of chemical reactions. Vapour pressure, the volatility, of water is influenced directly by temperature: an increase in the vapour pressure of water results in an increase in water vapour's rate of movement, in or out of organic materials. Infrared rays can penetrate opaque surfaces, heating materials internally. This is the basis of infrared photography, which allows one to see previous versions of a painting under the final painted surface.

The temperature of ambient air in rooms, in macroenvironments, is controlled by air conditioning, cooling or heating, and may be influenced by outdoor temperatures. Temperature changes occur in microenvironments because of the diffusion of heat from small heat sources, such as radiators, light bulbs, electrical appliances, sunlight, stratification (warm air rising and cold air moving downwards), limited air circulation or the infrared absorbency of the material of the heritage object.

Materials absorb heat according to the colour of their surface. A black surface absorbs infrared rays from a light source and a white surface reflects them. Thus the colour of the material of the heritage object, or materials adjacent to it, e.g. a container or display mount, will influence the temperature in the microenvironment of the object.

2.2.3 Effects of radiations on heritage eaters

We are concerned about the effects of temperature on heritage objects, but we must also be aware of their influence on insects and fungal pests. A general rule is that growth occurs from about 4–37°C, with optimum growth around 20°C.
Infrared absorption on material surfaces may create a conducive microenvironment for insect and fungal pest activity due to an increase in local temperature.

Light plays a role in the behaviour of insects and in the growth of fungi. Larvae shun light, whereas some of the adults are attracted to it. Some adult insects can see infrared and ultraviolet rays. Ultraviolet light traps are used successfully in orchards and forests to attract adult insects: the insect sees the ultraviolet light as sunlight reflecting off the ground of open spaces. (This is discussed in more detail in 10.2.) Some developmental aspects of the growth of fungi are also influenced by light. Some species of fungi, when subjected to light, produce pigments, while others are unaffected.

In microbiology, ultraviolet rays have been used to kill micro-organisms, but the levels used would damage the organic materials of heritage objects.

From even this little information it is obvious that the microenvironments of heritage objects may support insect and fungal activity while the macroenvironment does not.

2.3 WATER VAPOUR IN AIR

2.3.1 Holding capacity of air

The holding capacity of air is the amount of water that a given volume of air can hold at a given temperature and pressure. Air temperature influences the water-holding capacity of the air, as shown in the hygrometric chart (Figure 2.1). The actual amount of water in a given volume of saturated air varies with temperature: more at higher temperatures and less at lower. When the temperature of air is increased, the air expands and there is more space between the gas molecules for water to enter as water vapour. When the temperature decreases, the air contracts, the gas molecules are more densely packed and there is less space between them to which water can attach itself, so the holding capacity of the air is decreased.

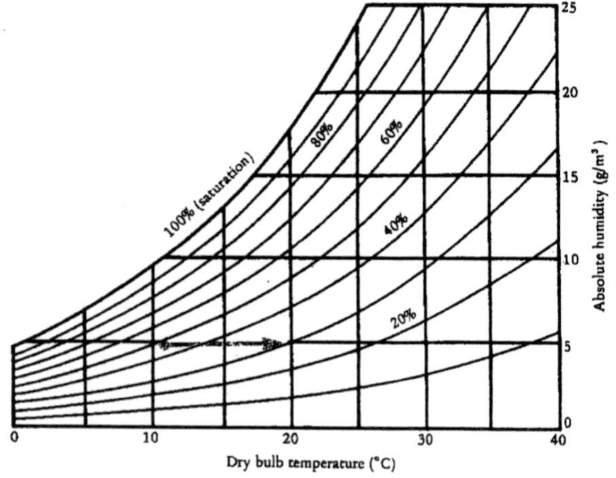

Figure 2.1. Hygrometric chart: relates the temperature of the air in a room (dry bulb temperature) to its RH and absolute humidity (after Thomson, 1988).

Water vapour moves into the air from adsorbent materials (see 2.4.2 for explanation of adsorb and absorb), water bodies, etc., according to a diffusion gradient, from a region of high concentration to a region of low concentration, until an equilibrium is reached. If the air has all the water it can hold, i.e. is at 100% of its holding capacity, at a specific temperature and pressure, it is saturated. Above saturation, it will rain.

The water in the outdoor air comes from water bodies, clouds and organic materials. In buildings housing heritage objects it comes from the organic materials of the heritage objects, air-conditioning units and people.

What is the relevance of the holding capacity of air to insect and fungal growth? As one example, when there are temperature changes, specifically reduction in temperature, the holding capacity of the air is decreased and the excess water vapour goes into organic materials. The more moisture in materials, the greater the potential of insect or fungal attack. Another example is when infested heritage objects in polyethylene bags are placed in freezing temperatures for insect eradication (see 12.1). It is important to know that, as the air in the bag around the object cools, its holding capacity is reduced. The excess water vapour is adsorbed into the materials of the object; it does not form frost or condense on surfaces.

2.3.2 Relative humidity (RH)

2.3.2.1 MEASURING RH

Temperature and RH of air are so closely linked that one cannot be discussed without the other.

RH is measured as the percentage of water vapour in a given volume of air relative to its maximum holding capacity. Thus, at a given temperature, 20°C (see Figure 2.1), a cubic metre of air has a holding capacity of 17g of water: it is 100% saturated. But if there is only 8.5g of water in the cubic metre, which is 50% of what it could hold, its RH is 50%.

In an empty, closed system, i.e. a sealed showcase, with no new water vapour entering, temperature alone can alter the RH and the amount of moisture in the air will be the same.

For example, for a cubic metre of air with 8.5 g of water:

- at 25°C, the RH is 37%;
- at 20°C, the RH is 50%;
- at 15°C, the RH is 68%.

If the showcase were filled with adsorbent objects made from cotton, leather and wool and the above temperature changes occurred, there would be very little change in the RH in the case, even if the seal was broken and outside moisture entered the showcase. The reason is that the adsorptive organic materials act as a buffer preventing RH fluctuations by adsorbing moisture when the RH rises and giving off moisture when the RH falls. This explains the buffering reaction of wood that is often used to maintain constant RH in display cases and transport containers (Stolow, 1966; Thomson, 1986; Weintraub, 1981). Silica gel is a common buffer used in many situations in museums (La Fontaine, 1984; Stolow, 1966), homes and industry to maintain a constant RH in packages, containers, cases, etc. containing moisture-sensitive materials.

2.3.2.2 OPEN AND CLOSED ENVIRONMENTS

We often try to interpret aspects of indoor environments from personal experience. Our environment outdoors is an open system, not a confined system like a building, room or freezer chest. Besides experiencing hot, humid days, we have also felt how dry the air seems when the temperature outdoors is freezing. Actually, cool air should feel damp but, outdoors, freezing air feels dry.

Three things happen to make the air dry:

1 Because of the low temperature the holding capacity of water vapour in freezing air is low.
2 In the open system outdoors, water vapour condenses on cold surfaces as frost or forms ice and water vapour is withdrawn from the air.
3 Organic materials adsorb more moisture at low temperatures, withdrawing water vapour from the air.

Thus the freezing cold air holds less water vapour, there is less water vapour available and the RH can drop dramatically. When this cold, dry air comes into our furnaces or air-conditioning units and is heated, it feels drier, and is drier.

The example of air conditioning illustrates this. With air conditioning, there is always a need for outside air, replacement air, to come into the building. If replacement air from outdoors is at 0°C with 1.8g of water and RH 50%, when heated to 20°C the RH decreases to 20%, and that's dry. In some heating units water vapour is added to compensate for this dryness.

The hot, humid and the cold, dry days are examples of an open system in which the air has no limit but the atmosphere. Museums, heritage houses and your home are basically closed units and the amount of water vapour held in the air depends not only on the temperature but on how much water vapour is available. Water vapour comes from adsorbent materials, air-conditioning units and people but, with sophisticated air conditioning in buildings, the amount of water vapour is controlled by dehumidification and humidification units.

It is in this outdoor, open-air system of hot, humid and cold, dry days that the ancestors of our insect and fungal pests evolved. Their behavioural and physiological responses are still based on this open system, even though they have adapted to buildings. The key to this adaptation is their ability to enter periods of low metabolic activity, quiescence or diapause, and wait for us to inadvertently cause conducive indoor environments to occur. When this happens, they hurry to take advantage of it. Many endemic beetle species that are pests in museums, even though they do not see the light of day or feel the daily and seasonal fluctuations of temperature and humidity, still go through seasonal pupation times.

2.3.2.3 RELEVANCE TO HERITAGE EATERS' ACTIVITY

The interrelationship of organic materials, temperature and RH to pest problems is relevant. Outdoors, insects respond to temperature and moisture changes and have complex feedback mechanisms that can trigger development. For example, some pupal cocoons can adsorb moisture from the air, which will initiate adult emergence or, as another example, the conidia of fungi may need fluctuations of temperature and moisture before they can germinate. These feedback mechanisms can also occur in buildings with temperature and RH changes, which cause adsorption and desorption of moisture in insects as well as in materials. Most outbursts of insect pest and fungal activity observed in buildings have occurred after some environmental change, which suggests that there is a real interaction.

A scenario: In a large museum, one Christmas holiday, the floor maintenance crew thought it would be a good idea, while the staff were away, to strip off the wax from the floors of their offices, on all 14 floors, and apply new wax. This was a water cleaning process. The chief conservator was informed only on return from the holidays, by reading the hygrothermographs of that week. The RH change was dramatic but short. Twelve to fourteen days later an unusual number of varied carpet beetle adults appeared on the window light traps. The population peaked and waned in a few days. The computer record of previous years did not show a population peak for this time of the year, so it can be assumed that it was caused by the dramatic increase in RH.

For further information on water vapour in air and RH, see La Fontaine and Michalski (1984), Michalski (1994) and Thomson (1986).

2.4 WATER IN MATERIALS

2.4.1 Equilibrium moisture content (EMC) of organic materials

In discussion of RH, adsorptive organic materials had to be included because of their role in buffering RH fluctuations.

Organic materials of heritage objects, if exposed to an environment containing water vapour, will eventually arrive at a steady-state moisture-content condition, called equilibrium moisture content (EMC). The EMC depends on the RH and temperature of the surrounding air, and physical conditions in the material. It fluctuates with change in either RH or temperature or both. Figure 2.2 shows how the EMC varies with temperature and RH changes. General principles are that an increase in temperature decreases the EMC and vice versa, and increasing the RH increases the EMC and vice versa. It is possible to maintain a constant EMC in a material by altering both temperature and RH.

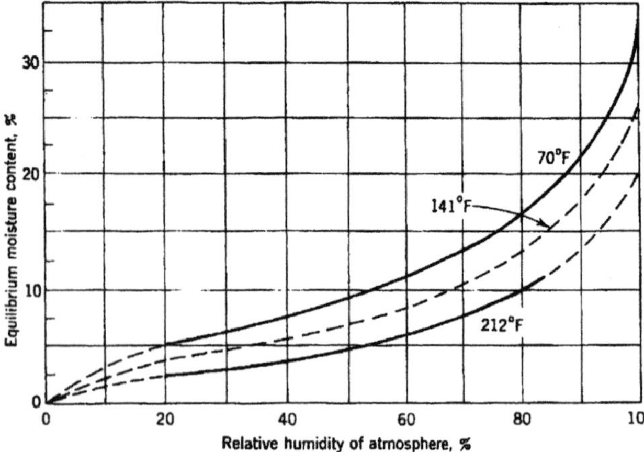

Figure 2.2. Sorption isotherms for wood at three temperatures (from Panshin and de Zeeuw, 1970).

If there is more moisture in organic materials than in the air, there is a diffusion gradient and the moisture will diffuse out of the materials into the air. This is simply the drying of materials. Eventually, an equilibrium will be reached at which equal amounts of water vapour move in and out of the materials. If the temperature of the air decreases, the excess water in the air diffuses into the materials until, again, an equilibrium is reached. The water in materials in equilibrium with that in the air is the EMC. This refers to the amount of moisture in a material at equilibrium with a specific RH and temperature. When materials are oven-dried the weight lost is the EMC and represents all the moisture, bound or free, in the materials.

In *dry organic materials*, such as wood, the EMC is its water content measured as a percentage of dry weight. This water is called EMC because some of it moves to reach equilibrium.

$$\frac{\text{weight of water} \times 100}{\text{dry weight}} = \text{\% MC of oven-dry weight}$$

Example:

wet weight	= 110g
dry weight	= 100g
weight of water	= 10g

$$\frac{10 \times 100}{100} = \text{10\% MC of dry weight or 10\% EMC}$$

Water in *living materials* is usually measured as a percentage of body weight (which may also be called live weight or wet weight).

$$\frac{\text{weight of water} \times 100}{\text{wet weight}} = \text{MC as \% of body weight}$$

Example:

wet weight	= 100g (weight of an individual)
dry weight	= 10g
weight of water	= 90g

$$\frac{90 \times 100}{100} = \text{90\% water of body weight, live weight or wet weight}$$

The movement of this water in a living organism is controlled by life processes and is not directly influenced by RH or temperature.

For further information on EMC, see Panshin and de Zeeuw (1970) and Thomson (1986).

2.4.2 MOISTURE IN ORGANIC MATERIALS – FREE, SURFACE ON SURFACE AND BOUND

Organic materials can adsorb just so much moisture. The amount depends on their chemical and physical structure. For example, woods can only adsorb water vapour up to 28% EMC of their dry weight. Over this amount, they become wet. The EMC water is in molecules in cell walls, associated with chemicals and other water molecules. If the wood is wet there is free water inside the lumen (central empty region inside the wood cell).

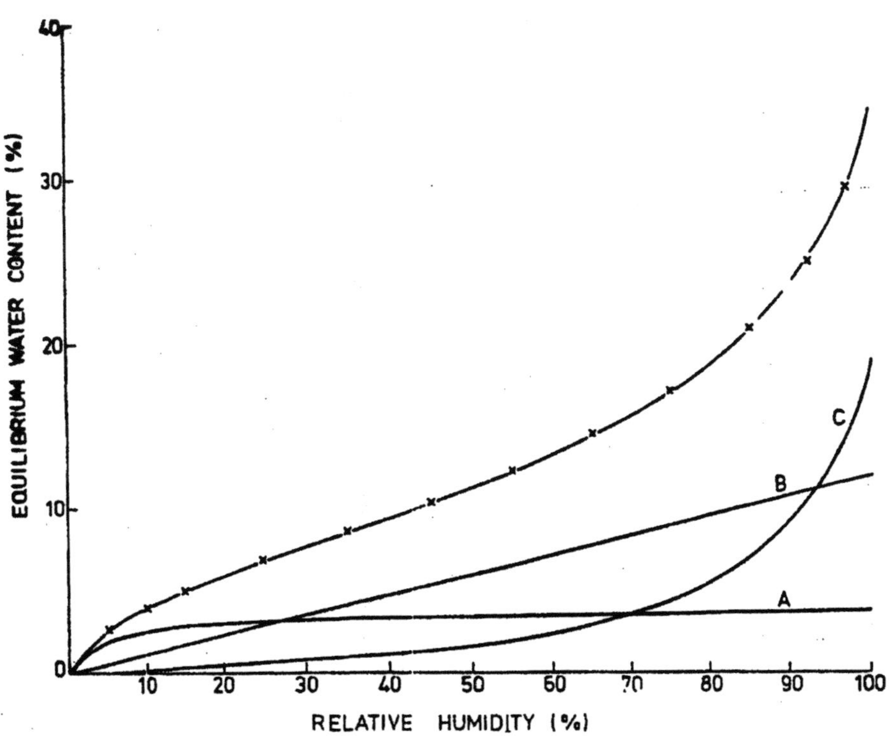

Figure 2.3. Water vapour adsorption curves of Merino wool. The top curve shows the processes as a result of the three curves: A is bound water adsorbed by strong hydrophilic bonds, B is monolayer water adsorbed by weak hydrophilic bonds and C multi-layer formation by weak hydrogen bonds (after Watt, 1980, originally from D'Arcy R. L. and Watt I. C. 1963. Trans. Faraday, 66, 1236).

The water involved in this 28% EMC has different physical forms according to its attachment in the materials. This is shown in Figure 2.3. Some water molecules are bonded by strong chemical bonds to the molecules of the organic material, i.e. cellulose, protein, etc. This is called bound water. Some water molecules are bonded by weaker hydrogen bonds to the surfaces of the these molecules and some water is attached to other water molecules by very weak electrostatic bonds (multi-layered water). The water that wets materials is free water in the pores or capillaries and lumina of cells of the materials. All the water, except the molecularly bound water, is adsorbed water.

Adsorption is a special type of absorption in which surfaces act as the absorber. Absorption is the uniform penetration of one substance into another by chemical or molecular action. Radiation, gases, heat, chemicals in solution as well as fluids in biological systems are *absorbed* because they are involved in chemical or molecular reactions. Whereas water, water vapour and chemicals that are on surfaces of animal and plant fibres, colloidal and crystalline polymers, chelators and such chemicals as charcoal are *adsorbed* to the surface. Fibres have many levels of adsorbing surfaces, from micro and macro fibrils to the complex fibre.

For further information on moisture in organic materials, see Rockland and Stewart (1981).

2.4.3 Sequence of water removal with drying

When wet wood is oven-dried, the water is removed in a sequence reflecting the strength of its bond attachment to molecules and surfaces in the material.

Free water is the first to go. It is free in the lumina of the cells or capillaries and takes the least energy to remove, coming off rapidly by evaporative drying. The wood is now below fibre saturation point (28% EMC) and feels dry.

If the drying of this relatively dry wood is continued, the next water to come off is the multi-layered, electrostatically bonded water, which moves freely in and out of the material according to the RH changes in the air.

As the drying process carries on, the next water to be removed is that bonded by hydrogen bonds. This water takes heat energy equivalent to the strength of the bonds to be released.

Finally, the last water to come off, and hardest to remove, is the chemically bound water.

The multi-layered, electrostatically bonded water and the hydrogen bonded water are the only types of water that move to reach an equilibrium, but we use the term EMC to include all the water in materials. Weight changes in organic materials occuring during small fluctuations in the environment involve only these weakly attached types of water.

Only free water and some of the weakly bonded multi-layered water are available for the growth of micro-organisms and most insect pests.

2.4.4 Hysterical hysteresis

When moisture is adsorbed into materials because of an increase in RH, and then desorbed because of a decrease in RH, the rate of desorption is much slower than the rate of adsorption. The graph in Figure 2.4 shows that the process of adsorption has a lower EMC than when in the process of desorption (drying). This normal characteristic of organic materials is called the hysteresis sorption curve.

It is important to be aware of the process of hysteresis when drying wet materials. Even if they have come to equilibrium with ambient conditions, they may still have a much higher EMC than we expect, which could make them vulnerable to insect and fungal attack. This is also the case when a humidification treatment has been used to soften materials for manipulation.

In the freezing process for eradication of insects (Florian, 1986), the organic materials subjected to the temperature reduction will adsorb water vapour, resulting in a small increase in EMC. When the material is removed from the freezer and it reaches equilibrium with the room temperature,

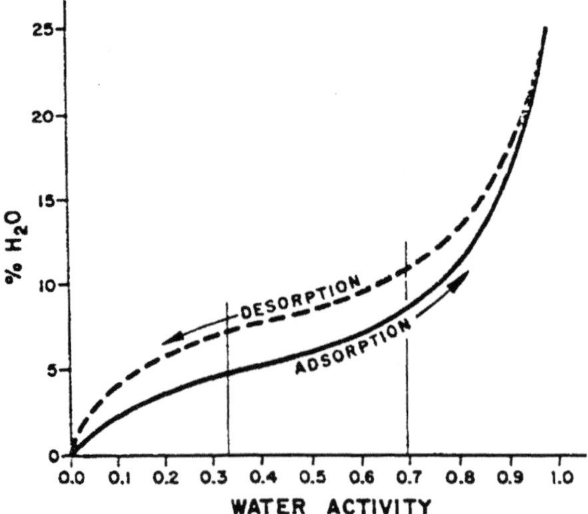

Figure 2.4. Schematic representation of a moisture sorption hysteresis loop. Water activity can be converted to 0 to 100% RH (Kapsalis, 1987). (For an explanation of water activity see section 2.4.6)

Table 2.3. Percent equilibrium moisture content (EMC) of different materials held at 50% RH and 100% RH, shown to illustrate the different adsorbency of materials (Florian, 1986).

Material (Reference)	Temperature (°C)	EMC 50% RH	EMC 100% RH
Unmodified merino wool (1)	35	11.3–12.3	34.2
Methylated wool (79%) (1)	35	9	46.0
Collagen (2)	35	15	55
Merino wool (3)	20	11	35
Merino wool (3)	65	9	31
Merino wool (3)	100	7	28
Wool (4)	no data*	11–13	35
Cotton (4)	no data	5.5–6.5	23
Jute (4)	no data	8.5–11	35
Cellulose acetate rayon (4)	no data	4.5–5	17–18
Viscose rayon (4)	no data	11–12	40
Cuprammonium rayon (4)	no data	11–12	40
Nylon (2)	35	4.5	10
Nylon (4)	no data	3.5–4	8
Silk (4)	no data	7.5–8	30
Wood (5)	no data	9	31
Silica gel, grade 03 (6)	no data	30	35
Silica gel, grade 59 (6)	no data	5	15

* no data – assume 20°C.

References: 1. Watt (1979). 2. D'Arcy and Watt (1981). 3. Watt (1980). 4. Carlene (1944). 5. Hoadley (1980). 6. La Fontaine (1984).

it will lose, desorb, most of the water vapour it adsorbed. The EMC will be higher than when it was put into the freezer because of hysteresis. Eventually, the original equilibrium will be reached.

For further information on hysteresis, see Kapsalis (1987), Rockland and Stewart (1981), Troller and Christian (1978) and Watt (1979).

2.4.5 Regain

Regain is a term describing the adsorbency of materials. Old materials tend to be brittle and dry. Over time, materials are exposed to many fluctuations in gain and loss of moisture due to environmental fluctuations. Each time a loss occurs, some of the organic material's molecular bonds, which would normally hold water, bond instead to each other (cross-link). Water can no longer fit in and the material becomes stiff and dry. These old materials have thus lost some regain ability. The hysteresis sorption curve has become smaller and smaller, as is seen in Figure 2.5. This material has a reduced EMC and is consequently more resistant to insect or fungal attack.

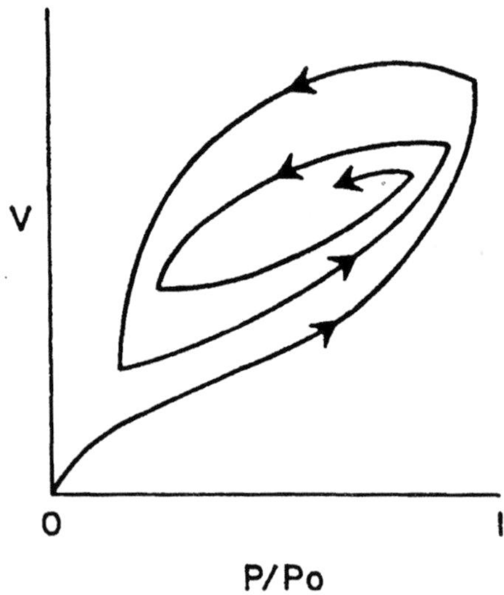

Figure 2.5. Scanning paths of repeating adsorption and desorption curves in hysteresis (after Kapsalis, 1981). P/Po = water activity a_ω or % RH, V = equilibrium moisture content (EMC).

Wood from different species or different types of leathers, textiles or papers, at the same RH and temperature, may each have a different EMC. Table 2.3 gives examples of the EMCs of a variety of similar and dissimilar materials. The moisture content of the materials is dependent on their many characteristics, i.e. physical structure or porosity, inherent chemicals and those used in manufacture or during use, deterioration and the sorptive history. Physical characteristics are: available hydrogen bonding sites; protein denaturation; degree of polymer crystallinity or amorphous regions; and available surface area. Chemical alterations are caused by: tannage; alkylation; acetylation; deamination; and humectants. Deterioration can involve mechanical breaking, physical shrinkage, and oxidation and photochemical degradation. The sorptive history of materials is a result of successive adsorption and desorption cycles, which may result in loss of hysteresis and reduced moisture regain, and changes in molecular structure. There are many other possible alterations to materials.

At the same RH and temperature, some materials will have enough moisture to support fungal activity and others will not, another example of a microenvironment. The major influence on the rate of development and the activity of insects and fungal pests is moisture in the materials, the substrate on which they are growing.

The role of the microenvironment in supporting pest activity is often overlooked in the assessment and prevention of pest problems. The logical approach in evaluating vulnerability is to examine the range of EMCs reported for the different groups of materials under scrutiny.

2.4.6 'Water, water, everywhere. Nor any drop to drink'

Some chemicals, when added to materials, increase their moisture content but not their vulnerability to heritage eaters.

In the organic material of heritage items there are sometimes water-soluble chemicals, either inherent or added during use or treatment, that change the vapour pressure of the water. For example, a water solution of glycerine is often used as a humectant to keep objects soft and pliable. The glycerine lowers the vapour pressure of the water, as the water is strongly bonded to the glycerine molecules and cannot move according to changes in the RH and temperature of the air around it. There may be a great quantity of water in the material but fungi cannot use it because they cannot compete with the strength of the bonds between the glycerine and the water.

The glycerine changes the vapour pressure of the water or, in other words, alters the water activity (a_ω) (Rockland and Stewart, 1981): a_ω is an expression of the ratio of the vapour pressure of the water in materials relative to pure water, thus it ranges from 1 to 0. Pure water has a high vapour pressure and easily evaporates, but water mixed with sugar or salt has a low vapour pressure and it takes extra energy and a long time to evaporate. Most fungi cannot utilize water below a_ω 0.65. (Water activity and fungi are discussed in detail in 17.1). In the fungi physiology and food industry literature, a_ω is used to describe water in materials.

2.4.7 The heat of wetting

Adsorption is an exothermal reaction. When we go outside on a damp, cool day with a wool coat on, the wool will adsorb moisture from the cold air and become warm. The adsorption of the water in the organic material is an exothermic reaction which creates heat. The opposite happens when water is evaporated, an endothermic reaction. It utilizes heat for evaporation; for example, when we sweat our body heat is utilized in evaporation and the heat loss cools our skin.

These exothermic and endothermic reactions, caused by adsorption and desorption respectively, occur in the organic materials of heritage objects during fluctuations of EMC. This phenomenon, which changes the microenvironment, is commonly overlooked when we examine the vulnerability of these materials to insect and fungal damage. Could the temperature/EMC cycles be involved in breaking dormancy or quiescence in insects or cause activation of the conidia of fungi? We are aware that the heat of wetting causes shrinkage in badly deteriorated leathers, and use this as a method of determining deterioration, but we do not consider it on the micro-level of insects and fungi.

2.4.8 Heritage eaters do not drink water

The water in materials influences their vulnerability to biodeterioration by insect and fungal heritage eaters. Insects may obtain some water vapour from the air they breathe, but there is no strong evidence that fungi adsorb water vapour from the atmosphere. Thus they are dependent on the water in the materials they eat.

Fungi give off enzymes dissolved in their cytoplasmic water, but they will reabsorb this water, as well as some substrate moisture, with the digested nutrients. Some insects, for example booklice and some wood-boring beetles, feed on living fungi growing on materials and benefit from the ability of these fungi to remove water from the substrate. Some stored grain beetles can live on dry grain, with less than 5% EMC, by using the bound water in the cellulose and starch molecules of the grain as a source of water. Organic materials with a high moisture content must be texturally easier to chew, which would make them more attractive to some insects. The bottom line is that water is needed for life.

Even if the RH around a material is not conducive for growth, if the material has sufficient moisture it will support pests. With our tunnel vision we always look at the influence of the ambient air RH on the growth and development of pests and overlook the influence of moisture in the materials themselves.

In the food industry moisture in foodstuffs is controlled to prevent fungal activity. In the lumber industry wood is kiln-dried to lower the EMC and protect it from specific wood-attacking beetles. Anyone with experience in maintaining an insect colony knows how critical it is to maintain just the right moisture in the materials on which the insects are feeding.

We do an excellent job when documenting heritage objects of recording information about the type and condition of the materials, but we rarely note their weights – unless they are made of gold. We should be recording the weight of objects, plus the RH and temperature at the time of weighing. The RH and temperature may vary but the three pieces of information, taken together, will be significant. Over time, a number of weighings will tell us about regain changes and may be a valuable reference point for drying objects after accidental wetting.

There are, unfortunately, no easy, non-destructive methods of determining the EMC of our priceless heritage items. X-ray densitometry and determination of electrical resistance are two non-destructive methods used to determine moisture in wood, but these are not suitable for heritage objects because they are either damaging or give information only regarding the one spot analysed.

2.5 DUST

The word 'pollutants' makes us think of acid rain, sulphur dioxide and nitrous oxide, present in the outdoor environment as a result of gas pollution. In museums, heritage houses and our homes events involving these pollutants rarely occur. There is, however, a major problem in museums and houses caused by particulate pollution – dust.

Dust contains all sorts of airborne particles that settle out and are deposited on or adjacent to heritage objects. Depending on where the building is the dust can contain any of the following: human epithelial cells (skin debris), textile fibre fragments, starch grains, fungal conidia and spores, pollen grains, carbon soot and inorganic crystal of all kinds. In a museum that is visited by thousands of people, the dust will contain many skin epithelial cells; if there are wall-to-wall carpets, there will be lots of rug textile fibres; if it is an agricultural region, there will be fungal conidia, starch grains, etc. Some particulate pollutants are removed by air filters but others gain access to buildings with people and through open doors, windows, docking bays, etc.

Dust may be a source of nutrients for some insects or fungi and it may form a microenvironment on surfaces as it prevents normal air flow over them and the large surface areas of the small dust particles will adsorb moisture. Both these factors will improve the environment for pests.

The dust, *per se*, does not cause a problem for heritage objects but the organic material within it is fodder for pests. Some infestations of insects and fungi on objects can be solely supported by organic materials in the dust.

For further information on dust, see Thomson (1986).

2.6 AIR CIRCULATION

Air circulation, of course, influences the moisture content on the surface of and within materials. If we want to dry things rapidly, we use fans, as well as heat. Movement of air also prevents accumulation of dust, and the fungal conidia contained in it, on surfaces. The application of air circulation to prevention of insect and fungal pests in heritage collections is in its infancy. Sakomoto *et al.* (1995) reported on tests conducted in storage facilities and in chambers with a controlled, weak air flow. Use of the air flow resulted in restrained fungal growth. Arai (1995) used on cabinets a type of louvre that encouraged air circulation and was able to show how this reduced fungal activity. Both cases must involve the elimination of microenvironments of high moisture content and/or the simple removal of conidia. These are further examples of the importance of microenvironments.

REFERENCES

Arai, H. 1995. Personal communication.

Brill, T.B. 1980. *Light, its Interaction with Art and Antiquities.* Plenum Press, New York, London.

Carlene, P.W. 1944. The moisture relation of textiles, a survey of the literature. *Journal of the Society of Dyers and Colourists*, 60:232–237.

D'Arcy, R.L. and I.A. Watt. 1981. Water vapor sorption isotherms on macromolecular substrates. In *Water Activity: Influences on Food Quality*, Eds R.L. Rockland and G.F. Stewart. 1981. Academic Press, New York, pp 111–142.

Florian, M-L.E. 1986. The freezing process – effects on insects and artifact materials. *Leather Conservation News*, 3(1):1–13,17.

Hoadley, R.B. 1980. *Understanding Wood.* The Taunton Press, Newton, Connecticut.

Kapsalis, J.G. 1981. Moisture sorption hysteresis. In *Water Activity: Influences on Food Quality*, Eds R.L. Rockland and G.F. Stewart. 1981. Academic Press, New York, pp144–165.

Kapsalis, J.G. 1987. Influences of hysteresis and temperature on moisture sorption isotherms. In *Water Activity: Theory and Application to Food*, Eds L.B. Rockland and L.R. Beuchat. Marcel Dekker Inc., New York, pp171–213

La Fontaine, R. 1984. *Silica Gel.* C.C.I. Tech. Bull. No. 10.

La Fontaine, R.H. and S. Michalski. 1984. The control of relative humidity: recent developments. *Preprints, ICOM Committee for Conservation, Copenhagen*, 2:84.17.33–37.

Michalski, S. 1987. Damage to museum objects by visible radiation (light) and ultraviolet radiation (uv). In *Lighting in Museums, Galleries, and Historic Houses.* The Museums Association, London, pp3–16.

Michalski, S. 1989. A light damaged slide rule. *Proceedings of the 14th Annual IIC-CG Conference*, p22.

Michalski, S. 1994. Relative humidity in museums, galleries and archives: specification and control. In *Bugs, Mold and Rot II: A Workshop on Control of Humidity for Health, Artifacts, and Buildings.* National Institute of Building Sciences, Washington, pp51–62.

Panshin, A.J. and C. de Zeeuw. 1970. *Textbook of Wood Technology*, Vol. 1. 3rd Edition. McGraw-Hill Book Company, New York.

Rockland, R.L. and G.F. Stewart. 1981. *Water Activity: Influences on Food Quality.* Academic Press, New York.

Sakamoto, K., N. Kurozumi and T. Kenjo. 1995. A simple method for temporary conservation of art objects: effect of air flow for preventing fungal growth. *3rd International Conference on Biodeterioration of Cultural Property, 4–7 July, Bangkok, Thailand.*

Stolow, N. 1966. *Controlled Environments for Works of Art in Transit.* Butterworths, London.

Thomson, G. 1986. *The Museum Environment.* 2nd Edition. Butterworths, London.

Troller, J.A. and J.H.B. Christian. 1978. *Water Activity and Food.* Academic Press, New York.

Watt, I.C. 1979. Water vapor sorption hysteresis in swelling substrates. In *Physics of Materials*, Eds D.W. Borland, L.M. Clarebrough and A.J.W. Moore. Commonwealth Assoc. and Industrial Research Organization, Australia.

Watt, I.C. 1980. Sorption of water vapor by keratin. *Journal Macromol. Sci.-Rev. Macromol. Chem.*, C 18(2):169–245.

Weintraub, S. 1981. Studies in the behaviour of RH within an exhibition case. Part 1. Measuring the effectiveness of sorbents for use in an enclosed showcase. *Preprints, ICOM Committee for Conservation, Ottawa*, 81.18.4.

3

Classification, Naming and Diagnostic Features of Common Insect Heritage Eaters

3.1 THE GROUPING OF ANIMALS

The animal kingdom is divided into 13 major groups, called phyla. The animals in each phylum have common characteristics, for example, all animals with an internal skeleton are in the phylum Chordata and all single-celled animals are in the phylum Protozoa.

A phylum is subdivided into smaller groups of animals that have similar structural features and these groups are subdivided in turn into still smaller groups of animals until the individual species is reached.

The sequence of groups is as follows: phylum, subphylum, class, subclass, division, order, suborder, superfamily, family, genus and, finally, the individual species.

3.2 THE PHYLUM ARTHROPODA

Insects are included in the phylum Arthropoda. The arthropods include not only insects but other animals, e.g. spiders, crabs, lobsters, centipedes, etc.

The animals in this large group have the following morphological features in common:

- a segmented body
- segmented, jointed, paired appendages
- bilateral symmetry
- chitinous exoskeleton.

3.3 CLASS INSECTA

There are many classes in the phylum Arthropoda. The insects are all grouped in the class Insecta (or Hexapoda). The existence of two alternative names for the class demonstrates how the naming of organisms is an ongoing discipline and new names are being introduced continuously to give clarity and to utilize new information about the relatives of insects.

Insecta (Hexapoda)

Figure 3.1 illustrates the parts of an adult beetle.

Adult insects have a distinct head, thorax and abdomen. Three pairs of jointed appendages, or legs, developed on three body segments form the thorax. The head segments, bear a pair of antennules, antennae, mandibles (jaws), maxillae and the labium. The abdomen may have up to 11 segments.

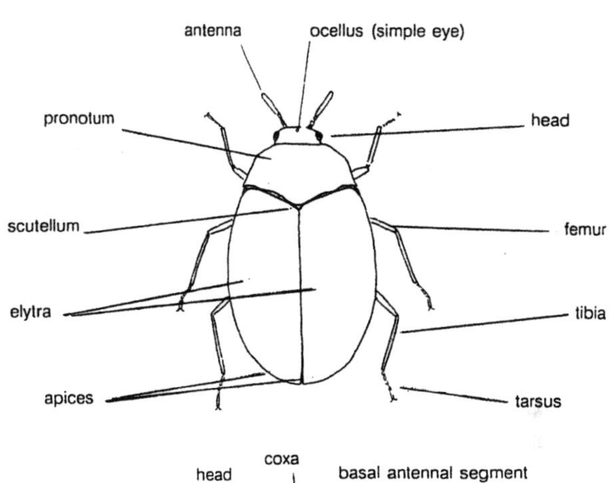

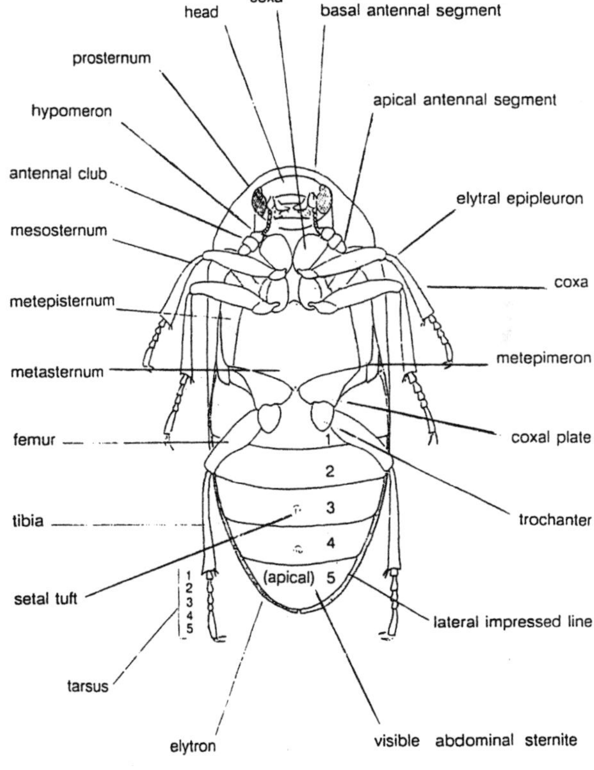

Figure 3.1. Top, dorsal view of a carpet beetle, Anthrenus fuscus. *Bottom, ventral view of a hide beetle* Dermestes *sp. (Peacock, 1993, with permission).*

The typical lateral compound eyes are present in adults and nymphs but absent in the larvae. Simple eyes, ocelli, may be found on adults: one medium and two laterally placed dorsal ocelli.

3.4 CLASSIFICATION OR NAMING OF INSECTS

There are probably millions of insect species. The task of naming or classifying them is as enormous as their numbers. The information presented here is, basically, the classification of the heritage-eating insects discussed in this book. The value of knowing their classification is as a means of communication so that it is clear exactly what insect is being discussed. It also makes possible logical groupings of insects with similar characteristics, at the same time enabling specific differences to be shown.

Many insects do not have a common name or the same common name may be given to several different insects. These problems are overcome by using the Linnaean system of binomial nomenclature, which gives every insect two Latin names: genus and species. The genus is a generic name for related species, and the species name is that of a group of individuals that interbreed. These two Latin names are always used together and are italicized, as in this book.

The combination of a generic and a specific name gives a unique name for each kind of insect. Examples are shown below with: *Blatta orientalis*, the oriental cockroach; *Blattella germanica*, the German cockroach; and *Tineola bisselliella*, the common clothes moth. *Blatta*, *Blattella* and *Tineola* are generic names, and *orientalis*, *germanica* and *bisselliella* are species names. The two insects with the common name of cockroach are not of the same genus and do not interbreed. In textbooks the first time the insect is mentioned both the generic and species names are given in full, but in subsequent references the generic name may be abbreviated to the first letter, e.g. *T. bisselliella*. Sometimes the name of the scientist who described the insect is included after the species name, e.g. *Blatta orientalis* Linnaeus, *Tineola bisselliella* (Hummel). The full scientific names of the common heritage eaters are listed in 3.6.

The full classifications of the cockroach and common webbing clothes moth are given as examples, to show all the subdivisions:

Class Insecta
Subclass Apterygota – wingless

Order Thysanura – silverfish, firebrats
Subclass Pterygota – winged insects

Division Exopterygota:
simple, incomplete metamorphosis, wings develop externally
Order Isoptera – termites
Order Psocoptera – psocids, booklice
Order Blattodea – cockroaches
Suborder – Dictyoptera
Superfamily – Blattoidea
Family – Blattidea
Genus – Blatta
Species – *Blatta orientalis*
Linnaeus
Oriental cockroach
Superfamily – Blaberoidea
Family – Blattellidae
Genus – Blattella
Species – *Blattella germanica*
(Linnaeus)
German cockroach
Division Endopterygota:
complete metamorphosis, wings develop internally
Order Coleoptera – beetles
Order Diptera – flies
Order Hymenoptera – ants
Order Lepidoptera – moths
Suborder – Ditrysia
Superfamily – Tineoidea
Family – Tineidae
Genus – Tineola
Species – *Tineola bisselliella*
(Hummel)
common clothes moth

3.5 CLASSIFICATION BASED ON METAMORPHOSIS AND ANATOMY

The classification of insects is based on anatomical features of the adult and type of development of egg to adult.

In the groups of insects listed in 3.6 there are two types of development or metamorphosis:

3.5.1 Metamorphosis

INCOMPLETE METAMORPHOSIS

In incomplete metamorphosis the egg develops into a minute immature stage that looks like a small adult. There are many moults and each new nymph looks more like the adult. When the nymph changes into the sexually mature adult stage it undergoes only slight morphological changes, usually only the development of reproductive organs. The life cycle of a cockcroach (Figure 3.2) illustrates incomplete metamorphosis.

COMPLETE METAMORPHOSIS

In complete metamorphosis the egg hatches into an immature form, a larva, which does not resemble the adult form. The larva goes through many moults: each time the result is a larger larva. In its last moult the larva body is completely reconstructed into a pupa, an immature adult in a pupal case, and from the pupal case a mature adult emerges. The life cycle of a moth (Figure 3.3) illustrates complete metamorphosis.

3.5.2 Anatomical features

The class Insecta is subdivided into 29 orders; only the eight orders that include the insects discussed in this book are listed in Box 3.1.

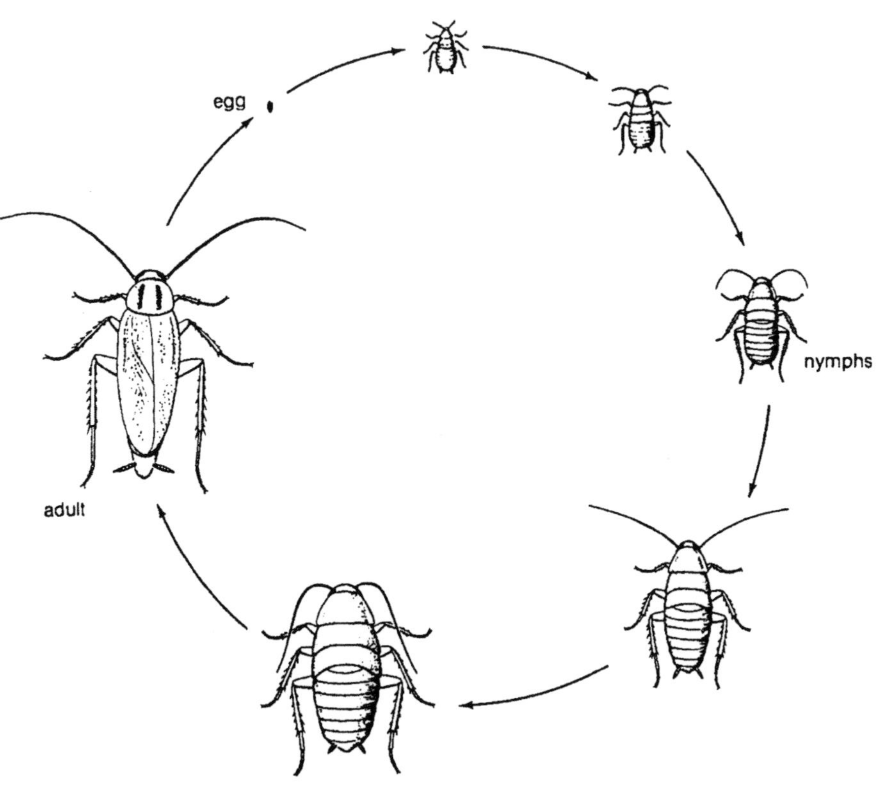

Figure 3.2. The life cycle of a cockroach, illustrating incomplete metamorphosis. The egg hatches into a nymph, which resembles the adult but is smaller and sexually immature. The nymph goes through a series of moults, each time increasing in size and resembling more the adult form. During the last moult, a sexually mature male or female adult is formed, which lays or fertilizes the eggs to repeat the cycle (after Bennett et al., *1997).*

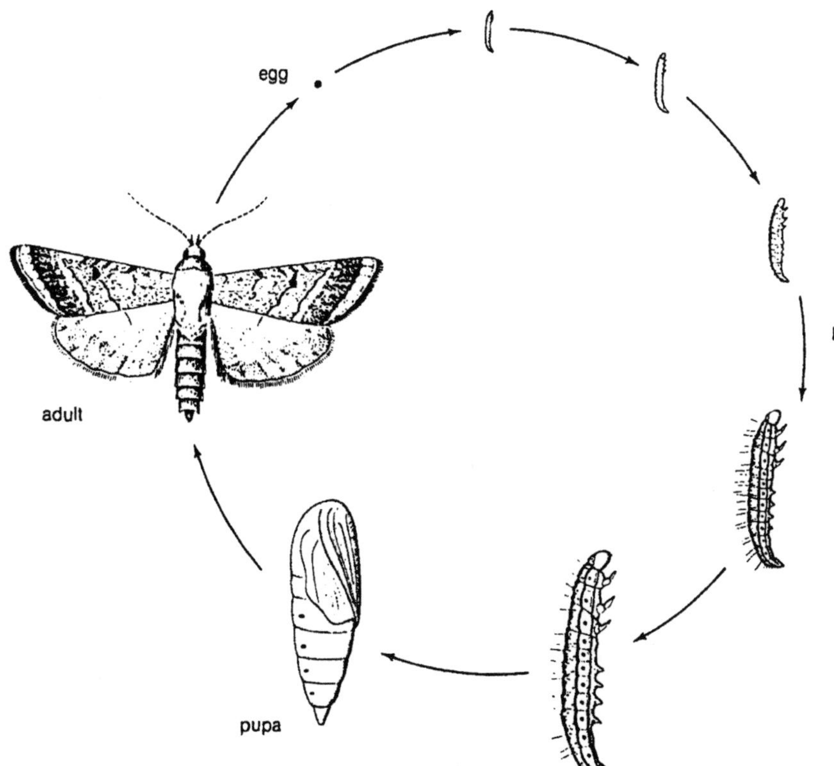

Figure 3.3. The life cycle of a moth, illustrating complete metamorphosis. The egg hatches into a worm-like larva. The larva moults several times; each time it is larger but retains its larval form. In its final moult the larva forms a pupa, which may be a partially or fully formed, dormant adult. When the pupa breaks dormancy, it goes through pupation and a sexually mature adult emerges to repeat the cycle (after Bennett et al., *1997).*

3.6 THE COMPLETE SCIENTIFIC AND COMMON NAMES OF INSECT HERITAGE EATERS CITED

CLASS INSECTA:
SUBCLASS APTERYGOTA – wingless insects
Order Thysanura – silverfish, firebrats
Family Lepismatidae
Acrotelsa collaris (Fabricius) – large silverfish
Ctenolepisma lineata pilifera (Lucas) (= *quadriseriata* Packard) – fourlined silverfish
Ctenolepisma longicaudata Escherich (=*urbana* Slabaugh) – grey silverfish, giant silverfish
Lepisma saccharina Linnaeus – common silverfish, silvermoth
Lepismodes inquilinus Newman – firebrat
Thermobia domestica (Packard) – firebrat
SUBCLASS PTERYGOTA – winged insects
DIVISION EXOPTERYGOTA – simple, incomplete metamorphosis, *wings develop externally*
Order Isoptera – termites
Family Hodotermitidiae
Zootermopsis spp. – dampwood termites
Family Kalotermitidae
Calcaritermes spp. – powderpost termites
Cryptotermes spp. – powderpost termites
Kalotermes spp. – drywood termites
Incisitermes spp. – drywood termites
Neotermes spp. – dampwood termites
Paraneotermes spp. – dampwood termites
Family Rhinotermitidiae
Reticulitermes spp. – subterranean termites
Order Psocoptera – psocids, booklice
Family Liposcelidae
Liposcelis divinatorius (Muller) – booklouse
Order Blattodea – cockroaches
Family Blattides
Blatta orientalis Linnaeus – common oriental cockroach
Periplaneta americana (Linnaeus) – American ship cock roach
Periplaneta australasiae (Fabricius) – Australian cockroach
Family Blattellidae
Blattella germanica (Linnaeus) – German cockroach

DIVISION ENDOPTERYGOTA – complete metamorphosis, *wings develop internally*
Order Coleoptera – beetles
Family Bostrichidea
Heterobostrychus aequalis (Waterhouse)
Lyctus brunneus (Stephens) – brown powderpost beetle
Lyctus planicollis LeConte – southern lyctus beetle, true powderpost beetle
Family Anobiidae
Anobium punctatum (De Geer) – common furniture beetle, false powderpost beetle, furniturewoodworm
Hylotrupes bajulus (Linnaeus) – old house beetle
Lasioderma serricorne (Fabricius) – cigarette beetle
Stegobium paniceum (Linnaeus) – drugstore beetle, bread beetle, biscuit beetle
Xestobium rufovillosum (De Geer) – deathwatch beetle
Family Dermestidae
Anthrenus flavipes LeConte – furniture carpet beetle
Anthrenus fuscus Olivie – furniture carpet beetle
Anthrenus museorum (Linnaeus) – museum beetle
Anthrenus scrophulariae (Linnaeus) – common carpet beetle
Anthrenus verbasci (Linnaeus) – varied carpet beetle
Attagenus brunneus Faldermann – two-spotted carpet beetle
Attagenus megatoma (Fabricius) – black carpet beetle
Attagenus pellio (Linnaeus) – fur beetle
Attagenus piceus (Olivier) – black carpet beetle
Attagenus unicolor (Brahm) – black carpet beetle
Dermestes ater De Geer – black larder beetle
Dermestes lardarius Linnaeus – larder or bacon beetle
Dermestes maculatus De Geer – hide beetle
Dermestes vulpinus Fabricius – leather beetle
Megatoma undata Linnaeus – carpet beetle
Reesa vespulae (Milliron) – museum nuisance, carpet beetle
Thylodrias contractus Motschulsky – odd beetle
Trogoderma inclusum LeConte (= *vericolor* [Creutz.]) – large cabinet beetle
Trogoderma granarium Everts – khapra beetle
Trogoderma ornatum (Say) (= *tarsalis* Melsheimer) – cabinet beetle
Trogoderma variabile Ballion (= *parabile* Beal) – ware house beetle, hide beetle
Family Tenebrionidae
Tenebrio molitor (Linnaeus) – yellow mealworm, grain beetle
Tenebrio obscurus (Fabricius) – dark mealworm
Trilobium castaneum (Herbst) – grain beetle
Trilobium confusum Jacquelin du Val – confused flour beetle
Family Ptinidea
Gibbium psylloides (de Czenpinski) – hump spider beetle, shiny spider beetle
Mezium americanum (Laporte) – American spider beetle
Nitpus hololeucus (Falderman) – golden spider beetle
Ptinus clavipes Panzer (= hirtellus Sturm) – brown spider beetle
Ptinus fur (Linnaeus) – white-marked spider beetle
Ptinus ocellus Brown (= *tectus* [Boieldieu]) – Australian spider beetle
Ptinus villiger Reitter – hairy spider beetle
Family Odemeridae
Nacerda melanura (Linnaeus) – wharf borer
Order Diptera – flies
Family Muscidae
Musca domestica Linnaeus – common house fly
Order Hymenoptera – ants
Order Lepidoptera – moths
Family Tineidae
Tinea pallescentella (Stainton) – large pale clothes moth
Tinea pellionella (Linnaeus) – case-making clothes moth
Tineola bisselliella (Hummel) – webbing clothes moth, common clothes moth
Trichophaga tapetzella (Linnaeus) – tapestry moth
Family Oecophoridae
Endrosis sarcitrella (Linnaeus) – white-shouldered house moth
Ephestia cautella (Walker) – almond moth, dried currant moth
Hofmannophila pseudospretella (Stainton) – brown house moth

BOX 3.1 DIAGNOSTIC FEATURES OF ADULT INSECT HERITAGE EATERS

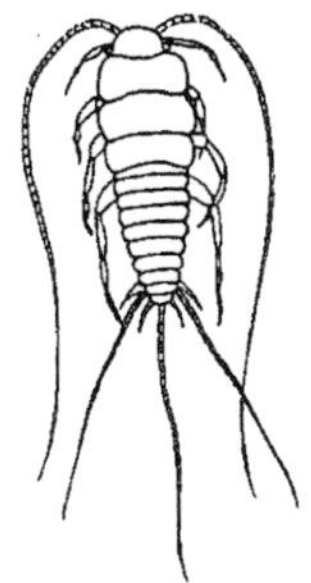

Order Thysanura – silverfish, firebrats

Incomplete metamorphosis, nymphs like small adults, all stages cause damage with chewing mouthparts, flattened fish-shaped, less than 10mm long, long antennae directed forward, three tail-like cerci of equal lengths.

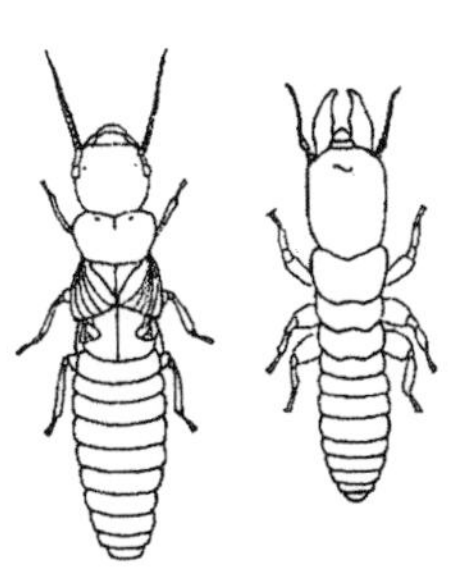

Order Isoptera – termites

Incomplete metamorphosis, social insects, workers and soldiers wingless and light-coloured, swarmers dark-bodied with four equal length wings. No waist between abdomen and thorax, chewing mouthparts, workers cause damage.

Order Psocoptera – psocids, booklice

Incomplete metamorphosis, nymphs like small adults, all stages cause damage. Small, 1–2mm, soft-bodied, antennae long and slender, light-coloured, usually wingless, chewing mouthparts.

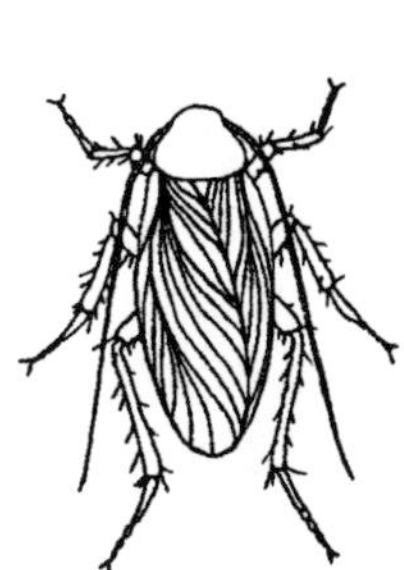

Order Blattodea – cockroaches

Incomplete metamorphosis, nymphs like small adults, all stages cause damage. Flattened dorsoventrally, chewing mouthparts, prothorax large and shield-like, usually four wings, when present the front pair is thickened and leathery and the back pair is membranous and folds beneath the front wings, legs adapted for running.

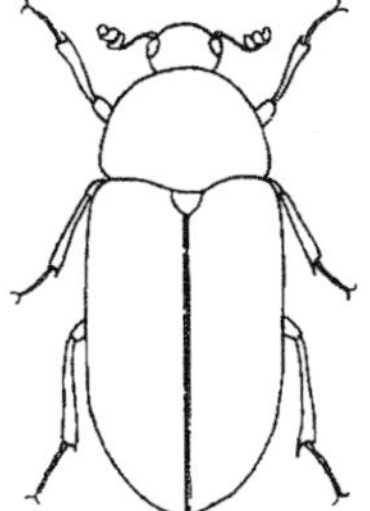

Order Coleoptera – beetles

Complete metamorphosis.
Adults: hard shell-like front wings (elytra) which meet, when in rest, on a straight line down the back, hind wings fold under front wings, adults may or may not feed.
Larvae: vary, may be grub-like to caterpillar-like, three pairs of articulated thoracic legs. Head, hard, sclerotized capsule; ocelli, no compound eyes. Mouthparts opposable mandibles, larvae usually cause damage.

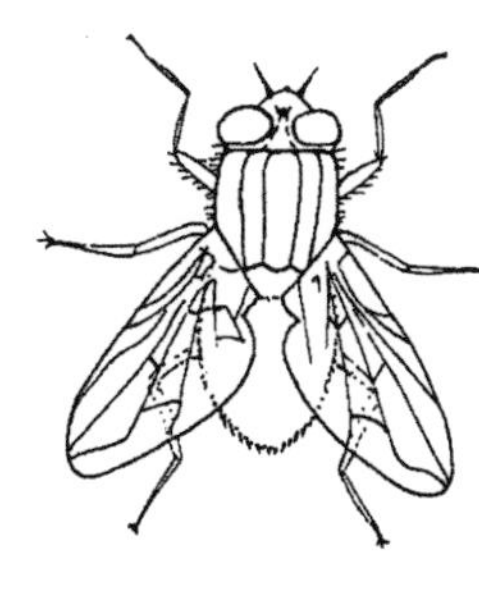

Order Diptera – flies

Complete metamorphosis.
Adults: Two pairs of wings, front pair membranous, back pair forming knobs called halters, mouthparts for piercing, sucking or sponging. May damage heritage materials by soiling with faecal material (fly spots), carpet beetle larvae may be harboured in dead adult's abdomen.
Larvae: maggots, grub-like, live on moist dead organic material.

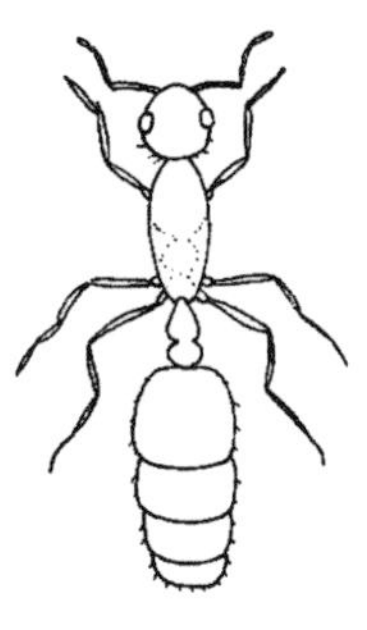

Order Hymenoptera – ants

Complete metamorphosis.
Adults: Social insects, different castes, worker ants are wingless, reproductive adults have four wings. Mouthparts adapted for chewing or lapping, damage caused by adults tunnelling in wood or scraping organic material from surfaces.
Larvae: vary, may be grub-like without legs, may have mandibles, adults feed larvae.

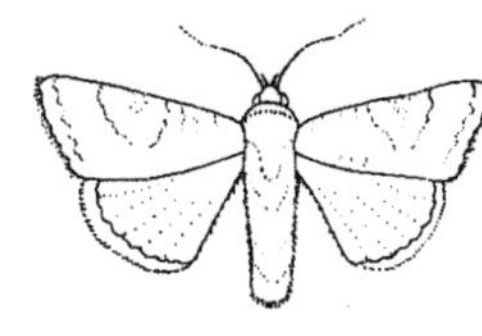

Order Lepidoptera – moths

Complete metamorphosis
Adults: four wings, membranous and covered with overlapping scales. Adults have mouthparts adapted to sucking, do not cause damage.
Larvae: vary, grub-like to caterpillar-like, three pairs of prolegs, some with hooked crochets in circles or rows on the pad of each proleg. Head, dark, sclerotized capsule, soft body. Mouthparts with opposable toothed mandible, silk spinnerets present, cause damage.

Illustrations by Lori Graves

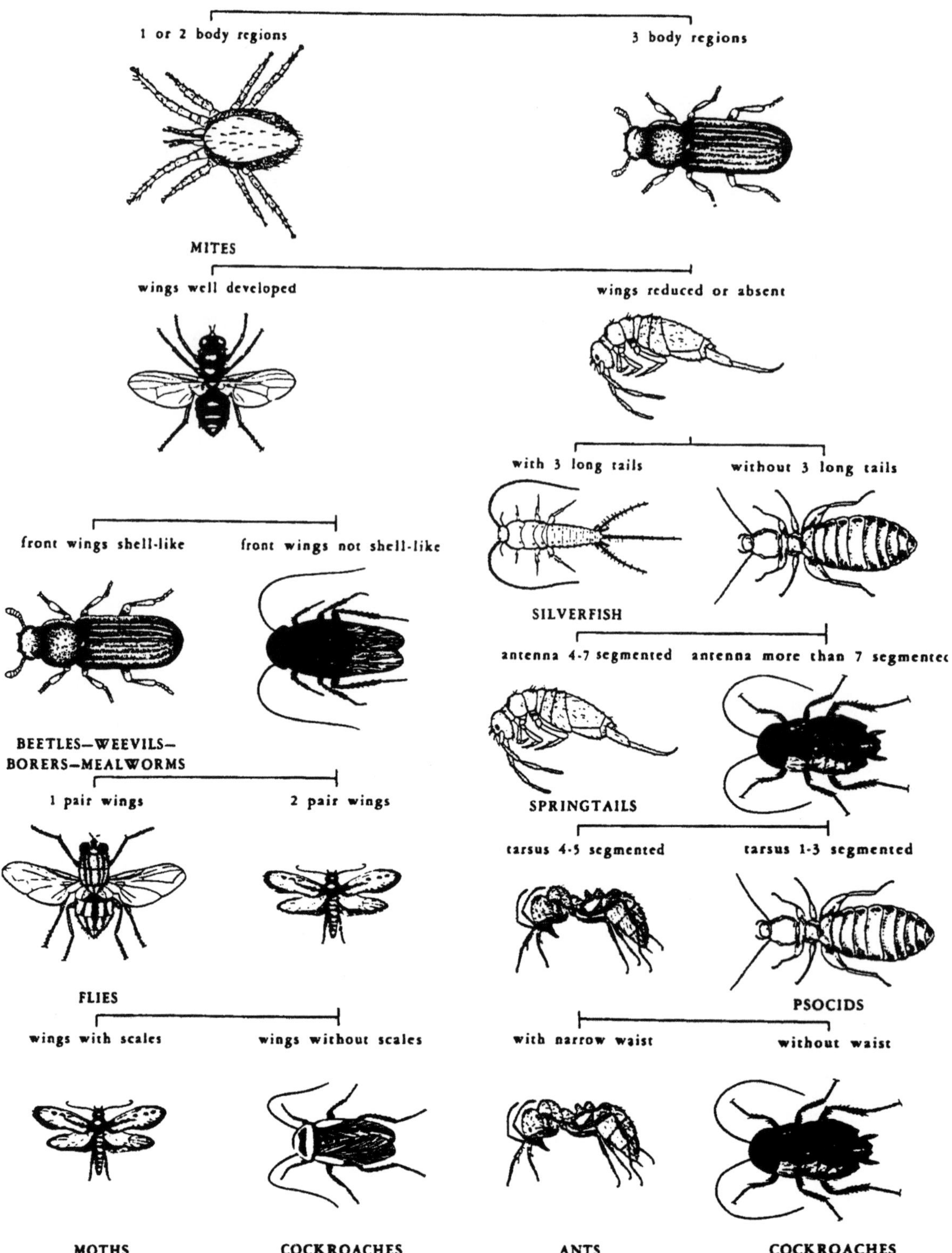

Figure 3.4. A key to common insect types (Scott, 1959, U.S.D.H.E.W).

Figure 3.4 shows a key to common insect types (Scott, 1959).

REFERENCES

Bennett, G.W., J.M. Owens and R.M. Corrigan. 1997. *Truman's Scientific Guide to Pest Control Operations*, 5th edition. Advanstar Communications Inc., Cleveland, Ohio.

Gullan, P.J. and P.S. Cranston. 1994. *The Insects: An Outline of Entomology*. Chapman and Hall, London, New York.

Peacock, E.R. 1993. *Adults and Larvae of Hide, Larder and Carpet Beetles and their Relatives (Coleoptera:Dermestidae) and of Derodontid Beetles (Coleoptera: Derodontidae)*. Handbooks for the Identification of British Insects, Vol.5, Part 3,. Royal Entomological Society of London, London.

Scott, H.G. 1959. *Household and Stored-Food Insects of Public Health Importance and their Control.* U.S. Department of Health, Education and Welfare, Atlanta, Georgia.

4

Exoskeleton and Moulting

4.1 INTRODUCTION

The outer surface of insect nymphs or larvae, pupae and adults is called the exoskeleton or integument. For the insect, the role of the exoskeleton is fundamental: it is the basis for their survival and evolutionary success. It acts as the skin, defines the insect and, like a skeleton, gives support to its soft body and muscles. The exoskeleton prevents body water and oxygen loss, aids in body temperature control and protects the insect body from parasites, micro-organisms and ultraviolet light. It must be soft and flexible to allow for movement and extensible to permit growth. In some parts, it must be thin to allow oxygen diffusion to individual cells and, in others, hard and horny for mandibles and claws. The exoskeleton is the site of many sensory organs involved in detecting water, chemicals and movement, and can even be used as a food source for its own and other species' larvae.

Because many insect eradication methods use chemicals, gases or abrasive and adsorbent powders, whose actions are influenced by the exoskeleton, relevant information about its structure is presented here. Despite the fact that it is usually the larvae that are the heritage eaters, because we rarely see the larvae until after the fact, we concentrate on the adults. Most of the information in the literature, reviewed here, is about adults but it is applicable to other life stages.

4.2 STRUCTURE OF THE CUTICLE

The exoskeleton is made up of three layers (Figure 4.1): an outer, non-cellular *cuticle* (*procuticle* and *epicuticle*) of unique chemicals; an underlying layer of cells called the *epidermis* that secretes the chemicals of the cuticle; and the non-cellular *basal membrane* below the epidermis.

The epidermis is a layer of cells that secretes the chemicals used for moulting of the cuticle and also supplies all the chemicals used in forming the different layers of the new cuticle. The epidermis cells do not divide but they grow in size with larval growth.

The cuticle, the non-cellular outer layers of the exoskeleton, is our main concern. There are three main regions in the cuticle: the *endocuticle*, *exocuticle* and *epicuticle*.

The endocuticle is the region, accounting for about two-thirds of the cuticle, adjacent to the epidermis. It is made up of chitin-protein polymers and is responsible for the extensibility and flexibility of the exoskeleton.

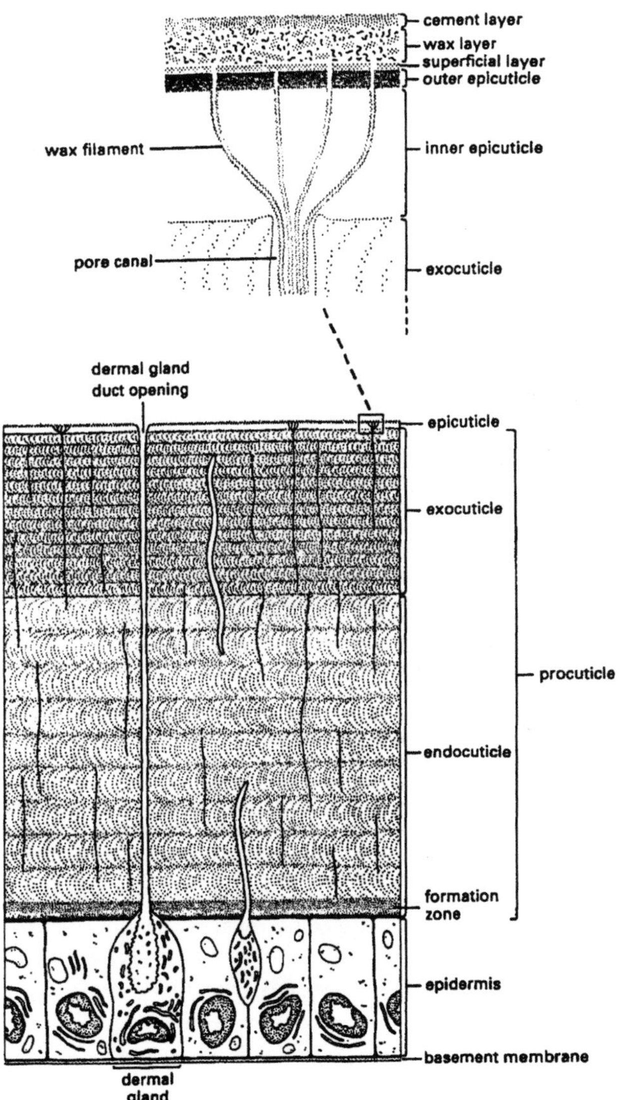

Figure 4.1. General structure of insect cuticle: the enlargement above the main diagram shows details of the epicuticle (Gullan and Cranston, 1994, with permission).

The exocuticle is the dark, hard, outer one-third of the cuticle. It is made up of chitin and quinone-tanned proteins. It provides rigidity for the hard parts of the head and legs.

The epicuticle is the thin surface on the exocuticle, consisting of a wax layer about 0.1–3.0μm in thickness or a varnish-like cement. It is this extremely thin wax layer that is so critical in preventing body water loss.

The trachea are invaginations of the epidermis, so their lining is continuous with the exocuticle. The chemistry of the tracheal cuticle resembles the exocuticle, but with a few exceptions: there is no epicuticle wax or cement present and in the finer branches, the tracheole, chitin is absent. (See chapter 5 on the tracheal system).

For further information on cuticle structure, see Andersen (1979), Gullan and Cranston (1994), Locke (1974) and Wigglesworth (1984).

4.3 THE CHEMICALS IN THE CUTICLE

The chemicals of the layers each play a specific role in the protective nature of the cuticle.

4.3.1 Chitin-protein polymers

Chitin-protein polymers are in the endocuticle and exocuticle, but not in the epicuticle. Chitin is a colourless polymer which is insoluble in water, dilute acid or alkali, alcohols and all organic solvents. The chitin polymer is in the form of submicroscopic crystallites aligned to form larger rodlets, which align to form larger microfibrils, and these form fibrils that in turn form lamellae. Protein binds all the levels together. In the chitin-protein complex, chitin gives strength and protein acts as a plasticizer.

It is this dense alignment of chitin crystals that protects the chitin against solubilization. The only thing in nature that can dissolve it is the complex mixture of enzymes (including chitinase, glucanase and protease) found in the moulting fluid and also produced by a few insect-eating bacteria and fungi.

4.3.2 Sclerotization

The exocuticle contains chitin-protein polymers and a protein component, which have been converted to a horn-like material called sclerotin in a hardening process is called sclerotization. The proteins are tanned, like leather, by phenolic quinone tanning agents, which create one of the strongest protein cross-linkage bonds known. If the exocuticle is sclerotinized it cannot be digested even by the moulting fluid and is left behind as the exuvium or moult. Tyrosine is the main protein and its presence contributes to the amber colour, along with melanin. Melanin, the same brown pigment found in our hair, is commonly present in the insect cuticle and adds a black or brown colour. It is usually involved in the formation of colourful and metallic physical colours. Melanin protects the soft body of the insect from ultraviolet damage and from micro-organism attack. Melanin also inhibits the enzyme mixture that digests chitin.

For further information on sclerotization, see Ricketts and Sugumaran (1994) and Wigglesworth (1985).

4.3.3 Epicuticle wax and cement

There are minute tubes throughout the cuticle that bring lipids and proteins to the surface of the exocuticle. The lipoproteins and the crystalline wax surface, which form the epicuticle, cover the exocuticle and make it waterproof. The waxes are chemically different in different insect species (Gilby, 1980). In some insects there is a varnish-like substance over the epicuticle called cement. Shellac is a commercial product made from the cement of the lac scale insect *Kerria lacca* and is used like a varnish to finish wood surfaces on furniture.

The waxes vary from the soft, greasy material on the cockroach to the hard, crystalline wax found on *Tenebrio* larvae.

The chemical composition of the waxes varies with different species. The melting points, or transition temperatures, of the waxes also vary. When the waxes melt, the cuticle appears to lose its water impermeability and this is expressed in the different heat tolerances of different species.

For further information on cuticle chemicals, see Andersen (1979), Hackman (1978) and Wigglesworth (1984).

4.4 MECHANICAL PROPERTIES OF THE CUTICLE

When the cuticle is first laid down by the epidermis, it is soft and white but the exocuticle usually quickly becomes dark and hard through sclerotization. It remains soft and white in some larvae and in some adult insects, i.e. booklice or subterranean termites, but in most adult insects the exocuticle becomes dark and hard. Lepidoptera (moths and butterflies) and Coleoptera larvae have a soft plastic cuticle throughout the instars (the larval or nymph stage between the moults) with great extension ability to accommodate larval growth. The cuticle of adult Coleoptera is brittle and hard as a result of sclerotization: plasticity and increase in size is limited to brief periods before hardening, immediately after pupation.

There is evidence that the cuticle plasticity can be altered by a shift in the pH of the diet: when acidic it is hard and when alkaline soft (Andersen, 1979). In addition, there are regions of the whole cuticle that are more plastic than others: abdominal intersegmental membranes of female termites can extend 10-fold to accommodate egg production. In the exuvium of the common carpet beetle, intersegmental bands of hard, brown, sclerotized cuticle are obvious between plastic, white segments.

For further information on mechanical properties of cuticle, see Locke (1974).

4.5 WATER PERMEABILITY OF THE CUTICLE

The ability to adsorb water vapour through the cuticle is dependent on the insect species, its stage and size, the structure of the epicuticle, nutritional state, environmental temperature and relative humidity (RH). To generalize is impossible, but active water uptake does occur through the cuticle, which does not have an epicutical surface wax lipid/protein layer. Brown, ridged, sclerotized exoskeletons usually have an epicuticle but white, soft nonsclerotized exoskeletons of larvae, booklice, white termites and ants are without it. Subterranean termites and drywood termites maintain their body water by adsorption of water vapour through the exoskeleton from the humid air in the galleries of the wood in which they live. Strangely, firebrat and mealworm larvae can absorb moisture through the anal opening.

Table 4.1. Relative humidities (RH) at which insects have been shown to adsorb water vapour from the air

Insect species	RH (%)
Cigarette beetle larva – *Lasioderma serricorne*	43
Firebrat – *Thermobia domestica*	45
Prepupa of flea	50
Booklice – *Liposcelis divinatorius*	60
Yellow mealworm larva *Tenebrio molitor*	90
Cockroach nymph	82
Psocid booklice	53–58

At the RHs shown in Table 4.1, the insects specified, partially hydrated, have been shown to adsorb water vapour from the air, without eating and drinking, causing an increase in body weight.

For further information on cuticle water permeability, see Ebeling (1974) and Gilby (1980).

4.6 VULNERABILITY OF THE EPICUTICLE TO TEMPERATURE

Knowing the structure of the cuticle allows us to pinpoint its weakest or most vulnerable part, and helps us to design eradication methods based on this weakness. The presence of the extremely thin wax layer of the epicuticle makes the insects vulnerable to abrasion, fat-soluble chemicals and heat.

Abrasive dusts of borax or diatomaceous earth are used as insecticides because they remove the extremely delicate epicuticle and cause lethal dehydration (Ebeling, 1971, 1974). Soaps are also used in insecticides because they dissolve the wax of the epicuticle and the insect dies of dehydration. Surfactants and wetting agents are used in insecticidal preparations to wet this wax, so the toxic insecticides can be more easily absorbed into the body of the insect.

Heat treatments for eradication of insect pests are also used. Temperatures of 40–60°C have been shown to cause rapid loss of body water, leading to death, in a variety of insects. Death has been attributed to dehydration because the heat melts the wax in the epicuticle. The waxes of different insect species have different melting temperatures. Cockroaches show a rapid loss of body weight due to water loss attributed to the transformation of the epicuticle wax at 30°C.

Figure 4.2 shows how three types of grain beetle demonstrated a dramatic increase in weight loss due to water loss at the temperature that disrupted the molecular orientation in the lipid layer of the epicuticle.

Gilby (1980) discussed the problem of interpreting the literature with reference to the role of temperature transition and transpiration. As with the literature on lethal freezing temperatures (see chapter 12), Gilby (1980) wrote of the literature on transpiration, 'For a rigorous analysis of experimental results it is necessary to know the physical properties of the insect ... in addition to environmental parameters'. He suggested that the evidence in the literature shows no abrupt change, as at a critical temperature, or melting or crystalline change of the waxes, but a gradual increase in permeability with temperature.

Temperature increase may have many possible results, which must be considered: increase in metabolic activity, increase in rate of external respiration, heat damage of cellular components, increase in vapour pressure of water, etc. (Machin and Lampert, 1989).

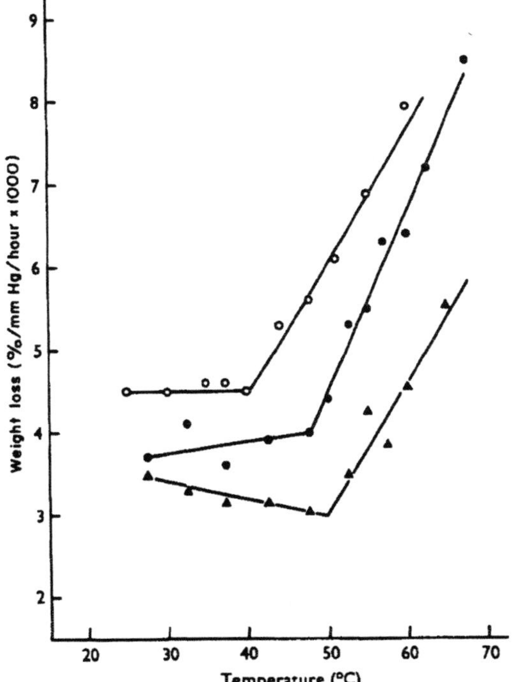

Figure 4.2. Abrupt rise in rate of weight loss due to water loss for three species of tenebrionid beetles at critical temperature points. O Eleodes armata; ● Centrioptera muricata; ▲ Cryptoglossa verrucosa *(from Ahearn, 1970).*

The presence of lipids has been demonstrated by application of solvents and abrasion, but the molecular architecture and the theory of its function are not clear, according to Machin and Lampert (1989). These authors showed from their research that permeability increases occurred between 35 and 40°C and were irreversible in pieces of excised cuticle and that the permeability increased as the temperature rose, with no distinct transition. So much for the melting wax theory.

4.7 MOULTING OR ECDYSIS

The cuticle gives the larvae and nymphs its many protective features but, because it cannot expand or grow once it is formed, it has to be shed periodically and a larger new cuticle formed to accommodate growth. The shedding of the cuticle is called moulting.

Moulting is a complex process involving hormonal, behavioural, epidermal and cuticular changes. The end result is the shedding of the old cuticle or exuvium. A new cuticle is laid down by the epidermal cells.

The hormones and their concentrations during the life of a larva are shown in Figure 8.1 (in chapter 8). A hormone called the juvenile hormone (JH) is needed for the larva to go through the necessary instar growth. High titres of JH inhibit the expression of adult features, so they are associated with a larval–larval moult; low titres of JH cause a larval–pupal moult. Following the last instar moult, there is a dramatic reduction in JH, which insures that the moult goes into a pupa.

During moulting, an increase in ecdysteroid hormone stimulates the epidermis, which leads to the formation of a new cuticle.

JH is used as a form of insect pest control, to prevent adult formation in insect populations. It does not kill the larvae immediately, but the metabolic imbalance will eventually do so.

The cuticle of most larvae remains soft and flexible and may not have a sclerotized or waxy epicutical. If present, a sclerotized exocuticle is usually confined to the head or dorsal segment plates. A differentiated exocuticle and endocuticle appear when the pupa is clothed (pharate) in the larval–pupal moult. This last instar is often a wandering stage, during which the larva wanders away from its feeding site to find a suitable place to pupate.

The sequential steps in the process of moulting are:

1 Enzymatic digestion of the endocuticle, between the epidermal cells and exocuticle, by the moulting fluid;
2 Absorption of the dissolved endocuticle;
3 Formation of a new cuticle by the epidermal cells;
4 Rupturing and removal of the insoluble exocuticle and epicuticle (the moult or exuvium);
5 Expansion of the new instar and of the new cuticle;
6 The hardening and sclerotization of parts of the exocuticle.

The exuvium is composed of the sclerotized exocuticle and epicuticle. These structures contain lipids that are free, not bound to the protein-chitin complex, and, if the exuvium is eaten by a larva it can utilize the lipids for nutrition. Sometimes these lipids can also be absorbed back into the body of the larva if it is under stress from lack of food.

REFERENCES

Ahearn, G.A. 1970. The control of water loss in desert tenebrionid beetles. *The Journal of Experimental Biology*, 52:573596.

Andersen, S.O. 1979. Biochemistry of insect cuticle. *Annual Review of Entomology*, 24:29–62.

Ebeling, W. 1971. Sorptive dusts for pest control. *Annual Review of Entomology*, 16:123–158.

Ebeling, W. 1974. Permeability of insect cuticle. In *The Physiology of Insecta*, Vol. 6, Ed. Morris Rockstein. Academic Press, New York, pp271–345.

Gilby, A.R. 1980. Transpiration, temperature and lipids in insect cuticle. *Advances in Insect Physiology*, 15:1–33.

Gullan, P.J. and P.S. Cranston. 1994. *The Insects: An Outline of Entomology*. Chapman and Hall, London, New York.

Hackman, R. H. 1974. Chemistry of the insect cuticle. In *The Physiology of Insecta*, Vol. 6, Ed. Morris Rockstein. Academic Press, New York, pp215–270.

Locke, M. 1974. The structure and formation of the integument in insects. In *The Physiology of Insecta*, Vol. 6, Ed. Morris Rockstein. Academic Press, New York, pp123–215.

Machin, J. and G.J.Lampert. 1989. Energetics of water diffusion through the cuticular water barrier of *Periplaneta*: the effect of temperature, revisited. *Journal of Insect Physiology*, 35(5):437–445.

Ricketts, D. and M. Sugumaran. 1994. 1,2-Dehydro-N-B-alanyldopamine as a new intermediate in insect cuticular sclerotization. *The Journal of Biological Chemistry*, 269(35):22217–22221.

Wigglesworth, V.B. 1984. *Insect Physiology*, 8th edition. Chapman and Hall, London, New York, p191.

Wigglesworth, V.B. 1985. Sclerotin and lipid in the waterproofing of the insect cuticle. *Tissue and Cell*, 17(2):227–248.

5

The Tracheal System

5.1 STRUCTURE OF TRACHEAL SYSTEM

The function of the tracheal system may be summarized as: oxygen in, carbon dioxide out; water in, water out.

Insects, like all oxygen-utilizing animals, must obtain oxygen and eliminate carbon dioxide. This process is called gas exchange (breathing) or external respiration. Internal respiration involves the use of oxygen in the actual chemical processes of aerobic respiration or metabolism (see 12.2.5).

In adults, larvae and pupae of insects with complete metamorphosis (holometabolous), such as beetles and moths, gas exchange occurs by means of tubes (tracheae (pl)) branching throughout the insect body that form the tracheal system (Figure 5.1). Eggs also require oxygen for development and maintenance and have special shell structures for gaseous exchange (see Chapter 6).

Knowledge of the structure and function of the tracheal system is needed to devise logical eradication methods that involve gas exchange, including altered atmospheric gases, anoxic environments and some fumigants.

Air-carrying oxygen enters into the tracheal system through a series of openings located along the sides of the body, called spiracles (Figure 5.1a). There is usually one pair per body segment, though the numbers vary up to 10 pairs. The spiracles have valves (Figure 5.1c) that are opened or closed according to internal and external influences. The tracheal system rami-

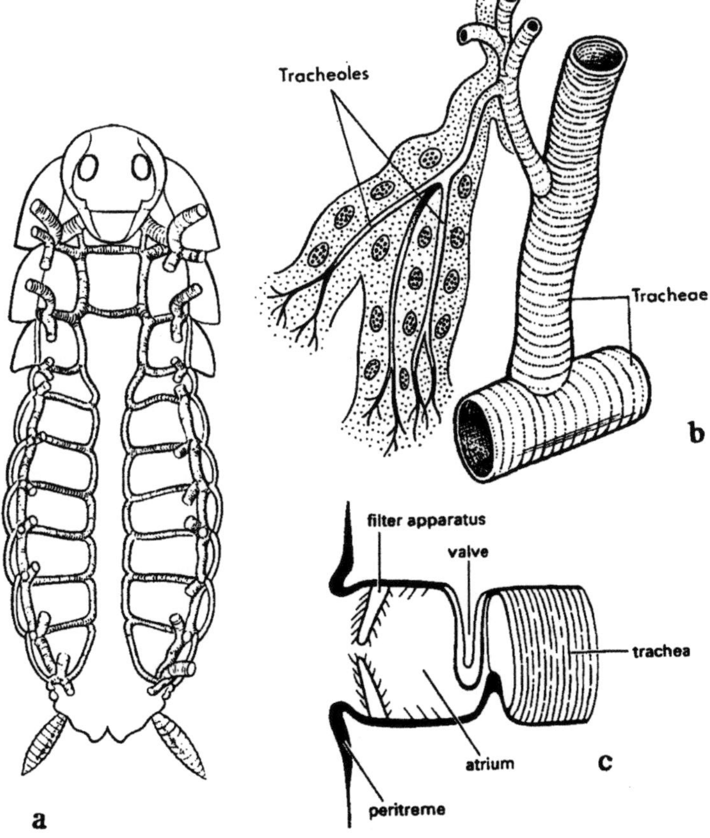

Figure 5.1. The tracheal system: a, overall arrangement of the branches of the tracheal system in a cockroach; b, details of the relationship of tracheae and tracheoles; c, details of a spiracle with a closing valve adjacent to the trachea (a, b from The Rentokil Library, *Munroe, 1966 and c from Gullen and Cranston, 1994, with permission).*

fies throughout the body of the insect. It is made up of a network of tubes, tracheae, which branch repeatedly and become smaller and smaller, terminating in tracheoles (Figure 5.1b), which are the size of individual body cells.

The tracheae are invaginations of the chitinous exoskeleton and are thus impermeable to oxygen and water. The terminal tracheoles are not lined with wax or chitin and are thus permeable to water, oxygen and carbon dioxide, which diffuse freely, according to the diffusion gradient, in and out of the body cells and body fluid.

The tracheae tubes have spiral, ridged thickenings (Figure 5.1b), called taenidial bars, along their length for strength and flexibility, and to prevent the collapse of the tubes and allow free passage of air. There are also air sacs, without the taenidial bars, which can increase in size for gas storage. This air storage is also a method of reducing water loss.

In larval moulting, the old tracheal tubes are pulled out through the new spiracular opening. New tracheal structures are formed around the old ones immediately after the latter have separated from the epidermis. Despite the difference in the gross morphology of the holometabolous larvae and adult, the larval tracheal system is preserved in a modified form in the adults. It has been suggested that, in some puparia (hardened, protective larval skins), the spiracular structures are larval structures that have been retained in the pupal stage. The tracheal system of the nymphs is the same as in the adults, except for minor size differences. Very little definitive work has been done on the structural changes of the tracheal system from the larva to the pupa.

5.2 AIR MOVEMENT THROUGH THE TRACHEAL SYSTEM

The movement of air through the trachea is by simple diffusion, according to a diffusion gradient, but can be augmented by abdominal contractions which act like a pump, as well as spiracular valve fluttering. Both oxygen and carbon dioxide gases diffuse into the haemolymph (blood) but there are no special cells or chemicals in the blood that are involved in active gas transport.

5.3 THE SPIRACULAR VALVE

5.3.1 Opening and closing of the spiracular valve

The closing of the spiracles is essential for terrestrial insects to prevent body water loss. The opening and closing of the spiracles is caused by muscles which contract or relax to open and close a valve at the opening of the trachea. (A valve is shown in Figure 5.1c). If the valve is made of elastic cuticle the muscles have to pull it open, but if not the muscles open the valve and there is an opposable ligament to close it.

The spiracles are usually closed to prevent water loss. The opening of the spiracles for gaseous exchange may be just a fluttering of the valve. In some diapausing pupae it has been shown that the carbon dioxide can periodically be mechanically blown out of the spiracles. This cyclic discharge of carbon dioxide is called the Prague cycle (Slama and Coquillaud, 1992).

Opening and closing is controlled by an interaction of many endogenous and exogenous factors, i.e. exogenous: temperature, relative humidity, atmospheric pressure, concentration of oxygen, carbon dioxide and nitrogen; and endogenous: insect age, stage, metabolic rate, water reserves and internal oxygen and carbon dioxide concentrations.

(For further information see Nikam and Khole, 1989).

5.3.2 THE INFLUENCE OF OXYGEN, CARBON DIOXIDE AND NITROGEN ON SPIRACULAR VALVE OPENING

Air contains approximately 21% oxygen, 78% nitrogen, 1% argon and 0.03% carbon dioxide, by volume.

Both oxygen and carbon dioxide influence spiracular behaviour. The spiracle opens when the concentration of oxygen is lower or carbon dioxide is higher in the body fluid than in normal atmospheric air.

During oxygen depletion and anaerobic respiration in the insect, lactic acid accumulates, which can also stimulate the spiracles to open. An increase in carbon dioxide may cause body fluid acidic conditions, which are suggested to trigger opening of the spiracles. Because carbon dioxide is more soluble in the haemolymph than oxygen, it may be the major initiator of spiracle response. Pure nitrogen causes the spiracles to open.

Carbon dioxide or nitrogen are often combined with fumigants to keep the spiracles open and enhance the insecticidal effect.

5.3.3 THERMOREGULATION – TEMPERATURE INFLUENCES SPIRACULAR VALVE OPENING

Insects must maintain a body temperature within an appropriate range for the performance of normal metabolic activities. They must gain heat but avoid high body temperatures. The environment of the insect may be hot or the internal temperature of the insect may increase due to raised metabolic activity. The insects have little ability to compensate for environmental temperatures. Insects' behavioural patterns, posture, avoidance of light, etc. usually reflect their thermal sensitivity to their environment. The regulation of internal high body temperature generated by an increase in muscle activity involves haemolymph circulation as well as the spiraculotracheal system.

Studies of insect respiration have shown that the tracheal network of insects ventilates excessive air volume at high temperatures and during raised metabolism (after flight). When exposed to abnormally high temperatures, insects may die because of the temperature effect or dehydration. The effects of temperatures over 40°C can cause death due to denaturation of proteins, enzymes and DNA, all of which are required for life processes. Large insects can sometimes control their body temperature by evaporation of moisture from the body. They do this by opening the spiracles.

At reduced temperatures the spiracles respond to oxygen and carbon dioxide down to -5°C but below -5°C the spiracles are frozen shut. At temperatures just above -5°C the spiracular valves should close to conserve body temperature but, if placed in 2% carbon dioxide, the spiracles remain open.

High temperatures are now being tested as a method of insect pest eradication. The above information suggests that temperature elevated to around 40°C may cause lethal dehydration and temperatures about 50°C may cause other lethal cellular temperature effects. Any insect pest eradication treatment is as intrusive to the heritage object being treated as to the insect. Research is needed to determine the influence of such a treatment on the materials of the heritage objects.

5.3.4 BODY WATER INFLUENCES SPIRACULAR VALVE OPENING

Insects may obtain water in various ways: with ingested food; from oxidation of ingested food; by drinking it; via the tracheal system; via the cuticle; and via the anal opening. Water loss occurs through the tracheal system and the cuticle.

In most insects the exoskeleton or cuticle is water impermeable because of a surface lipid or wax layer or wax. If this wax layer is destroyed by heat or mechanical abrasion, body water can be easily lost. Only a few insects, i.e. booklice, firebrats and silverfish, normally adsorb moisture through the cuticle. The cuticle of these insects does not have a surface waterproofing lipid or wax layer. Body water loss occurs mainly through the tracheal system by simple diffusion from the haemolymph into the air in the trachea. The direction of diffusion is dependent on the diffusion gradient between the relative humidity of the air in the trachea and of the external air. There is an interesting conflict between the need to obtain oxygen and at the same time conserve water: opening the spiracular valves brings in oxygen but causes loss of water. Fluttering of the spiracular valves may be a method of conserving water and yet obtaining needed oxygen.

The water reserves or state of hydration of the insect influences the spiracular response to oxygen and carbon dioxide. Hydrated dragonflies in 2% carbon dioxide keep the spiracles open to eliminate the excess carbon dioxide but, if the insect is dehydrated, the spiracles remain closed. This suggests that protection against dehydration has first priority over gases. Insects usually die of dehydration when their body moisture is reduced to about 50% of their total body weight: insects' normal water content is around 80% of total body weight. Spiracular valve closing, a water-impermeable cuticle and excretion of dry faeces are considered the main methods of conserving body water.

5.3.5 SPIRACULAR VALVE ACTIVITY AND FUMIGANTS

Even though fumigants have been used for nearly a hundred years, spiracular valve activity under fumigation is still a neglected field. Fumigants may act as an anaesthetic, a nerve or respiratory inhibitor or a metabolic toxin. Thus there will be a different spiracular valve response to each specific fumigant. It may be that the toxic fumigants themselves do not cause the death of the insect but they are killed by lack of oxygen or by dehydration. The response of the spiracular valve of the insect pests to eradication treatments using fumigation or altered atmospheric gases is critical to the success of the treatment.

For more details on the tracheal system see Bursell, 1974a,b; Gullan and Cranston, 1994; Keister and Buck, 1974; Miller, 1974; Slama and Cocquillaud, 1992.

REFERENCES

Bursell, F. 1974a. Part A. The insect and external environment. Chapter 2. Environmental aspects – humidity. In *The Physiology of Insecta*, Vol. II, Ed. Morris Rockstein. Academic Press, New York, pp44–84.

Bursell, F. 1974b. Part A. The insect and external environment. Chapter 1. Environmental aspects – temperature. In *The Physiology of Insecta*, Vol. II, Ed. Morris Rockstein. Academic Press, New York, pp2–43.

Gullan, P.J. and P.S. Cranston. 1994. *The Insects: an Outline of Entomology*. Chapman and Hall, London, New York.

Keister, M. and J. Buck. 1974. Respiration: some exogenous and endogenous effects on rate of respiration. In *The Physiology of Insecta*, Vol. VI, Ed. Morris Rockstein. Academic Press, New York, pp470–509.

Miller, P.L. 1974. Respiration – aerial gas transport. In *The Physiology of Insecta*, Vol. VI, Ed. Morris Rockstein. Academic Press, New York, pp346–402.

Munroe, J.W. 1966. *Pests of Stored Grain Products, The Rentokil Library*, Hutchinson, London.

Nikam, T.B. and V.V. Khole. 1989. *Insect Spiracular Systems*. Ellis Horwood, Chichester, p136.

Slama, K. and M.S. Coquillaud. 1992. Homeostatic control of respiratory metabolism in beetles. *Journal of Insect Physiology*, 38(10):783–791.

6

The Insect Egg

6.1 EGGS AND HATCHING

Most insects are oviparous, that is, the young hatch from internally fertilized eggs that have been laid externally from the female body. Only in a very few insects do the eggs develop in the body of the female and living young are laid.

The appearance of the eggs varies with species. They may be oval or elongated and the shells vary in thickness, sculpturing and colour. The design of the sculpturing is species-specific and it assists in species identification. Box 6.1. shows the sculpturing on some common moth eggs. Certain insects, for example the cockroaches, enclose the eggs in a protective coating or capsule.

Most insects lay from a few to hundreds of eggs. The eggs are laid in a specific spot, an oviposition site, where there is some protection, a suitable environment and nutrients for the development of hatched young. The eggs in the oviposition site undergo embryological development and, when this is completed, a young larva or nymph emerges. Many of the museum insect pests – clothes moths and beetles – lay their eggs in the materials of heritage objects. The foraging insects, such as cockroaches and booklice, lay their eggs in a different environment from where they feed. The cockroach is known to look after and feed the newborn nymphs for a day or two.

The insect eggs are rich in yolk. There are enough nutrients and water for embryological development to the nymph or larval stage, but gaseous diffusion must occur.

The eggshell is made up of three envelopes: the inner serosal cuticle of the embryo, the vitelline membrane of the egg and the outer hard chorion shell (Figure 6.1). The eggshell serves to regulate the rates of exchange of gases between the surrounding atmosphere and the inside of the egg and to conserve water. The oxygen molecule is larger than the water molecule so there must be some system to allow free movement of the larger oxygen and at the same time to restrict the loss of water.

6.2 EGGSHELL STRUCTURE

The serosal cuticle of the embryo acts as a living membrane with its permeability controlled by osmosis. It separates the amniotic fluid of the developing larva from the vitellin membrane. Sonobe and Nakamura (1991) suggested that the serosal cuticle formed after 24–36 hours of incubation may be involved in the control of oxygen absorption.

The vitelline membrane and chorion are non-living and act as permeable membranes involved in passive diffusion. The wax layer covering the vitellin membrane functions to prevent water loss. In dermestids' eggs without a chorion there are a large number of slightly raised regions (0.5μm in diameter) on the exposed vitelline membrane. These regions have a multitude of wax canals, which replenish wax lost by abrasion or predators (Furneaux and Mackay, 1976).

The chorion is made up of a structural protein called chorionin. It derives its strength and insolubility from disulphide-crosslinked or quinone- tanned proteins. The majority of terrestrial eggs have a meshwork in the chorion, which holds a layer of air (Figure 6.1). The meshwork is made up of aeropyles or holes that extend throughout the shell to give a continuity of atmospheric and chorion gas. Aeropyles, tubes of very small diameter, connect the meshwork of the inner chorion with the outside atmosphere. It is the aeropyle openings on the surface of the chorion that give the chorion the sculptured surface (see Box 6.1). The innermost layer is a thin, solid sheet of chorion. The chorion with its aeropyles functions as a plastron, an air bubble gill, like the air bubble the diving beetles carry with them when they dive in water. Some insects

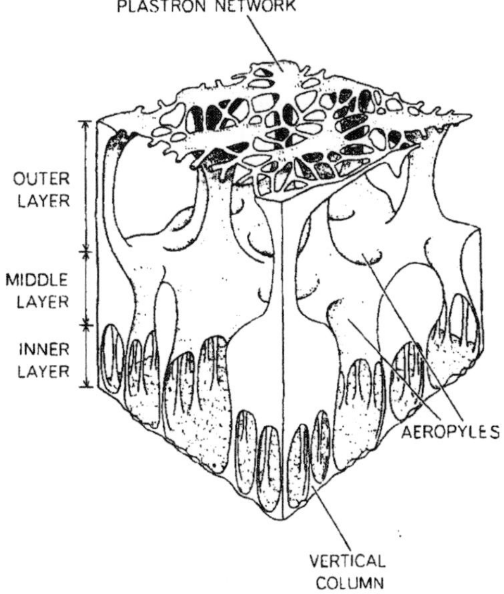

Figure 6.1. Section of the chorion shell of an insect egg showing the plastron network and air-filled outer layer underlying it, the meshwork of vertical columns of the inner layer and the aeropyles between (after Hinton, 1970).

have the plastron restricted to a respiratory horn or localized regions on the chorion. The plastron also prevents an oxygen deficiency when the egg becomes wet. The chorion additionally acts to protect the intactness of the wax layer of the vitelline membrane.

At the anterior end of the egg, the micropylar area, there are a number of openings for the entrance of sperm. Their ornate shapes, shown in Box 6.1, assist in species identification. Lepidoptera eggs may have meshworks so fine (Furneaux and Mackay, 1976) that they cannot be seen with a light microscope, whereas in other insect eggs the aeropyles are easily visible. In *Dermestes*, the chorion is very thin or absent.

For further information on eggshell structure, see Arbogast *et al.* (1980), Arbogast *et al.* (1983), Arbogast *et al.* (1984), Arbogast and Brower (1989), Hinton (1969, 1970) and Furneaux and Mackay (1976).

6.3 FUNCTION OF THE EGGSHELL

6.3.1 Introduction

The following reviewed studies, on the function of the eggshell regarding oxygen and water permeability and temperature tolerances, are on specific insect species. They describe activities that must be common to other insects. There is species variability but the underlying phenomena must be universal.

The purpose of this review is to provide a background for understanding the actions of eradication methods using altered atmospheres, reduced oxygen and temperature extremes. Unfortunately, there is a great lack of information directly applicable to the heritage eater insect species, but this review will act as a knowledge base on which to add.

6.3.2 Oxygen permeability

Oxygen requirements vary with the size of embryo and stage of development. Daniel and Smith (1994) studied the oxygen requirements of developing eggs and compared the results with adults. *Callosobruchus maculatus*, Yemen strain, eggs 1–2 days old had an oxygen requirement of 8.59μl per day and those 6–7 days old required 23.52μl/day. They attributed the increase in oxygen to the change in metabolites used, from carbohydrates to fats. Fats require up to three times the amount of oxygen when used in anaerobic respiration. This type of increase was also shown in the oxygen needs of the pupae during diapause (see chapter 8). Non-feeding adults used 75–82μl per hour, at a constant rate. The weight differences were 25.5μg for eggs and 5.3mg for adults. The eggs during development required one third more oxygen per unit of body weight than adults.

The respiratory quotient (RQ) has been observed during the development of the egg and the general picture is that, at initiation, the RQ is close to 1, with a rapid drop. This has been attributed to the utilization of different energy sources, i.e. first carbohydrates then fats converted to carbohydrates.

6.3.3 Oxygen requirements during diapause

Insect eggs usually go through an obligatory stage of development delay called diapause. It is a stage of low metabolism and low oxygen consumption. If the egg in early embryonic development goes into diapause, the assumption has been that the permeability of the chorion would decrease just before diapause. Recent work (Sonobe and Nakamura, 1991) on the silkworm egg shows, however, that the permeability of the chorion to oxygen does not change appreciably with the onset of diapause, even though oxygen consumption decreases. These researchers also demonstrated that it is not caused by the lack of acceptance of oxygen in the electron transfer system in oxidative respiration (see chapter 5). They suggested that the serosal membranes play a role in oxygen absorption control.

6.3.4 Prevention of water loss

Even though the water molecule is smaller than the oxygen molecule and the pore size of the chorion has to enable the larger of the two molecules to move through the shell, water loss is minimal. The most important aspect of egg survival is prevention of water loss. In some dry terrestrial insect eggs only small specialized areas of the shell may be permeable to gas and the majority of the shell is hard, smooth and impermeable. This is the case in the bean weevil, *Callosobrochus maculatus* (Daniel and Smith, 1994). These investigators showed that a single opening in the chorion, the egg pore, was solely responsible for gas diffusion by plugging it with oil; the egg suffocated and died.

The gas permeability of the insect eggs makes them vulnerable to altered atmospheric gases used as a method of eradication.

6.4 RESISTANCE OF EGGS TO LOW TEMPERATURE

Low-temperature insect pest eradication methods are covered in 12.1. With silkworm eggs, Yamashita and Yaginuma (1991) showed that the number of days of incubation influences resistance to low temperatures. Eggs were initially incubated at 25°C for various lengths of time prior to 24 hours' treatment at -20°C, then returned to 25°C to continue incubation. For eggs with an initial incubation of one day 78% hatched after cold treatment, with 2 days' initial incubation 15% hatched, and with nine days incubation 0% hatched. Earlier stages were more resistant to low temperatures than later stages.

Yamashita and Yaginuma (1991) also showed that the diapause egg was more resistant to low temperatures than the non-diapause egg because of their lower super cooling point (the temperature at which their body fluids freeze). On the other hand, Gray *et al.* (1995) reported no difference in resistance to low temperature of the diapause and non-diapause eggs of the gypsy moth. This limited information demonstrates the variability of responses to low temperature due to egg physiological state and species.

6.5 IMPLICATIONS FOR ERADICATION METHODS

The literature on eradication methods by temperature extremes and anoxic environments (see chapter 12) contains many reports on the success of the treatments. Such success is determined by the death of the insect tested. Unfortunately, in

BOX 6.1. EGGS OF SOME COMMON MOTH SPECIES

Scanning electron micrographs, showing (left) a lateral view of the whole egg, oriented with the anterior to the right, and (right) the micropylar area of the egg (Arbogast, 1996, with permission)

a, Tineola bisselliella *(Hummel), webbing clothes moth*

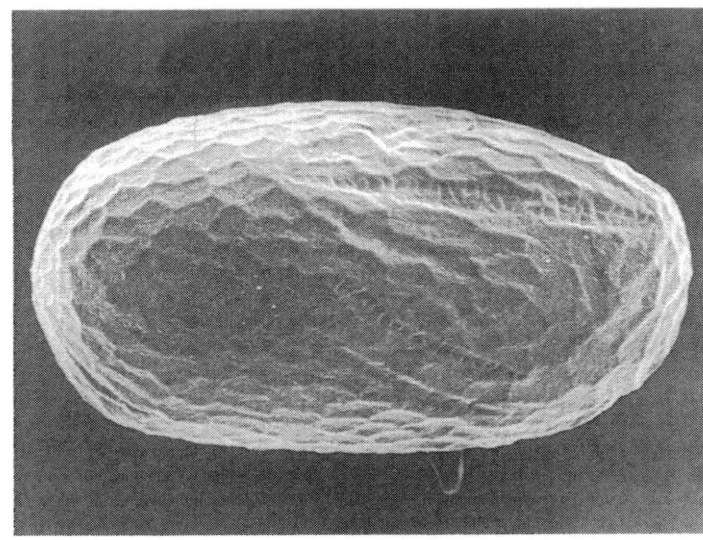

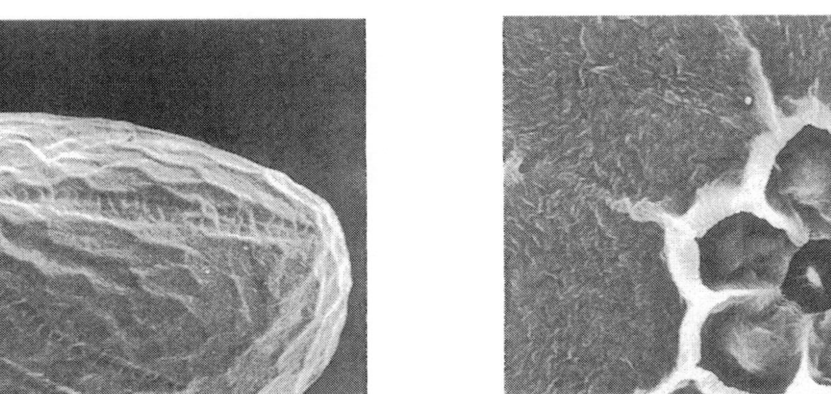

b, Tinea pallescentella *(Stainton), large pale clothes moth*

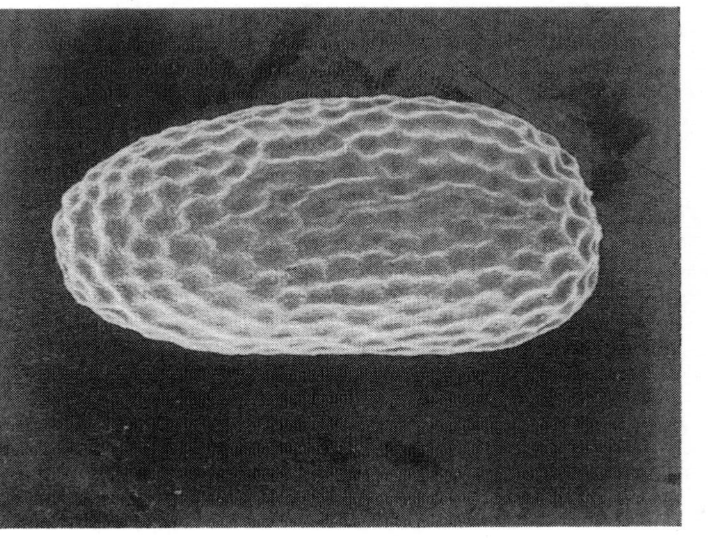

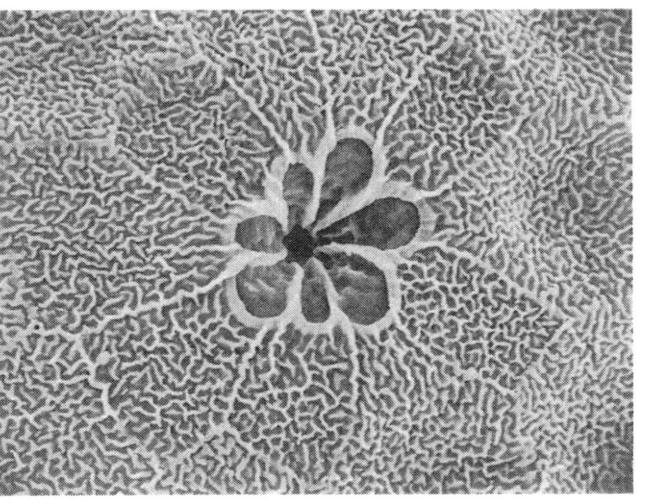

BOX 6.1 (cont.) *EGGS OF SOME COMMON MOTH SPECIES*

c, Tinea occidentella *Chambers*

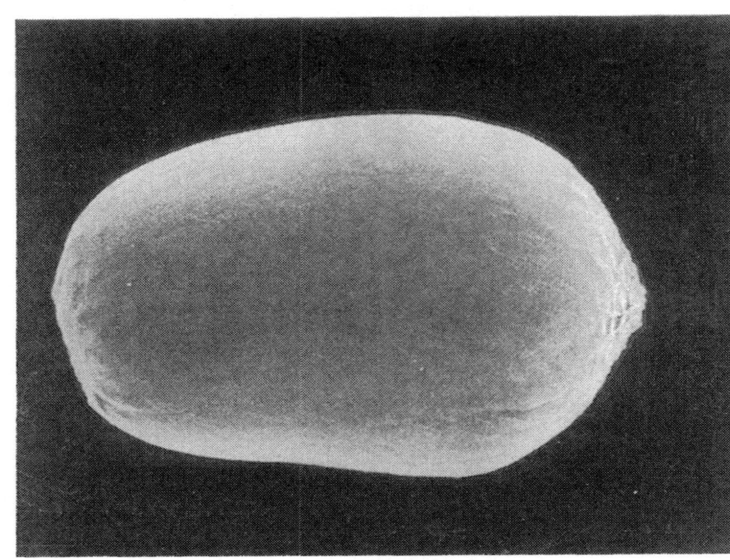

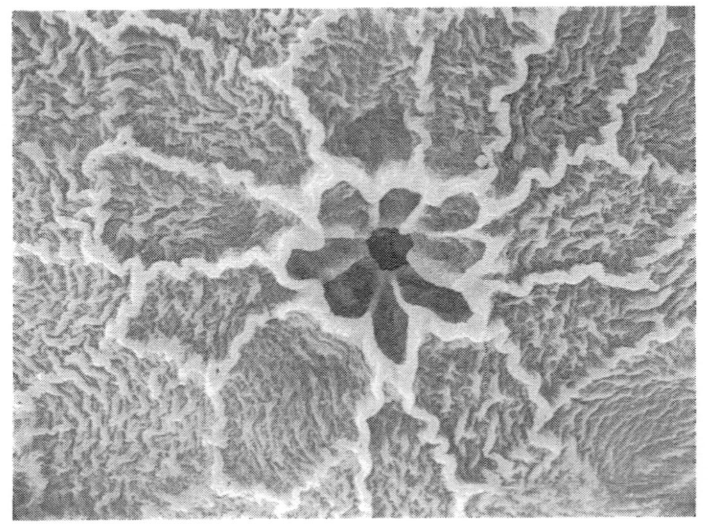

d, Endrosis sarcitrella (*L.*), *white-shouldered house moth*

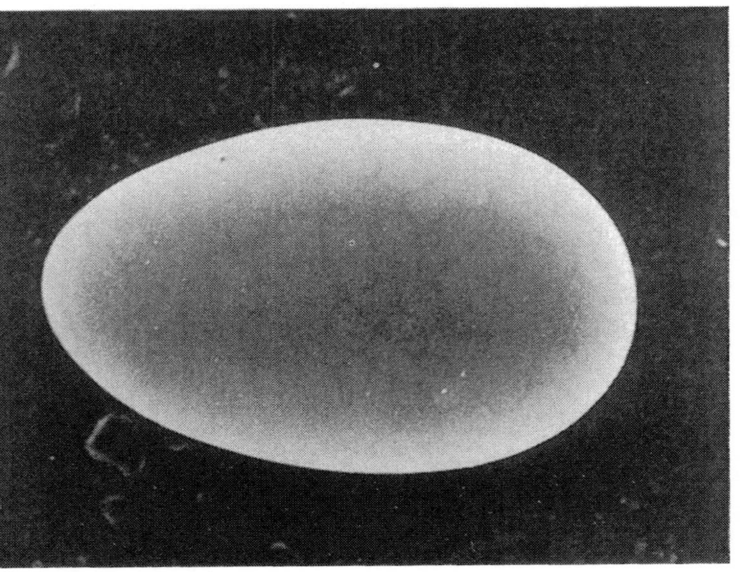

BOX 6.1 (cont.) EGGS OF SOME COMMON MOTH SPECIES

e, Hofmannophila pseudospretella *(Stainton) brown house moth*

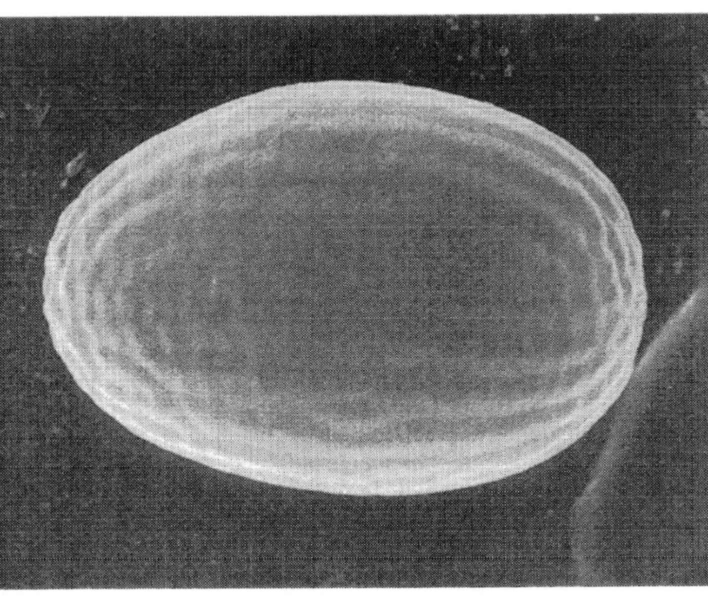

f, Niditinea fuscella *(L.)*

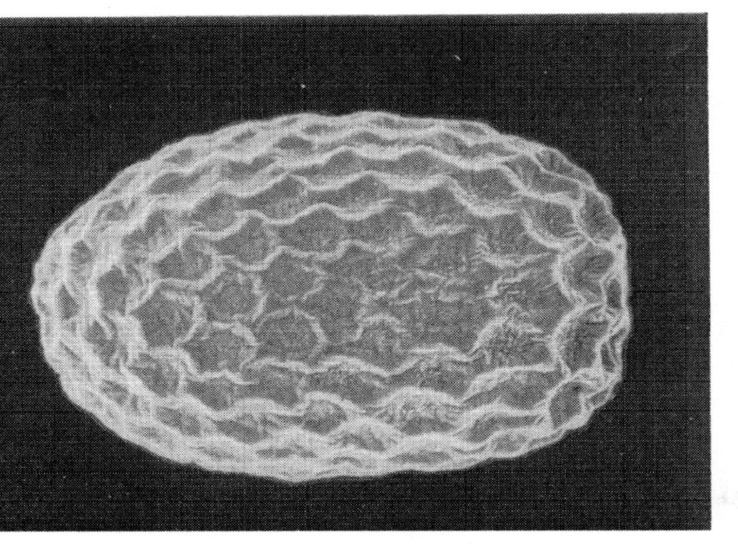

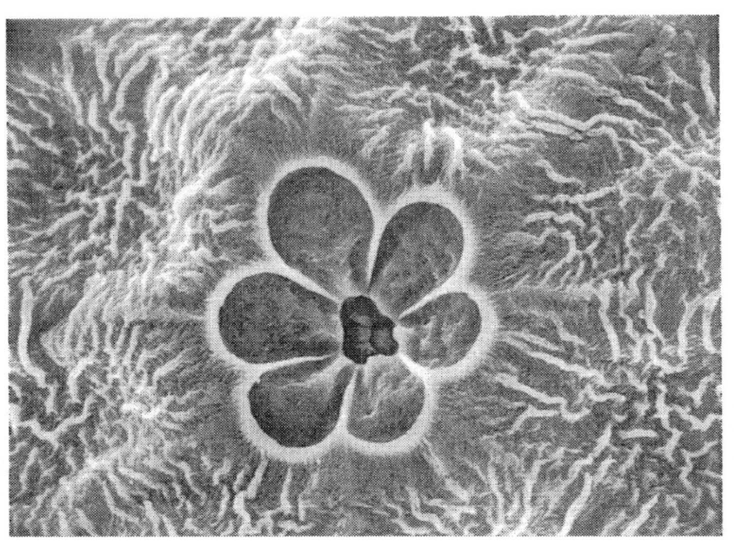

nearly all cases the cause of death is not known. It is possible that low and high temperatures, as well as anoxic conditions, could result in death due to dehydration. It is also reported that large amounts of the anaerobic carbohydrate metabolism products polyols, alanine and lactate, accumulate prior to diapause. These are substrates that can be used without oxygen, by anaerobic respiration, to produce adenosine triphosphate (ATP) needed for cellular maintenance. It is important to note that these same chemicals are produced when insect larvae are subjected to stress from low or high temperatures and from dehydration. This further supports a common response to stress from different origins.

6.6 BIOLOGY OF EGGS OF COMMON HERITAGE-EATING INSECTS

The size of the eggs, length of incubation and number laid will vary greatly with the nutritional state of the adult and the environmental parameters, so these data are not used as a means of identification. However, the following information from the literature may help to identify the origin of the eggs or aid in the process of removing eggs.

- *Tineola bisselliella*, webbing clothes moth. The eggs are about 1mm long, oval, ivory white, with narrow ridges. The eggs are attached to threads by a gelatinous material and are not easily shaken off. The time of hatching varies with environmental parameters: 4 days–3 weeks.
- *Dermestes maculatus*, hide beetle. The eggs are 2mm long, creamy in colour.
- *Attagenus megatoma* (= *piceus*), black carpet beetle. The eggs are very fragile: a vigorous brushing or shaking will remove and kill most of them, whereas moth eggs are more sturdy and withstand more abuse.
- *Anthrenus verbasci*, varied carpet beetle. The eggs are 0.27mm wide by 0.55mm long; the egg surface is rough with a short spine-like projection at one end. Eggs are white when first laid but become cream-coloured during development.
- *Trogoderma inclusum*, large cabinet beetle. The eggs are 0.5mm long, with a hair-like projection at one end, which adheres to any surface it contacts.
- *Anobium punctatum*, common furniture beetle. The eggs are whitish, ellipsoid, 0.35mm wide and 0.55 long. They resemble an acorn, with the cup being an alveolate area with small pits, aeropyles.
- *Ptinus tectus*, spider beetle. The eggs are sticky when first laid and become covered with particles of food and debris. They are 0.47–0.55mm in length and 0.29–0.40mm in width, and are opalescent.
- *Tenebrio molitor*, yellow mealworm. The eggs are bean-shaped and sticky but become covered with meal and debris.
- *Blatta orientalis*, oriental cockroach. An ootheca, an egg case in which fertilized eggs develop, is carried by the female until the young are ready to hatch. The mother tends the young nymphs for several days in their nursery.

REFERENCES

Arbogast, R.T., G.L. Lecato and R.V. Byrd. 1980. External morphology of some eggs of stored-product moths (Lepidoptera: Pyralidae, Gelechiidae, Tineidae). *Int. J. Insect Morphol. Embryol.*, 15: 165–169. 1996.

Arbogast, R.T., G. Chauvin, R.G. Strong and R.V. Byrd. 1983. The egg of *Endrosis sarcitrella* (Lepidoptera: Oecophoridae): Fine structure of the chorion. *J. Stored Prod. Res.*, 19: 63–68.

Arbogast, R.T., R.V. Byrd, G. Chauvin and R.G. Strong. 1984. The egg of *Hofmannophila pseudospretella* (Oecophoridae): Fine structure of the chorion. *J. Lepid Soc.*, 38: 202–208.

Arbogast, R.T. and J.H. Brower. 1989. External morphology of the eggs of *Tinea pallescentella* Stainton, *Tinea occidentella* Chambers and *Niditinea fuscella* (L.) (Lepidoptera: Tineidae). *Int. J. Insect Morphol. Embryol.*, 18 (5/6): 321–328.

Arbogast, R.T. 1996. Personal communication. Research Entomologist, Center for Medical Agricultural and Veterinary Entomology, U.S. Dept of Agriculture, Gainesville, Florida.

Daniel, S.H. and R.H. Smith. 1994. Functional anatomy of the egg pore in *Callosobruchus maculatus*: a trade-off between gas-exchange and protective functions. *Physiological Entomology*, 19: 30–38.

Furneaux, P.J.S. and A.L. Mackay. 1976. The composition, structure and formation of the chorion and vitelline membrane of the insect eggshell. In *The Insect Integument*, Ed. H.R. Hepburn. Elsevier Scientific, Amsterdam, Oxford, New York, pp157–176.

Gray, D.R., F.W. Ravlin, J. Régnière and J. A. Logan. Further advances towards a model of gypsy moth (*Lymantria dispar* (L.)) egg phenology: respiration rates and thermal responsiveness during diapause, and age-dependent developmental rates in postdiapause. *Journal of Insect Physiology*, 41(3):247–256.

Hinton, H.E. 1969. Respiratory systems of insect eggshells. *Annual Review of Entomology*, 14:343–368.

Hinton, H.E. 1970. Insect eggshells. *Scientific American*, August, pp84–91.

Sonobe, H. and M. Nakamura. 1991. A re-visitation of the oxygen permeability of the chorion in relation to the onset of embryonic diapause in the silkworm, *Bombyx mori*. *Journal of Insect Physiology*, 37(10):727–731.

Yamashita, O. and T. Yaginuma. 1991. Silkworm eggs at low temperatures: implications for sericulture. In *Insects at Low Temperatures*, Eds. R.E. Lee and D.L. Denlinger. Chapman and Hall, New York, London.

7

The Larva: the Eating Machine

7.1 INTRODUCTION

An insect egg hatches into either a larva or a nymph. The larva is the feeding stage of insects that have complete metamorphosis (holometabolous), such as beetles and moths. The larvae are caterpillar, wire worm or grub-like in appearance. Nymphs are sexually immature juveniles of insects with incomplete metamorphosis (hemimetabolous), such as cockroaches, silverfish and booklice.

Both larvae and nymphs undergo a series of moults as they grow. The young insect that hatches from the egg is called the first instar. This stage ends with the shedding of the old cuticle and from it emerges the second instar. Thus an instar is the growth phase between two successive moults. The different larval instars, of one species, are similar in appearance but vary in size. They never resemble the adult form, whereas the nymph instars always do, and, after each successive moult, there is a stronger resemblance to the mature adult.

The larvae have a different diet and lifestyle from their adults, whereas nymphs usually compete with their adults for the same food and habitat. It is mainly the larvae of the holometabolous insects and the nymphs and adults of the hemimetabolous insects that are the heritage eaters. Details of the biology of nymphs are discussed under their adult forms (see chapter 9).

7.2 THE LARVA

Even though larvae cause nearly all the damage in holometabolous insect infestations, rarely are they studied or identified. We have a mind-set directed towards the 'adult' insect, which rarely causes direct damage to heritage objects. Their role in life is distribution and reproduction, which is of course a concern in control of insect pests at all levels: buildings, storage areas and drawers. Our fixation on the adult insect must be because they fly – we see them, we can catch them. In contrast, we rarely see larvae, catch them, or even look for them.

In most books or articles on museum and household insect pests (Freeman, 1980; Hickin, 1972; Hinton, 1945; Hinton and Corbet, 1972; Pinniger, 1994) there are elegant illustrations, biology and identification keys for the adults, with often only a little information on the identification and biology of the larvae. If present, this information is often from a few sources such as Hinton (1943, 1956) and Rees (1943, 1947).

In entomological taxonomic literature, Peterson's (1967) and Stehr's (1987) works discuss the taxonomic features of larvae in all insect families and have excellent photographs and illustrations, but there is very little information on the biology and identification of the larvae of museum or household insect pests. In treatises on specific groups or families of insects, such as Robinson's (1979) work on *Tinea pellionella* complex, and Scoble's (1992) *The Lepidoptera*, there is some information, but again it is buried in the taxonomic literature along with the larvae of a multitude of other species. Peacock (1993) has presented excellent illustrations of the hide, carpet and larder beetle larvae and has made points on identification, but again there is little on the biology of the larvae. Even in this entomological literature the authors often refer to Hinton (1943) and Rees (1947).

There is, however, a large group of papers on the digestion of keratin by the larvae of clothes moths and dermestid beetles, triggered by the economics of the wool industry. There is also an extensive body of literature on cold-hardiness and anoxic tolerances of larvae, triggered by the need for non-chemical eradication methods in the stored food industry, as well as basic biology.

The following is a compilation of relevant information from all of this literature and general entomology text books (Gullan and Cranston, 1995; Wigglesworth, 1984): it is sparse but significant.

7.2.1 General morphology of larvae

There are three common functional forms of larvae, polypod (many legs), oligopod (few legs) and apod (without legs).

- *Polypod* larvae have cylindrical bodies with three pairs of short thoracic legs and abdominal prolegs. The most common examples are Lepidoptera: butterfly caterpillars and moth larvae.
- *Oligopod* larvae lack abdominal prolegs and have functional thoracic legs. The most common examples are in Coleoptera: larvae of dermestid beetles, carpet beetles and stored food beetles.

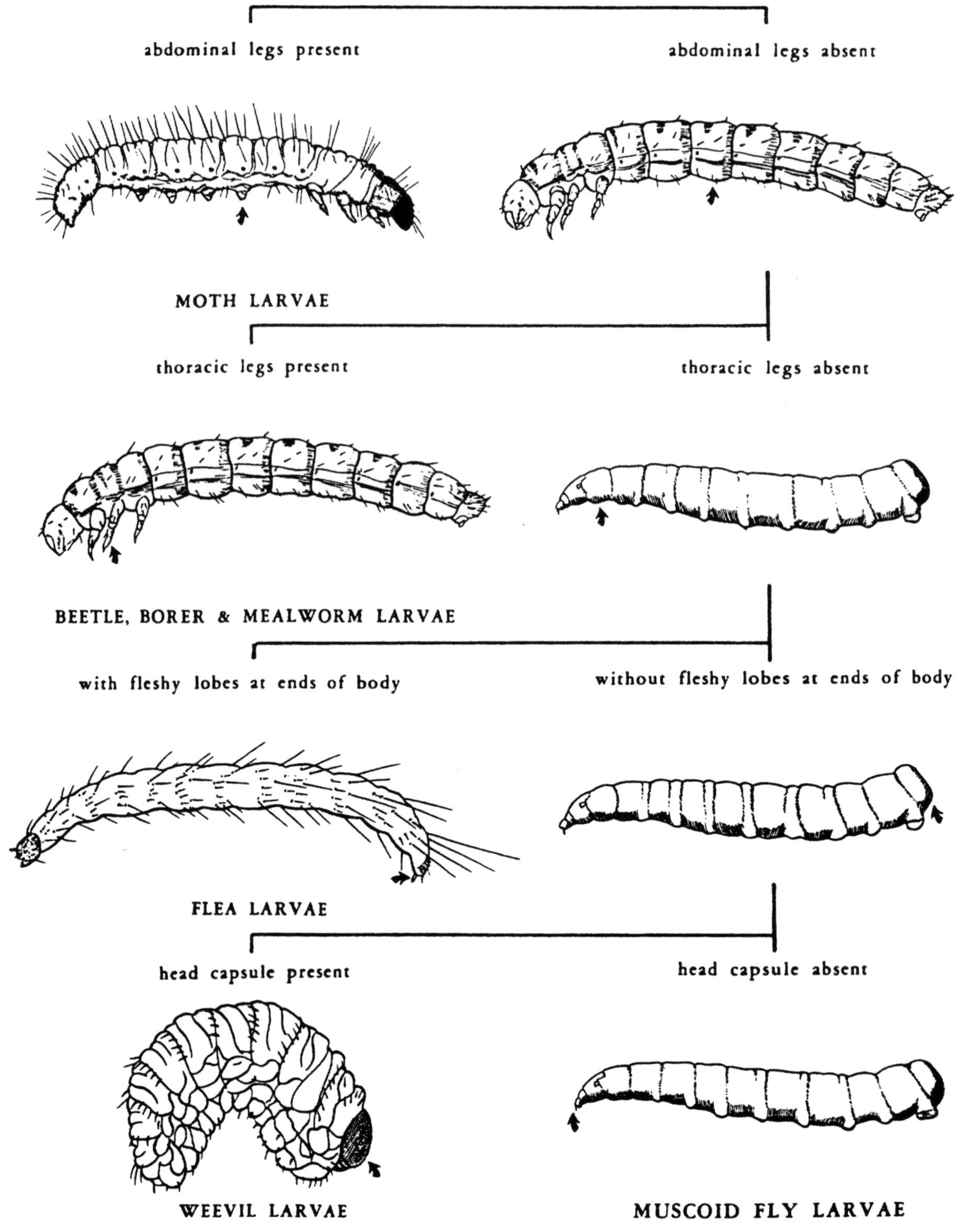

Figure 7.1. Pictorial key to common groups of household and stored food pests: larval stages (Scott, 1959, U.S. D.H.E.W.).

- *Apod* larvae lack true legs and are usually worm-, maggot- or grub-like. The most common examples are wood beetle and weevil larvae, bee and wasp grubs and fly maggots.

In Figure 7.1 a pictorial key to common groups of household and stored food pest larval stages illustrates these three types of larvae.

7.2.2 Biology of larvae

The biology of the immature stages of insects is covered in full in general entomology textbooks and journals (e.g. Gullan and Cranston, 1995; Wigglesworth, 1985; Wipking *et al.*, 1995). Only relevant aspects that aid understanding of the prevention and eradication of insect heritage eaters are presented here.

7.2.2.1 FEEDING, FOOD AND FAT

a *Feeding*

A list of the types of heritage objects and materials that have been infested by insects would be too lengthy to be practicable and would tell us little more than that nearly all organic materials and soiled synthetics, as well as metals, can be attacked. Some of the material damaged has been eaten by larvae and adults for food, some by larvae digging out pupation sites and some by larvae tunnelling through it.

The insect heritage eaters can be grouped according to where they live and the type of food they appear to eat – but remember, there is an exception to every rule.

1 The environmental indicators: those that live and breed in one place in the building and visit foodstuffs and materials elsewhere. Both nymphs and adults feed and their presence tells us there is something wrong, somewhere, in the building's environment.

   Nymphs and adults of cockroaches, ants, crickets, booklice, silverfish, termites.

   Food: starch, sugars, oils, protein gelatin, fungi, wood, etc.

2 Those that live and breed in the foodstuffs and in some cases move away from the food to pupate. Adults and larvae feed.

   For example: *Dermestes lardarius*, larder beetle; *Ptinus tectus*, Australian spider beetle; *Tenebrio* species (spp), mealworm; *Trogoderma* (spp), hide beetle; *Stegobium paniceum*, drugstore beetle; *Lasioderma serricorne*, Cigarette beetle.

   Food: stored dry food products (spices, dried plant and animal material, cereals, nuts, dried fruit). Occasionally these insects damage wood for pupation.

3 Those that feed and breed in natural organic materials of which heritage objects are composed or synthetics soiled with natural organic materials. Adults may fly and feed on pollen or nectar but not on the food of the larvae; some larvae may move away from food to pupate.

   For example: clothes moth and house moth: *Tineola bisselliella*, *Tinea pellionella*, *Hofmannophila pseudospretella* and the carpet and fur beetles: *Anthrenus verbasci*, *Attagenus pellio*.

   Food: keratin in fur, feathers, wool, etc.; skin, dried animal tissue and blood; soiled natural and synthetic fabrics; some plant materials.

4 Those with larvae that bore into wood and are able to subsist on wood kept in buildings. Only larvae feed.

   For example: woodworm, *Anobium punctatum*; powderpost beetle *Lyctus brunneus*.

   Food: cellulose, starch and protein in wood, fungi in wood.

5 Lost souls: fortuitous wanderers from the garden or elsewhere outdoors.

   For example: house fly, *Musca domestica*, ladybird beetle, fungus gnat, etc.

b *Food and food supplements*

Nearly every type of organic material is eaten by some insect larvae, but it is not always clear if they digest what they eat. For example, some larvae eat large quantities of wood but digest only the fungi present, while others may utilize only the associated starches and proteins in the wood.

Many insect larvae may attack keratin materials (wool, horn, tortoiseshell, feathers) but cannot digest this protein. These larvae and adults, i.e. termites, silverfish, larder beetles, khapra beetles and white-shouldered moths, are eating through the materials to get to the other side or are eating the associated materials or soil spots on the materials.

The larvae that attack insect collections do not have the ability to digest the chitinous exoskeletons, but feed on the fatty materials normally present in the adult insect specimens.

The only animals that can digest keratin are insects and, in the insect world, only a few can do this. The protein keratin of wool, hair, horn, etc. is resistant to normal digestive proteolytic enzymes, and is insoluble in most solvents. *Tineola bisselliella*, the common or webbing clothes moth, has been shown to digest keratin (Waterhouse, 1958). It has digestive juices that are alkaline (pH 10) and a reducing environment in the midgut that causes the initial breakdown of the keratin protein. The strong disulphide bonds in the keratin are reduced to more soluble sulphydryl bonds, which are then acted upon by the proteolytic enzymes that digest the protein. The midgut does not have any trachea and has a thickened wall that is basically impermeable to oxygen, so it is able to maintain anoxic conditions for a reducing environment. Some carpet beetle larvae (*Anthrenus verbasci*, the varied carpet beetle, and *Attagenus piceus*, the black carpet beetle) have also been shown to digest keratin.

Keratin is not a very nutritious food and the larvae that eat it also eat other materials such as dried fish or meat, ground grains, casein, protein in bones, dead rodents, etc. The salts and vitamins in urine and sweat stains on wool are also very attractive to the keratin eaters.

Synthetic fabrics are often thought to be insect-proof but it has been demonstrated that both clean and soiled synthetic fabrics can be destroyed by clothes moths and carpet beetles. Bry (1991) showed that larvae of the furniture carpet beetle (*Anthrenus flavipes*), the black carpet beetle (*Attagenus unicolor*) and the webbing clothes moth (*Tineola bisselliella*) grazed lightly on synthetic fibres of dacron, nylon, viccara, dynel and rayon but as a comparison they fed extensively on mixtures of wool/nylon, wool/orlon and wool/viscose rayon. These same insect species were given a group of synthetic textiles (100% acetate, 100% polyester, 100% nylon, 100% acetate tricot, 50% polyester/50% acrylic, 50% polyester/50% rayon, 80% triacetate/20% nylon and 60% rayon/30% polyester/10% linen bonded to acetate tricot), which had spots of acidic perspiration, artificial alkaline perspiration, ketchup, chicken bouillon, mustard, and 5% sugar. The larvae of the three species damaged the synthetic textiles and the black carpet beetle and webbing clothes moth did most damage when the textiles were spotted with ketchup. The most feeding occurred on 100% acetate contaminated with ketchup and the least on clean or soiled polyester fabric. The moral of the story is that their favourite food was ketchup. These six contaminants are only a token sample of the possible spots that occur on textiles, but the results show that these insect species can damage soiled synthetic textiles, supporting the necessity to clean textiles before storage.

Another feature of the digestive system of the clothes moth larva is that it is able to ingest large amounts of metals and then detoxify itself. This is of importance regarding the resistance of the clothes moth to metal-based mothproofing chemicals.

Which nutrient supplements insect larvae can synthesize is still not well documented. What the larvae cannot synthesize, e.g. sterols and fat soluble vitamins, they need in the food they eat. Sterols are required for structure, moulting and development and vitamins have a variety of activities. Perspiration and urine are common sources of these supplements.

Symbiotes living in the larva's gut, for example yeasts and bacteria, may supply vitamins (the vitamin B group) and some amino acids that they cannot synthesize. It has been shown that bacteria digest cellulose for utilization by the termite and the *Lasioderma serricorne* (cigarette beetle) larva has symbiotes that produce the vitamins it requires.

c *Fat – the fat body*

The instar larvae are the active, growing, food-consuming stages of the insect's life. The purpose of the larva is to eat and to store enough food energy for pupation and the emergence and maintenance of the reproductive adults. Not all larvae reach this goal because of insufficient food, bad genes or adverse environmental conditions.

Inside the larva, the most conspicuous structure is a large fat body made up of loose sheets or ribbons of fat cells. The fat body in the larva is like the liver in mammals, a group of specialized cells in which fat, glycogen and proteins are stored, and the site of intermediary metabolism. The tissue is stuffed with mitochondria, suggesting its metabolic role. The fat body reaches its full development in the late stages of the last instar of the larva: the stored chemicals are used for pupation and adult emergence. Some adult insects that do not feed, e.g. carpet beetles and clothes moths, have remnants of the fat body, which supplies the energy for flight and reproductive activities. The adult house fly, even though it feeds, has a large fat body (carpet beetle larvae are commonly found inside the abdomens of dead house flies, which obviously take advantage of this free energy source).

The fat body is an organ with a multitude of functions: metabolism of carbohydrates, lipids and nitrogenous compounds; storage of glycogen, fat and protein; synthesis of blood sugar, egg yolk, and blood and storage proteins. The amounts of the chemicals in the fat body change during larval development. Glycogen accumulates towards the end of larval life, reaching up to 33% of dry weight. Fat or lipid levels fluctuate: they are high in the early stages, drop and rise again at maturity. Protein levels drop if the larva builds a cocoon. Uric acid, the waste product of protein metabolism, is usually stored as crystals in the fat body. The crystals accumulate in the larval instars and are passed on to the pupa or adult for final elimination. Trehalose is the sugar commonly stored in the fat body and its level fluctuates with metabolic activity.

In the last instar the fat body cells become dissociated, but sometimes reassociate during the formation of the pupa, to form a fat body for the new adult.

d *Oxygen requirements*

Larvae have shown unusual resistance to low levels of oxygen as an adaptive response to environments of low oxygen, such as rotting logs (0.5% oxygen), stored grain (1.8% oxygen) and in animal stomachs. The larvae of the horse bot fly can tolerate levels of 0.1% oxygen in the horse stomach (Wigglesworth, 1984). By comparison there is 21% oxygen in air.

During diapause and exposure to low temperatures the larval oxygen requirement is reduced, reflecting a reduced metabolic rate (see Figure 8.4 in chapter 8).

High temperature and muscular activity cause an increase in oxygen demand. The rate of larval development may be influenced by reduced amounts of oxygen. Tests with the larvae of the grain beetle (*Tenebrio molitor*) showed that, when exposed to levels of 10.5% oxygen, the rate of larval growth was slower and they underwent more moults but reached the same size as larvae in 21% oxygen (Loudon, 1988).

Altered atmospheric gases, including low oxygen or anoxic conditions, are suggested as methods of insect pest eradication for museum and household insect pests. Details of these methods are given in 12.2.

For further information on larval oxygen rquirements, see Wigglesworth (1984).

e *Water – nor any drop to drink*

Larvae do not drink water, so they obtain water from their food (dietary water), from water vapour through external respiration or surface absorption or from water bound in chemicals (metabolic water). They must conserve water in their body by reabsorption of the water in their gut and by prevention of loss through defecation, respiration and transpiration.

Some organic materials are more vulnerable to insect attack not only because of their odour but also their moisture content. Certain adults and nymphs (booklice, silverfish) have sensory organs that detect moisture, but most larvae appear to have only odour-detecting olfactory sensilla on mouthparts, which help them with food selection.

The energy expenditure of larvae depends on the amount of dietary water (Van't Hof and Martin, 1989). Low water content in food causes reduction in growth rates, and increases in respiration rates and oxygen assimilation. Higher metabolic activity is required for reabsorption of water from the gut and an increase in the time required for feeding to obtain sufficient water. This illustrates the importance of moisture content (MC) in the food of larvae. There are many reports on water content (MC) tolerances in the food of some insect heritage eaters, but the parameters are so variable that the information is not very useful. Environmental fluctuations in temperature and relative humidity (RH) that alter the MC of materials can cause developmental changes in larvae, such as periods of quiescence, moulting and pupation. The bottom line is: the drier the material, the less vulnerable to insect attack. The interaction between the RH of ambient air and the structure of the organic materials of heritage objects with reference to MC is discussed in chapter 2.

Water vapour absorption does occur in the soft-bodied booklice and silverfish, and the larva of *Tinea pellionella* is able to adsorb water vapour through the cuticle from unsaturated air at 93% RH (Chauvin and Vannier, 1980).

Under water stress some insects can extract water from chemicals, e.g. the last instar larvae of the wax moth (Jindra and Sehnal, 1990) was shown to extract metabolic water from the food it was eating. Metabolic water is a byproduct of oxidative catabolism of carbohydrates and fats.

Larvae under stress from cold temperatures or anoxia produce polyols (glycerol or sorbitol) in their body fluids, which help to conserve water. The polyols bind water, which lowers the vapour pressure, preventing normal diffusion and conserving the water (see 12.1.1).

For further information on larvae feeding, see House (1974) and Wigglesworth (1984).

7.2.2.2 *Environment: temperature and RH*

The fact that we find insects in objects in heritage collections of all types tells us that microenvironments support their development. There may not be optimum conditions but the heritage eaters survived. We can try to determine why the insects were able to live in this specific microenvironment and, if it was because of an environmental (temperature and RH) problem, we can solve it. Booklice and silverfish are excellent indicators of problems in building environments.

As mentioned above, the most critical aspect of the environment for the insect is the moisture content of the material, which depends not only on the environment but on the material itself.

In most cases the environment does not determine the location of the insect activity: it is probably by chance that infested materials were placed in that spot and the insects survived. The environment we supply in our museums and homes doubtlessly provides optimum conditions for most insects; we cannot change this, but we can stop the insects from entering. The integrated insect pest programme discussed in chapter 13 is a preventive approach which does just that.

7.2.2.3 *Sight and light*

Larvae do not have the ocelli or compound eyes found in adults, but they may have one or several pairs of stemmata on each side of the head (Figure 10.3). Stemmata are different from the simple eyes, the ocelli, of the adult. A typical stemma is composed of a single light-refracting unit (cuticular lens), a few light-isolating structures (crystalline body or three rhabdoms) and the light-sensing components (ocular nerve) (Scoble, 1992). The stemmata produce a well-focused image with poor resolution because of the few cells involved. Lepidoptera larvae usually have six stemmata on each side of the head. When they turn their head back and forth they obtain a mosaic of the visual field. Larvae usually move away from light.

7.2.2.4 *Dormancy, diapause, quiescence*

The development from an egg to an adult insect is often interrupted by a period of dormancy. If brought about by the environment, this is called quiescence, but if it is caused by an internal physiological state, it is called diapause. Quiescence is a slowing down or halting of development as a response to an adverse environment, e.g. low moisture, and is broken as soon as the external environment is suitable for continued development. Diapause is the halting of development by some internal physiological state. Any one of the stages (egg, nymph, larvae or pupa) can pass into a more or less prolonged state of arrested development or diapause: this can last a few days or months. It is most common in overwintering insects where a photoperiod response is sometimes needed to increase a hormone level to break the diapause. In developing prepupal larvae there is a juvenile hormone present which inhibits moulting, thus maintaining diapause (see 8.3). Once the juvenile hormone is metabolically broken down, the moulting hormone, ecdysone, is produced, the diapause is broken and moulting and then pupation occur. The use of the juvenile hormone has been researched as a method of insect population control by preventing pupation.

The cause of dormancy may not be obvious: it is difficult to determine if a dormant period is a period of quiescence or diapause.

The larvae of different instars and developmental stages suggest a potential for a large variation in metabolic states, but there is a clear difference between diapause and non-diapause larvae. Wipking *et al.* (1995) compared the physiological states of diapause, initiated by short daylengths of LD 8:16 (8 hours light: 16 hours darkness), and non-diapause moth larvae (LD 16:8). At 20°C, in the diapause, compared with the non-diapause larvae, the respiration rate was reduced by about 77%, the levels of lipids, glycogen and water by 50% and the oxygen consumption by 70–80% (varying with weight). Even though this work was carried out on a specific moth, these results suggest a clear characterization for diapause. They are similar to those presented for the pupa in diapause (see 8.4 and Figure 8.2).

It is suggested that diapause occurs in insect populations in museums and homes. The cause may be an adverse environment, most probably related to low moisture in the materials of the objects – the insects' food – or it is genetically controlled. An increase in the numbers of adult insects occurred about two weeks after an accidental increase in humidity in a museum (see 2.3.2), suggesting that the increase in moisture broke the diapause of the last instar or pupa and adult emergence was triggered (see 2.3.2.3 for more details). Diapause has a population survival benefit if pupae are synchronized so that adults emerge at the same time to ensure partners for mating.

7.3 MORPHOLOGY OF LARVAE OF SOME HERITAGE EATERS

The larvae of the Lepidoptera and Coleoptera are the main heritage eaters. Details of morphology are summarized here; for further information, see Peacock (1993), Peterson (1967), Scoble (1992) and Stehr (1987).

7.3.1 Lepidoptera larvae morphology: General characteristics

- polypod form
- distinct head sclerotized
- chewing mouthparts, mandibles opposable, toothed and visible

- one pair of short antennae
- typically six stemmata
- protruding labial spinneret
- three pairs of five-jointed thoracic legs
- 10 abdominal segments
- pairs of prolegs with crochet on segments 3, 4, 5, 6 and 10
- spiracles on prothorax and abdominal segments 1–8

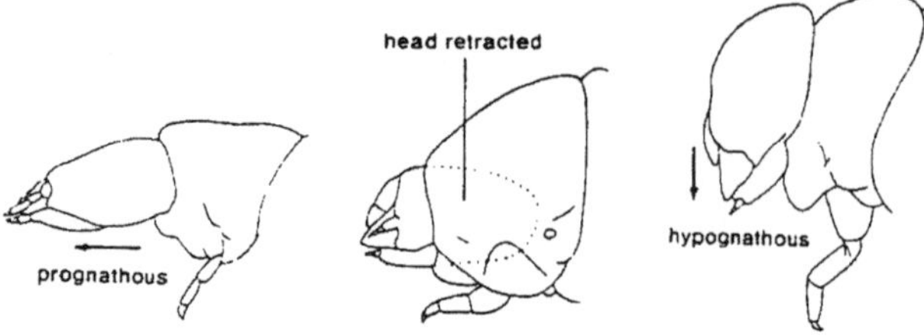

Figure 7.3. The head position of larvae and adult insects (after Stehr, 1987).

CLASSIFICATION OF COMMONEST LEPIDOPTERA HERITAGE EATERS

Tineoidea
  Tineoidea
    Tineidae
      Tineola bisselliella, Tinea pellionella, Trichophaga tapetzella
  Gelechiodea
    Oecophoridae
      Hofmannophila pseudospretella, Endrosis sarcitrella

There may be many other species that are of particular concern to you. By using the references cited it is possible to research these species and add a personal appendix to this book.

TINEIDAE (CLOTHES MOTH, CEREAL MOTH, WOOL MOTH) LARVA – MORPHOLOGICAL FEATURES

Figure 7.2 shows the overall structure of *Tinea pellionella*, the casemaking clothes moth and *Tineola bisselliella*, the webbing clothes moth. Mature larvae range from 6–50mm long. The body is cylindrical, moderately slender and naked except for primary setae (hairs). The cuticle appears smooth but with minute spinules. The body is usually whitish except for an almost black head and thoracic plates. Round spiracles are located along the abdomen.

The head capsule, shown in Figure 7.2, is heavily sclerotized. It has setae and sensilla (sensory hairs) in specific arrangements which assist in identification of the species. The head is hypognathous (pointed downwards; Figure 7.3) in position: that is, the head is directed vertically, with mouthparts directed ventrally.

The larvae have chewing mouthparts, even though their adult form has sucking or vestigial mouthparts. In Figure 7.4, scanning electron micrographs show the awesome complexity of a moth larva's mouthparts (*Tinea translucens*). No wonder they are called heritage eaters. The mandibles are well developed, heavily sclerotized and bear molar and incisor areas. They are opposable and, when brought together, they interlock. The labrum (lip), which overlays the mandibles, and the jointed maxillae located below the mandibles, both push the food into the grinding mandibles. Sensilla, olfactory hairs, are located by the mandibles so they brush up against the food to assess its mechanical and chemical qualities.

Silk is exuded from large silk glands in the thorax and head, into the tube-like spinneret (Figure 7.4) situated on the underside of the head between the maxillae.

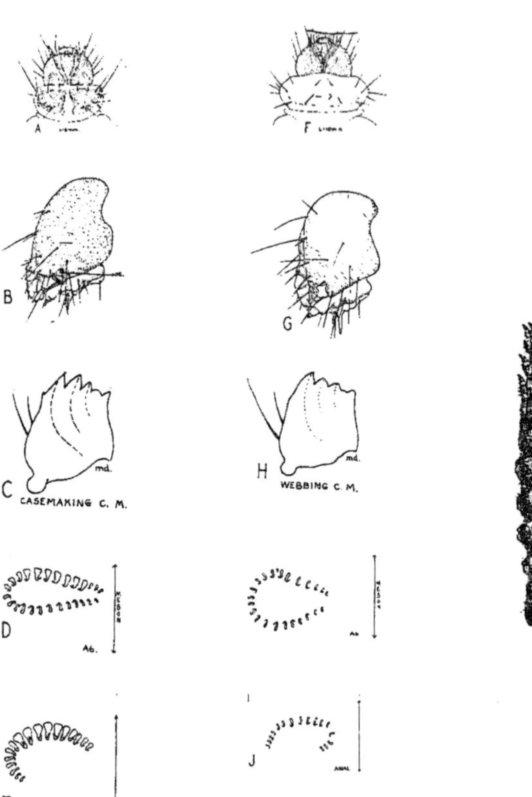

Figure 7.2. The overall structure of the larvae of Tinea pellionella, *the casemaking clothes moth (A–E) and* Tineola bisselliella, *the webbing clothes moth (F–J). A and F, dorsal view of head and prothorax; B and G, lateral view of head; C and H, middle view of right mandible; D and I, crochets of sixth abdominal, right proleg; E and J, crochets of right anal proleg. (Larvae, Royal British Columbia Museum, by Ann Howatt-Krahn; A–J, Peterson, 1967, with permission.)*

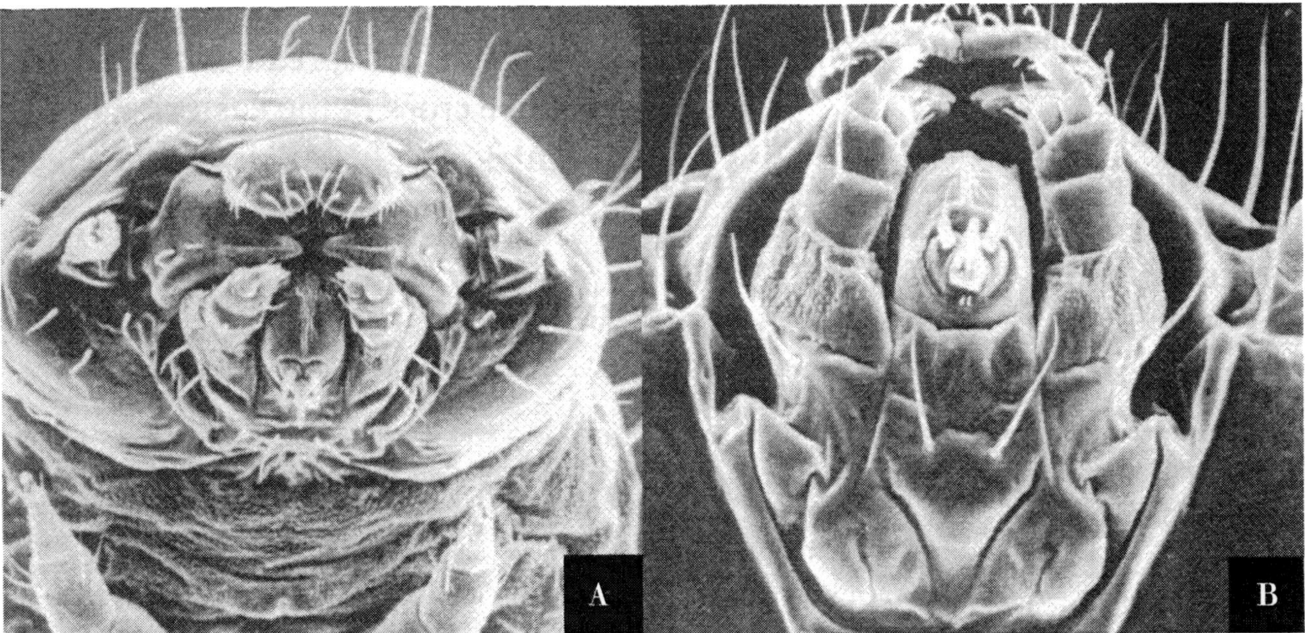

Figure 7.4. Scanning electron micrographs of the mouthparts of the larva of Tinea translucens *Meyrick.* A *shows the frontal view with the mouth cavity surrounded by the bottom spinneret and the maxillae at its sides, and the top labrum, below which are the paired mandibles. Small antennae are at each side of the mandible.* B *shows details of the spinneret and paired maxillae (from Davis, 1987, with permission).*

Some larvae live for all or part of their lives in silk cases, which offer some means of protection. Larvae usually build a silk cocoon for the developing pupa. A web of silk threads is often associated with cereal moths and webbing clothes moths.

There are one to six stemmata (the number depending on the species), which give a mosaic impression of the field of vision. The antennae are short, at segments 3–4. Sensory openings are usually located on the second segment.

There are three segments to the thorax. A thoracic spiracle is located in the first segment. Each segment has a pair of well-developed, five-jointed legs, which terminate in a claw. These legs are similar to the adults'.

The abdomen usually has 10 segments. Five of the abdominal segments, 3, 4, 5, 6 and 10, have a pair of soft prolegs, fleshy outgrowths of the body wall (Figure 7.5) . Each proleg has a base and terminal planta (sole). The planta bears a circle of small retractable hooks called crochets, structures by which the larva hold on to the material on which it is feeding. The crochets allow the larva to walk firmly over a surface, and they can even walk on vertical, smooth surfaces by secreting a silk pad which sticks to the surface and gives a firm grip. The arrangement of the crochets is related to the larva's mode of life and in the Tineidae they are in a uniserial ellipse or circular arrangement (Figure 7.5). The crochets and silk pads make the larvae tenacious wall climbers.

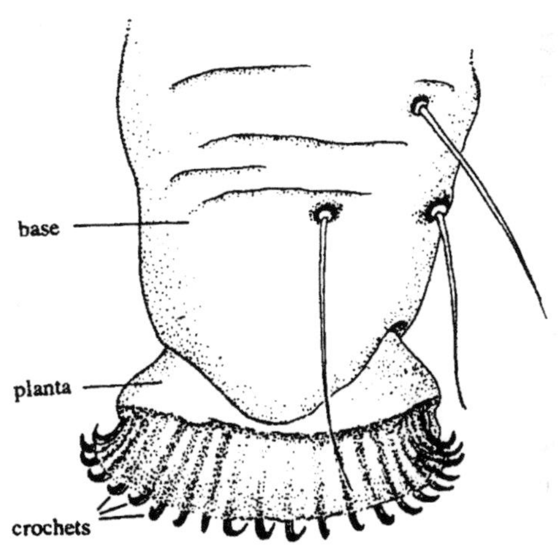

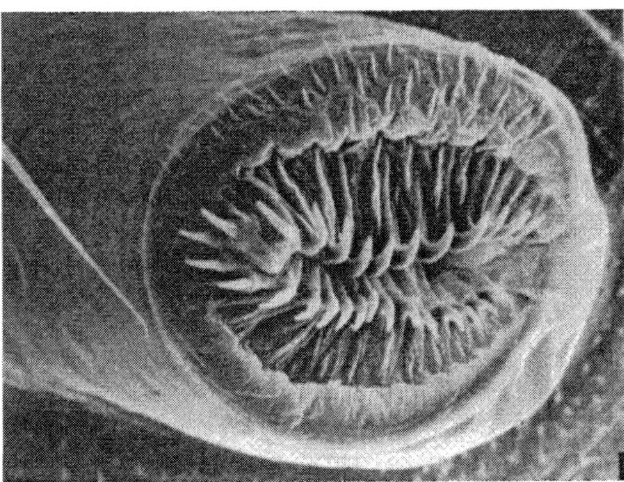

Figure 7.5. Prolegs of Tineidae larva. Above, diagram of the whole proleg (after Scoble, 1992). Below, scanning electron micrograph showing the uniserial, uniordinal arrangement of the crochets (from Davis, 1987, with permission).

BIOLOGY AND ILLUSTRATIONS OF SOME LEPIDOPTERA LARVAE HERITAGE EATERS

The Lepidoptera family is large and information on the larvae sparse. The most useful reference is Hinton (1956).

Trichophaga tapetzella, tapestry or white-tip clothes moth

The larvae usually infest coarse materials such as horsehair upholstery stuffing and skins. They construct rough silken tunnels in the infested material that are smooth inside but outside appear rough because of the camouflaging pieces of fibre or hair and faecal pellets. The larvae spin a tough cocoon for pupation.

***Tineola bisselliella*, webbing clothes moth (Figure 7.2)**

The larvae are caterpillar-like, creamy white with a golden brown head. They are extremely small, 0.1mm when hatched, and can crawl into crevices equally as small. Larvae spin a loose webbing, by which they are recognized, and may make feeding tunnels. The larvae are active and may be found on the floor below an infestation, hunting for a pupation site. The larvae drop and move away quickly when alarmed. They crawl away from light.

***Tinea pellionella*, case-making clothes moth (Figure 7.2)**

The larva is easily recognized by the case it spins, which is open at each end, and the larva drags it wherever it goes. The larvae die, probably from dehydration, if they are removed from their cocoons. They may move to a protected area, such as ceiling or floor crevices, to pupate; they pupate in the case after sealing it at both ends. The larval cocoon is made of silk to which the larva attaches chewed pieces of the material it is eating, so the cocoon mimics the colour of the material.

Other species: *Tinea pallescentella*, large pale clothes moth.

***Hofmannophila pseudospretella*, brown house moth**

General body colour is white and uniformly glossy, with head and first dorsal plate sclerotized and chestnut brown. The larvae are seldom less than 16mm. Before pupation, the larvae go into diapause, which can last 71–145 days. The life span of larvae is 192–140 days in cultures, 12 months in nature. The larvae remain naked until they enter diapause or pupation, when they spin a cocoon (that tears like paper) and remain in the tube while feeding. The last larval instar is a wandering stage, which leaves its food to hunt for a hiding place (e.g. corrugated cardboard) for pupation. The larvae have been reared on a wide variety of both animal protein and plant carbohydrate. The best development occurred on dead adults.

***Endrosis sarcitrella*, white-shouldered house moth**

The larva is dull white, with rows of shiny spots representing the dorsal plates; it rarely exceeds 14mm in length. The larva eats carbohydrates, proteins and dead insects. There is no diapause: the larva wanders for a short period of time and then spins a cocoon and forms a pupa. Corrugated cardboard has been used for larvae to spin their cocoons on; the cocoon tears like cotton-wool.

7.3.2 COLEOPTERA LARVAE MORPHOLOGY: GENERAL CHARACTERISTICS

- oligopod form
- head capsule well-developed and sclerotized

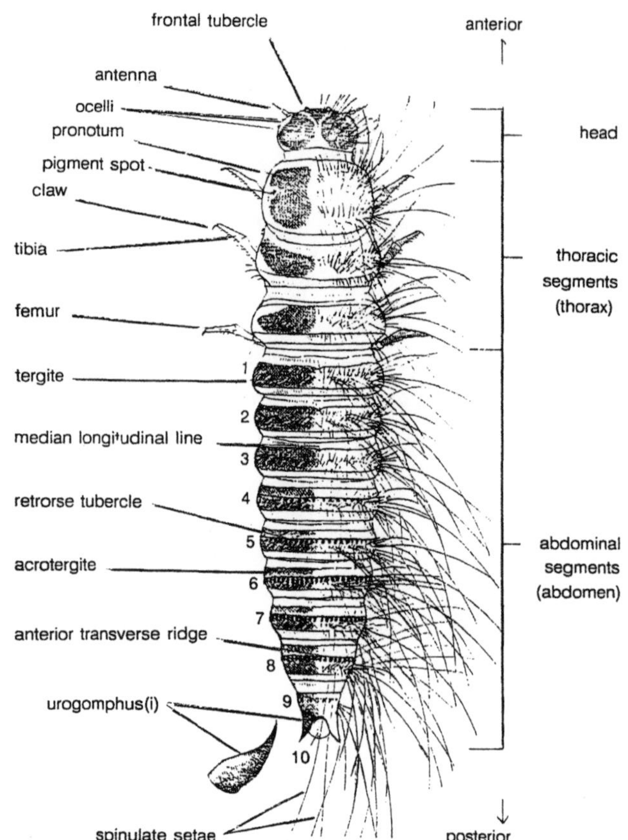

Figure 7.6. Dermestes maculatus, *hide beetle, larva, to show morphology (from Peacock, 1993, with permission).*

- antennae almost always with four segments or fewer
- number of stemmata on each side six or fewer
- mouthparts chewing with opposable mandibles moving in a transverse plane
- labial silk gland and spinneret always absent
- thoracic legs usually five-segmented
- abdomen usually 10 segments
- prolegs absent
- spiracles with accessory openings

The larva body form varies from elongated and slightly c-shaped to fat, grub-like and strongly c-shaped.

Figure 7.6 shows the larva of the hide beetle, *Dermestes maculatus*, to demonstrate Coleoptera morphology.

CLASSIFICATION OF COMMONEST COLEOPTERA HERITAGE EATERS (Stehr, 1991)

Bostrichoidea
- Dermestidae
  - *Dermestes, Trogoderma, Anthrenus, Attagenus, Ptinus, Thylodrias, Megatoma*
- Bostrichidae
  - *Lyctus*
- Anobiidae
  - *Anobium, Xestobium, Stegobium, Lasioderma*
- Ptinidae
  - *Ptinus, Menzium, Gibbium, Nipusi*

Tenebrionoidea
Tenebrionidae
Tenebrio

MORPHOLOGY, BIOLOGY AND ILLUSTRATIONS OF SOME COLEOPTERA LARVAE HERITAGE EATERS

Dermestidae, dermestid beetles (hide, larder and carpet beetles)

The most valuable sources on dermestid morphology are Hinton (1945), Rees (1943) and Peacock (1993), who provides an excellent illustration and discussion of the anatomy and characteristics used for identification, as well as keys for identification and the biology of the adult Dermestidae beetles and larvae. The majority can be recognized by their hairy appearance and brown dorsal plates. The larvae are oligopod larvae (they lack abdominal prolegs) and have functional thoracic legs. The general morphology of the dermestid beetle larvae is shown in Figures 7.6 and 7.7.

The body is elongated and subcylindrical not curved when viewed from the side. It is densely covered with long or short spiny setae (hairs) and sometimes with hastisetae (see Figure 7.10) (hastisetae are spear-shaped segmented setae unique to Dermestidae). Three pairs of thoracic legs are five-jointed, with tarsus and claw fused into a single claw-shaped terminal segment. The abdomen is 8- to 10-segmented without prolegs. Some species have caudal brushes of hastisetae or long straight spicisetae (barbed setae) at the tip of the abdomen.

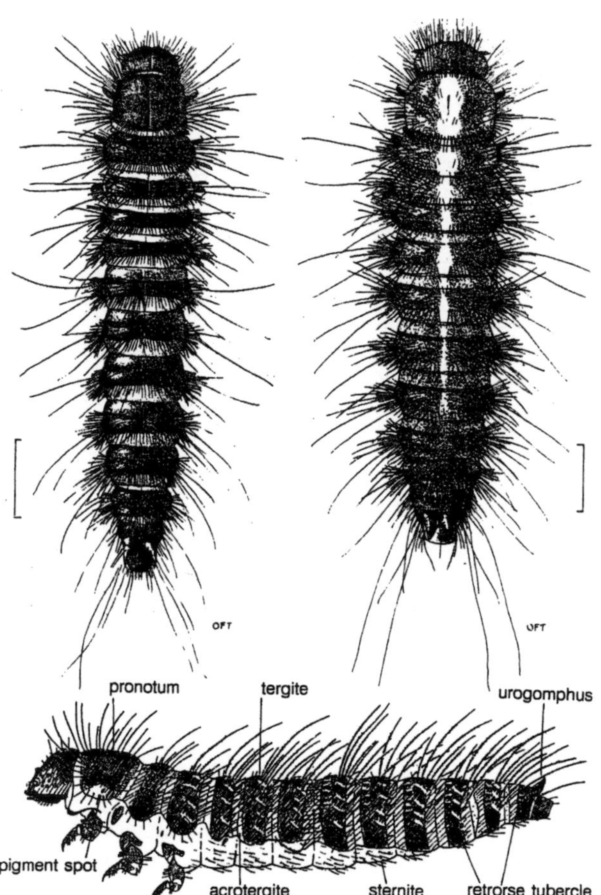

Figure 7.7. Dermestes *larvae. Above left,* D. lardarius, *larder beetle; above right and below,* D. maculatus , *hide beetle. (From Peacock, 1993, with permission.)*

The head is visible from above, free and hypognathous (pointed forwards; see Figure 7.3), that is, directed vertically with mouthparts directed ventrally. It has a pair of opposable, brown, sclerotized mandibles which are more brown on top than on the bottom, and are distally rounded with 2–3 apical teeth. There are no silk glands or spinnerets.

The thorax is short, one-quarter–two-fifths of the length of the abdomen, and has three pairs of five-segmented thoracic legs, with the claw fused with the terminal segment. The abdomen has nine or ten segments and no prolegs, and there are conspicuous tufts of setae on the posterior tergites (segments).

The larvae eat mainly dried animal matter, e.g. woollens, feathers, hides, dried meat, dead insects and exuviae (cast skins) of insects. These pests are cosmopolitan and have spread through commerce. Most adults eat only pollen and nectar but some species (e.g. *Dermestes* and *Thylodrias contractus*) are found feeding in the same habitat as the larvae.

The following are the most common Dermestidae larvae reported to be heritage eaters. Their diet is mainly proteinaceous material of all kinds. Only salient features are mentioned.

Thylodrias contractus, odd beetle

This larva (Figure 7.8) feeds on feather, fur, carrion, dead insects, zoological collections of insects, birds and dried animals. It is oval-shaped and light golden brown, with a row of hairs on each body segment that are club-shaped, clavate spiciseta. The female adult may be mistaken for a larval form because of its soft, larviform structure. The larvae curl up when disturbed.

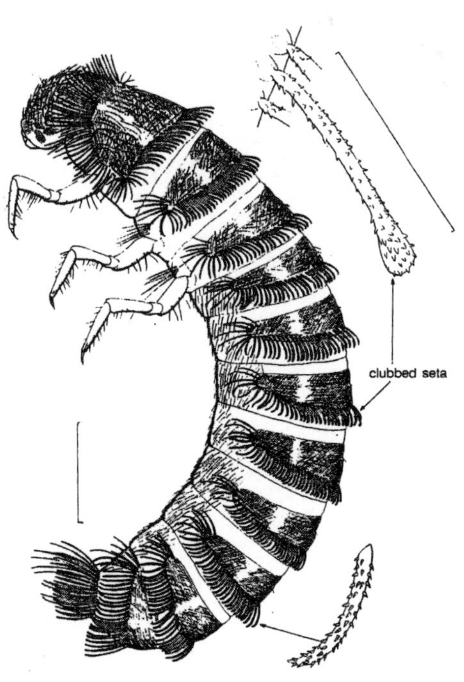

Figure 7.8. Larva of Thylodrias contractus, *odd beetle (from Peacock, 1993, with permission).*

Dermestes lardarius, larder or bacon beetle; _Dermestes maculatus_, hide beetle

Larvae (Figures 7.6 and 7.7), when hatched, are white but soon become dark. They are very active in the dark but feign death in the light. The last instar larva moves away from the feeding site and bores into surfaces to make pupal chambers. Both adults and larvae feed together. Before it lays eggs the adult female eats the same food as the larvae. When there is adequate food, faecal pellets are excreted in bead-like chains. The larva (Figure 7.7) has dark, strong, bristle-like tufts of hair along its body, which is 10–15mm in length and has dorsal extensions, urogomphi, on the ninth abdominal segment. The last abdominal segment is encircled by a sclerotized ring.

Attagenus unicolor, black carpet beetle

The larvae are hairy and characterized by posterior tufts of long hairs, caudal setae. They avoid light and feign death if disturbed (curl up and play possum). They have a banded appearance and their exuviae show this feature.

Other species: *Attagenus pellio*, fur beetle, two-spotted carpet beetle (Figure 7.9).

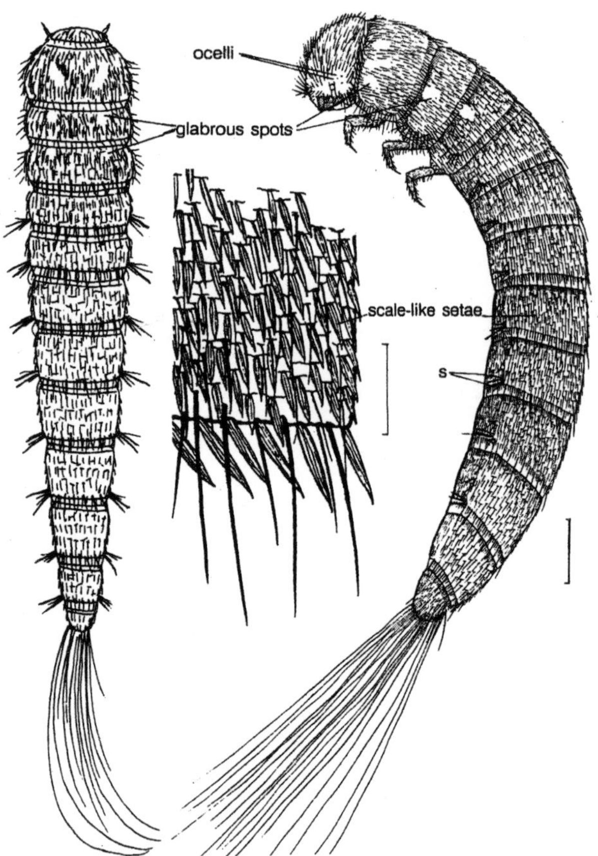

Figure 7.9. Larva of Attagenus pellio, *two-spotted carpet beetle. Left, dorsal view; centre, scale-like setae; right, dorsal lateral view (from Peacock, 1993, with permission).*

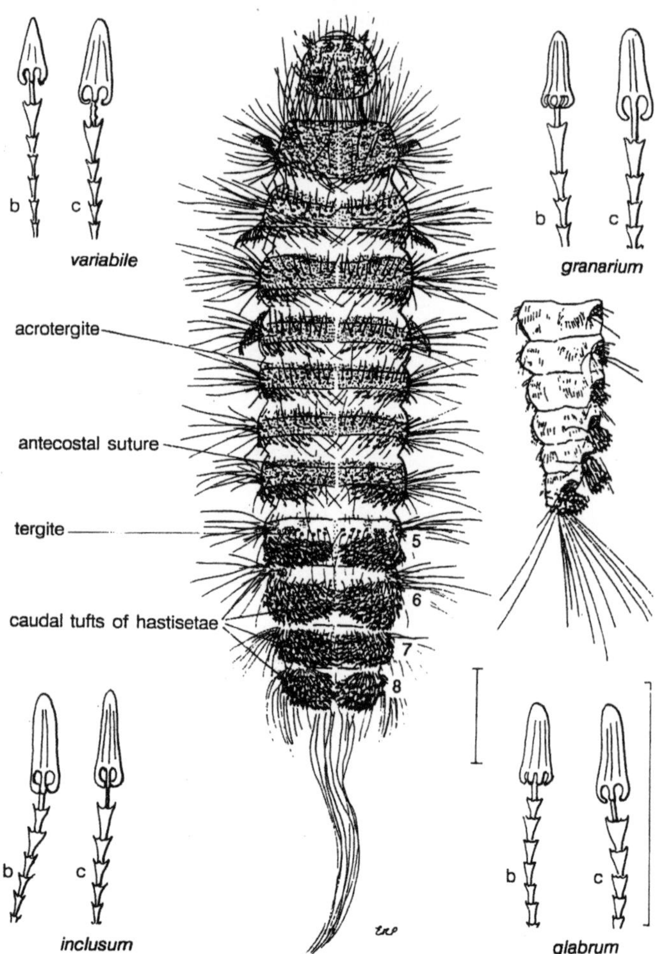

Figure 7.10. Larvae of Trogoderma *spp., cabinet beetles. Centre, T.* glabrum, *dorsal view; middle right, side view of apical abdomial segments. Enlargements of hastiseta from* Trogoderma *spp., as marked: b, seta from abdominal sergite 1; c, seta from caudal tuft of abdominal tergite 6 (from Peacock, 1993, with permission).*

Trogoderma inclusum, large cabinet beetle, mottled dermestid

This light brown larva (Figure 7.10) is spear-headed, with setae and hastisetae present on the back and a long brush of hairs, spicisetae, extending from the posterior of the abdomen. It has dorsal extensions, urogomphi, on the ninth abdominal segment. The last abdominal segment is encircled by a sclerotized ring. Adults and larvae appear to feed together. Larvae wander to a pupation site.

Other species: *Trogoderma granarium*, khapra beetle.

Reesa vespulae, museum nuisance, carpet beetle

This larva is light brown, a similar colour to *Trogoderma*, and found on all types of museum collection: botanical, entomological, skin, fungi, seeds, as well as in paper and textiles.

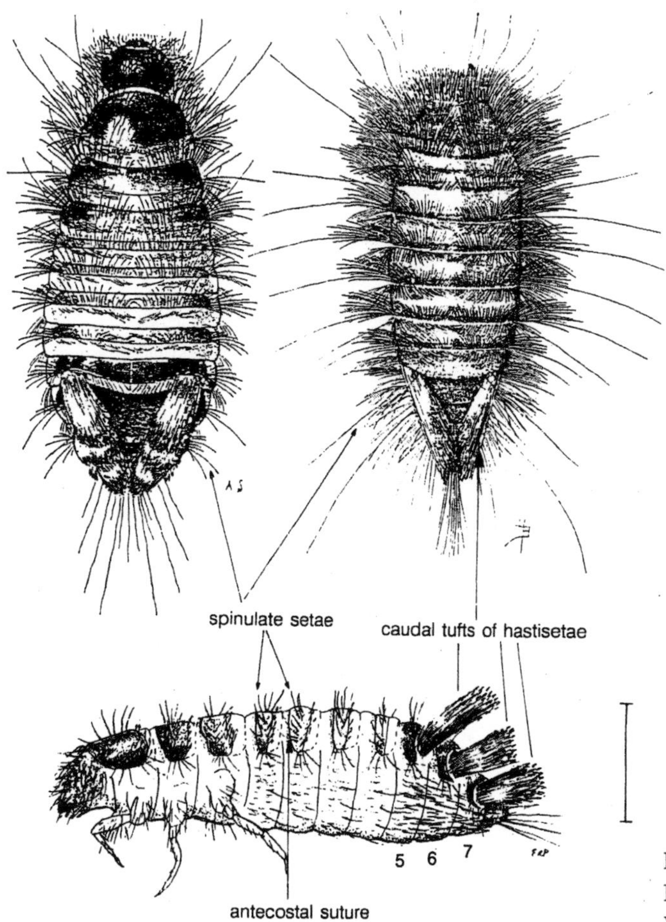

Figure 7.11. Larvae of Anthrenus *spp., carpet beetles. Above left,* A. verbasci, *dorsal view; above right,* A. verbasci, *side view; below,* A. flavipes, *dorsal view (from Peacock, 1993, with permission).*

***Anthrenus verbasci*, varied carpet beetle**

The larvae (Figure 7.11) are 4–5mm in length, much fatter than *Attagenus* larvae and are often called woolly bears. They are often found in cracks in wooden floors and under base boards in dust. They are brown and hairy, with a bunch of special golden hairs, a caudal brush, on each side of the rear abdominal segment on the supra-anal organ. The larva is able to raise and vibrate this fan-shaped mass of hastisetae as a defence mechanism. The hairs are shaped like arrows and their details assist in identification of different species. The spiny setae deter predators and the hastisetae may become attached to the attacker and, while it is cleaning them off, the larva can escape. If the larva is disturbed, it rolls up and fans out the posterior hairs. The larvae avoid the light and pupate in their food, commonly when this food is a dead insect. The larvae are very active and move around quickly and widely.

Other species: *Anthrenus flavipes*, furniture carpet beetle (Figure 7.11); *Anthrenus fuscus*, furniture carpet beetle; *Anthrenus scropulariae*, common carpet beetle, buffalo moth. *Megatoma undata*, carpet beetle.

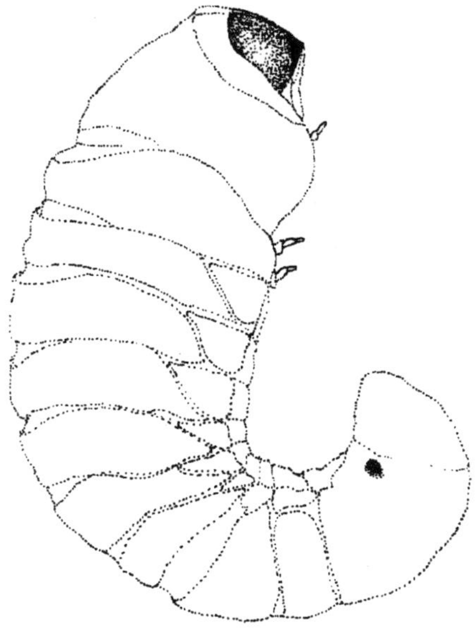

Figure 7.12. Larva of Lyctus brunneus, *brown powderpost beetle (Royal British Columbia Museum, by Ann Howatt-Krahn).*

BOSTRICHIDAE (BOSTRICHOIDEA), WOOD BEETLES, POWDERPOST BEETLES, TWIG AND WOOD BORERS

The larva (Figure 7.12 shows an example) can be 3–60mm in length, but is usually less than 20mm. The body is elongated, subcylindrical or slightly flattened, moderately or strongly curved ventrally (c-shaped), lightly sclerotized except for a dark mouth with a whitish to yellow cuticle and a few scattered dorsal simple setae. The head is retracted and prognathous, elongate and somewhat flattened, with three-segmented antennae.

***Lyctus brunneus*, powderpost beetle**

The larva (Figure 7.12) lives its life in wood. When it is first hatched in a crevice or pore of the wood, it is creamy white and less than a centimetre in length. It has dark brown, sclerotized mandibles and a strongly arched body. The thoracic legs have three segments, the last of which is paddle-shaped. A pair of breathing spiracles on the last, eigth abdominal segment are large and easily seen. The larva usually eats along the grain but does cut across other tunnels. It cannot digest cellulose and hemicellulose; it lives on cell contents, starch, sugars and some proteins and thus is restricted to sap wood (hardwoods). The larva attacks parquet floors and oak panelling. It is frequently imported in hardwoods from the tropics. The moisture content of wood is 8–30%; the optimum for this larva is 16%. Kiln-dried wood is protected from *Lyctus brunneus* attack. The frass consists of fine particles with a silky feel.

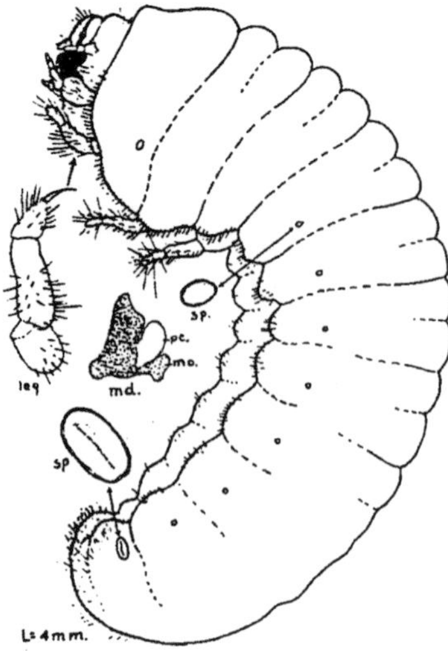

Figure 7.13. Larva of Lyctus planicollis, *southern lyctus beetle. sp=spiracle, md=mandible (from Peterson, 1967, with permission).*

Lyctus planicollis, southern lyctus beetle, true powderpost beetle

This larva (Figure 7.13) infests many kinds of dry, seasoned hardwood, especially ash, hickory and oak.

ANOBIIDAE (BOSTRICHOIDEA), FURNITURE, DEATHWATCH, DRUGSTORE AND CIGARETTE BEETLES

Powderpost beetles, spider beetles and anobiids have the following in common: strongly c-shaped, well-developed legs, lightly sclerotized body and a pair of longitudinal, oval anal pads or cushions just below the anal opening, which prevent the abdomen from touching defecated faeces. Anobiids differ from lyctids by having protracted and hypognathous heads and very short antennae.

The anobiid larvae can be from 2–12mm in length, having a c-shaped body that is lightly sclerotized with a nearly black, heavily sclerotized mouth, and, usually, fine hairs. The thorax has three pairs of well-developed, five-segmented legs. The head is globular to flattened; the mandibles are symmetrical, robust and unidentate to tridentate.

WOOD BEETLES

Anobium punctatum, common furniture beetle, false powderpost beetle, furniture woodworm

The larva (Figure 7.14) lives its whole life in wood. It can only be observed by breaking open the wood in which it is living. It is arch-shaped and has three pairs of well-developed thoracic legs, each with five segments. The larva usually tunnels up and down the grain of the wood. The tunnels are filled with rejected wood fibres and barrel-shaped faecal pellets, which give the frass a grainy feel.

Figure 7.14. Larva of Anobium punctatum, *common furniture beetle, woodworm (Royal British Columbia Museum, by Ann Howatt-Krahn).*

Xestobium rufovillosum, deathwatch beetle

This larva is similar in appearance to *Anobium punctatum*, the common furniture beetle. It has two black spots on each side of its head, while *A. punctatum* has just one. The larva is creamy white and strongly hook-shaped, is covered with erect golden hairs and grows to about a centimetre in length. The newly hatched larvae move over the surface of the wood to find a crevice or trough to enter the wood. Frass is in the form of bun-shaped pellets.

CEREAL- AND PROTEIN-EATING BEETLES

Stegobium paniceum, drugstore beetle, bread beetle, biscuit beetle

This larva (Figure 7.15) has a head that is protracted and hypognathous. It is nearly white, except for short, light-coloured setae (hairs) all over the body. Larvae and adults move around freely in stored food, spices, dried soup mixes, flour, etc. The larvae mature in 4–5 months and grow to 5mm.

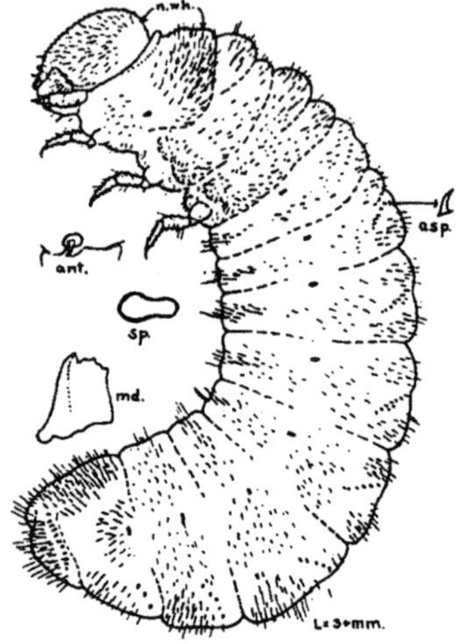

Figure 7.15. Larva of Stegobium paniceum, *drugstore beetle (from Peterson, 1967, with permission).*

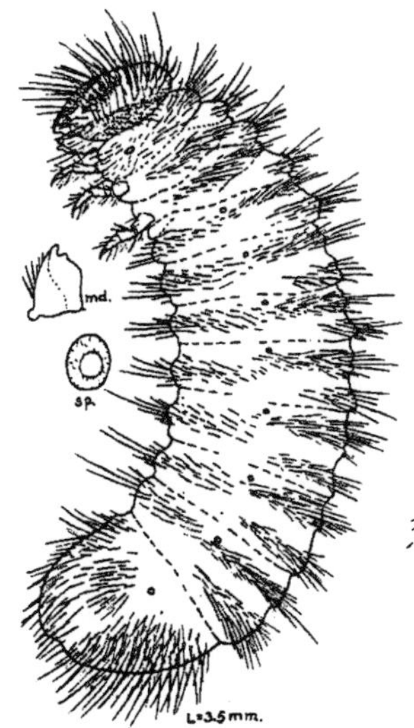

Figure 7.16. Larva of Lasioderma serricorne, *cigarette beetle (from Peterson, 1967, with permission).*

Lasioderma serricorne, cigarette beetle

The larva (Figure 7.16) is nearly white, except for many long setae on the body. They shun light. Larvae and adults appear to feed together. They are commonly found in tobacco, where the larvae make long cylindrical galleries in the compacted leaves, but they also feed on other plant material and spices.

PTINIDAE (BOSTRICHOIDEA)

SPIDER BEETLES

The spider beetle adults and larvae feed on the same food. They are scavengers of a wide variety of animal and plant material: faeces, hair, feathers, textiles, exuviae, dead insects, etc.

The larva can be 2–6mm long (see Figure 7.17 for example). Its body is elongated, moderately curved ventrally (c-shaped) and lightly sclerotized with fine hairs. The head is protracted and hypognathous, and it is heavily sclerotized. Stemmata are absent, antennae are very short and mandibles are symmetrical, robust and wedge-shaped, with a simple unidentate apex. The abdomen has anal pads.

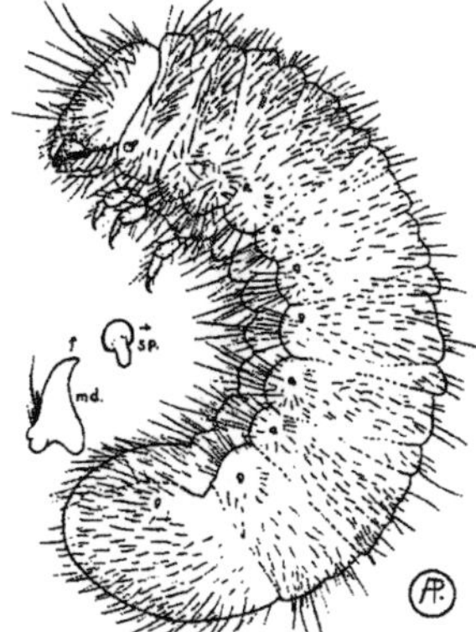

Figure 7.17. Larva of Ptinus brunneus, *spider beetle (from Peterson, 1967, with permission).*

Okumura (1982) discussed the biology of adult spider beetles. There is very little reference to the larva.

Ptinus tectus, Australian spider beetle

The larva is a whitish, fleshy grub that is strongly curved. It rolls up into a tight ball when disturbed. The body is covered with hairs and the thoracic legs have claws. When mature, the larva wanders away from food to find a suitable pupation site. It may eat its way through tough materials such as sacking, cellophane and cardboard for pupation, at which time it builds a spherical, thin-walled, tough cocoon.

Other species:

Gibbium psylloides, hump spider beetle
Mezium americanum, American spider beetle (Figure 7.18)
Nitpus hololeucus, golden spider beetle
Ptinus brunneus, spider beetle
Ptinus fur, white-marked spider beetle
Ptinus hirtellus, brown spider beetle
Ptinus villiger, hairy spider beetle

Figure 7.18. Larva of Mezium americanum, *American spider beetle (from Peterson, 1967, with permission).*

REFERENCES

Bry, R.E. 1991. Synthetic fabrics and fibre pests. *Journal of Entomological Science*, 26(1):51–58.

Chauvin, G. and G. Vannier, 1980. Absorption of water vapour by the larvae of *Tinea pellionella* (L.) (Lepidoptera: Tineidae). *Experientia*, 36:87–88.

Box 7.1 KEYS FOR IDENTIFICATION OF LARVAE OF COMMON CLOTHES MOTH AND BEETLE HERITAGE EATERS

Clothes moths (Tineidae)

Abbreviated key for identification of the commonest clothes moths, according to silk structures:

a Larvae live in elliptical, flattened cases covered or spun with infested material, open at both ends:
Tinea pellionella, case-making clothes moth

b Larvae live in silken fibres and rough tunnels in the infested material:
Trichophaga tapetzella, tapestry moth
naked larvae
not hairy
may form a silken tube or burrow through material

c Larvae associated only with webbing:
Tineola bisselliella, webbing clothes moth
naked larvae
not hairy
associated with webbing and faecal pellets
head yellow to light brown without ocelli

Hofmannophila pseudospretella (brown house moth) and *Endrosis sarcitrella* (white-shouldered house moth) are in the family Oecophoridae, which differs from the family Tineidae by arrangement of setae on the thorax and of crochet hooks. Tineidae have an elliptical or circular uniserial crochet arrangement and Oecophoridae an elliptical or circular biordinal arrangement.

Beetles (Coleoptera)

Abbreviated key for identification of the commonest Coleoptera larvae (collated from Stehr, 1987):

A Larvae are not fuzzy, the head is protracted and prognathous (pointed forwards), they have two pygopods present on the 10th abdomen segment and are without sclerotized ring, and they are associated with stored products:
a exoskeleton stiff, wire worm-like
i dark brown
Tenebrio obscurus, dark mealworm
ii yellow, golden brown
Tenebrio molitor, yellow mealworm, grain beetle
b exoskeleton soft
i yellowish white
Trilobium castaneum, rust-red flour beetle, grain beetle
Trilobium confusum, confused flour beetle

B Larvae are fuzzy, not grub-like, the head is free and hypognathous (head pointed downwards):
a larvae is spear-headed with setae (hastisetae) on back
i long brush of hairs extending backwards from posterior of abdomen; spear-headed setae arise from abdomen segments
Trogoderma
T. granarium, khapra beetle
T. inclusum, large cabinet beetle
T. ornatum, cabinet beetle
ii three pairs of caudal tufts or brushes at posterior region of abdomen; spear-headed setae arise from between abdomen segments
Anthrenus (larvae indistinguishable)
A. flavipes, furniture carpet beetle
A. scrophulariae, common carpet beetle
A. verbasci, varied carpet beetle
b Larvae without spear-headed setae on back
i long brush of hairs (spicisetae) extending backwards from posterior, head free and hypognathous
Attagenus
A. megatoma, black carpet beetle
A. pellio, fur beetle
A. piceus, black carpet beetle
Megatoma vespula, carpet beetle
ii larvae are fuzzy, have long spicisetae, with pair of processes at the tip of the abdomen, urogomphi on the ninth segment, sclerotized ring encircling the last abdominal section, reassociated with protein material
Dermestes lardarius, larder or bacon beetle
Dermestes maculatus, hide beetle
c larvae with short, thick hairs (lanceolate spicisetae) across rear edge of each body segment, head free and hypognathous
i hairs are club-shaped on rear edge of the prothorax, rolls up like a pill-bug
Thylodrias contractus, odd beetle

C Larvae are not fuzzy, lightly haired, grub-like, they have three pairs of well-developed thoracic legs, no prolegs, head is protracted and hypognathous, stemmata are absent:
a Thoracic spiracles located near front of prothorax
i larvae with light-coloured or colourless setae all over the head, peanut-shaped spiracles
Stegobium paniceum, drugstore beetle, bread beetle, biscuit beetle. No distinct colour markings, mouthparts and underside of are head brown
ii larvae have yellowish brown setae in a face-like pattern on head, spiracles annuliform to oval
Lasioderma serricorne, cigarette beetle. Long, light-coloured, more fuzzy than above, setae located on all parts of the body
b Thoracic spiracles located near posterior of prothorax
Spider beetles
Ptinus fur, whitemarked spider beetle
Ptinus tectus, Australian spider beetle

The wood beetles are not included here because larvae are rarely found; also, the bore holes on infested wood are commonly used for wood beetle identification.

Davis, R.D. 1987. Tineidae. In *Immature Insects*, Vol. I, Ed. F.W. Stehr, F.W. Kendall/Hunt Publishing Company, Iowa, USA, pp362–365.

Freeman, P. 1980. *Common Insect Pests of Stored Food Products. A Guide to their Identification*, 6th Ed. British Museum (Natural History) Economic Series, London, No. 15.

Gullan, P.J. and P.S. Cranston. 1995. *The Insects: An Outline of Entomology*, Chapman and Hall, London, New York.

Hickin, N.E. 1972. *The Woodworm Problem*. The Rentokil Library, Hutchinson, London.

Hinton, H.E. 1943. The larvae of the Lepidoptera associated with stored products. *Bulletin of Entomological Research*, 34:163–212.

Hinton, H.E. 1945. *Monograph of the Beetles Associated with Stored Products*, Vol. 1. British Museum (Natural History), London.

Hinton, H.E. 1956. The larvae of the Tineidae of economic importance. *Bulletin of Entomological Research*, 47:251–346.

Hinton, H.E. and A.S. Corbet. 1972. *Common insect pests of Stored Food Products*. British Museum (Natural History) Economic Series No. 15, London.

House H.L. 1974. Nutrition. In *The physiology of Insecta*, Vol. 5, 2nd Ed., Ed. Morris Rockstein. Academic Press, New York, pp1–62.

Jindra, M. and F. Sehnal. 1990. Linkage between diet humidity, metabolic water production and heat dissipation in the larvae of *Galleria mellonella. Insect Biochemistry*, 20(4):389–395.

Loudon, C. 1988. Development of *Tenebrio molitor* in low oxygen levels. *Journal of Physiology*, 34(2):87–103.

Okumura, G. 1982. Stored product pests. In *Handbook of Pest Control*, 6th Ed., Ed. A. Mallis. Franzak and Foster Publishing Comp., Cleveland, Ohio.

Peacock, E.R. 1993. *Adults and Larvae of Hide, Larder and Carpet Beetles and Their Relatives (Coleoptera:Dermestidae) and of Derodontid Beetles (Coleoptera: Derodontidae)*. Handbooks for the Identification of British Insects, Vol. 5, Part 3. Royal Entomological Society of London, London.

Peterson, A. 1967. *Larvae of Insects*, Parts 1 and 2, 6th Ed.. Edward Bros, Ann Arbor, Michigan.

Pinniger, D. 1994. *Iinsect Pests in Museums*. Archetype Publications, London.

Rees, B.E. 1943. Classification of the Dermestidae based on larvalcharacteristics, with a key to the North American genera. U.S. Department of Agriculture. Miscellaneous Publication 511:1–8.

Rees, B.E. 1947. Taxonomy of the larvae of some North American species of the genus Dermestes (Coleoptera: Dermestidae). *Proceedings of the Entomological Society of Washington*, 49(1):1–14.

Robinson, G.S. 1979. Clothes moths of the *Tinea pellionella* complex: a revision of the world's species (Lepidoptera:Tineidae). Bulletin of the British Museum (Natural History), Entomol. Series, 38(3):57–128.

Scoble, M. 1992. *The Lepidoptera Form, Function and Diversity*. Oxford University Press, New York.

Scott, H.G. 1959. *Household and Stored-Food Insects of Public Health Importance and Their Control*. U.S. Department of Public Health, Education and Welfare, Atlanta, Georgia.

Stehr, F. W. 1987/1991. *Immature Insects*, Vols I and II. Kendall/Hunt Publishing Company, Iowa, USA.

Van't Hof, H.M. and M.M. Martin. The effect of diet water content on energy expenditure by third-instar *Manduca sexta* larvae (Lepidoptera:Sphingidae). *Journal of Insect Physiology*, 35(5):433–436.

Waterhouse, D.F. 1958. Wool digestion and moth proofing. *Advances in Pest Control Research*, 2:207–262.

Wipking, W., M. Viebahn and D. Neumann. 1995. Oxygen consumption, water, lipid and glycogen content in early and late diapause and non-diapause larvae of the Burnet Moth *Zygaena trifolii. Journal of Insect Physiology*, 41(1):47—56.

Wigglesworth, V.B. 1984. *Insect Physiology*, 8th Ed. Chapman and Hall, London and New York, pp191.

8

The Pupa

8.1 PUPATION SITE

When a mature larva is committed to metamorphosis it continues to feed to reach its critical size. It then ceases to feed and leaves the food in search of a pupation site. This is called the wandering stage and is triggered by hormones (see Figure 8.1). The wandering larva decides on the pupation site, possibly the feeding site on the heritage object or it may seek out a suitable protected pupation site away from the feeding site. Often the pupae are not seen because they are in chambers or cocoons made by the larva, or away from the larval feeding site.

Pupation sites can be tunnels or pupation chambers made by the larva beneath the surface of compact materials, such as wood, or in cracks and crevices in the walls, ceiling or floor close to the larval feeding site.

The fact that the pupation site may not be on the infested heritage object means that, in the event of an infestation, one must inspect the insect remains to be sure that all stages of the life cycle, including the pupae, have been found and removed. There have been frequent instances where the pupae have not been located and, after a clean-up, there was a reoccurrence of the infestation from these hidden pupae. This has often been blamed on unsuccessful eradication methods.

8.2 PUPATION

In the group of insects that have complete metamorphosis (holometabolous), the final instar or mature larva that has completed feeding, called the prepupa, goes through structural and morphological changes in preparation for metamorphosis. This period is called pupariation and is still a larval stage. It is during the larval–pupal moult that metamorphosis occurs and the pupa is formed; this process is called pupation. The pupa is an intermediate, non-feeding stage that moults to produce an adult insect.

Commonly during pupation, the larval structures are dissolved and new adult structures develop from a group of undifferentiated embryonic cells called imaginal discs. These cells divide, differentiate and form the pupa, which is encased in a new, heavily sclerotized cuticle (see 4.3.2). It may be further protected by a larval cocoon or a puparium. The cocoon is spun silk and the puparium the sclerotized moult of the prepupa larva.

The pupa can be an immature or fully formed adult. If fully formed, it usually remains dormant in the pupal case for a period of time. The dormant period, called the diapause, allows the pupa to survive adverse environmental conditions, e.g. overwintering. When environmental conditions are conducive, the adult emerges. This is a way to synchronize the emergence of many adults at one time to ensure mating and survival.

In museums or homes the occurrence of a large number of adult insect pests of one species, at one time, suggests that there has been an environmental change, usually an increase in relative humidity, which has broken the diapause of pupae and triggered emergence of the adults.

For further information on pupation, see Denlinger and Zdárek (1994) and Gullan and Cranston (1995).

8.3 PUPATION UNDER HORMONAL CONTROL

Pupation is controlled by the relative amounts of the juvenile and ecdysteroid hormones (Figure 8.1). These two hormones are secreted internally from the endocrine gland, the corpus allatum, located behind the brain. The juvenile hormone (JH) is required to ensure that, when a larva moults, it remains as

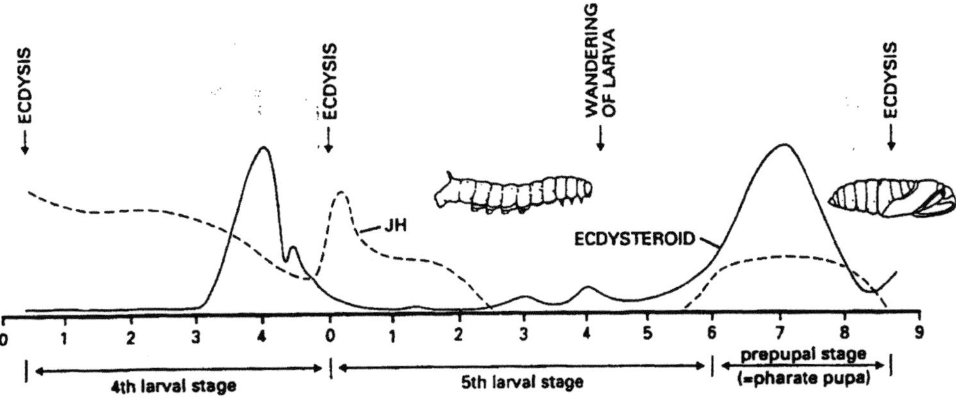

Figure 8.1. Fluctuations in the relative amounts of the juvenile hormone (JH) and ecdysteroid (ES) during the last two larval stages and the prepupal stage. The diagram shows the presence of high JH and low amounts of ES coinciding with ecdysis (moulting) of the larval stage. The reverse, low JH and high ES, triggers the development of the larva to the prepupal stage (after Gullan and Cranston, 1995).

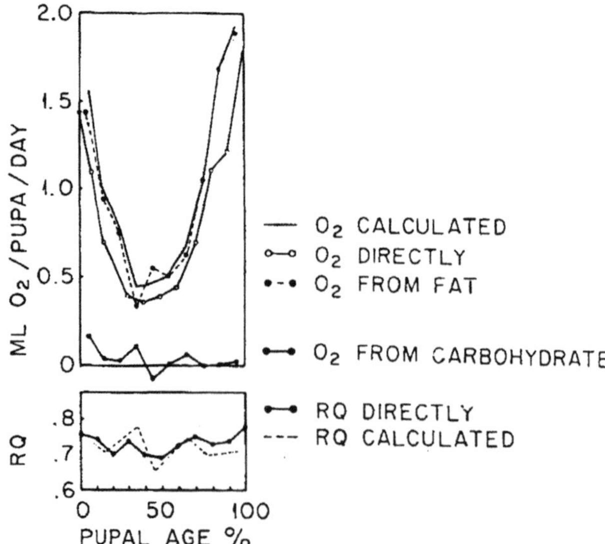

Figure 8.2. The oxygen consumption and respiratory quotient during metamorphosis of the fly Calliphora erythrocephala, *directly measured on living pupae and calculated from estimations of the gradual disappearance of fat and carbohydrate (from Agrell and Lundquist, 1973).*

a larva in the next stage. JH is no longer produced in the final instar larva but there is an increase in the ecdysteroid hormone (ES). The reduced amount of JH and the presence of ES activate the imaginal discs and direct the larva to proceed to the prepupal stage and undergo pupation. The production of these hormones is triggered internally in the endocrine gland, probably by the nutritional status of the larva and environmental conditions (Gilbert and King, 1973).

JH is used in agriculture and forestry to control insect pest populations by preventing pupation. However, this extends the life of larva, the reverse of what is required for the control of heritage eaters.

8.4 METABOLISM OF PUPA

The pupae of the common insect pests of heritage objects are inactive; their body movement is restricted to the abdominal segments, probably related to external respiration or breathing. The pupa is a non-feeding stage. The food needed for emergence comes from the fat body, proteins and glycogen of the mature larva. The goal of the larva was to accumulate these nutrients for the development and reproduction of the adult.

Research has shown (Agrell and Lundquist, 1973) that during pupal life the main food utilized is fats. This is measured by the amount of oxygen required and the amount of carbon dioxide produced to convert this nutrient into heat energy. The ratio of these two gases is called the respiratory quotient (RQ), the ratio of CO_2 evolved to O_2 consumed. The RQ is dependent on the source of energy being utilized, e.g dextrose 1.00, protein 0.8, fats 0.7. In Figure 8.2 the ratio is around 0.7, suggesting utilization of fat for energy.

During pupal life, oxygen is required for respiration to produce the chemical energy for metabolic processes. Figure 8.2 shows that oxygen consumption is high at the initiation of pupation, then drops to a low level and remains there until just prior to emergence, at which time it rapidly becomes high again. The period of low oxygen consumption is the diapause. The length of time of diapause varies with insect species and environmental conditions. Figure 8.2 illustrates the adsorption curve of oxygen for pupae of one insect species, but this u-shaped curve is common to many species.

The relevance of this information to heritage eaters is in relation to anoxic insect pest eradication treatments. The low oxygen consumption of the diapause pupa suggests that it may require a longer treatment time than active stages. It is possible that, in the future, pretreatment to induce breaking of diapause would make the anoxic treatment more rapid. Details of the effects of anoxic conditions are reviewed in chapter 12.

8.5 PREVENTION OF WATER LOSS

The pupa has no way of obtaining water, so it must conserve as much internal water as possible. The sclerotized cuticle, puparium or cocoon of the pupa must prevent body water loss. Body metabolic wastes are not eliminated during pupal life, also conserving water.

There is, however, water loss when tracheal spiracles open to acquire essential oxygen. Beetle pupae have spiracle valves to control the opening. Some diapause pupae store carbon dioxide and eliminate it in one daily burst, which shortens the time needed for spiracles to be open, thus reducing water loss. The low consumption of oxygen during diapause also limits water loss. Tests have demonstrated that an increase in carbon dioxide in the ambient air causes beetle pupae spiracles to open. It is the open spiracles that cause body water loss and eventually lethal dehydration, not the gas conditions.

This information assists in understanding the vulnerability of the pupal stage to eradication methods using altered atmospheric gas concentrations. In tests with modified atmospheric gas concentrations the cause of death is often not determined, but in most cases it is probably due to body dehydration.

For further information on insect spiracular systems, see 5.3.1.

8.6 TYPES OF PUPAE

Pupae vary in appearance but have been grouped in two basic types; exarate and obtect. Coarctate are special exarate pupae with a puparium. For further information, see Peterson (1967) and Stehr (1987).

8.6.1 Exarate

- most pupae are exarate
- with appendages free or not glued to the body
- with distinct and free antennae
- with legs and wing cases held close to the body
- look like mummified adults
- non-articulated mandibles (adecticous) are common but rarely there are articulated mandibles (decticous), which cut through the cocoon;
- all the Coleoptera pupae are of typical exarate type.

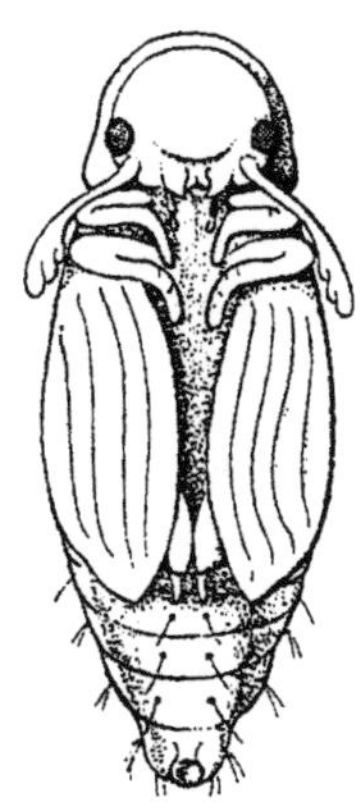

(with permission from The Rentokil Library, *Munroe, 1966)*

8.6.2 Coarctate (exarate adectitious)

- essentially like exarate pupae, but remain covered by the hardened exuviae of the last larval instar
- always adecticous
- example: puparia of flies.

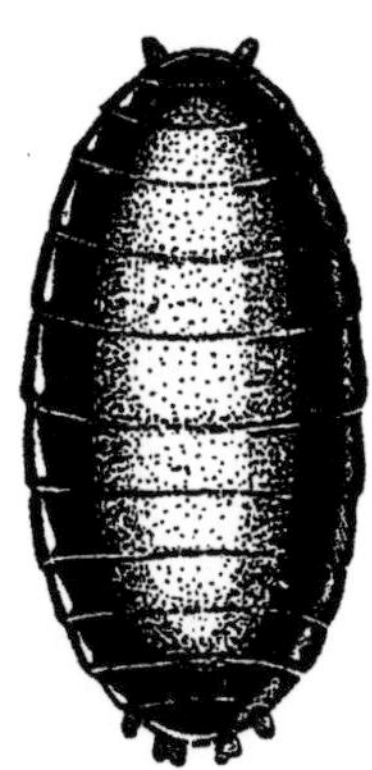

(with permission from The Rentokil Library, *Munroe, 1966)*

8.6.3 Obtect

- with appendages more or less glued to the body
- the cuticle is often heavily sclerotized as in almost all Lepidoptera
- the pupae of Lepidoptera (moths) may be covered by a silken larval cocoon
- always adectitious (non-articulated mandibles).

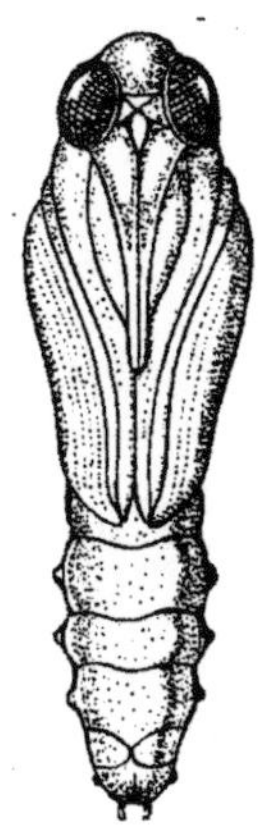

(with permission from The Rentokil Library, *Munroe, 1966)*

8.6.4 Summary of salient features of pupae types of some insect orders *(all illustrations are from Peterson 1967, with permission)*

COLEOPTERA (BEETLE) PUPAE

Beetle pupae are always adecticous (without functional mandibles) and typically exarate (with free antennae, and legs and wing cases held close to the body). Pupae may develop in or on materials of the larval feeding site, in pupal cells or partially enclosed within the prepupa larvae exuviae, which are usually covered by hairy setae or spines for protection.

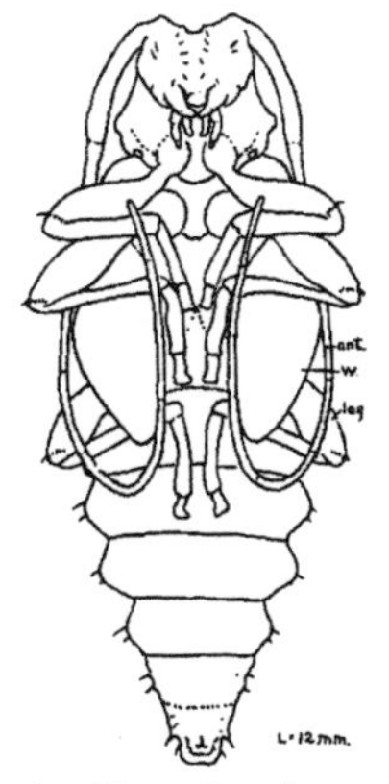

Cerambycidae – Longhorned beetle

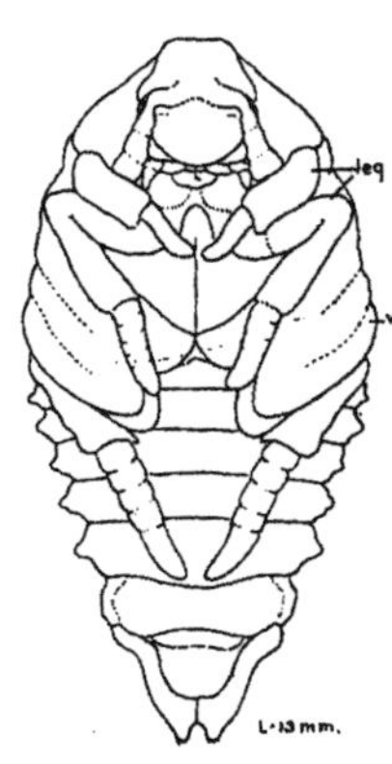

Scarabaeidae – Japanese beetle

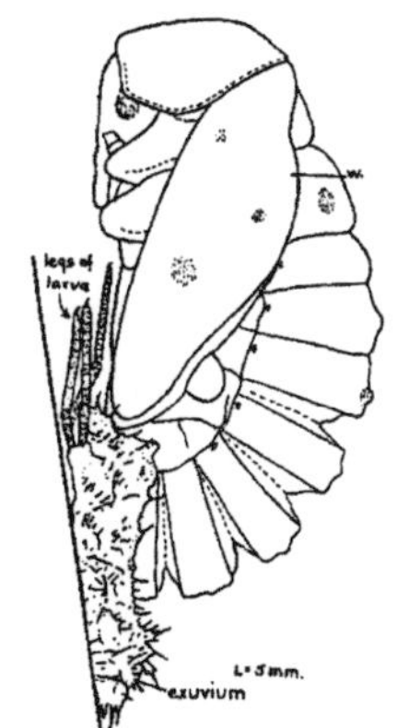

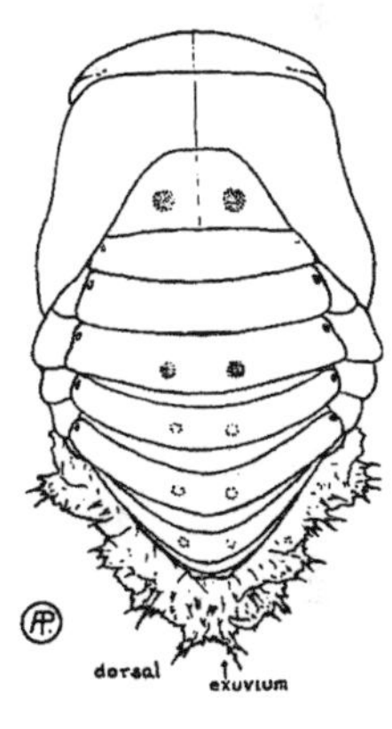

Coccinellidae – Ladybird beetle

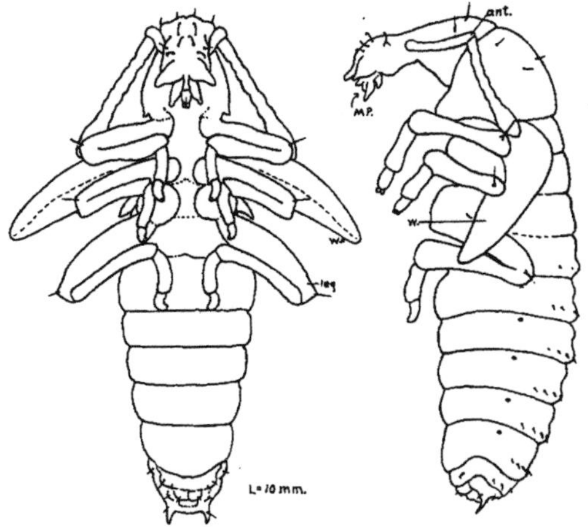

Curculionidae – weevil

LEPIDOPTERA (MOTHS AND BUTTERFLIES) PUPAE

The pupae are obtect pupae with mouthparts, legs and wing cases fused to the body wall. Most pupae of moths are found in cocoons or pupal cells, both of which are made by the prepupal larvae. The cocoons are spun silk covered with bits of feeding material and the pupal cells are lined with silk. Adults dissolve the silk for emergence. The butterfly pupa, called a chrysalid, is naked and attached to some object above ground.

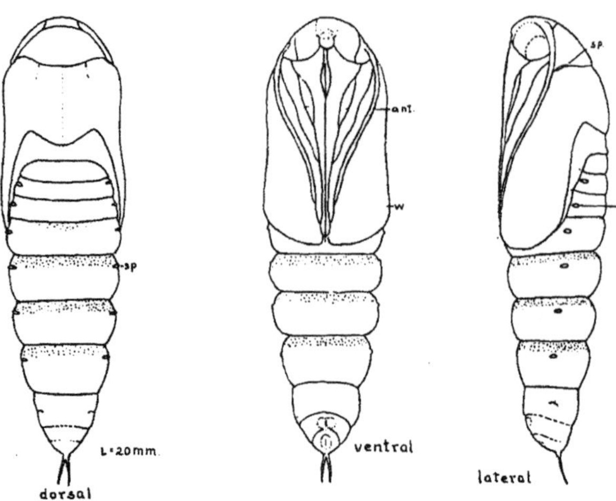

Moth (Heliothis sp.)

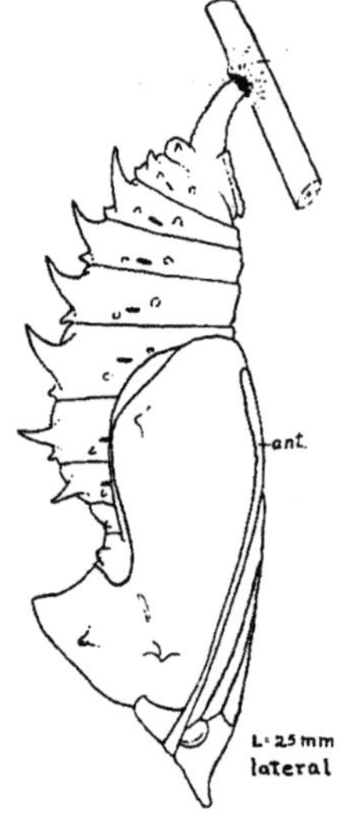

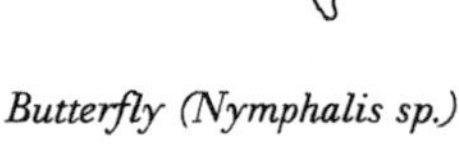

Butterfly (Nymphalis sp.)

DIPTERA PUPARIUM AND PUPAE

These are basically adecticous (without functional mandibles) and typically exarate (with free antennae, and legs and wing cases held close to the body) but the pupa is inside a puparium, the sclerotized moult of the prepupal larva.

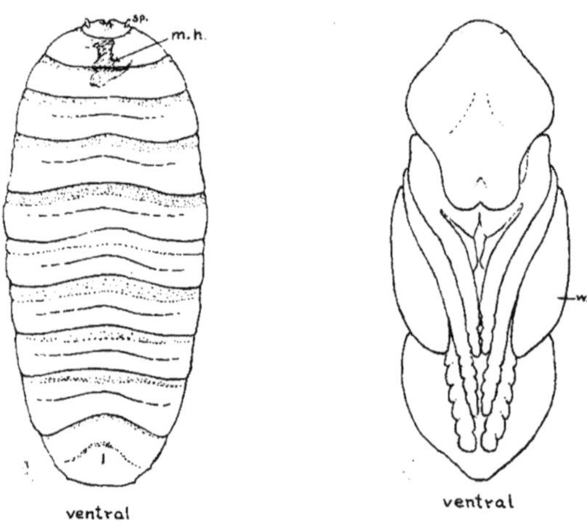

Metopiidae (Blowfly) puparium and pupa inside

HYMENOPTERA PUPAE

The pupae are adecticous (without functional mandibles) and typically exarate (with free antennae, and legs and wing cases held close to the body), but have fairly conspicuous antennae.

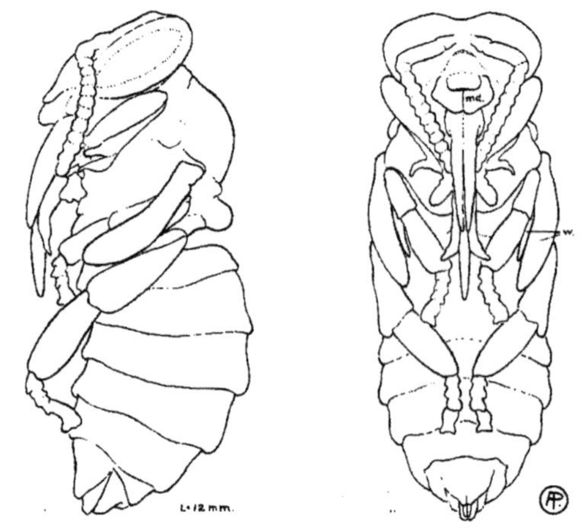

Apidae - Honey bee (lateral and ventral view)

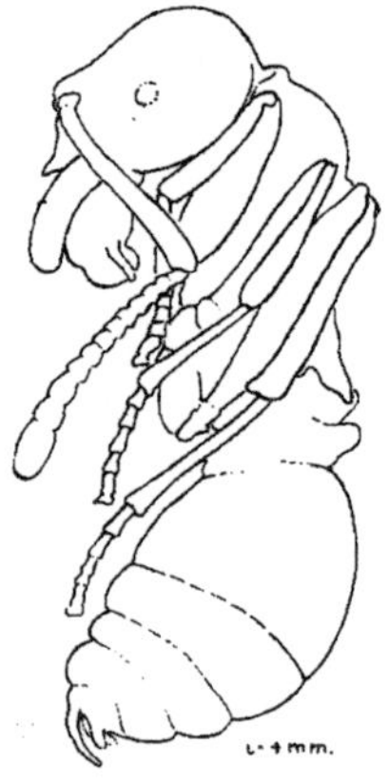

Formicidae - wingless worker ant

BOX 8.1 SALIENT FEATURES OF PUPAE OF SOME COMMON HERITAGE EATERS

The characteristics selected are pertinent to problems of control in museums or homes. There is limited information and illustration of the heritage eaters' pupae in the literature, so the following material may seem incomplete. Sources used are Mallis (1982), Monro (1966), Mosher (1969) and Peterson (1967).

EXARATE PUPAE

WOOD BEETLES

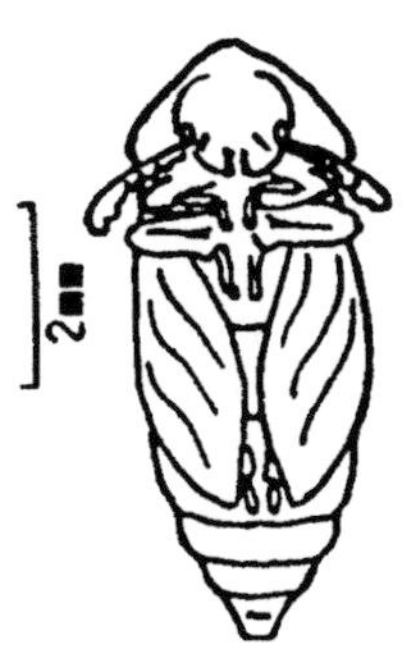

(from Koeller, 1973)

***Anobium punctatum*, common furniture beetle, woodworm**

- The mature larva builds a pupal chamber close to the surface of the wood.
- The pupa is milky white when first formed but soon darkens.
- After rupturing the thin transparent pupal case the adult remains in the pupal chamber until its exoskeleton has hardened.
- The mature adult bores a flight hole about 2mm in diameter for emergence from the pupal chamber.

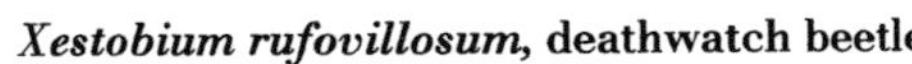

***Xestobium rufovillosum*, deathwatch beetle**

Similar to *A. punctatum*, above.

- Pupae are creamy white and resemble the adult beetle in shape but the legs and antennae are held down (though not adhered to the body) by the thin, transparent pupal skin or case.
- The mature larva enlarges a gallery immediately beneath the wood surface for a pupal chamber.
- The adult bites its way out, forming a circular exit hole in the pupal case.

***Lyctus brunneus*, powderpost beetle**

- The mature larva finishes feeding near the surface of the wood and builds a pupal chamber.
- The pupa is first of all white but darkens before emergence.
- The adult bores its way out of the wood, pushing sawdust (not frass with faecal pellets) in front of itself.

STORED DRIED FOOD BEETLES

***Stegobium paniceum*, drugstore beetle**

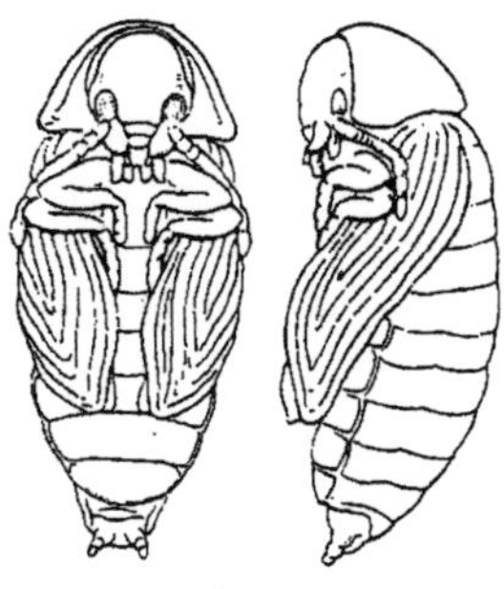

(from Linsley and Michelbacher, 1943)

- The mature larva builds a cocoon of food particles, cemented together with secretion from its mouth.
- Pupation occurs in feeding site.
- Pupal stage lasts 12–18 days.
- Adult bites its way out of the cocoon.

BOX 8.1 (cont.) SALIENT FEATURES OF PUPAE OF SOME COMMON HERITAGE EATERS

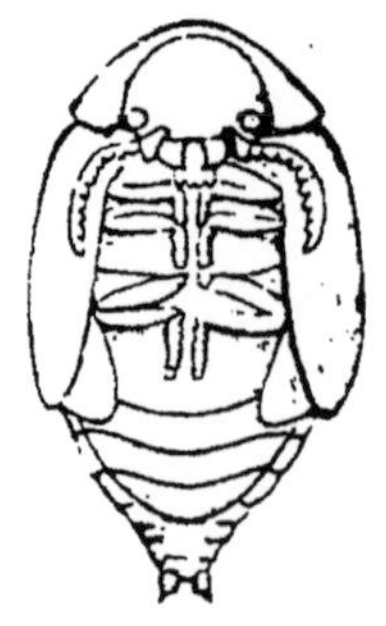

(from Chittenden, 1911)

***Lasioderma serricorne,* cigarette beetle**

- Pupation occurs in feeding site.

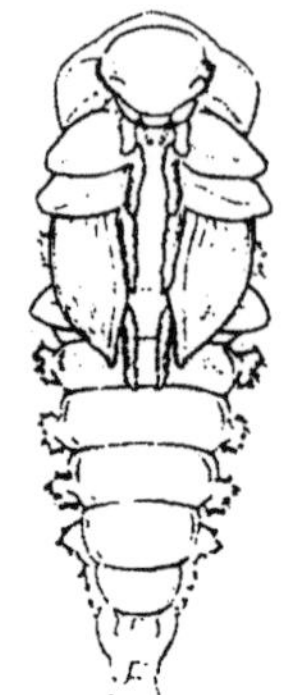

(from Linsley and Michelbacher, 1943)

***Tenebrio molitor,* mealworm**

- Pupation occurs in feeding site.
- The curved pupa lies on its side among foodstuffs.

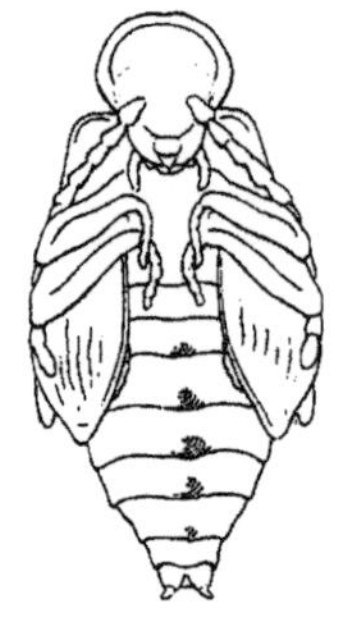

(from Linsley and Michelbacher, 1943)

***Ptinus sp.* spider beetle**

- The pupa is extremely delicate; it is first white then turns golden yellow.
- The prepupal larva wanders to a hiding place and burrows in wooden walls or dense material and builds a spherical, thin-walled but tough cocoon for pupation.
- The adult remains in the pupal case for a few days then bites its way out.

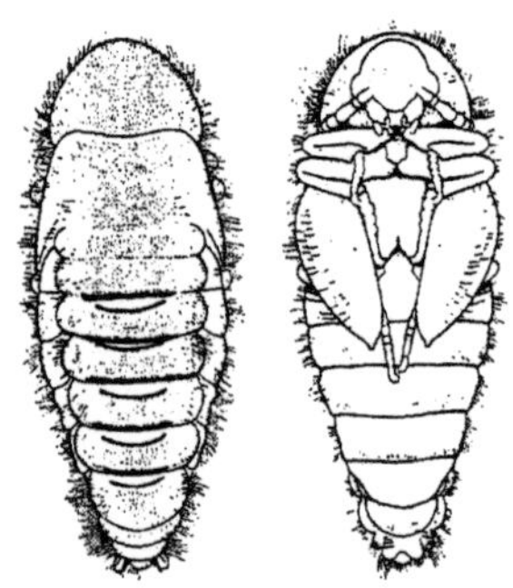

(from Waterhouse, 1991)

HIDE, FUR AND CARPET BEETLES

***Dermestes maculatus,* hide beetle**

- The last instar larva usually moves away from the feeding site to a pupation site.
- The pupation site consists of some compact material.
- The larvae make short tunnels in any surfaces: wood, leather, soft metals, dried meat, etc.
- The naked pupa rests in the tunnel plugged by the mature larva's skin.
- If the pupa is exposed on the surface the larva skin remains attached to the pupa.

BOX 8.1 (cont.) SALIENT FEATURES OF PUPAE OF SOME COMMON HERITAGE EATERS

***Attagenus pellio*, fur beetle; *Attagenus megatoma*, black carpet beetle**

- Pupae are never visible because they remain in last larva instar skin.
- The adult may stay in the skin for 3–20 days.

MUSEUM AND CARPET BEETLES

***Anthrenus verbasci*, varied carpet beetle**

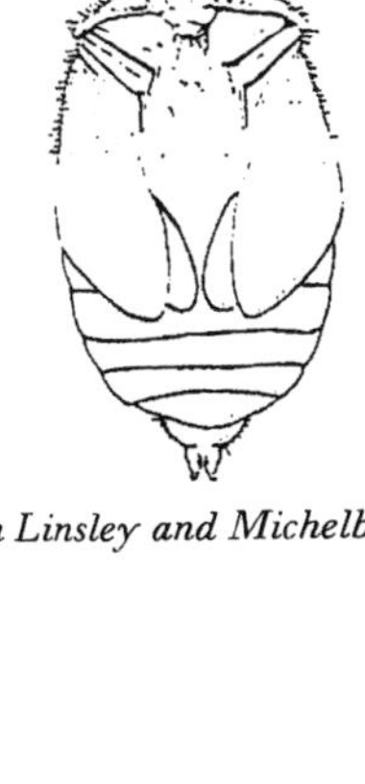

(from Linsley and Michelbacher, 1943)

- Pupation usually occurs in the feeding site.
- The last larval skin is not shed but remains and completely covers the pupa, so the pupae are often mistaken for larvae.
- The adult remains in the larval skin for 4–30 days.

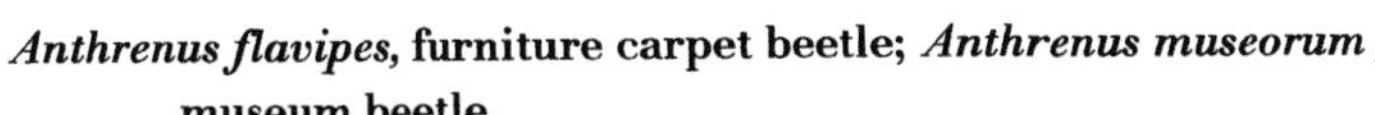

***Anthrenus flavipes*, furniture carpet beetle; *Anthrenus museorum* , museum beetle**

Similar to *Anthrenus verbasci*, above.

***Anthrenus scrophulariae*, common carpet beetle**

- Pupation does not necessarily occur in the larval feeding site, but often found in crevices, e.g. in the floor beneath the infested material.
- The adult remains in the pupal case for up to 18 days.

OBTECT PUPAE

CLOTHES MOTHS

***Tineola bisselliella*, webbing clothes moth**

- Prepupal larvae usually pupate hidden in cracks or folds in material in the feeding site.
- The prepupal larva spins a cocoon of silk, smooth inside but with bits of textile or other materials from the feeding site.
- The length of pupation varies greatly depending on temperature and relative humidity.
- The pupae are reddish-brown in colour and obtect, i.e. appendages adhere to the body.
- On emergence the adult leaves the pupal case protruding slightly from the cocoon.

***Tinea pellionella*, casemaking clothes moth**

- The larva is always in a cocoon, which it drags around wherever it goes.
- Incorporated into the silk cocoon are fragments of the material it is feeding on.
- The prepupal larva cocoon is used for pupation.
- When ready to pupate, the larva seeks a protected place away from the feeding site, such as crevices on walls or ceilings.
- The cocoon is sealed at both ends prior to pupation.

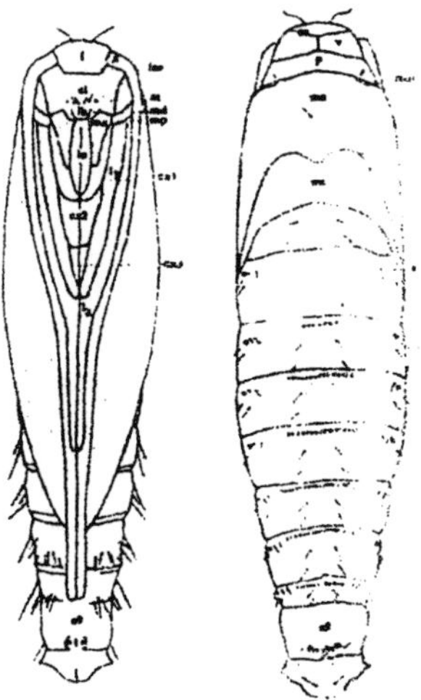

(from Mosher, 1969)

***Trichophaga tapetzella*, tapestry moth**

Similar to *Tinea pellionella*, above.

REFERENCES

Agrell, P.S. and A.M. Lundquist. 1973. Physiology and biochemical changes during insect development. In *Physiology of Insecta*, Vol. 1. Ed. Morris Rockstein. Academic Press, New York, pp159–249.

Chittenden, F.H. 1911. *Stored Food Pests*. USDA Bulletin 8.

Denlinger, D.L. and J. Zdárek. 1994. Metamorphosis behaviour in flies. *Annual Review of Entomology*, 39:243–266.

Gilbert, L.I. and D.S. King. 1973. Physiology of growth and development: endocrine aspects. In *The Physiology of Insecta*, Vol. 1, Ed. Morris Rockstein. Academic Press, New York, pp250–370.

Gullan, P.J. and P.S. Cranston. 1995. *The Insects: An Outline of Entomology*. Chapman and Hall, London, New York.

Koeller, G.K. 1973. *Tratado de la Prevision del Papel y de la Concervacion de Bibliotecas y Achivas*. Servicio de Publicaciones del Ministerio de Educacion y Cienca, Madrid.

Linsley, E.G. and A.E. Michelbacher. 1943. Insects affecting stored food products. *California Agriculture Experimental Station Bulletin*, Number 676.

Mallis, A. 1982. *Handbook of Pest Control*, 6th Ed. Franzak and Foster Company, Cleveland, Ohio.

Munro, J.W. 1966. *Pests of Stored Products*, *The Rentokil Library*, Hutchinson, West Sussex, UK.

Mosher, E. 1969. *Lepidoptera Pupae. Five Collected Works on the Pupae of North America Lepidoptera*. Entomological Reprint Specialists, East Lansing, Michigan.

Nikan, T.B. and V.V. Knole. 1989. *Insect Spiracular Systems*. Ellis Horwood, Chichester.

Peterson, A. 1967. *Larvae of Insects*, Parts I and II. Printed for the author by Edward Bros, Ann Arbor, Michigan.

Stehr, F.W. 1987. *Immature Insects*, Vol. 1. Kendall/Hunt Publishing Co., Dubugue, Iowa.

Waterhouse, D.F. 1991. *The Insects of Australia*. 2nd Ed. The Melbourne University Press, Melbourne, Australia.

10

The Adult: Trapping and Monitoring

10.1 THE ADULTS

10.1.1 Introduction

In trapping adults in heritage collections the common insects that are a concern are moths and beetles. We see the adults only on traps and, occasionally, a flying moth. Adults are rarely found in infestations.

Books on the control of insects in museums all have excellent illustrations of the adults. The identification of all the adult insects that are found in museums would form a book in itself. This chapter will discuss only the biology of the adults that is pertinent to trapping and monitoring, i.e. light responses for light traps, sex odour attraction for pheromone traps and feeding site odour for oviposition sites.

The general morphology of some common beetle and moth heritage eaters is shown in Figure 10.1. Figure 10.2, a pictorial key to some common beetles and weevils, includes stored grain and food product pests.

The role of the adults is reproduction: rarely do they eat. The insect pests have a variety of patterns as to when and where the females mate. Some mate as soon as they emerge and lay eggs in the feeding site. Some females move away from the site and the male flies to the female, either at night or during the day, and they mate away from the feeding site. The female then must find an oviposition site for egg laying with a new potential feeding site for the new generation. Some adult insects fly to flowers for a pollen meal before or after mating.

To cover all the variables there are three main methods of trapping, based on insect physiology: light responses for light traps, sex odour attraction for pheromone traps and feeding site odour attraction for oviposition sites. The traps are made up of the attractant – light, pheromone or food – and a method of catching the gullible insect, such as a sticky landing surface, water or electricity.

10.1.2 Reasons for trapping insects

Capturing, trapping and other sampling methods of insect populations in the field have been used for the basic studies of insect biology: population dynamics, ecology and behaviour in nature. The greatest thrust in trapping technology has come from applied entomology, i.e. the study of agriculture and forest insect pests, of stored food insect pests and medical entomology. According to the species of insect involved and the nature of the investigation, many different sampling methods and designs of traps have evolved, and trapping systems are being revised constantly. Against this continually

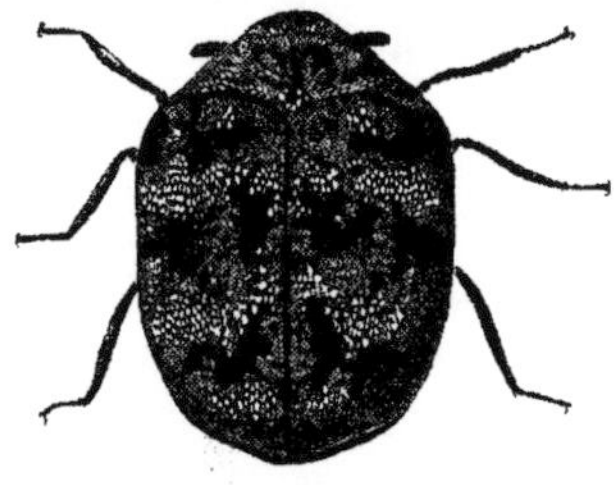

Anthrenus verbasci *(L.), varied carpet beetle.*

Anthrenus scrophulariae *(L.), common carpet beetle.*

Attagenus pellio *(L.), black carpet beetle.*

Lyctus brunneus *(Steph.), brown powderpost beetle.*

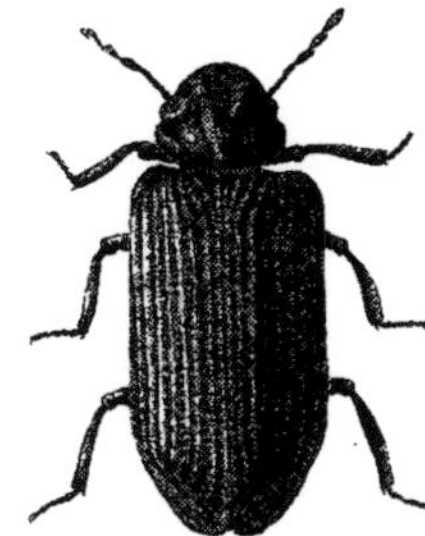

Anobium punctatum *(De Geer), common furniture beetle.*

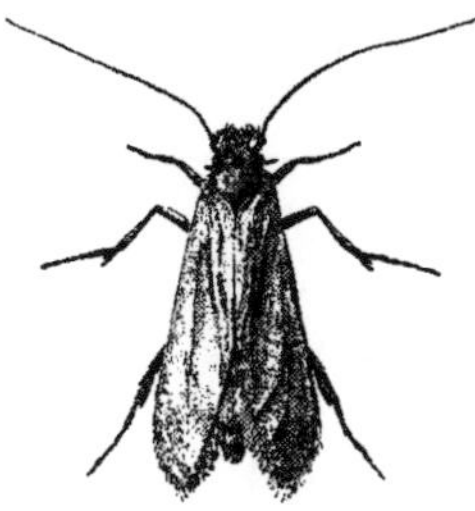

Tinneola bisselliella *(Hummel), webbing clothes moth*

Figure 10.1. General morphology of some common adult heritage eaters (Royal British Columbia Museum, by Ann Howatt-Krahn).

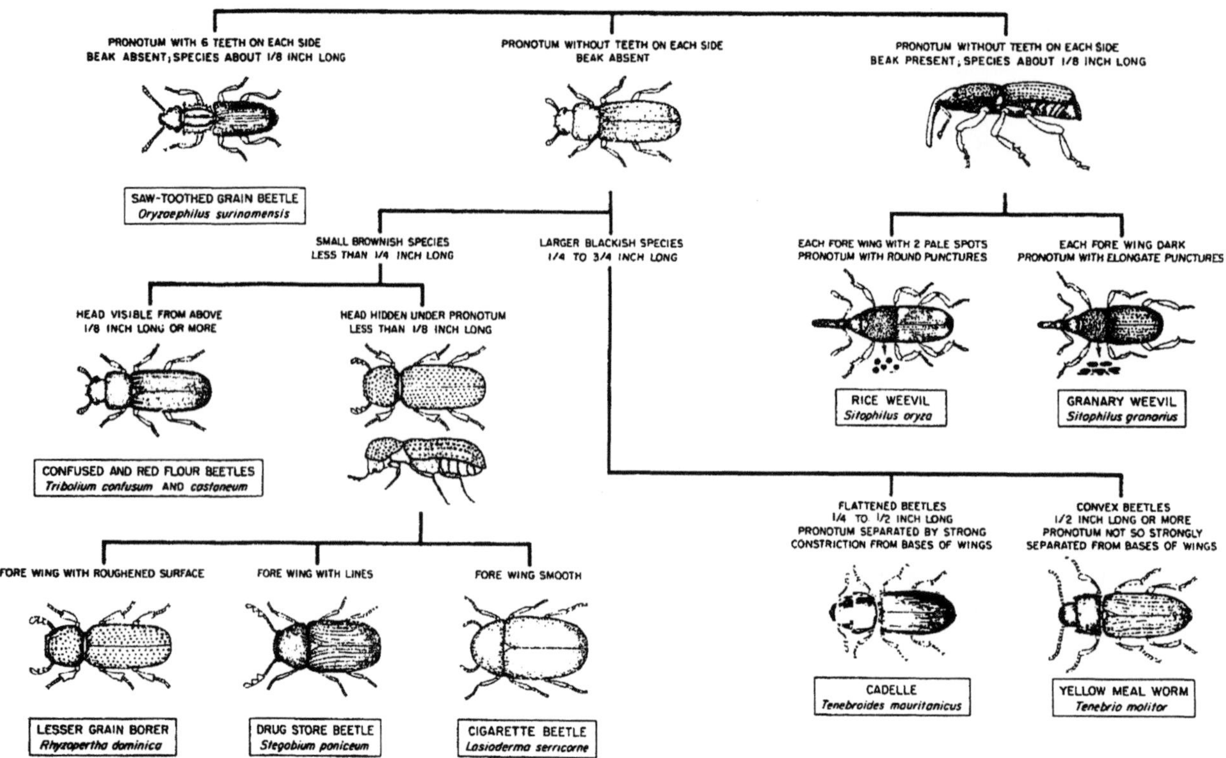

Figure 10.2. Pictorial key to some common beetles and weevils (Scott, n.d., U.S. Dept Public Health Services)

changing background it is inappropriate to offer firm instructions for all circumstances. Methods developed for a specific species in a specific environment are very often unsuitable for the same species or a closely related one in another environment.

In the museum world and in our homes we have transferred this technology to our own insect pest problems. We must, however, question whether the use of these techniques is helping us obtain our goal of prevention of insect pest damage or whether we doing things without knowledge of their full consequences.

In the food warehousing industry, trapping insects is used for monitoring and sometimes for eradication or population size control. The goal is reduction of product loss, not complete elimination of loss. In forestry and agriculture trapping is carried out not only to determine insect activity but also population size and the sexual maturity of individuals. This information is used to determine when best to release insecticides or biological organisms (parasites, disease organisms) for population control.

In the heritage collection, the value in monitoring insect activity is determining if there is a problem and also the location of the problem. The next and most important step is inspection of the collection, in order to locate the infestation, the source of the insects that were trapped. Inspection of collections of heritage objects is the most important aspect of an integrated insect pest control programme.

The common types of insect traps are light traps, pheromone traps and food traps.

10.2 LIGHT TRAPS

10.2.1 Light response of insects

Light traps have been used as attractants, based on food-seeking responses, e.g. colour of flowers, UV radiation of sunlit spaces, low light intensity for moonlight flyers, etc. The trap includes a light source, and a method of capturing the insect once it has been attracted there.

The insect's reaction to light results in phototaxic behaviour, i.e. a body orientation to the light. The reactions are dependent on the light intensity, brightness, and wavelength content and on the insect's colour vision (spectral efficiency of the photopigments of the insect eye), and the insect's developmental stage. The larval stemma is like a basic unit of the adult's ommatidium and compound eye (Figure 10.3). They

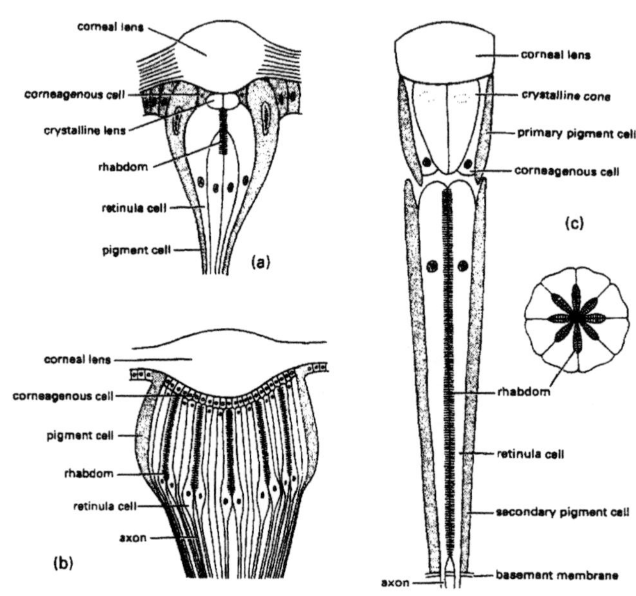

Figure 10.3. Longitudinal sections through the simple and compound eyes: (a) a simple stemma of a lepidopteran larva; (b) dorsal ocellus of a adult bug; (c) an ommatidium from a compound eye, with enlargement showing a transverse section. (From Gullan and Cranston, 1994, with permission)

both have lenses, light-gathering pigments and neurons for transmission of the stimuli. The ability to resolve an image depends on the number of ommatidia in the eye: the silverfish has around 12, whereas the dragonfly has 10,000. The ocelli and stemmata do not resolve images: they most probably detect only sudden changes in overall illumination.

Colour vision or wavelength discrimination means the ability to distinguish between spectral lights of different wavelengths independently of intensity. The spectral sensitivity of an insect's eye depends on the absorption of light of specific wavelengths in the photopigments.

Early experiments in behavioural studies gave variable results but suggested differences in insect colour vision: for example, they showed that the *Papilio* butterfly prefers purple and blue colours, whereas aphids and *Vanessa* butterflies prefer yellow colours. The presence of photopigments was demonstrated in the early 1960s. Since that time experiments dealing with individual ommatidia cells in the insect eye have revealed that they vary in responses to colour, or light wavelength.

Long wavelengths of light, 350 to 650nm, are visible to most insects, but there are peaks of sensitivity, which are due to types of ommatidia or receptors. The colour receptor types in the insect eye can be divided into three large groups: UV, blue and green receptors, of which the mean maximum sensitivities are around 350nm, 440nm and 510nm respectively.

Most insects show two colour sensitivity peaks. In cockroaches, *Blattaria* and *Periplaneta*, the sensitivity is over the range 365 to 507nm with two peaks, UV and green (Mote and Goldsmith, 1970). Figure 10.4 shows that the ommatidia of the drone bee can distinguish three groups of colours (Burkhardt, 1977). Moths show UV and possible blue and green-yellow receptors and beetles show UV and green-yellow receptors. Flies have an infrared receptor along with UV and blue receptors (Blum, 1985).

Most insects visualize UV in the range 300–400μm. Generally, UV light is most attractive to insects under natural conditions, leading to the success of trapping insects in the field using a UV- emitting 'black lamp'. The attraction to UV is possibly due to the resemblance of the light to open spaces

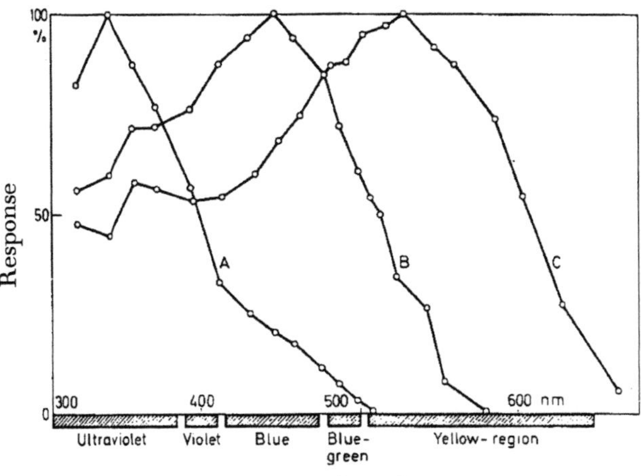

Figure 10.4. Visual cells of the drone bee, stimulated with light of different wavelengths show three receptor types with maximum spectral response: A – at 360 nm (UV receptors); B – between 420–460 nm (blue receptors); and C – at 530 nm (green receptors) (from Burkhardt, 1977).

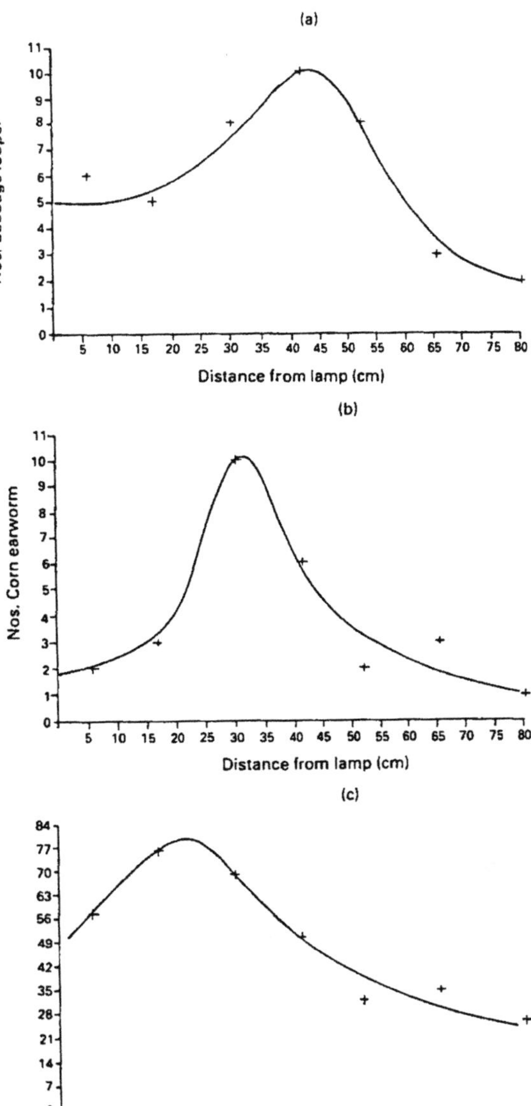

Figure 10.5. Radial density distribution of three species of moths on baffles round light trap (from Muirhead-Thomson, 1991).

in nature, which reflect UV light when flooded with sunlight. UV light traps are more effective than incandescent light traps for food storage beetles.

Besides wavelength, light intensity may also be involved. For example, below levels of 5–10 lux, diurnal (active during daylight) species have monochromatic vision (as humans do at twilight). The nocturnal species become colour-blind at light intensities 0.5–5 lux (moonlight is around 0.2 lux and a moonless night 0.0003 lux). Insects do not always fly to the brightest light but show preferences for specific colours. The structure of the moth's eye is developed for maximum sensitivity and adaptation to the dark and the beetle is adapted for bright light. Muirhead-Thomson (1991) showed that moths did not tend to be trapped immediately around light, but the maximum number trapped were at a distance of 40cm from the light source (Figure 10.5). This may be a response to light intensity. Hsiao (1972) showed that at low light intensities moths displayed positive phototaxic behaviour but at high intensities showed negative phototaxic response near the light source; they did, however, land at a peripheral dark margin of the light. This led to an improvement in trap design: simply painting the light baffles black.

For further information on insect light response, see Gullan and Cranston (1995), Mazokhin-Porshnyakov (1969), Menzel (1979) and Scoble (1992).

10.2.2 Light trap design and placement

Taking advantage of insects' specific attraction to light, we have designed effective light traps. Insect traps were first used outdoors, in nature, to collect insects for entomological and ecological studies. Outdoor light traps have very little real value for museums, but an exception is the use of a light trap outdoors to counteract a building light also acting as a light trap. Because so many of the insect pests that invade our heritage collections come from outdoors, some care must be taken to prevent them from coming inside. Outdoor night lighting of a building may attract these insect pests to the building. Gilbert (1984) suggests that a light trap that emits more UV than the building lights, placed 45-60m (150–200ft) away from the building will attract insects away from the building lights. The commonest outdoor light trap is the insect electrocutor type.

The design of commercial indoor traps varies. They are constructed usually for specific target insects. The light bulbs used in commercial light traps are usually blacklight bulbs (Gilbert, 1984), which emit a small amount of UV light, which is shown to attract most flying insects. There are many commercially available bulbs with an inside phosphorus coating, which is required to release the UV light.

The placement of the trap is critical, while the distance from the sedentary insect to the light is also important. The distance from which the light trap will attract the insect is dependent on the lamp type, the trap design and the visual acuity and nature of the target insect. Gilbert (1984) reported that most flying insects cannot respond to light from further away than 30m (100ft), and they respond at 6–7.5m (20–25ft) and more significantly at 3.5m (12ft). Placing traps about 15m (50ft) apart is the general rule in a warehouse, but this is only a broad rule because there are so many variables involved.

The placement of the light trap at a specific height above the floor may be significant (Keever and Cline, 1983). For day-flying flies, Gilbert (1984) suggests that, because of the surface-skimming flying behaviour of day-flying insects, the most effective traps are placed near the floor. Most night-flying insects fly at greater heights but exceptions are gravid female moths, which are not strong fliers and are captured close to or on the floor. At the Royal British Columbia Museum (Florian, 1987) female webbing clothes moths were captured close to the floor and males at a height of 1.2–1.5m (4–5ft). Keever and Cline (1983) reported that at 1.8 and 3.7m (6 and 12ft) above the floor there was no difference in the sex of moths captured.

Light traps can be strategically placed in bottlenecks, stairwells and corners of large storage facilities.

The insects caught in the light trap should be removed immediately and the insect numbers and species recorded on a computer database. This will collate information about the influx of new species or an abnormal increase in the numbers of one species, which could point to a specific problem related to the storage of the heritage collection.

In the pest control literature there is some pertinent information that will assist in designing light traps for particular insects. In Mallis (1982), besides useful data on moths and carpet beetles, the bibliography is extensive and cites many references on specific insects.

10.2.3 Light traps – summary

The most effective light for attracting flying insects is UV light in the range 300–400nm. High-intensity incandescent light repels night-flying insects; low- intensity light attracts them. Moths show UV and possibly blue and green-yellow receptors and beetles UV and green-yellow receptors. Flies have an infrared receptor along with UV and blue receptors.

The main value of light traps is that they can capture both sexes of a variety of species. The placement and design of traps should be adapted to the target insect. There is a limit to the distance for efficacy of the light trap.

10.2.4 Review of the literature on use of light traps in heritage collections

Light traps are recommended for use in insect pest monitoring in museums or other buildings where there are heritage objects. The most important fact impacting on your activities in purchasing or making insect light traps is that you do not know which insect species you are trying to catch. You will not know until you catch some, and even then you will not know if you have missed some that have not been attracted to the type of trap you have used. Thus, a variety of traps is the most logical approach. It is worth testing different colours of incandescent bulbs associated with different colours of sticky traps. Varying light intensity and height from the floor should also be tested.

There is very little definitive information about the light responses of common insect pests in museums but some results using light traps are reported by Gilbert (1984). Those attracted to light were the black carpet beetle, the cigarette beetle (*Lasioderma serricorne*), the drugstore beetle (*Stegobium paniceum*), reproductive winged termites and the house fly, but booklice and silverfish were not attracted to light. Cockroaches, pill bugs and ants are commonly found on light traps because they are foraging for other insects and smell them on the traps. This is another reason for removing insects as soon as they are captured.

Florian (1987) reported that the carpet beetle (*Reesa vespulae*), the varied carpet beetle (*Anthrenus verbasci*) and the house fly are attracted to windows and the webbing clothes moth (*Tineola bisselliella*) to diffusely lit yellow sticky traps.

At the Royal British Columbia Museum (Florian, 1987), tests were run in all collection areas, using sticky yellow strips, 90 × 10cm (3ft × 4in), installed hanging from every red exit light or small squares cut to fit behind blue, 4W nightlights that plug directly into the electrical outlet at baseboard level. The sticky strips, which are universally available, are made of yellow plastic coated with a tacky polyethylene glue. Gooseneck lamps with the sticky tape hanging from them were successful in capturing beetles. All the traps were professionally labelled showing they were put in place by the Conservation Section. These small traps could be placed anywhere in the collection

*Table 10.1. Distribution of the varied carpet beetle (*Anthrenus verbasci *[L.] by windows and floors of the Royal British Columbia Museum. Results of survey of May 5 to Sept. 20, 1986.*

FLOOR / WINDOW	1	2	2M	3	3M	4	4M	5	5M	6	6M	7	7M	**TOTAL**
1	1													**1**
2				1				1	1	1				**4**
3														**0**
4				1				1			1			**3**
5				6						3	8		1	**18**
6				5						4	5			**14**
7				1						3			1	**5**
8				1										**1**
9							1		2	2	1			**6**
10	1	1			1					1	7	4	2	**17**
11								1						**1**
12				1					2	1	1		1	**6**
13														**0**
14														**0**
15								1		2			1	**4**.
16														**0**
17	1													**1**
18														**0**
19										1				**1**
20	2									1	4			**7**
21												1		**1**
22	2				1		1		2	1			1	**8**
23					1	2			1	1			4	**9**
24	1				1		1							**2**
25							2		1				1	**4**
26			1	1		1							2	**5**
27														**0**
28						1			1			2		**4**
TOTAL	8	1	1	17	4	4	5	4	10	21	27	9	12	

1–7M represent the floor numbers, 1–28 are the window numbers on each floor window by window (1—5 east-facing windows, 9—19 south-facing windows, 20—28 west-facing windows).

area, their close proximity to potential insect captives making them more efficient.

A variety of light traps were tested in museums by Zaitseva (1991). It was determined that electrocution light traps were not successful but that traps using luminescent bulbs, filament bulbs and bulbs of DPC-50-1 specification could be used. The traps captured a large variety of insects from the families Dermestidae, Anobiidae, Latridiidae, Tenebrionidae, Tineidae and Floridae. An open-type container with a DPC-50-1 bulb attracted a large number of clothes moths. It was also reported that the windows in the building were successful light traps.

In forestry research (to monitor and study biodiversity of insects), a portable light trap is used. It is operated on a 6V battery or AC current (110V), and uses very small 1.8W light tubes. It hangs like a lantern and captures the insects in various ways in a container below the light. Besides the UV light tubes, there are light tubes available in blue, green and white light (Jobin and Coulombe, 1992). This seems like a sensible light trap for museums.

10.2.5 Case study – use of windows as light traps

Often the best light traps are windows, though they are limited to daylight-flying insects.

At the Royal British Columbia Museum, the large bank of windows on each floor of the Collection Building were used for light monitoring of insects (Florian, 1987). A computer database was used to record all insects collected, each week, on the window sills. The information has been useful in determining emergence patterns and new infestations. Other insects that do not infest the collection were also collected. The final results showed that there was an endemic population of interacting insects, combined with minor environmental problems.

The procedures involve numbering all the windows on a floor plan and recording information for each window. Table 10.1 shows the distribution of the varied carpet beetle (*Anthrenus verbasci*) and Tables 10.2–10.4 the distribution of the common house fly (*Musca domestica*), according to window and floor, over a period of three months.

Table 10.1 shows two distinct populations which were located in the areas where active infestations had been found. The one on the 3rd floor (windows 4–7) was very localized and the one at floors 6/6M (windows 5–8) was more diffuse, which suggests that it was a population that may have been active for a longer period and had spread out. These two populations were located on the southeast windows. The diffuse distribution on nearly all the floors by the southwest windows suggested a building problem. This type of data representation gives an excellent insight into insect populations.

This information led to an intensive inspection of the collections in the areas of highest concentration. Active infestations were located on floor 6M in an archaeological comparative faunal collection of seal skulls and on the 3rd floor in skeletal collections of small mammals.

Tables 10.2–10.4 show the distribution of house flies. They were found mainly on 7M, the highest floor, which suggested a building problem. An external examination of the building in this west corner showed that there was a small open seam

*Table 10.2. Distribution of the common house fly (*Musca domestica *[L.]) by windows and floors of the Royal British Columbia Museum. Results of survey of 26 January 1987.*

FLOOR WINDOW	1	2	2M	3	3M	4	4M	5	5M	6	6M	7	7M
1											3		
2												1	
3													
4													
5													
6											1		
7											1		1
8	1										2		
9													3
10									2	1			
11													2
12									1				1
13													1
14													
15													
16							1	2		1	1	1	
17								1		1	1	1	
18										2	2		
19								1					
20						1		1				1	
21									2	2	1		26
22							1				1	1	
23							3		1				
24								1	3	1			
25									1	7			17
26							4		1			2	
27					1			1	1		3	3	28
28							2	1			1	4	

1–7M represent the floor numbers, 1–28 are the window numbers on each floor window by window (1—5 east-facing windows, 9—19 south-facing windows, 20—28 west-facing windows).

*Table 10.3. Distribution of the common house fly (*Musca domestica *[L.]) by windows and floors of the Royal British Columbia Museum. Results of survey of 2–6 February 1987.*

FLOOR WINDOW	1	2	2M	3	3M	4	4M	5	5M	6	6M	7	7M
1													
2									2	1	1		1
3					1								
4										1	1		3
5											1		
6											1		1
7													1
8											1		7
9											3	1	
10													3
11											1		2
12													1
13										1	1		
14										1			1
15											1		2
16							2				1	2	
17							1						
18							1			1			
19								1					
20							1	1	1				
21							1			3	3		
22							1				1		
23						1	2						6
24							2						7
25					1		1			1			7
26						1	2						7
27							6						7
28							3			1			6

1–7M represent the floor numbers, 1–28 are the window numbers on each floor window by window (1—5 east-facing windows, 9—19 south-facing windows, 20—28 west-facing windows).

*Table 10.4. Distribution of the common house fly (*Musca domestica *[L.]) by windows and floors of the Royal British Columbia Museum. Results of survey of 16–20 March 1987.*

FLOOR WINDOW	1	2	2M	3	3M	4	4M	5	5M	6	6M	7	7M
1													
2						1							
3													
4													
5													
6													
7											2		3
8													2
9													
10													3
11													
12									1				1
13													1
14									1				
15													
16		1											
17													
18													
19													
20													
21													
22													2
23				1									2
24										1			3
25								1					3
26									1				3
27										1			3
28										1			3

1–7M represent the floor numbers, 1–28 are the window numbers on each floor window by window (1—5 east-facing windows, 9—19 south-facing windows, 20—28 west-facing windows).

between the last west window frame and the cement facade all the way up the building. This corner of the building is also the area catching the late afternoon sunlight. Both would seem to attract house flies. The flies were not pupating in the building or on the roof. The decreasing size of the population over the winter months suggested that they were coming from outside. In the areas of the highest concentration, the plastic protectors over the banks of recessed lights were cleaned, but only a few flies were collected. It still has not been determined how the flies were getting into the building but the main concern was that they are ovipositor sites for carpet beetles: live carpet beetle larvae have frequently been found in the abdomen of house flies. Because of this it is imperative that all flies are collected on one day each week and frozen as soon as collected.

There was no evidence that the insects came in with the air supply. There are two air filters, the finest operative down to the micron level. Tests with cotton cheesecloth placed over the air vents did not capture flies over a period of 1 month, and at the same time 10+ flies appeared on the windows.

10.2.6 Using information from traps

The information from light traps tells more about the population in your museum or collection area than any published literature. The information gathered over the years shows the annual fluctuation in population size of a specific species. There is a normal increase in population size due to the arrival of the adults freshly emerged from the pupae. Even though this occurs inside an air-conditioned building, it still seems to coincide with spring (March), but often a little earlier than it occurs outdoors. An abnormally high number of captured insects would alert you to a new infestation or some environmental problem. An example of this occurred at the Royal British Columbia Museum (see 2.3.2.3).

Over one Christmas period, because so many staff were away on holiday, the floor maintenance crew decided to strip the floor on 12 floors and rewax them. This process caused a humidity increase in the building which was obvious on the hygrothermograph charts but was not significant enough to be considered a problem and was easily stabilized by the air-conditioning system. But within 12–14 days after the humidity increase there was an increase in the number, higher than previous years for this time, of captured adult varied carpet beetles. From the literature we know that for this insect 12–14 days is the length of time that adult emergence would occur under conducive environmental conditions. Thus emergence must have occurred because of the high humidity resulting from the water used during the floor cleaning. Organic materials will adsorb moisture readily if the temperature is constant and the RH increases. One feature of organic materials is their opportunism: they take up moisture rapidly but give it up slowly. The rise in moisture in the pupae and in the adjacent organic materials must have triggered emergence. A second increase in the insect population occurred at the same time as in previous years but there were fewer individuals caught.

The appropriate response to the unexpected increase in population was to increase the number of sticky light traps in collection areas to determine if the insects were concentrated in one area and associated with an active infestation, and to carry out some inspection of the collection to ensure that the objects were protected from the flying adults. Remember that it is the heritage objects that are the food traps, the odour of the organic material of the objects that is the bait. Dense plastic boxes are impermeable to most odours, as are specially constructed biaxial plastic and plastic/aluminium foil laminate bags.

10.3 LURING THE SEXES

10.3.1 Introduction

Insects rely on their sense of smell for many of their behavioural patterns, e.g finding food, choice of site for laying eggs (oviposition site), mate selection and finding, courtship, social activities, alarm signals, etc. The chemicals produced and emitted by individuals that cause other individuals to vary their behaviour are called semiochemicals. There are three categories: allomones, defence secretions that repel predator species; kairomones, which attract predator species; and pheromones, sex attractants.

Synchronization of the sexual maturity of partners in any type of bisexual reproduction and the production of scents or pheromones, i.e. sex pheromones and aggregate pheromones are essential for reproductive success. The use of odours to attract insects to traps is based on these behavioural responses.

Pheromones are volatile, odiferous chemicals that are secreted by insects as a part of the communication system directing their behaviour. Most pheromones are sex attractants but there are others that influence behavioural patterns between the same species: alarm signals, trail marking, aggregation, social activities and predator attraction between different species. Thus, in nature, species-specific pheromones bring the sexes together but they may also attract predators of these insects.

For stored food insect pest species (Burkholder, 1984) in which the adults are short-lived and do not feed (moths, dermestids, bruchids and anobiids), the female produces the pheromones attracting the male. For the long-lived adults of the flour and grain beetles, a long-range aggregation pheromone is produced by the male, which attracts both sexes.

The pheromone for the black carpet beetle, *Attagenus megatoma*, was identified in 1967 and since then pheromones for nearly all the major insect pest species have been identified and most synthesized (Burkholder and Ma, 1985).

10.3.2 Commercial pheromone traps for forests, orchards and crops, and warehouses

The use of sex pheromones in attracting and capturing insect pests originates in agriculture, forestry and food product warehousing, in which large populations of insect pests need to be controlled or assessed.

Commercially available traps vary in construction and design but all contain synthetic sex pheromone lures incorporated with various controlled release mechanisms. The insects are usually captured on sticky traps, or crawl or are sucked through funnels into oil or some other liquid at the bottom of the trap. Pheromone traps are sometimes combined with food bait or light.

Outdoor pheromone traps have been developed for forest and crop protection as an alternative to chemical pesticides where pest resistance was a problem and in consideration of environmental issues. The traps are generally used as monitoring systems to determine: the presence, seasonal emergence patterns (start, peak and termination of the flight period) and density of a population. This monitoring is integrated with other control approaches, to determine when is the best time to use chemical pesticides or to release predator insects (biological control) to control the target insect. When used with an insecticide, follow-up monitoring assists in determining the success of the chemical treatment.

Indoor pheromone traps for flying and crawling insect pest control have also been developed for food product warehouses. The main purpose of these traps is for population control, which is achieved by monitoring to determine where active infestations occur, by capturing some insects to reduce the population size and by selectively trapping one sex to reduce mating possibilities or to cause mating disruption. Thus these traps do not eliminate the population but only give information about the infestation and achieve minimal population reduction.

Mass trapping with pheromone traps has been used for insect control. This involves placing a large number of traps in a small area with the aim of eliminating the population.

When pheromone traps are used in a building there are potential problems. Most of the insect pests in buildings have been found in large numbers outdoors, so the indoor traps could attract these insects from outside into the storage area. In warehouses this is partially prevented by placing the traps away from outside openings.

Another problem is the attraction of insects that prey on or are scavengers of the target insect. It is also important to remember that the traps may be specific to one sex or to only those adults in a specific hormonal developmental state and that the larvae are still causing damage.

Mass trapping by flooding the area with pheromone traps has been used in granaries, but the possibility has been mentioned of product contamination by the attractant pheromone in the product, thereby rendering the product prone to subsequent infestations (Burkholder and Ma, 1985).

For further information on commercial pheromone traps, see Burkholder (1984), Burkholder and Ma (1985), McVeigh et al. (1993) and Mueller (1982).

10.3.3 The chemical nature of pheromones

In discussing the use of pheromones against stored food insect pests, Burkholder (1984) categorized the main groups as: togodermal isomers, megatomoic acid isomers, dominicalure, sitophilure, tetradecadienoic acid (TDA) and serricornin, which were the major pheromones available at the time of publication. The chemical characteristics of these substances are: fat solubility, deterioration susceptibility (oxidation, etc.) and volatility.

This information is necessary because we need to know how long they are effective, their shelf life, and whether or not they can be absorbed into artifact materials such as oily skins, fur, leather, cellulosics, plastics (polyethylene), etc.

A true story: a forest entomologist worked for years on pheromone traps for the gypsy moth, so now when in the field the entomologist is the greatest pheromone trap. The pheromone has dissolved in his body fat and the moths just love him!

10.3.4 Using pheromone traps in buildings with heritage collections

Pheromone traps are commercially available against the following insects commonly found in museums or other buildings with heritage collections: common house fly (*Musca domestica*), German cockroach (*Blattella germanica*), warehouse and khapra beetles (*Trogoderma* spp.), furniture woodworm (*Anobium punctatum*, webbing clothes moth *Tineola bisselliella*), drugstore beetle (*Stegobium paniceum*, cigarette beetle (*Lasioderma serricorne*) and Indian meal moth *Plodia interpunctella* (Mueller, 1995). Pheromone traps against the varied carpet beetle (*Anthrenus verbasci*) are now being developed.

Pheromone traps have been suggested for use in museums by Child *et al.* (1994), Gilberg, 1992; Gilberg and Roach, 1991; Javovich, 1987; Kronkright, 1991. Museums, however, have little experience with these traps and they have often been brought into use without thought to the necessary research required before they can be safely recommended. Just because the trap attracts a specific insect is not enough.

10.3.5 Monitoring the value of pheromone traps

Pheromone traps do not achieve elimination of the population, which is essential when dealing with the protection of heritage artifacts.

The value of pheromone traps is in detecting and monitoring insects and locating active infestations. Constant monitoring of the population gives information about the time of emergence of adults and variations in the size of population. If there is a sudden or untimely change in the number of insects trapped, this suggests a problem. To locate the source of the insects, traps can be placed around an area of original insect capture, repeated in a smaller area and so on, to zero in on a specific area of the greatest insect activity which would then be visually inspected to locate the infestation.

The use of a great number of traps in the hope of eliminating the population is not appropriate because only individuals of one sex and in a specific physiological state are attracted.

10.3.6 Before use, consider carefully what the pheromone traps do

Attracting insect species that are not already in storage areas can be a problem. For example, the traps can attract a species of insects that prey on the target insect. Most buildings contain an endemic population of insects that interact with each other and are not necessarily in storage areas. The traps placed near heritage collections may expose the collections to potential extra infestation. Beetles and moths living in a natural history skeletal collection, for instance, may be attracted to a pheromone trap set in a collection of historical textiles or garments.

10.3.7 Is the species you are targeting the culprit?

Another disadvantage to the use of pheromones in the museum is that there may be many different species that could be overlooked if such a species-specific trap were used. In the museum or storage area there is usually a mixed population of endemic species. It is important to know all the species present, so species-specific traps are not efficient. They may have their use if, for example, all other methods of trapping are not showing an insect that you know is present. Specific pheromone traps would then be logical for this species but must be used with knowledge and prudence.

10.3.8 Trap results may be misleading

The interpretation of the insects trapped is important. It requires an understanding of the behaviour of the target insect and the type and effectiveness of the trap. The main value emerges in monitoring the target insect population over time to determine if there has been a change.

Because you have not caught any insects with the traps does not mean you do not have a problem. The problem may be with another species not targeted with the pheromone used. Also, there may be few insects in a reproductive state that would respond to the sex attractants, or there could be an imbalanced number of the specific sex being attracted. Remember that the pheromones most commonly used are those that attract only one sex.

10.3.9 Have the heritage objects become sex attractants?

We do not know if the heritage objects made of organic materials adsorb enough pheromone to be a potential attractant to insect pests. This is a question that should be answered before pheromone traps can be used in museums and heritage buildings. The heritage objects that are vulnerable are already, in a sense, bait traps. By using pheromones will we make them sex attractants as well? Pheromone traps are commonly used for long-term monitoring to determine the emergence patterns of the target insect, which means that there must be some adsorption of the pheromone on other materials.

10.3.10 Future and ethical responsibility to heritage objects

Pheromone traps are currently being developed for museum use.

To test the effectiveness of the trap in attracting the target species is a difficult job. Insects have to be reared, marked and freed to see if the trap works and, as an added complication, the physiological state of the freed insects plays an important role in their response to pheromones.

Because pheromones are natural products, it is automatically expected that their mode of action does not involve a toxic effect. This is not the case, and consequently synthetic pheromones are subject to the same registration and control as pesticides. In the use of pheromones where food is processed, for example, a zero tolerance in the food is required (Burkholder and Ma, 1985).

The pheromones must be used according to the label because they are registered products and subject to regulation by COSHH-UK (Control of Substances Hazardous to Health) in the UK, by EPA (Environmental Protection Agency) in the USA and by PCPA(Pest Control Products Act) in Canada. In Canada pheromones cannot be used for mass eradication, only for monitoring, but in the USA they can be used for mass eradication.

In addition, it is not known if there is any chemical interaction with the chemicals of the object that would enhance deterioration.

We must always consider all aspects of our action towards heritage objects, which we have an ethical responsibility to preserve.

10.4 OVIPOSITION TRAPS: BAIT TRAPS

Your heritage objects are the best food traps: they have proved themselves successful over thousands of years.

The odours from food traps have been designed to attract insects hunting for food and an oviposition site. Feeding behaviour involves food habit location, finding, recognition, acceptability and suitability. Oviposition involves a chain of behaviours, similar to feeding behaviour, resulting in the assessment of suitability and selection of the oviposition site.

In museums and other buildings with natural and cultural heritage objects made of organic materials such as fur, skin, bones, etc., these objects are food traps in themselves. If they are infested, this proves the point. An approach to this problem is to use storage methods that prevent odours from the organic materials escaping the object area. Storage cabinets and object containers made of special materials, e.g. plastics, glass, aluminium paper, etc., which are impermeable to odours, can be used. For example, tins or boxes of spices can be placed inside glass bottles. Commercially available polyethylene or polypropylene food storage quality containers are ideal because they prevent insects from entering and at the same time allow a view of the object without handling being required. If by accident infested materials are placed in the containers the infestation will not spread to adjacent materials.

REFERENCES

Blum, M.S. 1985. *Fundamentals of Insect Physiology*. John Wiley and Sons, New York, Chichester, Brisbane, Toronto, Singapore.

Burkhardt, D. 1977. On the vision of insects. *Journal of Comparative Physiology*, 120:33–50.

Burkholder, W.E. 1984. Use of pheromones and food attractants for monitoring and trapping stored-product insects. In *Insect Management for Food Storage and Processing*, Ed. F.J. Baur. American Association of Cereal Chemists, St Paul, Minnesota, pp69–86.

Burkholder, W.E. and M. Ma. 1985. Pheromones for monitoring and control of stored-product insects. *Annual Review of Entomology*, 30:257–272.

Child, R.E., D.B. Pinninger, R. Ashok and P. Smith. 1994. Insect trapping in museums and historic houses. *Proceedings of the 15th IIC International Congress; Preventive Conservation, Ottawa, September 1994*, pp129–131.

Florian, M.-L.E. 1987. Methodology used in insect pest survey in museum buildings – a case history. *8th Triennial ICOM Meeting, Biodeterioration Working Group, Sydney, Australia, September*, pp1169–1174.

Gilberg, M. and R. Roach. 1991. The use of a commercial pheromone trap for monitoring *Lasiderma serricorne* (F.) infestations in museum collections. *Studies in Conservation* 36(4):243–247.

Gilberg, M. 1992. Pheromone traps for monitoring insect pests in museums. Bulletin *IIC-CG*, 17(2):9–14.

Gilbert, D. 1984. Insect electrocutor light traps. In *Insect Management for Food Storage and Processing*, Ed. F.J. Baur. American Association of Cereal Chemists, St Paul, Minnesota, pp87–108.

Gullan P.J. and Cranston. 1995. *The Insects: An Outline of Entomology*, Chapman and Hall, London.

Hsiao, H.S. 1972. *Attraction of Moths to Light and to Infrared Radiation.* San Francisco Press, California.

Javovich, I. 1987. New facilities for the prevention of damage by insect pests. *Muzeumi Mutargyv* 17:199–212.

Jobin, L. and C. Coulombe. 1992. *The Luminoc® Insect Trap*. Information Leaflet LFC 2b, Ministry of Supply and Services Canada, Ottawa, Canada.

Keever, D.W. and L.D. Cline. 1983. Effect of light trap height and light source on the capture of *Catharus quadricollis* (Guerin-Meneville) (Coleoptera: Cucujidae) and *Callosobruchus maculatus* (F.) (Coleoptera: Bruchidae) in a warehouse. Journal of Economic Entomology 76(5):1080–1082.

Kronkright, D.P. 1991. Insect traps in conservation surveys. *Newsletter (Western Association for Art Conservation)*, 13(1):21–23.

Mallis, A. 1982. *Handbook of Pest Control*, 6th Ed. Franzak and Foster Company, Cleveland, Ohio.

Mazokhin-Porshnyakov, G.A. 1969. *Insect Vision*. Plenum Press, New York.

McVeigh, L.J., D.R. Hall and P.S. Beevor, Eds. 1993. *Insect Pheromones, IOBC/wprs Bulletin*, 16(10). Proceedings of the Working Group on "Use of Pheromones and Other Semiochemicals in Integrated Control". IOBC, Route de Marseille – B.P. 91, 84143, Montfavet, France.

Menzel, R. 1979. Spectral sensitivity and colour vision in invertebrates. In *Comparative Physiology and Evolution of Vision in Invertebrates. A: Invertebrate Photoreceptors*, Ed. H. Autrum. Springer-Verlag, Berlin, 6A:503–580.

Mote, M.I. and T.H. Goldsmith. 1970. Spectral sensitivities of color receptors in the compound eye of the Cockroach *Periplaneta.* Journal of Experimental Zoology, 173:137–146.

Mueller, D.K. 1982. Pheromones. New weapon against stored product insects. *Pest Control*, February: 22–24.

Muirhead-Thomson, R.C. 1991. *Trap Responses of Flying Insects.* Academic Press, London.

Scoble, M. 1992. *The Lepidoptera: Form, Function and Diversity*. Oxford University Press, New York.

Scott, H.G. n.d. *Household and Stored-Food Insects of Public Health Importance and Their Control.* U.S. Department of Public Health, Education and Welfare. Atlanta, Georgia.

Zaitseva, G.A. 1991. Control of insects in museums: the use of light traps. *Proceedings of the International Conference of Biodeterioration of Cultural Property, Lucknow, February 20–25, 1989*, Eds. O.P. Agrawal and S. Dhawan, pp469–477.

11

The Insect Infestation: Finding, Bagging, Eradicating and Clean-up

11.1 THE INSPECTION: BE PREPARED

11.1.1 Pinpoint the location of the infestation

Flying moths in a heritage collection or display areas means there is an infestation somewhere. It has to be found.

This requires an inspection and monitoring. Monitoring methods are described in chapter 10. If the collection area is large, monitoring, using sticky light traps of all sorts, may be needed to pinpoint the infestation. Once the area where the infestation is suspected to be is located, then an inspection of the individual heritage objects in that area follows. But before starting the inspection it is necessary to prepare the paperwork and paraphernalia needed to deal with the infestation when it is found.

11.1.2 Make a floor plan

First, make a floor plan or a drawing of the layout of the storage containers, cupboards, shelves, drawers, etc., and the location of the objects in or on them. The purpose of this is not only to mark the location of the infestation but also to mark the objects inspected. If the inspection takes several days this record will tell you where to start again. The location of an infestation should also be accurately recorded in the IIPC programme (see chapter 13).

11.1.3 Keep a permanent record

This record should be a permanent document and be included in a database, if possible. If objects are moved a record of their new location is necessary for object tracking. The record will be useful in the future for reference, to help with scheduling continual inspections and assessing the time required for inspecting the objects.

11.1.4 Take advantage of the inspection to clean and upgrade storage

Inspection of individual objects may seem labour-intensive but it can contribute to many care requirements of objects. It is an opportunity to observe any conservation problems with objects. It is also an opportunity to upgrade the storage to facilitate quicker and easier inspections in the future, for example, placing white paper under the objects on shelves or in containers makes the darker faecal pellets easier to see.

At the Royal British Columbia Museum a need to move the collection for asbestos abatement made us realize that storage is temporary and that objects in storage will eventually be moved. Thus the objects were stored individually in their own containers so that the objects would not have to be handled or packed and were always ready to be moved. These individual containers facilitate inspection of collections and prevent spreading of insect infestations to adjacent objects.

11.1.5 Prepare the bags

Prepare a variety of sizes of clear plastic bags on a tray or dolly (hand cart) for immediate access to facilitate rapid and easy bagging of any suspected infestation.

Clear polyethylene bags are needed for the freezing treatment (see procedures in this chapter). Clear or translucent, food quality, polyethylene containers with a tight lid seal can also be used. The object could be stored permanently in this type of container.

Large objects can be wrapped in polyethylene plastic and sealed with freezer tape. The reason clear plastic is recommended is because it is necessary to observe the object to give it the physical support it needs during handling or when storing it, and to observe any insect activity. Seals for the bags do not have to be airtight, ties, ziploc (self sealing) or freezer tape can be used.

Tags or labels should be attached to the bag with the date of bagging and any other identification needed. The tag can also be used to record the date and time that the bag started and ended treatment.

For small objects to be treated by anoxic treatment with an oxygen absorber (Gilberg, 1993; Gilberg and Grattan, 1994), gas-impermeable transparent bags (Burke, 1992) are needed.

In dealing with an infestation of extremely large objects the method recommended by Koestler (1995) using an anoxic gas can also be considered. The object can be isolated *in situ* by using a soft-walled enclosure system or bubble, custom-built around any size of infested object or group of objects. Large objects can also be wrapped in polyethylene and moved to a walk-in freezer.

If the objects are in boxes, bag the box. If the object is infested, the bagging will prepare it for the eradication treatment. No matter what treatment will be used, when an infestation is found it must be confined to a bag or container. The infested object should not be removed from the bag until after treatment to prevent contaminating other areas or objects. If the object is wet and infested, a rare event, a method of drying it must be devised using an insect-proof container, before the insect eradication treatment.

11.1.6 **Inspecting the objects**

The inspection of individual objects or specimens must be done slowly and thoroughly. Proceed from the top to the bottom of the cabinet, set of drawers or shelves.

In the process of inspecting heritage objects it is usually necessary to handle or move the objects. The greatest amount of damage to heritage objects occurs during handling. Proper handling and moving techniques, according to conservation standards, must be understood. This information is based on good common sense.

Insects know when there is some minute change in their environment and instead of waiting around to find out what it is, they scatter. If the infested material is agitated, larvae tend to move away rapidly or if the object is picked up they drop and crawl rapidly away. Adults fly away or hide. Insects, when disturbed, may give off an alarm scent which will alert other insects to your presence.

Being prepared helps prevent the infestation from spreading to other objects, maybe ones you have just inspected.

Because of the insects' startle response, it is necessary to be prepared to confine the infested material immediately when observed.

11.1.7 **What to look for – frass**

Frass is a give-away. First, without disturbing the object, look for frass (faecal pellets); then insect remains, exuviae (moult skins), webbing, cocoons; and material fragments, on the shelf or paper under and around an object. The presence of any of these remains indicates an infestation. The living insect stages are not commonly seen, they are always well hidden.

If frass or any other evidence of insect activity is found, get an appropriate bag, open it and bring it up to the object on the shelf and quickly slide the object into the bag and seal it with ziploc or tie.

If frass or other remains are not initially observed, examine the bottom and inside of the object. Often tweezers can be used for examination without disturbing the insects. If any insect remains are present, again using the precautions already mentioned, bag the object.

Do the bagging on the shelf without lifting the object away from the shelf. Place the bagged objects according to conservation standards – appropriate care in handling, packing, etc. – in a container which can be closed and easily moved to the place of treatment.

Objects close to the infested object should also be bagged for examination and treated, if necessary. The area where the infested objects were located should be thoroughly cleaned (see chapter 13 for suggestions on methods).

11.2 ERADICATION TREATMENTS

The infested object should be treated immediately. The bags are not intended to be insect-proof. Most insects will not leave the object, the feeding site, but in infestations with adults, i.e. larder beetles, stored grain beetles, the adults may attempt to escape. If wooden objects are infested with dry wood or powder-post termites, the termites may eat their way through the bag.

Anoxic (see section 12.2) and heat treatments (see section 12.1.3) for eradication are still in the research phase. For more information contact the authors of the research papers referenced for these treatments.

The following reduced-temperature treatment (Box 11.1) is recommended for heritage objects made of organic materials which are dry (see sections 12.1.1 and 12.1.2 for details).

11.3 THE CLEAN-UP – AFTER ERADICATION TREATMENT

Ideally, the cleaning of all evidence of insect activity in heritage objects should be undertaken in a positive-pressure fume hood to prevent the spread of the frass. The reason for this is that some people are allergic to insect frass and also predatory insects are attracted to odours which may still remain in the frass or other debris from the infestation.

It can be a long and arduous job to remove everything, especially cocoons embedded in textiles. If time prevents a complete removal of all evidence, a record and photographs showing what remains can be used as a reference point to determine if a new infestation has occurred after storage. Uncleaned objects should be placed in a dense plastic box to prevent the odour from attracting other insects.

11.4 THE EVIDENCE: WHO'S THERE, WHAT'S THERE?

In many cases it is possible to identify the culprit insect from the remains in the infestation.

Unfortunately, this book is not an illustrated guide to identification of the insects in the infestation. It is an example of what may be there and an aid to identification. If infestations are found in your home or institute, make a manual of the different insect infestations found. Each site will have only a few insect pests, thus it will be an easy job. After the infestation has been treated, remove some of the insect evidence and place it on coloured index cards with clear adhesive tape. Put the card in a ziploc bag and put this in the manual. Have it identified and use it to identify future culprits.

You will find: faeces (see Figure 11.1) and some insect remains including wings and wing scales of adults (see Figure 11.2) and cocoons, exuviae and hairs (setae) of larvae (Figures 11.3 and 7.10).

If insect stages are found the following chapters may help identify the insect species: eggs – chapter 6, larvae – chapter 7, pupae – chapter 8, and adults – chapters 9 and 10.

Heritage objects made of wood may show evidence of insect activity by insect holes in the wood and falling faecal pellets. Table 11.1 has descriptions of common wood beetle damage that will help identify the insect species.

With wood objects which show entrance and exit holes and falling frass, it is almost impossible to tell if wood beetle larvae are active inside. But some methods have been successful.

X-rays of bark on trees have been used in forest entomology studies to observe the difference between diseased and normal bark beetle larvae after attempts at biological control. Heritage

Box 11.1 PROCEDURES FOR FREEZING INSECT PESTS FOR ERADICATION IN DRY HERITAGE OBJECTS MADE OF ADSORBANT ORGANIC MATERIAL

1. A normal household (domestic) *chest freezer* which goes down to at least *–20°C* should be used. Temperatures lower than –20° to –30°C do not present a problem. Because a constant temperature must be maintained, do not use an upright freezer or one with a frost free cycle. The freezer must be maintained so that there is no frost build-up on the inside of the lid or sides.
2. The method of removing an infested object from storage requires that the object be placed in a clean, clear, polyethylene bag. Precautions should be taken when bagging infested materials, because as soon as the object is moved the insects will respond and try to escape. Prepare the bag in advance and seal it immediately when the object is placed in it. Sealing does not have to be airtight; ziploc, ties or tape are adequate. When the object is first bagged remove as much air as possible, the amount of remaining air will depend on the stability of the object and its tolerance to the pressure of the film against it. Bagging is also necessary to confine the infestation when using a specially constructed, controlled temperature and humidity freezing chamber. The object should remain in its bag during the freezing treatment.
3. If the object is large, with large air spaces around it, pre-treated silica gel or additional adsorbent material, such as clean cotton towels or sheeting, etc., can be included with the object in the bag.
4. Bagged infested objects should be kept at room temperature (above 18°C) and placed immediately in the chest freezer. The freezer temperature should already be at least –20°C. In an emergency they may be placed in a refrigerator at 5°C until freezer space is available, but should not be temporarily stored in a cold basement or cold storage with temperatures above 5°C. This temperature, 5°C, is the chill-coma temperature, the point at which the insects become inactive, do not feed, thus do no further damage. *It is imperative that these bagged objects held at 5°C are brought back to room temperature (approximately 20°C) before placing them into the chest freezer which is already at –20°C or lower.*
5. There should be adequate air circulation around the object to allow it to cool to at least 5°C in 4 hours. Dense objects, i.e. wood, boxes of newsprint or books, or a bag of flour, may need more time to reach a core temperature of –20°C. The extra time it takes for the materials to reach a core temperature of –20°C should be added to the treatment time.
6. Thermocouples can be used to record the time/temperature parameters of the freezing procedure, i.e. the rate of cooling and thawing, and the time at the minimum temperature.
7. The minimum temperature for insect eradication was established at –20°C, but a lower temperature of –30°C has been recently recommended. Because the reaction is time/temperature dependent the following are now recommended: *72 hours at –20°C to –30°C.* There is no need to adapt the freezer for the –30°C temperature, one can simply extend the treatment time. If there are any concerns about the effectiveness of these treatments or possible cold-hardiness of the insects one can, as a precaution, extend the time or immediately repeat the freeze/thaw cycle, that is bring the materials to room temperature and then place them back in the freezer to repeat the cycle. Repeating the cycles has the disadvantage of increasing the handling of the objects. Objects do not have to be removed after exactly 72 hours, they can be left in the chest freezer for a longer time, hours, days, or weeks without damage.
8. Remove the bagged objects from the freezer and place them in a secure area where there is good ventilation. Caution must be taken in handling and moving the cold objects. In some cases where a material has become stiff (plastics, acrylic glues, oil paints) extra precautions should be taken in handling these objects. Do not remove the bag until the object has reached room temperature and there is no condensed water on the outside of the bag. If possible, leave objects in the polyethylene bag for storage.
   A slow rate of thawing is desirable. The passive increase in temperature of objects that occurs when they are taken from the chest freezer (–20°C to –30°C) and placed at room temperatures, around 20°,C is slow enough. In an abnormal situation under high room temperatures, move materials directly from the freezer into a refrigerator or cold storage and leave them there until at ambient temperature. Another alternative is to turn off the chest freezer and leave the objects in the freezer until it has reached room temperature, but precautions must be taken to assure that there is no frost build-up inside which would melt and be a potential hazard to the objects.
9. All insect remains (frass, cocoons, exuviae (moults), larvae, etc.) must be removed from the treated object before re-storage. This establishes a reference point at which there are no insect remains, a zero point. This is the only way to know, for certain, that insect remains are from a new infestation and not from a previous infestation.
10. Because the freezing process is an interventive conservation treatment, details of the treatment should be recorded in the treatment documentation for the objects. The record should include: insect identification, stages and activity of the insect; packaging materials and method; time required to bring materials to 0°C and to minimum temperature; time materials were held at minimum temperature; time required to bring materials to room temperature; any physical changes observed, and the success of the treatment. It is not necessary to do this with every freezer load. The above information can be established for specific materials and object type and a standard treatment form used.

15KV 9601 1000.0U PFC

9602 PFC

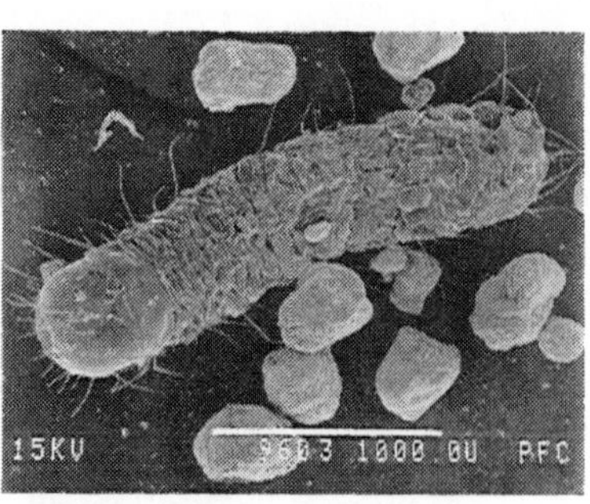
15KV 1000.0U PFC

a

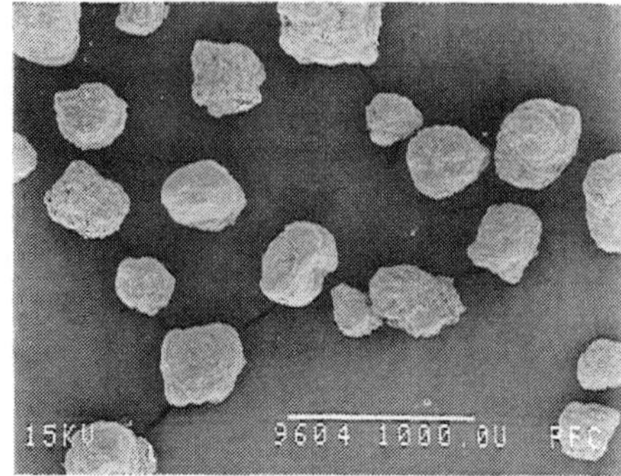
9604 1000.0U

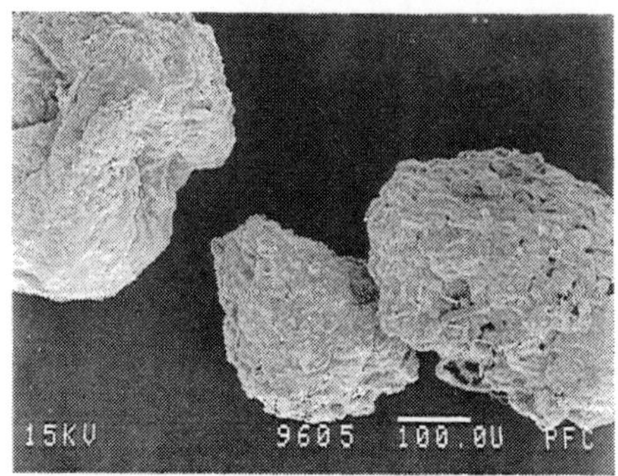
15KV 9605 100.0U

b

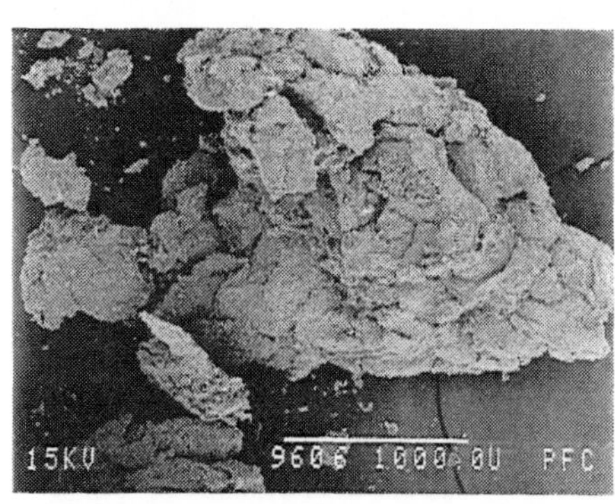
15KV 9606 PFC

c

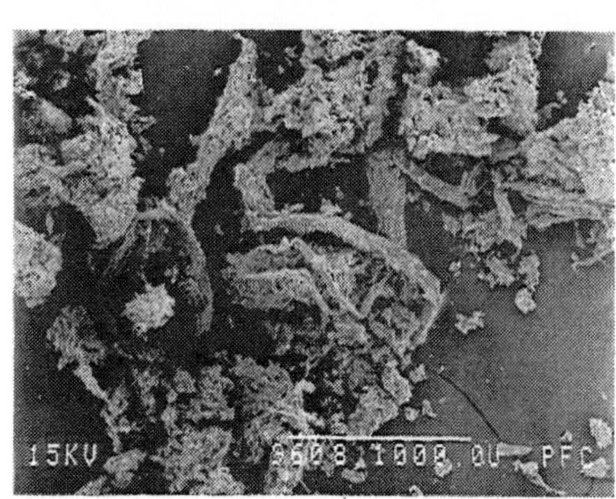
15KV

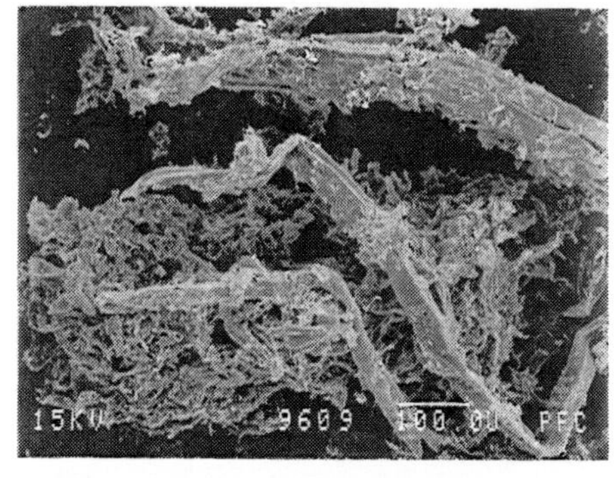
9609 PFC

d

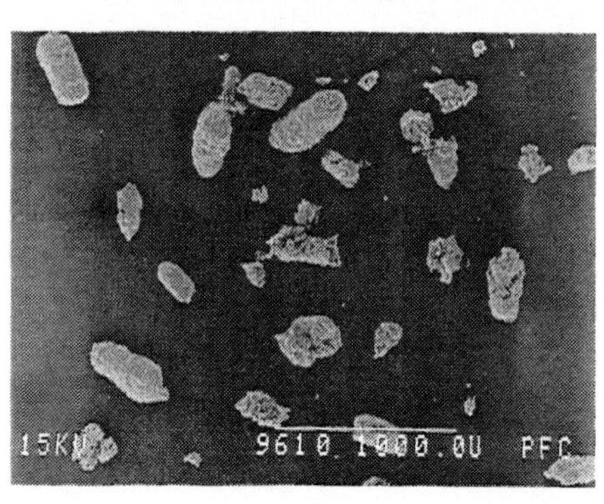
9610 1000.0U PFC

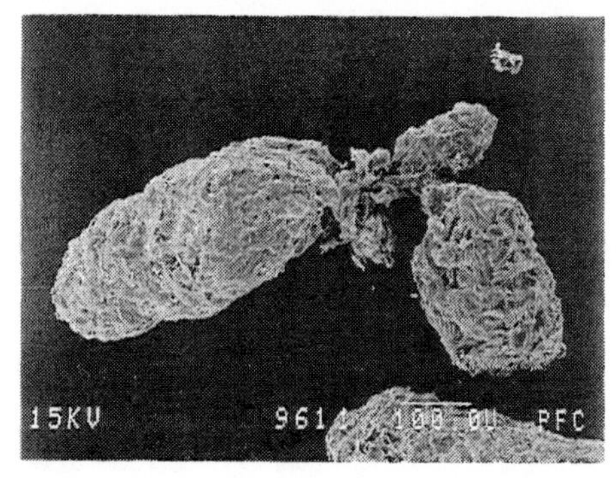
15KV PFC

e

Figure 11.1. Scanning electron micrographs of faecal pellets of beetle and moth larvae and termite adults.. a, Tineola bisselliella *(Hummel), webbing clothes moth (#9601–9603); b,* Tinea pellionella *(L.), case-making clothes moth (#9604–9605); c,* Reticulitermes hesperus, *Banks western subterranean termite (#9606–9607); d,* Hylotrupes bajulus *(L.), old house borer (#9608–9609); e,* Anobium gibbicollis *(LeConte), anobiid powder-post beetle (#9610–9611); f,* Zootermopsis angusticollis *(Hagen), damp wood termite (#9615–9616); g.* Heterobostrychus aequalis *(Waterhouse), oriental wood borer (#9617–9618); h.* Anthrenus verbasci *(L.), varied carpet beetle (#9743–9744); i.* Dermestes maculatus *(De Geer), the hide beetle (#9745–9746).*
(Micrographs taken in Scanning Electron Microscopy Laboratory, Pacific Forest Centre, Canada Forest Centre by Lesley Manning, Microtechnique Biologist.)

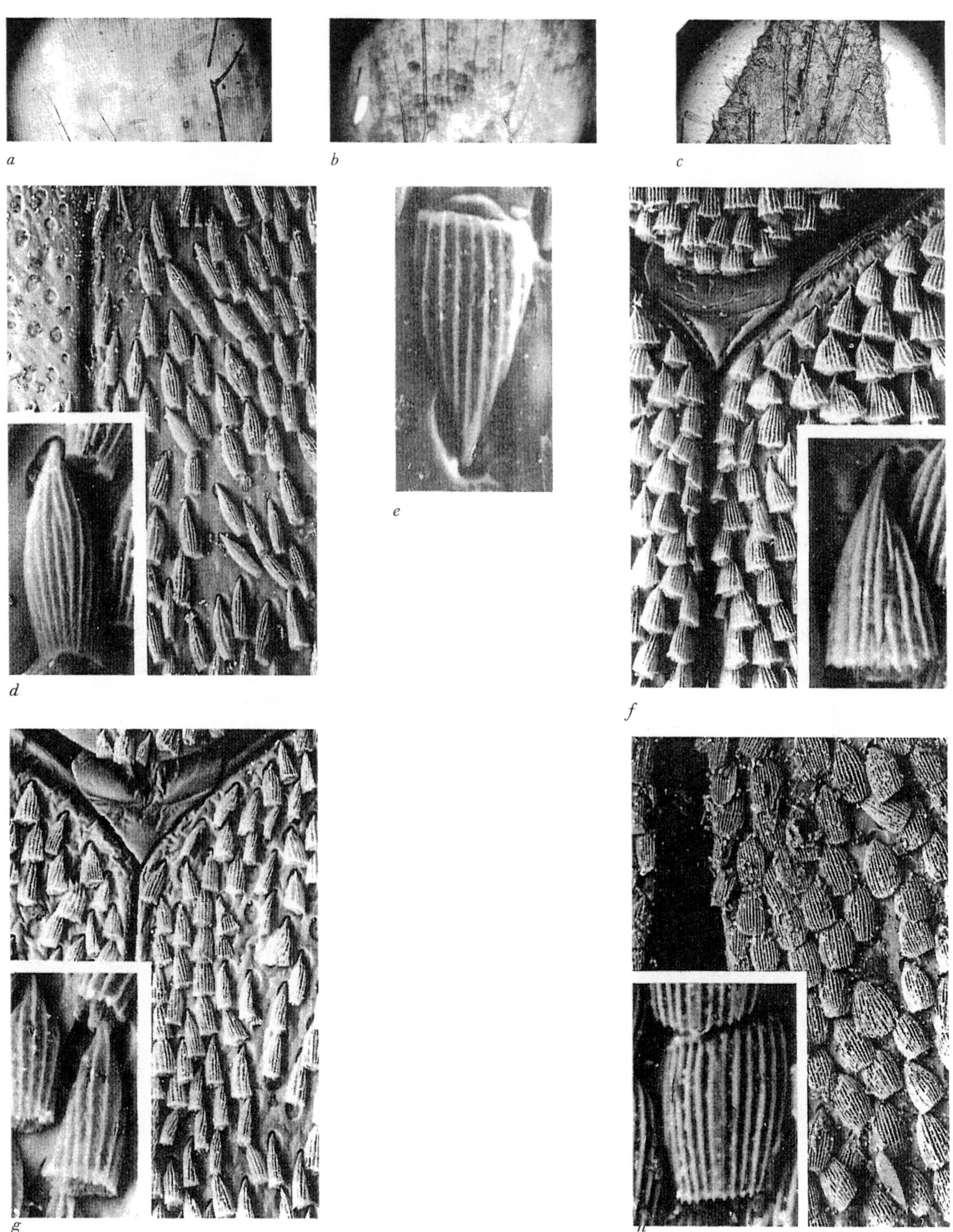

Figure 11.2. Wing scales of some common adult heritage-eating insect pests. a, Tineola bisselliella *(Hummel), webbing clothes moth; b,* Endrosis sarcitrella *(L.), white shouldered house moth; c,* Tinea pellionella *(L.), case-making clothes moth; d,* Anthrenus verbasci *(L.), varied carpet beetle; e,* Anthrenus museorum *(L.), museum beetle; f,* Anthrenus sarnicus *Mroczkowski; g,* Anthrenus fuscus *Olivier; h,* Anthrenus scrophulariae *(L.), common carpet beetle. (a–c, M-L. Florian; d–h, from Peacock, 1993, with permission.)*

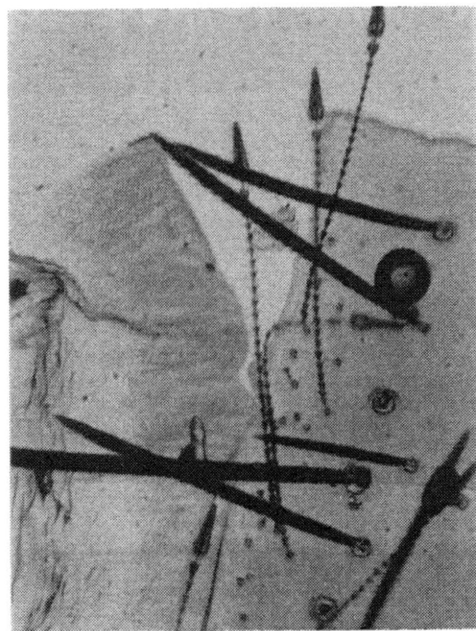

a

b

Figure 11.3. a, Light microscope photograph and, b, scanning electron micrograph of arrow-shaped hastisetae and thick spinulate setae of the larvae of Anthrenus verbasci *(L.) varied carpet beetle. (Light microscopy, M-L. Florian; SEM, Scanning Electron Microscopy Laboratory, Pacific Forest Centre, Canada Forest Centre by Lesley Manning, Microtechnique Biologist.)*

objects have been X-rayed with some success, but it is difficult to know if the larvae observed are alive or dead. Time-lapse X-rays have been used to demonstrate extension of the tunnels.

The sound of the rasping mandibles of the feeding larvae has been detected by stethoscopes and electronic sound devices.

Koestler (1993) reported that an infrared CO_2 analyser, FTIR (Fourier transform infrared spectroscope), has been used to detect insect activity in stored grain by the CO_2 they produce above the background of 0.03% (300ppm). Koestler (1993) has developed a modified CO_2-FTIR and has tested it with a wooden picture frame infested with termites. He was able to show that before treatment there was a CO_2 level above the background, but after treatment with an anoxic gas the CO_2 level dropped.

11.6 FINDING THE PUPA

After the insect has been identified check (see chapter 7) to determine if the larvae wander to build the pupation chamber away from the feeding site. If this is the case, a thorough inspection in the storage area where the infestation was located is essential. The pupae may be in wall cracks or under flooring and not easily seen.

Scenario: finding the pupa

In dealing with a webbing clothes moth infestation of natural history specimens of mountain sheep skulls with their horns, the author found that the larvae on the specimens and adults were caught on light traps. No thought was given to the pupae, expecting they would be in the interstices of the horn. Within two weeks after what was thought to be a thorough eradication of the infestation, new adults were caught on the light traps. On close examination of the walls and floor area around the skulls it was found that pupae were located in cracks of the cement, where the wall and floor meet. They were physically removed and there has not been a recurrence of the moth activity.

GENERAL AND CHAPTER REFERENCES

Bletchly, J.D. 1967. *Insect and Marine Borer Damage to Timber and Woodwork.* Ministry of Technology: Forest Products Research, Her Majesty's Stationery Office, London.

Burke, J. 1992. Vapor barrier films. *Newsletter, Western Association for Art Conservation*, 14(2):13–17.

Eberling, W. 1975. *Urban Entomology.* University of California, Los Angeles, p.695.

Florian, M-L.E. 1986. The freezing process: effects on insects and artifact materials. *Leather Conservation Newsletter* 3(1):1–13 and 17.

Florian, M-L.E. 1987. Methodology used in insect pest survey in museum buildings, a case history. *8th Triennial ICOM Meeting, Biodeterioration Working Group, Sydney Australia, September*, pp1169–1174.

Florian, M-L.E. 1992. Saga of the saggy bag. *Leather Conservation News*, 8:1–11.

Gilberg, M. 1993. Inert atmosphere disinfestation of museum objects using Ageless oxygen absorber. *2nd International Conference on Biodeterioration of Cultural Property, Yokohama, Japan*, pp397–406.

Gilberg, M.and D.W. Grattan. 1994. Ageless oxygen absorber: chemical and physical properties. *Studies in Conservation*, 39(3): 210–214.

Koestler, R.J. 1993. Insect eradication using controlled atmospheres and FTIR measurements for insect activity. *ICOM Committee for Conservation 10th Triennial Meetings, Washington, D.C.*, pp882–885.

Koestler, R.J. 1995. *Methods of controlling biodeterioation in fine art: an overview.* Kulturguterhaltung: Problemdefinition und Lösungsmoglichkeiten. Beiträge Workshop. Oktober in Wein, Veranstalted vom österreichischen EUROCARE Sekretariat. BIT-EUROCARE Sekretariat, Wiedner Haupstrasse 76, A-1040 Wein pp.7–14.

Mallis, A. 1982. *Handbook of Pest Control*, 6th Ed., Franzak and Foster Company, Cleveland, Ohio, p1099.

Mourier, H. and O. Winding. 1977. *Collins Guide To Wild Life in House and Home.* Collins, St. James Place, London.

Olkowski, W., S. Daar and H. Olkowski. 1991. *Common-Sense Pest Control.* The Taunton Press, Newtown, CT, p.715.

Osmun, J.V. 1984. Insect pest management control. In *Insect Management for Food Storage and Processing*, Ed. F.J. Baur. A.A. of Cereal Chemists, St. Paul, Minn. pp15–24.

Peacock, E.R. 1993. *Adults and Larvae of Hide, Larder and Carpet Beetles and Their Relatives (Coleoptera: Dermestidae) and of Derodontid Beetles (Coleoptera: Derodontidae).* Handbooks for the Identification of British Insects Vol.5, Part 3, Royal Entomological Society of London.

Table 11.1 Summary of diagnostic characters of damage caused by the commoner wood-boring insects and marine borers (from Bletchly, 1967).

	Type of timber attacked (sapwood & heartwood —exceptions given under remarks) S = Softwood; H = Hardwood	Flight holes	Tunnels	Bore-dust (Frass)	Type of insect or marine borer	Remarks
Tunnels without bore-dust	Chiefly imported S.	Absent or irregular	Partly concentric with the annual rings sometimes forming large cavities	—	Carpenter ants (*Camponotus* spp.)	Resembles termite damage but gallery walls are clean
	H, S	Absent	Rapidly enlarge from minute size on surface up to 1 in diam. within. Chalky lining often present	—	Shipworm (*Teredo* spp.)	Floated timber, harbour fixtures and boats attacked in salt water
	H, S	Absent	Honeycomb of small diam. ($\frac{1}{20}$ in) short ($\frac{1}{2}$ in) surface tunnels	—	Gribble (*Limnoria* spp.)	As for *Teredo*. Vertical timbers become eroded near water line to form a "waist"
	H, S	Circular ($\frac{1}{50}$ to $\frac{1}{8}$ in diam.)	Frequently across the grain. Diam. similar to entry holes. Walls darkly stained	—	Ambrosia beetles (Platypodidae & Scolytidae)	Wood surrounding tunnels sometimes also stained. Active only in green timber where bore-dust ejected through entry holes made by adults. Compare Lymexylidae
Tunnels with bore-dust	H, S	Absent	Sometimes enlarged into chambers. (Separated by septa of wood in case of damp wood termites)	Cemented mixture of bore-dust and wood chewings in mud	Subterranean termites	Tunnels connected to soil through mud galleries. Tunnel walls muddy. (Compare carpenter ant)
	H, S	Absent	Sometimes enlarged into cavities	Ovoid pellets with 6 longitudinal ridges	Dry wood termites	Bore-dust resembles small poppy seeds
	Chiefly S	Absent	Separated by septa of wood	Large wet pellets	Damp wood termites	In damp wood
	H, S	Circular ($\frac{1}{32}$ to $\frac{1}{4}$ in diam.)	Circular. Diam. (similar to flight holes) sometimes variable in same piece of wood. Walls unstained or slightly so	Sometimes absent from parts of tunnels	Lymexylid ambrosia beetles	Active only in green timber. Compare Platypodidae and Scolytidae
	H	Almost circular (about $\frac{3}{16}$ in diam.)	Oval	Longhorn type	Clytinid longhorn beetles	Little feeding under bark before penetrating into sapwood
	S	Perfectly circular ($\frac{1}{8}$ to $\frac{1}{4}$ in diam.)	Circular. Diam. as for flight holes. Surrounding wood sometimes partly decayed	Very tightly packed	Siricid wood-wasps	Live larvae present in green and recently seasoned wood. (Tunnels appear oval in section if cut obliquely)
	H, S	Oval (size depending on species)	Oval, separate and scattered	Mixture of coarse pellets and chips	Forest longhorn and Buprestid beetles	Feed under bark before penetrating into sapwood. Active attack in trees, logs and sawn timber whilst green. Attack by some species continues in seasoned wood. Compare house longhorn beetle

Table 11.1 (cont.)

	Type of timber attacked (sapwood & heartwood —exceptions given under remarks) S = Softwood; H = Hardwood	Flight holes	Tunnels	Bore-dust (Frass)	Type of insect or marine borer	Remarks
Tunnels with bore-dust	S	Oval (about $\frac{3}{8} \times \frac{3}{16}$ in diam.)	Oval, tunnels coalesce leading to breakdown of walls. "Ripple" marks on walls	Similar to some other longhorns. Sausage-shaped pellets	House longhorn beetle (*Hylotrupes bajulus*)	Serious structural damage in undecayed sapwood of seasoned softwoods. Characterised by a thin superficial skin of wood concealing internal disintegration
	H, S	Oval	Oval enlarged into cavities	Damp agglomeration of coarse pellets and shavings	Wharf-borer (*Nacerdes melanura*)	In damp decayed sleepers, poles, built-in timbers and harbour timbers
	Mostly in beech, elm, maple and sycamore	Circular ($\frac{1}{16}$ in diam.)	Circular $\frac{1}{16}$ in diam. numerous	Fine very densely packed powder	*Ptilinus pectinicornis*	Active in seasoned wood (Compare *Lyctus* powder post beetles)
	H containing starch	Circular ($\frac{1}{16}$ in diam.)	Circular $\frac{1}{16}$ in diam. numerous	Copious fine loosely packed powder	*Lyctus* powder post beetles	Active in partly and fully seasoned wood. Confined to sapwood in timbers where the heartwood is distinguishable. Wood disintegrated beneath superficial skin in severe cases. Compare house longhorn beetle
	Mainly H containing starch	Circular (up to $\frac{1}{4}$ in diam.)	As flight holes. Usually larger than *Lyctus*	As *Lyctus*	Bostrychid powder post beetles	See *Lyctus*. Mainly in tropical timbers. Unseasoned wood also attacked. Confined to sapwood in timbers where the heartwood is distinguishable.
	S	Circular ($\frac{1}{16}$ in diam.)	As flight holes	Mostly brown (with a few white) bun-shaped pellets	*Ernobius mollis*	In timber yards and recently-built houses. Often confused with *Anobium* but attack limited to bark and adjacent sapwood
	Mostly H	Circular ($\frac{1}{8}$ in diam.)	As flight holes	Larger bun-shaped pellets (easily visible to naked eye)	Death-watch beetle (*Xestobium rufovillosum*)	Common in old buildings especially in oak. Damage sometimes internal in large timbers and disintegration often severe
	H, S. (rare in most tropical H)	Circular ($\frac{1}{16}$ in diam.)	As flight holes; convoluted shape. Numerous	Small ellipsoidal pellets	Common furniture beetle (*Anobium punctatum*)	In wood usually more than 5 years old. Birch plywood very susceptible
	H, S	Irregularly oval to slit-shaped with ragged edges	Circular (about $\frac{1}{16}$ in diam.). Mainly straight—compare *Anobium*	Similar to but smaller than *Anobium*	Wood-boring weevils, *Euophryum* and *Pentarthrum*	In damp and decayed wood. Sometimes with *Anobium*

12

Insect Eradication Methods

12.1 TEMPERATURE EXTREMES

12.1.1 Freezing insect pests in heritage objects for disinfestation and eradication

12.1.1.1 Introduction

The use of sub-zero temperatures, usually referred to as freezing, to kill insect pests in stored food products was suggested by Mullen and Arbogast (1979), as a viable alternative to chemical control. For the same reason, freezing to eradicate museum and household insect pests on dry heritage objects composed of organic material (plant material, skin, fur, whole animals, bone, paper, textiles, wood, etc.) has been used (Billings, 1983; Crisfulli, 1980; Dawson, 1987; Florian, 1978, 1986; Ketcham-Trozak, 1984; Nesheim, 1984; Rasie, 1977; Remmington, 1983).

Chemical treatments (fumigants and insecticides) are no longer being recommended in museums (Florian, 1986, 1988, 1989). Human health hazards are a major concern because the chemicals are toxic and there is a lack of appropriate monitoring equipment to determine the presence of residual chemicals after treatment. Also, toxic by-products remain on the surfaces of treated objects. Many chemicals are banned by governments thus there are legal aspects to using chemical insecticides and fumigants. Finally, the chemicals used in the treatments may cause reactions with the chemicals of the materials of heritage objects, which can cause deterioration and destroy the research potential of these materials.

In a museum, collection managers have the legal responsibility to protect the collections. They must ensure the collections' documentation, security, accessibility and preservation (stability, longevity). There are two approaches to preservation: preventive measures and active interventive treatment against deterioration. Preventive measures include environmentally controlled storage, physical support, maintenance, insect pest control and conservation treatments, such as cleaning. Active intervention includes the preparation methods used specifically for natural history specimens, such as chemical fixing, tanning etc., and conservation treatments such as fumigating, sub-zero temperatures, impregnation or consolidation, etc. Thus use of sub-zero temperatures (freezing) for insect pest eradication is an active interventive treatment of heritage objects.

In the past, collection managers or curators have been involved in active interventive treatments of biological specimens, as have conservators with human history and fine art artifacts. No matter who executes these treatments or what the active interventive treatments are, there must be a realization of the preciousness of the heritage object, and the knowledge that the treatment will not destroy the aesthetic, cultural or research integrity, or the potential of the object. In this, there is no distinction between an object of natural or human heritage. Regardless of what we call a natural history collection (habitat, exhibit, educational, research, type, etc.), if it contains accessioned museum objects or unique specimens, they must be treated with as much care as human history objects.

To design an interventive treatment for heritage objects requires knowledge of the material being treated and knowledge of the interaction, immediate and long term, of the treatment on them. Before a treatment can be undertaken it must be established that it is necessary. Ethically, the above information must be known before using this treatment because lethal freezing of insect pests in heritage objects is an interactive treatment. After the treatment the details and success of the treatment must be recorded.

Freezing for insect eradication was first used with food products. The technology transfer of the application of freezing from food products to heritage objects requires some adaptations. The goal in food products is reducing the population size and limiting the economic damage. With heritage objects every insect must be eradicated with cessation of damage. Thus we need a treatment that will stop the damage immediately, will kill every insect (all stages), will not damage the object, can be executed simply and is not expensive.

To design a logical sub-zero temperature treatment, which we call a freezing treatment, for maximum lethal effect on the insect and minimum interference to the artifact material, it is essential to study the effects of the freezing process on the insect, the water relationships and the artifact material.

Florian (1986) presented the parameters and procedures for a freezing treatment for infested, dry heritage objects made of adsorbent organic material and reviews the essential information required to design such a treatment. The treatment is still under review (Brokerhof *et al.*, 1992, 1993; Brokerhof and Banks, 1993; Gilberg and Brokerhof, 1991; Strang, 1992, 1995). This chapter reports on this information and new information available on the topic.

A review of pertinent literature on the insect's response to low and sub-zero temperatures, and the effects of freezing on the insect and its cells and tissue, is presented to support the logic for the recommended parameters (Florian, 1986) for a lethal insect eradication treatment. A review of the effects of the freezing temperature on the moisture relationships and physical characteristics of the material of the dry heritage objects is presented also, to support the recommended procedures for the treatment. New information is reviewed, and conclusions and a synthesis of the information leads to recommendations for a logical freezing procedure.

Freezing procedures that have been used in museums to eradicate insect pests are also reviewed. The choice of equipment, which is readily available, easy to operate and inexpensive, is discussed. A clarification of the differences in freezing dry and wet materials and freeze-drying is also presented.

12.1.1.2 THE EFFECT OF FREEZING TEMPERATURES ON INSECTS

There are two main questions about the effects of sub-zero temperatures on live insects: the lethal aspect – how does it kill the insect, and the freeze-resistant aspect – can some insects survive freezing?

To understand the lethal effect of freezing on insects, it is necessary to look at the information on freezing of cells or tissues.

12.1.1.2.1 The state of water in cells and tissue

The water takes on three different states and each is located at specific regions in the cell or tissue (see sections 2.4 and 17.1). It may be bonded to polar sites of molecules; this is the molecularly bound water. The water may be bonded to the surface of molecules and to other water layers, this is called the multi-layer region. The third state is free water; this water is located inside capillaries, inside and between living cells, in cell vacuoles, between large fibres, etc.

a Bound water

Sinanoglu and Abdulnor (1965) explained that the water bonded to the polymer remains unchanged on freezing while the bulk or free water goes into ordinary alpha-ice. Meryman (1966) reports that in animal tissues 5–10% of the total water, the bonded water, normally does not freeze at -20°C. Zachariassen (1985) describes bound water as that water forming a shell around macromolecules which because of its altered state cannot be removed by freezing or drying at physiological temperatures, is osmotically inactive and does not act as a solvent for low molecular weight solutes.

Loss of structurally bound water in biopolymers (proteins, cellulose) may result in increased cross-linking. We are aware of this water loss in dry, brittle leather. Karow and Webb (1965) theorized that death due to freezing (in liquid nitrogen at −160°C) may be caused, primarily, by the extraction of bound water from vital cellular structures.

b Multi layer water

Water in the multi-layer region, weakly bonded to molecule surfaces and water layers, is similar to bound water in that it does not have solvent power and rarely freezes. It varies from bound water by having a different vapour pressure because of the weaker bond strength, is easily lost and regained with humidity or dehydration changes, and has higher viscosity and thermal expansion. This is the water that moves in and out of dry heritage objects with RH (relative humidity) changes and causes dimensional changes.

c Free water

Free water is involved as a solvent, it readily freezes, is quickly lost on drying and is active in osmosis. Free water can make up about 70% of the total water in living cells. In the dry organic materials of heritage objects there is no free water to freeze. In wet or waterlogged heritage materials there is free water which can freeze.

12.1.1.2.2 The effects of freezing on cells and tissue – the lethal and survival aspects

a Introduction

We are all familiar with the medical use of frozen cells and tissue; obviously they have survived freezing. The purpose of reviewing this subject is to determine the conditions under which they survive and to make sure that these conditions are not used when eradicating insects.

When living cells (80–90% water content) are subjected to low temperatures, depending on the rate of cooling and thawing and the final temperature reached, cellular physical and chemical changes occur and ice crystals may form. Some of these ice crystals may be lethal but the actual cause of death is not known. It still has not been shown conclusively whether it is a combination of events or a single one.

b Dehydration and concentration effects in cells may occur

If the rate of cooling is slow (1°C/minute), when eutectic temperatures (normal freezing temperature of the cell or body fluids) are reached, ice crystals are formed: first intercellular ice between the cells, then intracellular ice in the cell fluid. The removal of intercellular water, in the form of ice, causes free water in the cells to diffuse out into the intercellular region according to the diffusion gradient. In the cell, loss of this free water causes dehydration and changes in the concentration of the solutes in the cell fluid. The concentration effects may result in pH changes that may cause buffer precipitation. Proteins may undergo denaturation and precipitation causing colloidal disruption and molecular derangement. Zachariassen (1985) suggested that the increase in inorganic salts can cause changes in the structure and function of enzymes which have also been concentrated. Lindelv (1976) pointed out, in reference to frozen foods, that the rate of enzyme reactions may increase on initiation of freezing because of an increase in concentration of the enzyme and substrate.

c Ice crystals in cells may be lethal

When water freezes, ice crystals may form or the water may become a glass-like vitreous solid. Ice crystal shape varies from large hexagonal (or polyhedral) crystals to small evanescent spherulites. The shape of ice is dependent on the lowest temperature reached, the cooling rate, the concentration of the solute and the nature of the solute.

The shape of free ice will vary according to the rate of freezing (Luyet 1960, 1970), the slower the rate of freezing the larger the crystal. Meryman (1966) reviewed the literature and the consensus was that the large hexagonal crystals occur up to −60 to −80°C and the vitreous state occurs at −120 to −180°C. The large hexagonal crystals are most damaging to cells. Karow and Webb (1965) showed that these crystals physically rupture cell and organelle membranes. This leads to cell fluid loss and metabolic disruption. Ice spherulites cause little damage, if any.

Ice crystals need some particles, called nucleators, on which to start to grow or form. In air the nucleator may be a dust particle, in insects it may be a protein in a cell or food in their gut.

In slow cooling (1°C/minute or higher) of living tissue a few large ice crystals are formed, first in the extracellular fluid. The crystals in this location are not considered lethal or damaging, but may act as a nucleation particle or site for intracellular ice crystals that are considered lethal.

d Supercooling in cells lowers the freezing point of body water

Rarely do solutions freeze at 0°C. The temperature below zero at which they reach before freezing is called the supercooling point (SCP). The supercooling point is the temperature at which spontaneous nucleation occurs and ice is formed. The temperature of the supercooling point is dependent on the amount and kind of chemicals (solutes) dissolved in the water (solvent). Supercooling allows cells to withstand freezing temperatures without cell water freezing and thus may prevent the lethal aspects of freezing.

In both cryobiology and the frozen food industry, the chemicals glycerol or sorbitol, called cryoprotectors, are used to increase the solute concentration in solutions and lower the supercooling point. Cryoprotectors also alter the ice form to a less damaging form (Luyet and Gehenio, 1952).

In cryobiology, living cells are frozen for survival in long-term storage. This is possible because of the use of cryoprotectors. The procedure used for cell survival requires that the tissue cells are suspended in a glycerol solution which supercools to −15°C, then the solution is rapidly cooled to a very low temperature, −160°C. The water forms a vitreous sheet or, if ice crystals do form inside the cell, they are altered by the glycerol and are small and diffuse, and do not cause physical damage. In living cells cryoprotectors may protect membranes from lipid phase changes, and by bonding to large amounts of water in cells, protect them from water loss and desiccation. Thus cryoprotectors protect the living cell from cold-shock before the supercooled point is reached. Cold-shock, chilling injury, is a form of lethal cellular injury that occurs in cells immediately after rapid cooling to temperatures which are above the freezing temperature of their cell solution.

In conservation, polyethylene glycol, which acts as an antifreeze, is used to control ice types in freeze-drying treatment of wet or waterlogged archaeological wood. The polyethylene glycol lowers the freezing temperature of the liquid and influences the ice type and formation thereby preventing the damaging ice crystal formation.

Many organisms, eg. insects, fish, fungi, yeast and bacteria, produce glycerol and other polyols, which allow supercooling or control of cell water content. This allows them to live in sub-zero temperatures, but only up to their supercooling point, without freezing. Details of the role of glycerol and insect freeze-resistance is presented in the section below on supercooling point.

e The rate of freezing or thawing may reduce or enhance the lethal effects of freezing in cells

As mentioned above, for freezing tissue or cells for survival after storage or for medical purposes or research, glycerol or sorbitol is added to the suspending solution which acts as an antifreeze and allows supercooling to −15°C. The tissue in the glycerol solution is slowly cooled at a rate of 1°C/minute to the supercooling point −15°C. After supercooling, the solution is rapidly cooled, 150–200°C/minute, by plunging the material into frozen nitrogen or helium. Amorphous vitreous ice is formed, but no damaging ice crystals are formed. To thaw rapidly, the tissue is plunged into a warm (37°C) isotonic solution. This rapid rate of thawing prevents intracellular ice formation and allows the survival of the tissue. If the rates of freezing, or thawing after supercooling are slow, nucleation occurs and lethal ice formation occurs. Luyet (1970) reported that crystallization, upon thawing, may resume because crystal growth is temperature and time dependent. Once the ice crystal is seeded, the growth of the ice crystal is a time-dependent phenomenon. Mazur (1965) also reported that slow thawing of yeast cells after rapid cooling was lethal because intracellular water which had not already frozen could freeze during thawing.

12.1.1.2.3 The insect and freezing temperatures

a Categories of insects in reference to their response to low temperatures

Insects are basically bags of water containing over 70% free water which can easily freeze, but we are familiar with the resistance to freezing temperatures of some garden insects that overwinter, and ice fleas hopping on glaciers.

Zachariassen (1985) categorized insects as freeze-tolerant, freeze-sensitive and freeze-avoidance. *Freezing-tolerance* is the ability to tolerate formation of ice in the body fluid at temperatures equal to or below the supercooling capacity. *Freezing-sensitivity* is lack of tolerance to formation of ice in the body fluid. *Freezing-avoidance* is the survival strategy or cold-hardening of freeze-sensitive insects which occurs when they are exposed to low temperatures. Cold-hardening allows these insects to withstand lower temperatures than they could before cold-hardening. Freeze-hardening, freeze-resistance, cold-hardening and cold-acclimatization are synonymous with freezing-avoidance.

As the temperature is decreased an insect first will become inactive at their chill-coma temperature, will die when their cold-shock temperature is reached and their body fluids will freeze when the SCP is reached. Thus insects are killed before the SCP is reached.

Chill-coma results in loss of movement and feeding activity of insects which is reversed on warming.

During chill-coma oxygen consumption and the rate of metabolic activities is greatly reduced. Prolonged chill-coma may be lethal.

Cold-shock is a form of cellular injury which is lethal and occurs immediately after rapid cooling before ice formation (SCP) in the body fluids. The reasons for cold-shock have not been well defined.

Mechanisms of short-term cold-shock injury have been suggested: cold temperature lipid transformation in cell membranes resulting in leakage and loss of membrane function, the

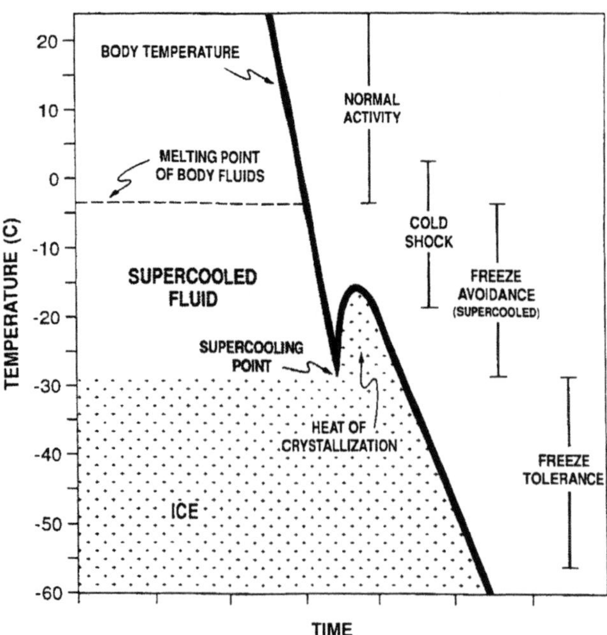

Figure 12.1. Insect body temperature (heavy line) during cooling to sub-zero temperatures in relationship to the melting point, supercooling point and the nucleation of ice in the body fluids. The bars on the right convey general ranges of insect response to low temperatures. Cold shock is usually lethal. The supercooling point is the point of body fluid freezing and is below the lethal point in most insects (from Lee, 1989).

loss of elasticity of the membranes and nerve injuries (Lee, 1991).

Lee (1989) reviewed insect cold-hardening and has illustrated the response of insects cooled to sub-zero temperatures (Figure 12.1). The limit of normal insect activity is just below zero. Cold-shock occurs from above zero to just above –20°C, or above the SCP. Cold-shock is a form of cellular injury which is lethal and occurs on rapid cooling without ice formation in the body fluids. Freezing-avoidance occurs in the supercooled range from just below zero to just above –30°C, whereas freezing-tolerance occurs from the lowest supercooled point to almost –60°C.

b *Freeze-sensitive insects which are killed from cold-shock at above freezing temperatures*

Typically, freeze-sensitive insects are the soft-bodied booklice, termites and silverfish which die at low but above freezing temperatures from cold-shock.

Mullen and Arbogast (1984) consider that stored product insects, because of their tropical origin, are the group which are killed at temperatures above freezing. Salt (1961), in discussing freezing of insects, maintains that household insect pests do not normally encounter cold temperatures and thus should not tolerate freezing temperatures. But in the literature there are many examples of the following insects surviving freezing temperatures: eggs of the cigarette beetle (Mullen and Arbogast, 1984; Gilberg and Brokerhof, 1991), clothes moths (Brokerhof *et al.*, 1993; Brokerhof and Banks, 1993), and larvae of the hide beetle (Ketcham-Troszak, 1984) which are heritage eaters. Strang (1992) has collated information from the literature on the lethal low temperature of many museum and household insect pest species. He has reported on 30 insect species where the range of lethal temperatures was below 0°, which shows clearly that museum and household insect pests are not freeze-sensitive.

In freeze-sensitive insects, Uvarov (1931) showed that the effects of cold-shock from low but above freezing temperatures are time dependent. In experiments on bedbug eggs the results showed that after 10 hours at 2°C, upon returning to room temperature, 80% hatched into normal larvae but after 39 hours at 2°C no larvae hatched. He also reported on the lethal time of above zero temperatures on two species of grain insects. For *Sitophilus oryzae* the lethal time was 60 hours at 7.2°C and for *S. granarius* L. it was 75 hours at 7.2°C. Thus the original suggestion that household insects are killed at above freezing temperatures may be right, but it depends on the time of exposure as well as the low temperature.

Howard (1896) discussed the use of low temperatures in cold storage to inactivate some common household insects. In experiments with *Tinea bisselliella*, the common clothes moth, the larvae were motionless below 5.5°C and survived after 2 months at temperatures varying from 8.8 to 2.7°C. It was also noted that the larvae did not die at a continuous temperature of 7.7°C, but did die if revived by warm temperatures and placed back in the low temperature. This showed that repeating the cold/warm cycle destroys their cold tolerance. Eggs did not hatch during treatment of 2.7°C and adults died after 5 days at –0.6°C.

With *Attagenus piceus*, the black carpet beetle, larval movement was observed at temperatures of 7.2°C to 8.8°C, but the larvae were motionless at temperatures from 3.3 to 6.7°C. After 20 days at temperatures from –3.3 to –8.8°C in cloth all larvae died, but in ground grain meal for 2 months at –1.6°C to –8.8°C all survived. The ground grain probably gave some thermal protection.

The larvae of *Dermestes vulpinus*, the leather beetle, were motionless from 2.2 to 4°C, and moved but did not feed at 4.4 to 7.2°C. However, they did feed at 8.3 and 8.8°C.

With *Trogoderma tarsale*, the cabinet beetle, pupation was not observed in pupae kept at 1.1 to 6.7°C for 3.5 months; adults were inactive at 1.1 to 6.7°C and after 2 months three of 10 died. This information is pertinent to cold-storage and exemplifies the fact that death due to cold-shock is time-dependent.

Howard (1896) concluded that temperatures of 4.4 to 5.5°C are adequate to inactivate common household insects. This is the chill-coma temperature at which insects are motionless and do not feed. This information is the historical basis for the use of cold-room storage to prevent insect damage.

c *Cold-hardening in freeze-sensitive insects*

There is a large group of freeze-intolerant insects which cannot withstand the freezing of their body fluid, but by cold-hardening they can prevent ice formation in their bodies at sub-zero temperatures. These are called freeze-avoidance insects. Cold-hardening is the acquisition of enhanced cold tolerance through biochemical and physiological processes, and it is initiated by exposure to low temperatures.

Hibernating (diapause) insects, in response to gradual lower temperatures of winter, undergo metabolic changes which increase their ability to survive freezing temperatures by cold-hardening. Details of the relationship between cold-hardiness and diapause are reviewed by Denlinger (1991). Diapause does not automatically mean that an insect can survive freezing temperatures, it has to cold-harden. The diapausing insects cannot tolerate body fluid freezing, but through cold-hardening they are able to prevent body fluid from freezing in the sub-zero temperatures to which they would normally be exposed. This occurs commonly in insects that overwinter in geographical regions where there are freezing temperatures during the winter.

Salt (1961) explained that prior to exposure to lethal sub-zero temperatures, the overwintering insects must be exposed to a gradual lowering of the temperature which has triggered these cold-hardening mechanisms. It is a slow process and may take weeks to complete.

d Supercooling point (SCP)

Zachariassen (1985) stated that normal, active summer insects from temperate, arctic and even tropical environments have freezing temperatures, or supercooling points (SCP), of their haemolymph ranging from −7 to −12°C, regardless of season. This is due to the presence of the solutes, proteins, ions, nutrients, etc. in solution.

Lee, *et al.* (1987) and Lee and Denlinger (1985) reported on the SCPs for the different non-diapausing stages of one species of flesh fly: feeding larva near −7°C; non-feeding, wandering last instar larva near −11°C; non-diapausing pupa near −23°C; pharate adult at −23°C, mature adult near −7°C. Freezing of the body fluid occurred in a few minutes at the SCP, which was lethal for all stages, but they also showed that the non-diapausing pupae and pharate adults died after a two-hour period of −10°C. Strong-Gunderson and Leopold (1989) showed that the range of SCPs of the developing house fly stages are: embryo, −27°C to −33°C; larva, −9°C to −16°C; pupa, −16°C to −24°C; and the adult, −17°C. However, all stages died when exposed to −5°C. Thus insects normally cannot survive a sub-zero temperature as low as their SCP. In many cases, the insect stage dies of cold-shock before the SCP is reached. To reduce or prevent cold-shock at sub-zero temperatures higher than their SCP, they must become cold-hardened.

Cold-hardening mechanisms are: lowering the SCP, preventing cell dehydration, and elimination of ice nucleation sites. It is important to understand how these mechanisms are initiated so that the freezing procedures used to kill the heritage-eating insects do not mimic these cold-hardening mechanisms. The most commonly occurring mechanism is lowering the SCP.

In the discussion of freezing tissue or cells for survival (12.1.1.2.2d), glycerol or sorbitol (polyols) is added to the suspending solution and acts as an antifreeze by lowering the freezing point or supercooling point of the solution from just below 0 to −15°C. These same cryoprotectors are synthesized in insects during cold stress.

Denlinger (1991) reviewed the relationship between cold-hardening and diapause. Diapausing, or hibernating, insects commonly have been found to increase levels of glycerol or sorbitol in their body fluid. Lowering of the freezing temperature (SCP) of their body fluids coincides with increases in the polyols and other low-molecular-weight solutes in their body fluids. The presence of these antifreeze polyols and the resultant decrease in the supercooling point is an important factor in determining freezing-resistance or cold-hardening. Zachariassen (1985) stated that an accumulation of polyols causes a steep drop in the lethal temperature due to a reduction in the amount of water by a colligative mechanism of the polyol.

There are two unique features of insects which make it possible for them to use supercooling to protect themselves from sub-zero temperatures. They have a non-living hydrophobic exoskeleton, which sheds water and prevents surface ice nucleation, and the tracheal system. The tracheal system simply brings air from outside into the insect's body where the diffusion of oxygen occurs directly in or out of cells. If a circulating, oxygen-carrying haemolymph was used, the increase in viscosity due to glycerol would interfere with circulation, but the viscous haemolymph is easily pumped in the large sinuses of the insects (Davenport, 1992).

Non-diapausing insect species have been shown to produce these antifreezes by a rapid mechanism to correspond with rapidly changing temperatures on a daily or even hourly basis (Lee *et al.*, 1987).

Synthesis of polyols can also be stimulated by anoxia, heat treatment, and chemical inhibitors of the electron transport system (see respiration 12.2.5) in oxidative respiration (Meyer, 1978).

Chen *et al.* (1990) compared the formation of glycerol and cold-hardening ability, due to cold stress, in tropical and temperate flies. The temperate fly was able to produce glycerol and become cold-hardened under cold stress whereas the tropical fly was not able to respond to cold stress.

e Dehydration and ice nucleating agents (INA)

Salt (1961) considered the two important aspects of freeze-resistance to be supercooling ability and dehydration. It seems obvious that water loss or dehydration in insects should increase their osmotic concentration and lower their freezing or supercooling temperature, but there is no clear evidence to support this theory.

Salt (1950) reported that RH does not influence the freezing temperature of insects, as shown in the example where the freezing temperature remained at −20°C in moist air and dry air over calcium chloride.

Freeze-tolerant insects may have low body water content. Some hibernating, dehydrated, freeze-tolerant chironomid larvae that live in arctic regions supercool to −45°C. Hinton (1960) reported that chironomid larvae, with water contents of 3 and 8%, survived liquid air at −190°C and liquid helium at −270°C. Ring (1982) reported that the relative water content of cold-acclimatized, freeze-tolerant beetles was 30%, which is lower than the lethal level of some desert species. This suggests that hibernating insects may be threatened by lethal dehydration rather than ice crystal formation. However, high solute concentrations and the accumulation of polyols may protect the insect against lethal aspects of dehydration. It is indeed a complex interaction.

Salt (1961) explained that the most important aspect of cold-hardening is prevention of ice nucleation. Ice nucleation readily occurs in actively feeding insects in the faeces within their digestive tract, thus they are less resistant to freezing than the non-feeding inactive stages. Hibernating insects usually evacuate their gut, eliminating these ice nucleators. Ring (1982) suggested that the survival of the freeze-tolerant alpine bark beetle, apart from the ability to supercool, is due to the absence of nucleators in the haemolymph and gut. Ice nucleating agents (INA) in haemolymph are special proteins and lipoproteins in body fluids which act as sites for ice crystal formation. Davenport (1992) reported that the difference between freeze-tolerant and freeze-susceptible insects is the presence or absence of INA. Freeze-susceptible insects have INA agents in their intestines, haemolymph and intracellular fluids. Their presence enhances ice formation before the supercooling point is reached. Freeze-tolerant insects seem to control the presence and placement of INA, i.e. in extracelluar spaces, and encourage ice formation outside the cell to protect the cell itself.

Lee (1991) suggest that the INA may function to encourage extracelluar ice and avoid injury from repeated freeze/thaw cycles that the insect normally experiences in nature, prior to hibernation.

In freeze-susceptible insects, the presence of polyols produced during cold-hardening may play a role in inactivating these INA (Baust and Morrissey, 1975).

12.1.1.2.4 Parameters of freezing process influence mortality of insects

a Ice formation and mortality are dependent on time/temperature and rate of cooling

In experimenting with the freezing and melting points of insect tissues Salt (1956) explained that for hibernating insects at −10°C, one can assume that about 75–80% of the body water is frozen, at −15°C about 85–90%, and at −20°C close to 90% or more is frozen. He commented that at −15°C there is no chance for the insects to survive freezing unless they belong to the small group of freeze-tolerant insects that can tolerate frozen body fluids and tissues. Zachariassen (1985) reported that freeze-tolerant insects become injured when 65% of their body water freezes, whereas freeze-sensitive insects show injury after 50% of their body water freezes.

Freezing will occur in the body fluid of insects held above the supercooling point, after a passage of time. Freezing is time dependent as the following examples illustrate. Salt (1950,1961) reported that with *Cephus cinctus* larvae held at −24°C, 25% froze in 30 minutes, and 50% in 60 minutes. With those held at -26°C, 50% froze in 10 minutes and 100% in 25 minutes. He also reported that adult insects freeze immediately when rapidly cooled to −20°C, but if the temperature reaches only −19°C they freeze in 1 minute, at −17°C it takes 1 hour, at −15°C a day and at −10°C a month. He explained this as the time/temperature required for nucleation and growth of ice crystals.

The above information is specifically about ice formation in the body fluid of insects. Insects normally cannot survive a sub-zero temperature as low as their SCP.

In many cases, the insect stage dies of cold-shock before the SCP is reached. As discussed before, cold-shock, or chilling injury, is a form of lethal cellular injury which occurs immediately after rapid cooling of insects, but above the freezing temperature of their body fluids. It may be caused by cold-temperature lipid transformation in cell membranes resulting in leakage and loss of membrane function, the loss of elasticity of the membranes, nerve injuries (Lee, 1991) or a low rate of metabolic activities and oxygen absorption. It is possible that only a few ice crystals may form and cause lethal damage. Cold-shock is also time/temperature dependent.

In most research on heritage eaters or stored food insects the reason for mortality from reduced temperature is not known, but it is shown to be time/temperature dependent.

Studying stored product insects, Mullen and Arbogast (1979) placed insect eggs in plexiglass probes into a domestic freezer at −10°C, and showed that the LT_{95} (lethal time for 95% mortality) was different for the different species, as follows:

7 hours – *Oryzaephilus surinamensis*, sawtoothed grain beetle;
8 hours – *Tribolium castaneum*, red flour beetle;
9 hours – *Ephestia cautella*, almond moth;
28 hours – *Callosobruchus maculatus*, cowpea weevil; and
62 hours – *Lasioderma serricorne*, cigarette beetle.

This illustrates the different species response to sub-zero temperatures. The results also showed time/temperature responses for all species, one example of LT_{95} follows:

Ephestia cautella, the almond moth
160 hours at 5°C
40 hours at 0°C
20 hours at −5°C
9 hours at −10°C, and
5 hours at −15°C

Studying museum insect pests, Brokerhof *et al.* (1992) placed two-day old *Tineola bisselliella* eggs in a domestic freezer set at different low temperatures. At specific times the eggs were removed to determine time/temperature mortality. There was no survival after 30 hours at −20°C, 72 hour at −15°C, 96 hours at −10°C, 240 hours at −5°C and 672 hours at 0°C. They were able to show that these results fit the same direct relationship between the natural logarithm of exposure time and reciprocal temperature, as in standard chemical reaction kinetics (i.e. it takes less time to dissolve a chemical as the temperature is increased). Thus the model can be used to estimate exposure time/temperature for disinfestation treatment.

b Rapid cold-hardening can occur

It is important to be aware that cold-hardening and the physiological change resulting in supercooling can occur very rapidly.

Wigglesworth (1972) stated that cold-hardening can occur in 4–18 hours as long as the insect is at a temperature at which it can still move and not in a chill-coma; insect movement is essential for cold-hardening. Chen *et al.* (1987) and Lee (1989) report on a rapid cold-hardening response in non-overwintering stages which protects these stages from the cold-shock injury that occurs at low temperatures, in the absence of tissue freezing. For species of flesh fly from a temperate environment, after direct exposure to −10°C for 2 hours, few survived, but if preceded by a 10-minute exposure to 0°C, 50% survived the 2 hours at −10°C. With these flies the glycerol titre increases two- to threefold after 2hours at 0°C. This rapid cold-hardening response protects the non-overwintering insect stages from cold-shock caused by exposure to low tempera-

Table 12.1. Summary of characteristics associated with cold-hardening for winter and the rapid cold-hardening response that protects against injury due to cold shock. (Adapted from Lee, 1989.)

Characteristics	Winter cold-hardening	Rapid cold-hardening
Differences		
Cold tolerance	Long-term freeze tolerance and/or supercooling	Short-term prevention of non-freezing injury
Stage	Only in overwintering stage	Present in more that one developmental stage (larva, pupa, adult)
Activity	Inactive (diapause, quiesence)	Active feeding and reproduction (sometimes diapause)
Timing	Seasonal	All year
Rate of cold-hardening	Slow (weeks–months)	Rapid (minutes–hours)
Similarities		
Cryoprotectant	Present	Present
Induction trigger	Low temperature	Low temperature

tures before they have become cold-acclimatized for prolonged winter survival. Table 12.1 (after Lee, 1989) compares this rapid cold-hardening with winter cold-hardening which may take weeks to develop. The significant feature of this rapid cold-hardening is that it occurs in non-overwintering insect stages: larvae, adults and pupae, and actively feeding individuals. This describes those insects which infest heritage objects. How universal this phenomenon is, is not known. The fact that the research was done on one species of thousands from a group with awesome variability in form is not as significant as the fact that all these different species must protect themselves from cold injury or overwintering: a uniform environmental variable (Baust and Rojas, 1985). In nature, insect populations with all life stages may be exposed to daily temperature fluctuations which may include low to sub-zero temperatures. A universal rapid cold-hardening response must protect non-overwintering stages from these low temperatures.

Mullen and Arbogast (1984) reported that stored grain insects, in grain silos, can become acclimatized to a gradual decrease in temperature which lowers the lethal low temperature. Brokerhof and Banks (1993) investigated the possible cold acclimatization with museum and household heritage eaters. In previous work (Brokerhof *et al.*, 1992, 1993) they used a domestic freezer for insect mortality studies and wondered if the rate of cooling would influence the cold acclimatization of insects. A preliminary study showed that when *Tineola bisselliella* eggs, which are the most low-temperature tolerant stage, were exposed to a gradual decrease in temperature from 25°C to 10°C over 10 days, or a 20-day period at 10°C, the lethal time at −20°C decreased from 1.1 to 0.7 hours, an insignificant amount compared with the time required to kill the eggs. In a more rigorous test, they used a rate of cooling of 2°C/hour to determine if it would cause cold acclimatization. The results, showed that the variations were insignificant experimental variations, and that cold acclimatization did not occur.

c Repeating cold/warm cycles destroys freeze-resistance ability

The following examples of repeated cold/warm or freeze/thaw cycles illustrate that this destroys the cold-hardiness or freeze-resistance ability of insects.

Howard (1896) reported that the common clothes moth at a continuous temperature of 7.7°C survived, but on repeating the warm/cold cycle died. Wigglesworth (1972) reported that after repeated freeze and thaw cycles, supercooling ability is eliminated and freezing occurs as soon as freezing temperatures are reached. Zachariassen (1985) stated that freezing and thawing during the winter may result in substantial physiological disturbances and suggests that extracellular ice nucleating agents may give some protection. Chen *et al.* (1990, 1991) showed that temperate flesh fly adults that were cultured at 25°C, chilled for 2 hours at 0°C or heated for 2 hours at 40°C to make them cold-hardened or heat-acclimatized, lost their cold-hardiness and heat-acclimatization if, after the above treatments, they were brought back up to 25°C.

Florian (1986) suggested that repeated freeze/thaw cycles could be used in freezing insect-infested artifacts to ensure lethal conditions for eradication, if cold-hardening is suspected. The literature suggests that if cold-hardening has occurred this repeat treatment is logical. Most importantly, it shows clearly that if bagged infested objects cannot be treated immediately and they have been temporarily stored in a refrigerator or cold storage at above freezing temperatures, the bagged objects must be brought up to room temperature (+/−20°C) before being placed in the freezer.

12.1.1.2.5 Variation in vulnerability to freezing of the different stages of the life cycle

The question always arises – are the different stages in the life cycle of the insect equally vulnerable to freezing?

Strang (1992) has collated the literature on eradication methods and research on lethal low temperatures of all stages of museum pests, and Asahina (1966) lists the freeze resistance of eggs, larvae, pupae and adults of different stored food insect species, but no general conclusions can be drawn. The main weaknesses of this literature have already been mentioned as the lack of the record indicating the rate of freezing and thawing, and the previous environmental history of the insects, both of which will influence the lethal low temperature.

Brokerhof *et al.* (1993), in exemplary research design, have shown results of time–mortality research using the commercial chest freezer at −20°C, with the different species and stages of two clothes moths, as well as the eggs of two species of clothes moths and two stored food pests. All stages and all species were killed in 30 hours at −20°C. They found that the adults were the least tolerant and that the eggs of *Tineola bisselliella* were the most tolerant. The larvae, pupae and adults did not survive after 1 hour at –20°C.

Gilberg and Brokerhof (1991) have shown the variation of time/temperature mortality of all stages of the drugstore beetle (*Stegobium paniceum*) using a chest freezer. The eggs are most resistant with a lethal time of 2 hours at –20°C, whereas with the adults, larvae and pupae the lethal time was 30 minutes at –20°C.

As previously mentioned, Lee and Denlinger (1985) and Lee *et al.* (1987) reported on the SCPs for the different non-diapausing stages of one species of flesh fly: feeding larvae near –7°C; non-feeding, wandering last instar larvae near –11°C; non-diapausing pupae near –23°C; pharate adults at –23°C, mature adults near –7°C, but all stages died at –10°C.

Salt (1961) reported that ice nucleation readily occurs in actively feeding insects in the faeces and their digestive tract. Thus actively feeding insects may be less resistant to freezing than the inactive stages.

We would expect that such structures as the cocoon would have some insulation advantage, but Asahina (1966) suggests that egg shells, hibernacula, cocoons and puparia prevent ice seeding in the pupae but not rate or degree of cooling. Brokerhof *et al.* (1993) report that the naked larvae of the *Tinea* clothes moth species were less resistant to low temperatures than the case-bearing larvae of the *Tineola* clothes moth species. This does suggest that stages with these coverings may be more resistant.

From the above examples it is apparent that there may be some differences in tolerance to low temperatures of the different life stages of the heritage-eating insects, but the –20°C for 72 hours used in the chest freezer for freezing treatment will be lethal to all stages.

12.1.1.2.6 The lethal low temperature and thermal ballast of materials infested

There are hundreds of references to lethal low temperature for as many insect species, some museum pests, some stored product pests and some agricultural pests. Unfortunately, the information is very difficult to use to establish lethal low temperatures because of the variability in results. The variability reflects the lack of well defined parameters for the tests, i.e. nutritional state of the insects, previous temperature exposures and, most importantly, the rate of thawing and freezing. Florian (1986) pointed out this weakness of the literature in reference to lethal temperatures. The problem with the literature relating to cold-hardiness is further explained by Baust and Rojas (1985). They stated that, of 1000 research papers, in all but six the experiments were made with uncontrolled post-freeze conditions and rates of freezing and thawing. They also consider that the methods of measuring survival are incorrect because the only accurate test of survival is reproductive capability. Strang (1992) also critiqued the literature and reported that the minimum time for 100% mortality, the variation in rates of cooling and interference with insulating materials associated with the infestation, are a problem.

The papers on clothes moths by Brokerhof *et al.* (1992, 1993) and Brokerhof and Banks (1993) are an exception. In these all the parameters of the experiments are reported and the research is applicable to the reality of the domestic chest freezer and the museum and household insect pests. Thus there are some papers which give sufficient parameters that are applicable to our problem with heritage eaters.

Mullen and Arbogast (1979) were concerned with the thermal qualities of the commodities the insects were infesting. They determined cooling rates for practical stored product commodities and suggested that the freezer should not be densely packed and that the disinfestation of any commodity can be accomplished by determining the time necessary for the temperature of the commodity to reach equilibrium in the freezer. That time would then be added to the chosen lethal time. For example, the time required to kill the eggs is 3 hours, plus 160 hours for a 50kg sack of flour to reach a core temperature of –10°C, is a total of 163 hours for treatment.

Florian (1992) placed the following items into individual ziplok bags: leather mukluks (Inuit boots), a plant leaf basket, a beaded purse and bone tools. The temperature and RH change were recorded with an ARC logger. Figure 12.2 shows that the materials of these objects reached the freezer low temperature in at least 2 hours. Shchepanek (1996) monitored the core temperature of a box of unmounted herbarium plant specimens with associated paper sheets and corrugated cardboard, sealed in polyethylene, and unsealed. In both cases, the temperature came to equilibrium with the freezer in less than 6 hours. Brokerhof and Banks (1993) reported on the calculated cooling rates of materials and the lethal temperatures of the eggs of *Tineola bisselliella*, the webbing clothes moth. Because insects may be protected by the materials they live in, temperature-estimated profiles of a number of common materials (cylinders of wool, wood, cork, wheat with a radius of 25cm and a 1cm-long wood slab) were recorded at the cooling rate of 2°C per hour to reach 253K (–20°C). By showing predicted cooling profiles of the materials and mortality curves of the insects, they predicted that complete mortality (30 hours) occurred before the core temperature of the material reached –20°C, at the cooling rate of 2°C per hour. Therefore, by adding the time for cooling of materials and the time to reach lethal temperatures for the insect the result is less than the 72 hours at –20°C.

Even though there are weaknesses with the reviewed literature, the chart developed by Strang (1992) is of value. It is a guide to the lethal temperatures for heritage eaters. Strang (1992) reported on 32 insect species. The range of lethal temperatures was 0 to –34°C: six species at 0–10°C, 21 species at –11 to –20°C, and five species lower than –20°C. Strang (1992) gives details of these last five species in the appendix of his paper: for a carpenter ant, –29°C was a measurement of the supercooling point; the low temperature for the powder-post or west Indian drywood termite was –34°C, the anobiid book beetle was –29°C, the dermestid beetle was –23°C, and the carpet beetle was –24°C. However, these were temperatures used in specific treatments and not necessarily the lethal temperature. Thus the sub-zero temperatures below –20°C are not necessary for lethal conditions. They were used because they were the low temperature of equipment or because of the packaging of contaminated products. As a result of these below –20°C temperatures, Strang (1992) suggested the use of –30°C in chest freezers, but stated that if this cannot be reached then repeated freeze/thaw cycles are recommended. He noted the disadvantage of excessive handling with the repeat treatments.

The temperature of –20°C for an insect pest eradication treatment for museums was recommended by Florian (1986). This temperature was chosen after a thorough review of the literature and because this is the temperature which most household chest freezers reach easily. A period of 48 hours at this temperature should kill all insects, but as a precaution the procedure requires that the treatment is repeated to ensure 100% lethal conditions. In reviewing the literature again, as well as new information, a longer period of time can be substituted for a repeat treatment. This would alleviate the problem of excess handling mentioned by Strang (1992). Thus –20 to –30°C (the temperature range of commercially available chest freezers) for 72 hours is now recommended. Personal communication with both Ring (1996) and Denlinger (1996) indicated that they felt the insects confronted in museums and households would be killed in one treatment of 48 hours at –20°C, but as a precaution, a 72-hour treatment could be used so a repeat treatment would not be needed.

Since 1985, the Royal British Columbia Museum has used one treatment of –21°C for 48 hours and has had 100% success with *Reesa vespula*, *Anthrenus verbasci*, *Tineola bisselliella*, and *Tinea pellionella* (L.) infestations. Brokerhof's work (Brokerhof *et al.*, 1992, 1993; Brokerhof and Banks, 1993) on clothes moths also supports the use of 48 hours at –20°C.

It is important to understand that the success of this treatment is not just the low temperature and time, but also the rate of freezing and thawing, and the room temperature acclimatization prior to freezing.

12.1.1.2.7 Summary of literature review

The temperature at which the cell and body fluid of the insect freezes, the supercooling point (SCP), is a dynamic physiological parameter of the insect body fluid. It varies with insect species and in individuals of a species. In an individual, it varies throughout the life of an insect, in the different stages and within the development of each stage. It can change in an individual in response to environmental parameters and nutrition, and it can be altered by cold-hardening.

SCP is measured by the heat of crystallization when ice is spontaneously formed in the insect's cell and body fluid. This method of measurement may not measure small amounts of extracelluar ice which may form prior to the rapid overall phase change.

Freeze-resistant insects die when their cell fluids freeze at the SCP, but most insects die from cold-shock before the SCP is reached. Thus SCP is not the lethal low temperature, it can be up to 20°C lower than the low lethal temperature.

Cold-shock, or cold injury, may be due to membrane damage, extracelluar ice, metabolic disruption and other physiological stresses. Freeze-sensitive insects, through cold-hardening, can prevent some degree of cold-shock damage and lower their lethal temperature, but the lowered lethal temperature is still not as low as the SCP.

Cold-hardening in non-overwintering insect stages is initiated by a rapid reduction of temperature in the insect. It allows these stages to withstand daily temperature extremes before overwintering. It coincides with a lowering of the SCP and increases in the cell fluid concentration of cryoprotectors, glycerol, sorbitol or other polyols. The polyols reduce cold-shock by protecting membranes, preventing cell dehydration, altering the ice form and lowering the SCP.

Cold-hardening can occur in diapause insects, slowly, over a long period of time. This allows the hibernating insect to survive the low winter temperature. In non-overwintering stages, cold-hardening can occur rapidly, in just a few minutes, which allows the insects to survive daily temperature fluctuations. Cold-hardening of non-diapausing insects stages will increase the lethal low temperature only a few degrees.

Cold-hardening is initiated by rapid cooling of the insect. It can be eliminated or cancelled out by the return of the cold-hardened insect to the original warm temperature (room temperature).

Some tropical and temperate flesh fly species have the same SCP. The temperate fly can undergo cold-hardening but the tropical fly cannot.

The rate of freezing and thawing, the age, nutritional state, and environmental history can alter the SCP and the lethal low temperature.

There are few published, precise lethal low temperatures for museum and household insects but the physiology of insects suggests that the lethal low temperature is most probably around –15°C for 48 hours.

Cold-shock and ice nucleation are time dependent. There are few published, precise times of exposure to sub-zero temperatures for lethal conditions, but it must occur within 48 hours at –20°C.

12.1.1.2.8 Relevance of literature review in designing the parameters of the freezing treatment to eradicate insects in infested heritage objects

Unfortunately, there is so much variation in the insects themselves, their ability to respond to environmental changes and the methods and parameters of the research that it seems to be beyond our ability to use the published information logically. But there are some suggestions and facts that can help design a successful lethal treatment for eradication of insect pests using sub-zero temperatures.

Ideally, the potential lethal freezing procedure for eradication of live insects in heritage objects should cause lethal cold-shock or ice crystal formation and prevent cold-hardening.

We assume that some damaging ice crystals are formed, thus the rate of freezing and thawing should be optimum for the formation of damaging ice crystals. The time held at the sub-zero temperatures should be long enough to ensure complete intracellular ice crystal growth.

The slow freezing and thawing which normally occurs when materials are placed in and taken out of a freezer chest will give maximum lethal conditions for insect eradication. It is suggested that a slower thawing would enhance the lethal aspects, thus the rate of thawing could be slowed by placing the frozen, bagged materials in a refrigerator to thaw. Slow thawing will enhance ice formation and lethal conditions.

The literature suggests that some museum, household or stored food product insect pests may be able to undergo rapid cold-hardening. Rapid cold-hardening of all stages of a flesh fly from a temperate environment was reported, but similar fly species from a tropical environment were not able to become cold-hardened. Many of the museum and household insect pests are of tropical origin but there are many local endemic species in temperate climates. Eggs of the case-bearing clothes moth were able to undergo slight cold-hardening, but only by a 0.3°C difference.

Thus in using freezing to eradicate these insects we must be sure that the procedures we use do not mimic those that naturally develop cold-hardiness. Caution should be taken to prevent exposure of insects to low temperatures prior to freezing. Examples of how cold-hardening could occur are by: temporarily putting bagged, infested artifacts, prior to freezing, outdoors where temperatures are considerably lower than the environment from which they came; storing the infested artifacts overnight, or for a few hours, in a cold basement prior to freezing; an extremely slow rate of temperature reduction during the freezing process; temporarily storing them, before treatment, in a refrigerator or cold-storage unit which has a temperature above the chill-coma temperature (5°C) of the insect.

It has been suggested that repeated freeze/thaw cycles break down the cold-hardening of insects and thus could be a component of the freezing procedure, however increasing the time of exposure would be just as effective, and would eliminate excessive handling.

Cold storage is commonly used to stop the activity of insects including feeding and moving. Common household insects will stop activity at 5°C. Cold is a relative term, but here it is considered as a temperature too low to support normal development or activity.

The lethal action to insects of low temperatures and freezing is time/temperature dependent, therefore, the time at the minimum temperature of the freezing procedure is critical. A period of 48 hours is a logical time, but as a precaution 72 hours is recommended.

In reference to the above information about the response and effect of freezing temperatures on insects, the following parameters for the freezing treatment to eradicate insect pests in an infested heritage object are recommended. To prevent cold-hardening or freeze-resistance, place the insect-infested object in a sealed bag or container and place it directly from room temperature into a freezer chest, already at –20 to –30°C. For lethal conditions use at least a temperature of –20°C for 72 hours then remove the container and slowly bring it to room temperature. To reduce the rate of thawing and further ensure that ice in the insect tissue is formed, the container can be placed directly from the freezer into a refrigerator until it reaches the ambient temperature of the refrigerator and then placed at room temperature.

If cold-hardening is a concern the whole procedure can be repeated immediately. For complete details of procedures see Box 11.1. Let logic prevail.

Some domestic freezers commonly go below –20°C and need not be altered, however any temperature between –20 to –30°C is acceptable. Bagged objects can be left in the freezer for longer than 72 hours. After equilibrium in temperature and humidity has been reached in the freezer, created by the low vapour pressure of water and low rate of chemical reactions, nothing happens that would cause a problem for the objects. Therefore, they can be left in the freezer for any period of time, but the minimum is 72 hours.

If the freezer is full to capacity and the materials of the object are dense, i.e. wood, books or textiles, then extra time is needed to reach –20°C in the core. Thermocouples should be used to monitor this to assure the full 72 hours at –20°C is completed. The materials that are treated must be dry and adsorbent.

The recommended parameters for a freezing treatment relate to the effectiveness of killing the insects. The care of the heritage object and procedures to protect it during the treatment as well as the effects of the reduced temperature on the materials and the changes in water relationships are presented in the next unit.

12.1.2 **The freezing treatment: its effect on dry materials of heritage objects**

12.1.2.1 Introduction

The recommended procedures for eradication of living insect pests in heritage objects made of adsorbent materials have been described in detail in Box 11.1. The reasons for the specific steps are discussed below.

In summary, the procedures are simple but precise. An infested object is sealed in a clear polyethylene bag in which most of the air has been removed. The bag is taken directly from room temperature and is placed in a domestic chest freezer, or other comparable unit, that is already at –20°C, but can range from –20°C to –30°C. If the infested object cannot be treated immediately because of lack of freezer space, it can be placed in a refrigerator that is at 5°C for temporary storage, but it must be brought back to room temperature before being placed in the freezer. The bagged object is left in the freezer for 72 hours and then removed directly to room temperature, or to a refrigerator for 24 hours then placed at room temperature. After the object in the bag has reached room temperature, the insect remains are removed from the object. The object is then ready to be restored in the bag or as storage methods require. Objects containing non-adsorbent or wet materials should not be processed.

12.1.2.2 Explanation for the specific steps in the freezing treatment

12.1.2.2.1 Water relationships in the bag

a Introduction

There are three aspects of water relationships which should concern us when freezing dry heritage objects made from organic materials: the freezing of water in the material; the freezing and condensation of water vapour in the air of the freezer or the bag in which the artifact is placed in the freezer; and the regain ability of the material. Polyethylene has very low permeability to water vapour and no thermal resistance. Thus it retains its own internal RH during storage and treatment, and the temperatures inside and outside of the bag are instantly the same (Florian, 1992). The heritage object in the bag is not influenced by the external RH, only the RH in the bag.

b Does ice form in dry materials?

In dry organic materials of heritage objects at equilibrium moisture content (50% RH and 20°C) with the museum or home, the amount of water in the artifact will depend on the regain ability of the material. Most organic artifact materials in the museum environment will have between 8 and 12% equilibrium moisture content (EMC). The moisture in the materials will be molecularly bound and multi-layer water which is not available for ice formation.

Other organic materials with a much higher EMC may not freeze at −20°C, i.e. dried beef meat with 20% EMC, gelatin gel with 35% EMC and motion picture film at 35% EMC. Fresh collagen samples (Dehl, 1970) with 45–60% EMC did not freeze at -50°C. The free water in these examples did not freeze because it is in fine capillaries below 30mμ in diameter and cannot freeze (Fisher, 1924). The water in the capillaries is physically altered; like bound water it does not have solvent power and does not form ice. It has a higher viscosity and thermal expansion, a lower water vapour, and is more stable than free water. The structure and reactivity of proteins found in heritage objects is discussed by Florian (1984).

Ice crystals will form in wet materials, such as waterlogged materials, when they are exposed to freezing temperatures because they are saturated with free water in large spaces. Ice could form in damp materials or newly applied adhesives, which have not come to equilibrium moisture content with ambient air.

c *Does water vapour freeze inside the bag?*

Water vapour freezes in dust-free air in the Wilson chamber at −41.2°C (Cwilong, 1947), in outdoor air at −32.2°C, and in smoke-filled air at −27°C. The freezing depends on nucleation particles. Neither the water vapour in the freezer chamber, nor in the air in the bag with the object should freeze at −20°C. However, if the temperature was near −30°C and there was particulate material to act as nucleation sites, the water vapour could possibly freeze, but the amount would be very small.

d *Does condensation occur inside the bag?*

We are familiar with water condensing on the surface of a cold bottle placed in warm, humid air. The warm air adjacent to the cold surface of the bottle is cooled, its moisture holding capacity is lowered, the excess moisture vapour condenses to form dew or water and, if it is frozen, frost on the surface. Temperature differentials between the air and the cold surface create rapid air circulation which continually supplies warm, moist air to the cold surface causing a visible build-up of water or frost.

When an airtight polyethylene bag filled with hot, humid air, such as your breath, is put into the freezer, the air cools and some frost will form on the inner surface of the bag which has become cold like the bottle. As the air cools, the holding capacity of the air in the bag decreases. When the air reaches 100% RH (saturated) the excess water condenses on the non-adsorbent, now cold, inner surface of the plastic bag. Condensation will also occur on non-adsorbent materials placed in the bag such as glass, metal, plastics, etc.

If an object made of adsorbent material is put in the bag under the same conditions, i.e. filled with hot, humid air, condensation may not occur if the object material is able to adsorb the excess water. Obviously, eliminating the humid air in the bag will reduce the amount of excess water dramatically. It is recommended in the freezing process for eradication of insects that all excess air is removed from the bags. The use of additional adsorbent materials (Thomson, 1986) or pre-treated silica gel (La Fointain, 1984) will ensure that the excess moisture is adsorbed and does not condense on surfaces.

When a cold, bagged object is removed from the freezer, condensation may form on the outer surface of the bag, but will disappear when it warms up and is at equilibrium with the ambient temperatures. The small amount of air inside the bag will also warm up, increase its moisture holding capacity and withdraw or take back the small amount of water vapour that went into the object during the freezing process.

It is essential that objects are not removed from the bag until everything has come to the ambient temperature, which takes at least 8 hours.

e *The regain ability, adsorbancy, of materials of objects*

If an object made of adsorbent material is placed in a polyethylene bag and the excess air is removed, condensation will not occur on the object as long as the regain ability of the material is able to adsorb the excess water from the cooling air. The regain ability of materials is variable and may be influenced by the material's inherent characteristics, treatment, deterioration and sorption history, as well as environmental parameters.

In the literature, regains of many materials are reported. Florian (1984) reviews moisture content of various materials.

The following list shows how much water can be adsorbed by 100g of material when subjected to a change from 50% RH to a saturated, 100% RH, at 20°C:

- 100g of nylon textile – adsorbs 4.5g of water
- 100g of methylated wool – adsorbs 35.0g of water
- 100g of collagen (skin) – adsorbs 40.0g of water.

This shows a range from relatively non-adsorbent nylon to readily adsorbent collagen. The amounts of water are the maximum the materials can hold without being wet.

In the freezing treatment, the amount of water adsorbed by a material is significant when related to the available water in the polyethylene freezer bag. If the temperature of the bag containing a square metre of air at 50% RH is reduced from room temperature to 0°C, it will have an excess of 8.5g of water. If the 100g of nylon were placed in this cubic metre of air, condensation would occur on it because it could only adsorb 4.5g of the 8.5g of water. The wool or collagen would readily adsorb the excess water. It would be extreme to place 100g of nylon in a cubic metre container. If the air volume was reduced by half, condensation would not occur. In reality, the air volume in the bag containing the infested object is going to be reduced by more than a half. The logical approach is to eliminate as much air as possible in the bag and not to freeze non-adsorbent materials.

Florian (1992) used environmental monitoring loggers placed inside the polyethylene bag with the objects to document the RH changes. Figure 12.2 shows the RH changes in four bags each with a different heritage object in them, during the freezing and thawing cycles, with a low temperature of −21°C in a domestic freezer. In the bags with the objects, the reduction of RH during freezing is a result of the reduction of holding capacity of the air and the adsorption of the excess water vapour by the materials. The RH was different for the different materials reflecting their specific adsorbancy. On warming, the increase in RH is due to the increase in holding capacity of the air and the release of water vapour from the materials of the objects.

12.1.2.2.2 Physical effects of subzero temperatures on dry materials of heritage objects

a Introduction

It is important to note that many heritage objects made from insect-vulnerable organic materials have gone through freeze/thaw cycles during use. The materials of the Inuit of the Canadian arctic: driftwood, soap-stone, seals' blood glue, antler, walrus, tusk, bones, untanned animal skins and sinew, during usage go through many freeze/thaw cycles without appreciable damage. Composite objects such as bone- or antler-laminated bows; arrows made of wood and feathers with copper, bone or iron beads; and sleds of wood, bone and rawhide all survived the freezing temperatures of the arctic during use.

It is likely that most of the material culture of the aboriginal people from temperate and arctic regions has been frozen, during use, without damage. Even so, it is our ethical responsibility as conservators to determine, to the best of our ability, whether additional freezing treatments would damage objects now in museum environments.

Information about the physical changes of materials at low temperatures is found in the literature on aeronautical research and materials research for the arctic, refrigeration, cryobiology and wood technology, and there are some important papers on testing the effects of the freezing process on materials in heritage objects.

The scientific information, presented below, is a guide. It is based on physical and chemical changes in new materials due to temperature and RH changes. Some of the materials are found in heritage objects, but they may be altered by fabrication, usage and deterioration. The general rule is that the more a material is altered, the more vulnerable it is to most environmental changes.

b Wood: the effects of sub-zero temperatures

When dry wood is subjected to −20°C two things can happen. There may be thermal shrinkage due to the temperature changes and there may be swelling due to an increase in EMC. The following reviews of research illustrate these reactions.

Mechanical properties of wood and wood products increase on cooling and moisture content. Sulzberger (1953) reported on tests on materials used in wooden aircraft over the temperature range of 60 to −20°C. The results of tests on wood and plywood showed that, with a decrease in temperature, an increase in strength properties occurred. In the case of wood, this increased with increase in moisture content. These changes in mechanical properties that occur are reversible on warming.

Beall (1982) studied the effects of temperatures in adverse environments on the structural use of wood and reported that in wood at 12% moisture content, the physical strength characteristics, i.e. modulus of elasticity and maximum crushing strength, increase with a decrease in temperature down to −185°C. Green wood and wood at fibre saturation point undergo greater increases.

Comben (1964) in studying the effect of low temperatures on the strength and elastic properties of timber, tested ash, Douglas fir and balsa at moisture contents of 12%, 18% and "green" (over 28% EMC) over a temperature range of 17 to −183°C. The findings showed that there is generally an appreciable increase in most strength properties with a decrease in temperature. Also, the higher the moisture content the greater is the strength-increasing effect of the low temperatures.

Because of the structure of wood there are different dimensional responses to the different wood surfaces (tangential, radial and longitudinal). Schirp and Kubler (1968) showed in their experiments the approximate dimensional changes of

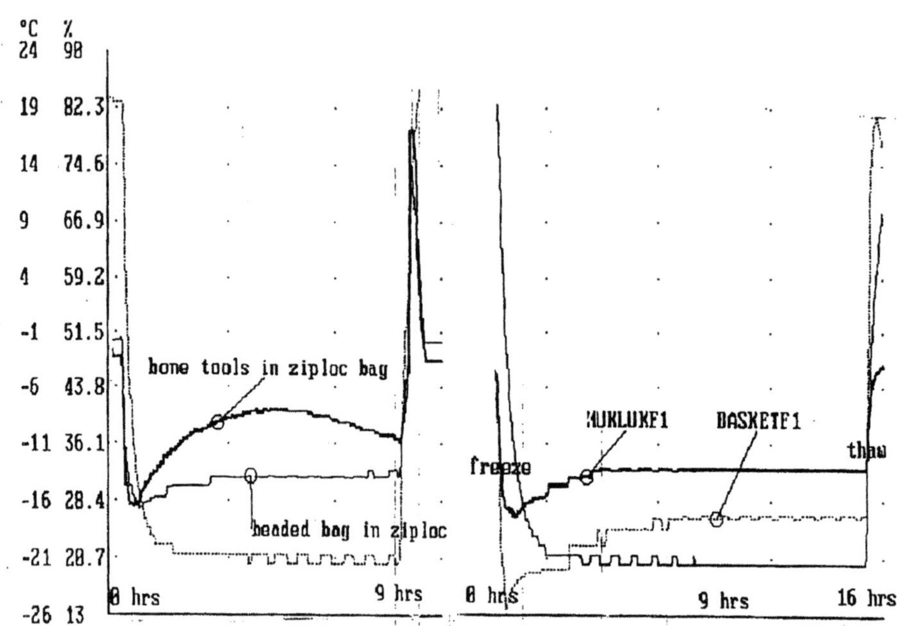

Figure 12.2. Computer printout of logger results of freeze/thaw cycle temperature and RH changes inside four polyethylene bags each with a different historical object.. The temperature is the bottom line. The RH is lowest with the most adsorbent material – plant material of a basket (Florian, 1992).

wood at different moisture contents (Table 12.2). The 12.8% moisture content best illustrates what would happen with wood in heritage objects. The change is very small and reversible on warming. The reduction in the dimensions is due to thermal shrinkage.

Schirp and Kubler (1968) describe causes of dimensional changes in wood produced by cooling, dependent on moisture content:

- oven-dry wood and air dry (0.1% and 12.8% MC) – thermal contraction is the determining factor
- medium moisture content (43–75% MC) – 'cold-shrinkage', a freezing-out of water from the cell walls and cavities is predominant
- high moisture contents (113–114% MC) – the formation of ice layers as well as volumetric expansion of freezing water becomes important.

Kubler (1962) showed that there were also longitudinal changes on cooling wood. In wood with 56% MC the changes from –20 to 40°C were less than 1%.

The dimensional changes of wood subjected to freezing temperatures will depend on the change in moisture content. Under conditions of freezing in a closed container the moisture in the wood will increase and the wood will swell (Hoadley, 1980), but the change is reversible on warming.

Dimensional changes in wood, due to thermal shrinkage, occur as a result of low temperature; for example wood at a constant 12.8% EMC (similar to EMC in the museum environment) subjected to –20°C shows shrinkage of –0.3% tangentially and –0.1% radially. This shrinkage is due to thermal contraction on the molecular level.

During the freezing process used for eradication of insects the EMC is not constant, the small thermal contraction in dry wood could be overcome by the slight swelling caused by increase in moisture content. The changes are small and do not present a problem.

The findings showed that there is generally an appreciable increase in most strength properties when there is a decrease in temperature and increase in EMC. Embrittlement of the wood occurs only at temperatures much lower than –20°C.

c Adhesives

In heritage objects with glue joints or paper with glued labels etc., there has been a concern about these bonds becoming separated or causing tension under –20°C temperatures (Kite, 1992; Michalski, 1991). Different adhesives respond differently to low temperatures. The following references illustrate these differences.

Table 12.2. Approximate dimensional changes of wood at different moisture contents (after Schirp and Kubler, 1968).

	Moisture content (%)			
	0.1	12.8	43–75	113–114
Tangential (%)				
-20°C	-0.2	-0.3	-0.6	+0.2–0.3
-40°C	-0.3	-0.4	-1.2	+0.2
Radial (%)				
-20°C	-0.1	-0.1	-0.4	-0.2
-40°C	-0.2	-0.3	-0.6	-0.3

Flanders and Tobiasson (1982) tested materials to be used in light-weight air-transportable arctic shelters and showed variable results with adhesives. A urethane-based construction adhesive used for cryogenic containers increased in strength up to –46°C, whereas a urea resin adhesive fell apart at the same temperature. Extrapolation from their graphs shows that the urea resin is still intact at –20°C. The authors also stated that metals and plastics become brittle only at –70°C.

Kubler (1962) showed that in glulam plywood (laminated wood) low temperatures appear to have no appreciable effect on glue line strength down to –65°C using phenol, melamine, resorcinol and casein-based adhesives.

Sulzberger (1953) reported on the effect of low temperatures on the shear strength of casein, urea-formaldehyde and phenol-formaldehyde glue joints at the different moisture contents of 8, 12 and 18% MC. Over the moisture range urea-formaldehyde and phenol-formaldehyde glue joints showed no change in shear strength, whereas casein joints showed a decrease of approximately 10% with increase of moisture content.

MacKenzie (1966) discussed the influence of solute concentration on freezing and stated that gelatin gel containing 35% MC cannot be frozen at all.

Acrylic glues with a high moisture content, used for preparation of herbarium specimens, have been observed to increase in tackiness after the freezing procedure, causing the herbarium sheets to stick to each other. When high moisture adhesives have been used it is imperative to test the freezing treatment on a sample herbarium specimen before doing mass treatments.

d Textiles

Taylor (1978) stated that the behaviour of textiles under low temperatures has been investigated for garments to be used in the arctic and outer space, and that fibres are strongest at the lower temperature and decrease in strength as the temperature increases. Dawley (1993) found no significant effects on new, dry wool subjected to the conservation freezing treatments used to eradicate insects. The yarn was exposed to freeze/thaw cycles and underwent continuous exposure to –25°C for 20, 30 and 60 days. It was then evaluated for tensile strength, extension at break, energy at break, moisture regain, solubility and morphological characteristics observed with scanning electron microscopy.

Okuma *et al.* (1991) tested the strength properties of a number of textile yarns exposed to temperatures from 20 to –50°C. The strength properties of silk, nylon, vinyon and polyester fibres increased with a decrease in temperature, but those of acrylic fibres decreased. They mentioned problems with testing equipment used at the low temperatures. Bulk wool cooled to –50°C and –70°C did not show a phase change. A phase change would indicate freezing of bound water.

e Photographs, motion picture film, paper

The effects of freeze/thaw cycling on motion picture films have been investigated. Empirical results of film stored at –20°C in heat-sealed, foil bags that were equilibrated to 50% RH showed that there were no adverse effects on the image stability of the film, based on annual inspections over a 10-year period. Experiments testing changes in wedge brittleness, mushiness and wet and dry adhesive tests showed no adverse effects on films put in heat-sealed, foil bags at 25–35% RH, stored in a taped film can at −12 to −15°C, after 6 months of daily cycling of thawing for 4 hours.

Hendriks and Morrow (1985) tested freezing on dry and wet photographs and negatives. The results showed adverse effects when wet material was frozen but no change when dry material was frozen.

The Swedish National Testing Institute (Antonsson and Samuelsson, 1996) tested three cotton/flax rag papers and three different types of chemical pulps papers from the period of 1910–1921. The tests were undertaken for M. Akerlund at the Swedish Museum of Natural History, Uppsala University. The results showed that repeated treatment of the freeze/thaw cycles did not decrease the folding endurance of the papers immediately after the treatment or after artificial aging of the treated paper.

f *Polymers*

The majority of polymers have low water permeability and regain, thus are basically non-adsorbent materials. In most cases they would not be damaged by insects. In cases where they are a part of a composite object which requires freezing treatment, precautions should be taken because some do become brittle on cooling.

Hartwig (1978) described brittleness in polymers: 'the chains of amorphous polymers are entangled. At low temperatures (much below −20°C) most degrees of freedom are frozen; the chains, therefore become stiff'. Under load without normal plastic flow, brittle fractures occur. It is important to realize that this brittleness is reversible on warming.

Kreibich *et al.* (1979) compared strength differences of a group of polymers and reported that polyethylene shows good flexibility, but polyvinyl chloride and cross-linked epoxy resin systems are brittle at low temperatures (200–400K [253K = −20°C]).

The stiffening point of most of the elastomers (rubber, latex except butyl, neoprene, fluorocarbon and polyurethane) is below −20°C, and the brittle point of all is below −50°C (Sehgal and Lindberg, 1973).

Street (1977) studied fibre composite materials in an arctic environment and explained that materials selected for arctic use today have to be strong and stiff materials at low temperatures and be resistant to thermal fatigue and freeze/thaw cracking, with top priority on toughness and low brittle failure. Fibre reinforced plastics, i.e. glass fibre-epoxy, get stronger and stiffer as the temperature decreases. Thermal contraction of glass fibre-epoxy is greatest at right angles to the fibre orientation and increases with decrease of temperature. The contractions at −20°C are extremely small, in the order of 10^{-4}. These fibre materials are used to replace brittle-matrix materials such as cement, concrete and ice which tend to fracture easily at low temperatures.

Strang (1995) wrote: 'polymeric materials do become stiffer and more brittle at low temperatures. The thermal response of coating is well characterized. Drying oil films have a glassy behaviour below −30°C and a glassy/rubbery transition between −30 and 0°C. Acrylics used in most paint formulations are glassy below 0°C and are leathery between 0 and 50°C (Michalski, 1991). This leads to the recommendation against the low temperature treatment of oil and acrylic paintings on canvas because of the increased brittleness in the image layer; these brittle layers may not fracture on their own, but will be vulnerable to external physical shock. If the risks associated with cold temperatures can be minimized by ensuring, for example, safe handling, then cold temperatures can be a viable method of pest control. Resin varnishes and glue have transitions higher than acrylic and are already glassy at room temperature and medium humidities. Therefore, assemblies with glued joints are of less concern than paint layers'.

The above information suggests that heritage objects, which contain polymeric materials, i.e. paintings and glued joints, treated with sub-zero temperatures become more vulnerable to physical shock, when cold, because of increase in stiffness or brittleness. Michalski (1991) brings to our attention that the risk associated with sub-zero temperatures can be minimized by ensuring safe handling. The brittleness is reversed on warming.

g *Seeds*

The preservation of seeds for future research and particularly plant breeding is of great importance. Special seed banks have been established, but rarely do they include weed or non-horticultural endemic species which would normally be present in native plant herbariums. Thus the freezing of plant material with seeds needs to be assessed independently.

A great deal of information is available on the effect of freezing on the viability of seeds, but this has not been reviewed for this book. The effects are variable and the important point is that some seeds will have drastic reduction of viability or germination percentage and others will have enhanced germination rates.

To give one example of the complexity of freezing seeds and viability, Scott (1923) reported on the relationship between the moisture content and viability of seed corn when subjected to low temperatures and concluded from his tests that corn seed with a moisture content of 30% are damaged on freezing at −12°C for 12 hours, and as the moisture content of the seed increases the damage is greater.

h *Summary of effects of subzero temperatures on the physical characteristics of dry organic material of heritage objects*

Inorganic materials that are not biodegradable would rarely be treated by freezing, i.e. metals, ceramics, glass etc. The group vulnerable to biodegradation includes the organic materials, textiles, wood, plastics and materials of animal (horn, baleen, feathers, etc.) and plant (leaves, seeds, fibres, etc.) origin.

With reference to wood, a decrease in freezing temperatures causes an increase in strength characteristics. Also, an increase in moisture content increases these strength characteristics. Swelling of wood will occur if an increase of moisture content accompanies temperature decrease. The physical changes caused by reduced temperature are minimal and reversible.

Most plastics, on cooling, will become brittle but not significantly at −20°C. Thermal brittleness is reversible.

Seed viability or germination percentage may be altered by freezing. The preservation of seeds for future research and particularly plant breeding is of great importance. Special seed banks have been established but rarely do they include seed from weed or non-horticultural endemic species that would be collected for native flora herbariums. Thus the freezing of herbarium plant material with seeds needs to be assessed independently.

12.1.2.3 SUMMARY OF EFFECTS OF SUB-ZERO TEMPERATURES ON DRY ADSORBENT ORGANIC MATERIALS IN A CLOSED PLASTIC BAG

1. Water in dry heritage objects made of adsorbent organic materials which have a moisture content in equilibrium with an ambient temperature of 15–20°C and up to 65% RH will not freeze at –20°C, thus ice damage cannot occur.
2. The procedures for freezing require that the object is placed in a clear (for visibility and low permeability) polyethylene bag. Then the bag is evacuated and sealed, before being placed in the freezer. This procedure prevents any dramatic moisture content changes which would cause dimensional changes due to swelling or shrinkage, as well as condensation forming on the object while in the freezer. The bagged object is placed in the chest freezer which is at –20 to –30°C for 72 hours. The procedures also specify that the object, after it has been removed from the freezer, should not be removed from the bag until it has reached room temperature. This procedure prevents condensation on the object.
3. Water vapour in the air in the bag with an artifact will not freeze at –20°C. If the air in the bag is filled with dust there may be some ice formed around –27°C.
4. Reducing the temperature of the air in the bag decreases its holding capacity. The adsorbent materials will adsorb the excess water, released by the cooling air, according to their regain ability. Thus condensation will not occur on the materials. The moisture content of the adsorbent materials will increase. The amount of water available for adsorption is small in comparison to the amount that can be adsorbed. Museum objects made of non-adsorbent materials should not be subjected to freezing because they cannot adsorb the excess water vapour and it will condense or form frost on the surface.
5. If the moisture regain of the material is in doubt, condensation can be prevented by eliminating the air through partial evacuation or vacuum-packaging, if the object is stable, or by controlling the RH of the cooling air with buffering adsorbent materials.
6. Research is needed to determine the regain ability or the amount and rate of adsorbancy of materials at below freezing temperatures, but regain does occur at –20°C and the rate is determined by the vapour pressure of the water in the materials.
7. Strength changes of wood, wood adhesives and polymers generally increase with a decrease of temperature and these strength changes are reversible on warming. The increase may be a reflection of the increase in moisture content. Minor (less than 1%) isodiametric thermal shrinkage and swelling of wood may occur during the freezing process but it is reversible. Acrylic adhesives with high moisture content do increase in tackiness, but this is lost after time.
8. Dry paper, textiles, photographs and films are not changed by sub-zero temperatures.
9. Non-adsorbent materials may become brittle at freezing temperatures, but –20 to –30°C is not sufficiently cold to make a permanent change. Also, it is immediately reversible on warming. If polymers become brittle with the treatment, special precautions in handling the objects must be taken.
10. Seed germination rates and viability are influenced by freezing. The freezing of herbarium materials, where the viability of seeds is a concern, needs to be assessed individually.
11. If dense materials are treated or the freezer is filled to capacity, the cooling rates of the material must be determined in order to ensure that the insects are held at the minimum lethal temperature for the right length of time (–20 to –30°C for 72 hours). Thermocouples or thermistor probes are recommended to monitor the temperature reduction of the museum object. Most materials if spaced well will reach 0°C, which is below the chill-coma temperature of insects, in less than 1 hour.

12.1.3 Heat treatment

Strang (1992, 1995) suggested that high temperatures, as well as low temperatures, are effective methods of eradication of insect pests in infested heritage objects. The information he presents for low temperatures is reviewed in section 12.1.1.

Strang (1992) has done an excellent job of collating information in heat eradication reports. The reports must be reviewed carefully if they are going to influence us in establishing heat eradication methods. The majority of the references are prior to the 1950s and many are experiences with heating buildings or storage rooms. They give temperatures which were feasible in heating the buildings and nothing in reference to the lethal high temperature of the target insects. For example, of the six references to clothes moths, the variations were 74 to 77°C for 5 hours, 72°C for 4 minutes, 60°C for 4 hours, 54°C for a short time, 49°C for 11 minutes and 48°C for 12 minutes. That is a broad range of temperatures and times. Proteins, lipids and DNA in insects are permanently damaged around 55°C, thus higher temperatures may be illogical, as long as the material treated reaches this temperature.

Strang (1995) and Michalski (1991) reviewed the high temperature effects on materials, some theoretical and some factual. Strang (1995) reported on heat treatments that have been used for clothes, herbarium specimens, wooden objects and buildings. Strang (1995) says: 'In spite of this extensive usage, these techniques [he refers to low and high temperature treatments] cannot be used carelessly, as they pose risks to certain museum objects, melting of materials, accelerated chemical deterioration at high temperatures, physical deterioration at high temperatures, changes in moisture content, dimensional changes due to heating and cooling in wood, dimensional changes in textiles and mould risk associated with bagged objects'.

We are early in the process of recommending this treatment as a mass treatment for insect pest eradication. Research is needed on the heat effects on materials, especially the moisture relationships, and research is needed on the lethal high temperatures on the insects themselves.

There is encouraging insect physiology literature which suggests that heat treatments may be done quickly and at moderate temperatures.

Denlinger *et al.* (1991) explained that with the flesh fly, a short heat shock (two hours at 45°C) can cause incomplete development of treated insects but a severe heat shock (one hours at 50°C) can be immediately lethal. After the short heat shock, thermoprotection occurs by the formation of heat-shock proteins (Chen *et al.* 1991).

Denlinger *et al.* (1991) reported that heat-hardening, like cold-hardening, also occurs. After a pretreatment of 2 hours at 40°C, before exposure to the extreme high temperature, there was about 85% survival after 120 minutes, whereas there were no survivors without pretreatment. The lethal effects of heat are time/temperature dependent thus a longer time would be required to overcome heat-hardening.

Vannier (1994) discussed the range of temperature tolerances of freeze-intolerant (freeze-sensitive) insect species. From his work he suggested that the thermobiological span (TBS), the number of degrees between the supercooling point (SCP) and the thermostupor point (TSP), may be a practical tool for comparison of insects of different origins. SCP is the point that the body fluid freezes, it is much lower than the lethal low temperature. TSP is the high temperature at which the insect becomes motionless. Thermal death immediately follows, which may be caused by protein denaturation and lipid melting.

The parameters of the test were extreme. The RH was maintained at 0% with silica gel and the temperature increase was 0.5°C per minute starting at 20°C. There were 40 insects for each test. It took an average of 1 hour to reach the termination of the experiment. Table 12.3 gives a list of these points of some freeze-intolerant insect species.

There are two significant findings in this work which are applicable to eradication methods of insects in heritage objects.

The first is the difference in the range of temperatures to reach TSP or SCP. The temperature range in which TSP was reached is significantly narrower than the range for SCP, i.e. the clothes moth larvae TSP range is 5° (47.5 to 52.5°C) and SCP is 20° (–24.5 to –5.5°C).

The second finding is the difference in range to reach SCP of the larvae and adults. There is much more variability in the larvae.

The TBS is like an identification card for freezing-intolerant species. The absolute range between SCP and TSP reflects the potential adaptive capacity of a species to withstand cooling or overheating in its environment. This may be a way of categorizing the insect pests in heritage objects to better understand their temperature tolerances. In the series of insects in Table 12.3, the saw-toothed grain beetle has the greatest resistance (the widest TBS range) and the collembolan springtail the least (the narrowest TBS range) to temperature extremes.

The biology of insects suggests that they are, indeed, vulnerable to temperatures around 50°C. The response is fast and the range of response is small, thus it looks like an excellent approach to eradication. We must look to the biology of our heritage eaters and devise logical methods of eradication.

There have been other heat-related methods reported in the conservation literature, e.g. microwave, infrared lamps used for insect eradication. Microwave ovens pose a threat of burns if, by chance, any metal fragments, pins or paper clips are in the materials. Volatile materials (resins) may cause minor explosions, some glues (acrylics) are not heat stable and bound water may be lost from organic materials. More research is needed; if these methods are to be used for treatment they must not damage the material of the object and they must be effective against the target insect. Remember our heritage objects are often priceless.

12.2 ANOXIC ATMOSPHERE FOR ERADICATION OF INSECT HERITAGE EATERS

12.2.1 Introduction

Air contains approximately 21% oxygen (O_2), 78% nitrogen (N_2), 0.9% argon and 0.03% carbon dioxide (CO_2) by volume. Anoxic or altered atmosphere treatment for eradication of insect pests involves the alteration of the proportions of these normal atmospheric gases to give a lethal atmosphere. The term 'anoxic' is used because the altered atmospheric gases have a reduced amount of oxygen.

In the history of grain storage, ground-buried pits or silos were used because they were easily made airtight. Airtightness was the significant factor in successful grain preservation. This allowed the atmospheric gases in the silo to be modified by the respiration of insects and micro-organisms, lowering the amount of oxygen and increasing the amount of carbon dioxide. Temperatures between 18 and 20°C were needed initially for biological activity. In such cases where airtightness had been obtained, almost complete kill of the insects occurred after 3 weeks (Shejbal, 1980). This is the basis of commercially controlled atmosphere storage, but instead of letting respiring organisms modify the atmospheric gas, a prescribed gas or mixture of gases is mechanically introduced into the silo or storage bin. An anoxic atmosphere has also been shown to enhance some conventional insecticides (Friedlander and Silhacek, 1983). Benefits from microbial eradication have also been reported in this storage method (Busta *et al.*, 1980; Di Maggio, 1980; Pelhate, 1980; Richard-Molard *et al.*, 1980; Serofini *et al.*, 1980).

Navarro and Calderon (1980) have shown that the success of the altered atmospheric gas system requires an integrated approach and not only is the toxicity of the gas important but also the exposure time, the temperature and relative humidity.

In the review article by Bailey and Banks (1980) on the use of altered atmospheres for insect eradication, the general conclusions are the following.

Table 12.3. Measurements of thermostupor point (TSP) mean and range, supercooling point (SCP) mean and range, and thermobiological span (TBS) between the two temperature extremes.

Species (adults except #2)	TSP (range)	SCP (range)	TBS
1. Saw-toothed grain beetle (*Oryzaephilus surinamensis*)	+55.4(4°)	-19.0(10°)	79.3*
2. Clothes moth (larvae) (*Tineola bisselliella*)	+50.0(5°)	-13.0(20°)	76.1*
3. Lacewing (*Nineta pallida*)	+46.9	-24.9	71.7
4. Springtail (*Orchesells villosa*)	+44.9(7°)	-9.0(11°)	64.2*
5. Collembolan springtail (*Caledonimeria mirabilis*)	+44.4	-8.0	52.4

* TBS includes mean of standard deviations. (Species 1, 2, and 4 (Vannier, 1994); species 3 (Vannier and Canard, 1989); and species 5 (Vannier and Najt, 1991).

1. The susceptibility of the insects varies substantially between species and between the different developmental stages, requiring different time exposures.
2. The gases are lethal to all life stages (egg, larva, pupa and adult) of the common stored grain insects.
3. The effectiveness of the gas is increased with an increase of temperature and a decrease in humidity.
4. Sublethal exposures may lead to developmental abnormalities.
5. There is a synergistic effect between low oxygen and carbon dioxide in some cases.

12.2.2 Review of some entomological research

The synergistic response between O_2 and CO_2 is reported

Bailey and Banks (1980) reported that at low oxygen levels the presence of a small percentage of carbon dioxide accelerates the lethal action of the atmosphere compared with a pure nitrogen–oxygen mixture. Calderon and Navarro (1979) reported that the time for mortality of adult stored grain beetles, *Tribolium castaneum*, was dependent on the quantity of carbon dioxide also present. For example, at 2% O_2, 90% mortality was reached with 5% CO_2 in 5 days but with 40% CO_2, in 1 day.

Weight loss is consistent with lethal treatments

Jay and Cuff (1981) compared four modified atmospheric gas combinations on the mortality and weight loss of larvae, pupae and adults of *Tribolium castaneum*. The results showed that at a constant RH of 50% and 27°C weight loss occurred in 72 hours with all treatments, the greatest weight losses were consistent with the greatest mortality.

Jay and Cuff (1981) also showed that by using the combination of 99% N_2, 0.6–1.2% O_2 and no CO_2, 100% kills of larvae, pupae and adults of *T. castaneum* were obtained in 72 hours, whereas with 97% N_2, 2.1–3.1% O_2 and no CO_2 kills of 25% pupae, 12% larvae and 0.8% adults occurred in 72 hours. Technically pure nitrogen may have up to 0.5% oxygen.

It has been demonstrated that temperature increase and RH decrease influence the lethal conditions

Rust and Kennedy (1993) showed that mortality was reached in 80 hours for all stages of *Drosophila melanogaster* subjected to 100% nitrogen at RH 75% and 25°C, and at RH 40% and 30°C in 28 hours. This showed that decreasing RH and increasing temperature shortened the time of treatment.

Jay *et al.* (1971) showed that with all treatments a reduction in relative humidity decreased the time of treatment for mortality.

Treatments stop feeding

In treatments of actively feeding insect infestations, it is imperative to stop the damage quickly. Soderstrom and Brandl (1982) found that feeding had stopped within 20 hours using modified atmospheres containing 1%, or less, O_2 for larvae of the Navel orange worm and the Indian meal moth.

Besides interfering with respiration rates, increased concentrations of carbon dioxide in the atmosphere are toxic.

Friedlander and Silhacek (1983) reported on the biochemical effects of CO_2 on insects. It was found that in oxidative respiration, 6-phosphogluconate dehydrogenase, a key enzyme, was inhibited by 10% CO_2. Their data indicate that susceptibility to CO_2 treatments seems to rely on the total mitochondrial oxidative capacity of insects.

Although the method of using CO_2 is regarded as non-chemical, this is evidence that CO_2 has significant biochemical effects and acts as a respiratory toxin.

In summary

The anoxic treatment must kill the insect adult, larva, pupa and egg. Even though there are many different insect species and stages involved in the research cited above, the basic biological phenomenon is the same. There may be more resistance of one species because of a morphological advantage, or a diapause stage with a low oxygen requirement. But there is always a need for oxygen in aerobic respiration, which is identical in all insect species.

The information from the limited literature review suggests that for maximum efficiency of insect pest eradication, the combination of low oxygen and an increase in carbon dioxide content of the treatment air, as well as an increase in temperature and a decrease in relative humidity from the ambient air would be most effective in increasing the rate of mortality.

Presently research on combinations of altered atmospheric gases and temperature extremes as a means of insect eradication is ongoing (Denlinger, 1996).

12.2.3 The influence of oxygen, carbon dioxide and nitrogen on spiracular valve opening

The most important aspect of survival for insects is retaining their body water. The opening and closing of the spiracular valves not only allows air movement in and out of the insect but also water vapour (see chapter 5). Fluttering of the spiracular valves is considered a method of preventing water loss. The spiracle opens when the concentration of oxygen is lower and carbon dioxide is higher in the body fluid than in normal atmospheric air. In research on altered atmospheres, it is well established that both a decrease in oxygen and increase in carbon dioxide and pure nitrogen causes the spiracles to open. However in insects, protection against dehydration has priority over concentrations of gases. Hydrated dragon flies in 2% carbon dioxide keep the spiracles open to eliminate the excess carbon dioxide, but if the insects are dehydrated the spiracles close.

Figure 12.3 shows that in air with an increase (15%) in carbon dioxide, increases in RH increase the rate of water loss in tsetse flies. Water loss is often considered the lethal condition, not toxicity of carbon dioxide

A 2.0% concentration of carbon dioxide is sufficient to produce sustained opening of the spiracles of adults of *Xenopsylla cheopis*, and larvae of *Tenebrio molitor* and *Tineola bisselliella*, but the same effect can be obtained by reducing oxygen concentrations below 1%. In the tsetse fly the threshold concentration of carbon dioxide for sustained opening depends on the physiological state of the insect, for example levels of 8% for one-day old and 20% for four-day old flies were required for lethal effects.

During oxygen depletion and anaerobic respiration in the insect, lactic acid accumulates which can also stimulate the spiracles to open. An increase in carbon dioxide may cause body fluids to become acidic, which has been suggested to

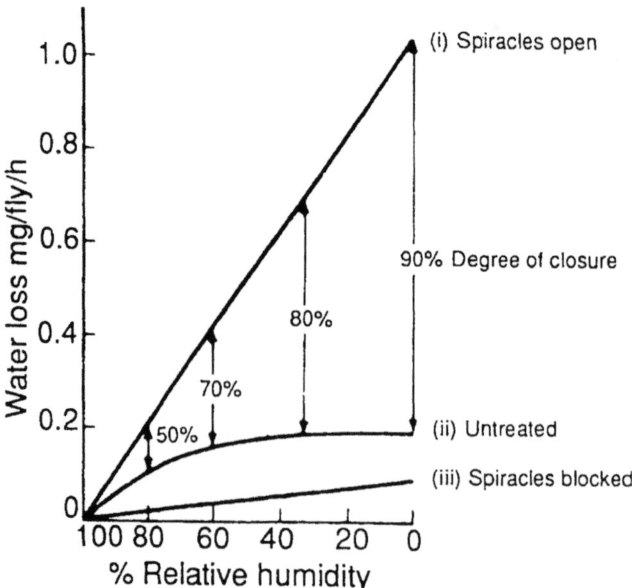

Figure 12.3. The rate of water loss from tsetse flies at different relative humidities (i) in air containing 15% CO_2, (ii) in air, and (iii) in air with spiracles blocked. The deduced degree of effective closures of the spiracles is indicated at four different levels of humidity (from Bursell, 1970).

trigger opening of the spiracles. Because carbon dioxide is more soluble in the haemolymph than oxygen, it may be the major initiator of spiracle response.

Carbon dioxide and nitrogen have been used to keep the spiracles open and enhance the effect of some fumigants.

For further information, see Nikan and Knole (1989) and chapter 5 of this book.

12.2.4 What is the cause of death under altered atmospheric gases?

The research on lethal conditions using different concentrations of atmospheric gases (carbon dioxide, nitrogen and oxygen) for eradication of insect pests, does not report on the cause of death. The research simply reports on its lethal effectiveness. Death can occur by dehydration, increased acidity due to lactic acid or carbon dioxide concentrations in the body fluids or lack of chemical energy for metabolic processes. Treatments have included: low or no oxygen; an increase in, or pure, carbon dioxide; or pure nitrogen. All of these would cause the spiracles to open, suggesting that dehydration is the most likely cause of death. Jay *et al.* (1971) showed that by using less than 0.1% oxygen and 38% carbon dioxide the increase in mortality with decrease in relative humidity was largely from desiccation.

It has been reported (Kukal *et al.*, 1991) that diapausing pupae of the flesh fly can withstand 14 days of anoxic treatment but cannot proceed from the pupal to adult stage. This same effect occurred after only 3 days of treatment with the non-diapausing pupae. This shows an effect on development, but the cause is not clear. It also shows that the diapausing pupa is more resistant to anoxic conditions than the non-diapausing state, a result of different oxygen and water demands.

There was also a marked increase in production of glycerol and alanine in both pupal types. In reviewing the effects of high and low temperature on insects (section 12.1), it was found that these chemicals also accumulate, suggesting a common response to different stresses. Glycerol has a role in preventing ice formation but it also alters the vapour pressure of cellular water, and alanine protects enzymes. In fungi, glycerol is synthesized under stress to tie up water molecularly to prevent water loss, to store water internally and to accumulate water in the substrate. The common response, the formation of glycerol, to all of these environmental stresses (freezing, heating and anoxia) by insects and fungi, is clearly protection against dehydration.

12.2.5 How long can insects live using anaerobic respiration?

The ability of the heritage-eating insects to go into diapause and low oxygen consumption, and to survive eradication by altered atmospheric gas conditions is a concern in their control.

There are some specialized insects, not among common museum or household pests, that can withstand low oxygen levels (2–5% compared with the 21% in air) for long periods of time. Research has still not explained how they maintain life functions at such low levels but there are some hints.

Metabolic respiration is a complex process. Simplistically, it is a sequence of chemical reactions in which glucose is broken down to produce chemical energy called adenosine triphoshate (ATP) for cell metabolic functions. Body cells don't use oxygen for energy – it is ATP that is the body fuel.

In oxidative respiration there are three groups of cyclic reactions: anaerobic, the Krebs cycle and the electron transfer system.

In the sequence of chemical reactions of oxidative respiration the first group does not require oxygen, thus is anaerobic. In these reactions a molecule of glucose is converted to pyruvic acid and six ATP molecules.

If oxygen is present the pyruvic acid enters the Krebs cycle and electron transport system, and is finally converted to 38 molecules of ATP, and carbon dioxide. However, if there is no oxygen, under anaerobic respiration, the pyruvic acid is converted back to glucose, but less than the original amount, which will again be converted to pyruvic acid and produce six molecules of ATP for limited cell functions. This backwards anaerobic cycle soon runs out but the six ATP molecules keep life going, giving the insect a chance to respond to the adverse situation by a feedback mechanism which produces glycerol, alanine, or other polyols, until oxygen becomes available.

Resistance to lack of oxygen occurs in insects of all kinds. Adult house flies can live without external oxygen for up to 12–15 hours and the insect *Gasterophilus* sp, which lives as a parasite in a horse's stomach, can withstand up to 17 days in the complete absence of oxygen. These insects accomplish this by temporary anaerobic respiration.

Chitin is the structural chemical in the exoskeleton of insects and the cell wall of hyphae of fungi. It is a strong chelator of metals and it has been reported, in fungi, to chelate oxygen as well. There is no report on its role in anoxic environments.

12.2.6 Do altered atmospheric gases influence the materials of the heritage objects?

Atmospheric gases at different concentrations than are present in the air must influence both the insects and the materials of heritage objects. Under anoxic conditions the oxidation state will change to a reducing environment. Carbon dioxide levels altered from the normal air concentration of 0.03% to higher concentrations will change the acid/base balance. This is a concern with grain (Storey, 1980). Yamamoto and Mitsuda (1980) reported that proteins in grain treated in silos with carbon dioxide absorbed the gas, but nearly all the gas was desorbed. We think of argon as being inert but it acts as a catalyst with iron to increase photooxidation reactions.There has been no definitive research on the effects of these gases on artifact materials. There are suggestions in the conservation literature that anoxic eradication treatments do not cause any damage, but these are only from visual observations. The chemical and physical effects of the treatment on the materials of the heritage objects must be researched.

12.2.7 Anoxic atmosphere treatment used to eradicate heritage-eating insects

12.2.7.1 The researchers

Since Gilberg's 1989 work with anoxic environments to eradicate insects in heritage objects, there has been a great deal of interest in the potential of this treatment and all of the following references report successful results (Daniel *et al.*, 1992, 1993; Daniel and Hanlon, 1995; Gilberg, 1989, 1990, 1991, 1993; Gilberg and Roach, 1993; Grattan and Gilberg, 1994; Hanlon *et al.*, 1992; Koestler, 1992, 1993, 1995; Rust and Kennedy, 1993; Valentin, 1990; Valentin and Preusser, 1990a, 1990b; Valentin *et al.*, 1992;).

Valentin and Preusser (1990b) have used an anoxic atmosphere for micro-organism control in heritage objects.

Burke (1993) gave an excellent review of all the current methods of insect eradication and discussed the research with anoxic atmosphere eradication at different museums.

12.2.7.2 The method

Anoxic atmosphere treatment is simply sealing the infested object in a gas impermeable container which contains the anoxic gas. The anoxic atmosphere can be accomplished by: removing the oxygen with an absorber, replacing the normal air with 100% carbon dioxide, argon or nitrogen, or by using a combination of carbon dioxide and nitrogen in place of the air.

Valentin *et al.* (1992) compared the lethal effectiveness of the three gases and reported that argon was most effective in a shorter time.

12.2.7.3 Enclosures: bags, bubbles, rooms and vacuum chambers

There are several approaches to enclosures. Gilberg (1989, 1990, 1993) and Grattan and Gilberg (1994) suggested small custom-made bags and the introduction of an oxygen absorber into the bag with the object. An anoxic environment, less than 0.1% oxygen, is reached and by using internal oxygen and RH indicators, the internal environment can be monitored. Special caution has to be taken to eliminate the hazard of the temperature increase caused by the exothermic reaction of oxygen absorption (Gilberg, 1990). These types of bag can also be continually flushed with a low nitrogen flow or flushed with oxygen and an oxygen absorber added. The plastic bags are made of a clear high gas barrier plastic laminate (Burke, 1992).

Another approach is bagging the object *in situ* with a high gas barrier plastic bubble and replacing the air with 100% nitrogen or argon. This method allows large objects to be treated without moving them. In the most recent tests, the gases are drawn through water to reach near 50% RH and the temperature of the enclosure controlled to ambient room temperatures. Gases in cylinders are at 0% RH and when they expand they are extremely cold. There is concern about maintaining ambient RH and temperature when treating heritage objects, but the use of slight changes may decrease greatly the time of treatment, which would be a great advantage. A polyethylene bubble has been developed commercially.

Koestler and Mathews (1994) discussed bagging a room full of documents using argon and the high gas barrier plastic.

Koestler (1995) realistically presented costs of undertaking anoxic eradication methods. Soft-walled bagging units would be custom-made and can cost from US$20,000–40,000 and hard-walled chambers require US$100,000–200,000.

G size cylinders of gas (about 4.5 cubic metres) range from US$15 for carbon dioxide, $20 for nitrogen, $40 for argon and $50 for helium. The amount needed would depend on the volume of the bagging or chamber system and whether it is just filled or requires continuous flow.

Other methods (Daniel and Hanlon, 1995) involve putting heritage objects into old fumigation vacuum chambers and evacuating the air and replacing it with the desired gas mixture, usually 100% nitrogen, to obtain a low oxygen (0.1%) level.

They suggest refurbishing the old vacuum chambers used in the past for ethylene oxide fumigation. Conversion for anoxic methods requires that they are leak-proof to maintain the low oxygen levels. At the Royal British Columbia Museum such a unit was found to lose internal pressure within 2 days.

12.2.7.4 The time factor

Most entomological research reports mortality in less than 4 days, yet the anoxic treatments for conservation require 20 days. However, if the equipment is airtight, less time should be required, even taking into consideration the density of materials. The density of the materials may not be an issue because if insects are living within, there is access to atmospheric gases.

A long treatment of 20 days is a logistic nightmare for busy museums that are involved in the general flow of objects coming in as new accessions, going in or out as loans, preparing for exhibit and continual inspection of collections, all of which may require some means of eradication of infestations or suspect infestations.

A responsible conservator, knowing the damage an active infestation can do in a day, could not ethically allow damage to occur for even a day. There is a suggestion that insects stop feeding after several days of anoxic treatment, but research is needed.

12.2.7.5 Case study: a failed experiment

It is interesting that the published literature always reports successes. At the Royal British Columbia Museum, an unpublished internal report dated December 1986, shows that the attempts of trying to kill insects by pure nitrogen in a commercial fumigation chamber failed miserably. Colonies of white fly, fruit fly, flour weevil and hide beetle were grown in 0.3 cubic meter portable cages. The cages appeared insect-proof because over the period of several months the insects never left the colony or escaped.

For the nitrogen tests the walk-in vacuum chamber, which had been adapted to use nitrogen, had been warmed to 20°C and was at 33% RH. The low RH was the nature of the cold metal chamber. The cages were transported to the chamber and the moment the cages were put on the floor of the chamber, the grain weevils escaped their cage and scattered. There was a great rush to close the chamber door. Two experiments were undertaken, one experiment of 48 hours with supposedly 100% nitrogen, in which all insects survived except those grain weevils which had escaped their colony; they were found dead on the floor. The second experiment was 21 days of supposedly 100% nitrogen, after which the flour weevils and hide beetles were alive. The pressure which was reached with the introduction of the nitrogen was lost during the treatment after 48 hours indicating a leak in the exhaust of the system.

There are several things which can be learned from this failed experiment. First, in dealing with infestations, it is essential that they are bagged or isolated prior to treatment. Infestations, when they are moved, have to be enclosed to prevent contamination of adjacent objects and areas.

The second and most important point is the question: Why did the insects that died, die? It wasn't the nitrogen because this escaped (monitoring methods are now used to determine the concentrations of the enclosed gases). If it wasn't the nitrogen it must have been the environment of the chamber. There are empirical reports that state that just bagging an infestation and leaving it for several weeks will kill it. It is difficult to culture insects. The natural history staff culture the hide beetle to clean skeletal material. These insects are very sensitive to environmental changes and it is always a battle to keep the temperature and moisture content in the materials just right for their activity. Any movement of an infestation will result in some environmental change. It is imperative for experiments on anoxic treatments that the environmental changes which the insects undergo are recorded and that the control insects have gone through the same environmental changes. One of the most difficult things in experiments with insects is to get valid controls.

12.2.7.6 *Final comments*

Many entomological research projects suggest that the death of the insect, whether under temperature extremes or anoxic conditions, may be due to dehydration. If this is the case there may be much simpler methods than using anoxic gases.

The equipment for anoxic treatments using controlled RH and temperature is expensive, but it has great potential for treating large objects and rooms full of archival materials. The small bags with the oxygen absorber have great potential for small objects.

REFERENCES

References for *Freezing insect pests in heritage objects for disinfestation and eradication*

Asahina, E. 1966. Freezing and frost resistance in insects. In *Cryobiology*, Ed. T. Meryman. Academic Press, London: New York. pp451–486.

Baust, J. G. and R.E. Morrissey. 1975. Supercooling phenomenon and water content independence in the overwintering beetle, *Coleomegilla maculata. Journal of Insect Physiology*, 21:1751–1754.

Baust, J.G. and R.R. Rojas. 1985. Review-insect cold hardiness: facts and fancy. *Journal of Insect Physiology*, 31(10):755–759.

Billings, C.J. 1983. Insect control by freezing. Correspondence, April 25,1983.

Brokerhof, A.W. and H.J. Banks. 1993. Cold tolerance of *Tineola bisselliella* (Lepidoptera: Tineidae) eggs at a slow cooling rate. *Journal of Stored Products Research*, 29(4):305–310.

Brokerhof, A.W., H.J. Banks and R. Morton. 1992. A model for time-temperature relationships for eggs of the webbing clothes moth, *Tineola bisselliella* (Lepidoptera: Tineidae), exposed to cold. *Journal of Stored Products Research*, 28:269–177.

Brokerhof, A.W., R. Morton and H.J. Banks. 1993. Time-mortality relationships for different species and development stages of clothes moths (Lepidoptera: Tineidae), exposed to cold. *Journal of Stored Products Research*, 29(3):277–282.

Chen C., D. L. Denlinger and R.E. Lee. 1987. Cold-shock injury and rapid cold-hardening in the flesh fly *Sacophaga crassipalpis. Physiological Zoology*, 60:297–304.

Chen C., R.E. Lee and D. Denlinger. 1990. The comparison of the responses of tropical and temperate flies (Diptera: Sacophagidae) to cold and heat stress. *Journal of Comparative Physiology*, B 160:541–547.

Chen C., R.E. Lee and D. Denlinger. 1991. Cold-shock and heat shock: comparison of the protection generated by brief pretreatment at less severe temperatures. *Physiological Entomology*, 16:19–26.

Crisafulli,S. 1980. Herbarium insect control with a freezer. *Brittonia*, 32(2):224.

Davenport, J. 1992. *Animals at Low Temperatures*. Chapman and Hall, New York.

Dawson, J.E. 1987. *A Review of the Use of Freezing/Low Temperature in Insect Control*. Department of Communications, Canadian Conservation Institute, EDR Report No. 1266, p5.

Denlinger, D.L. 1991. Relationship between cold hardiness and diapause. In *Insects at Low Temperatures*, Eds. R.E. Lee and D.L. Denlinger. Chapman and Hall, London, pp174–198.

Denlinger, D.L. 1996. Personal communication. Professor, Department of Entomology, Ohio State University, Columbus, Ohio.

Florian, M-L.E. 1978. Biodeterioration of museum objects. *Museum Round-up*. Autumn, pp35–43, British Columbia Museum Association, Victoria, B.C., Can.

Florian, M-L.E. 1986. The freezing process – effects on insects and artifact materials. *Leather Conservation Newsletter*, 3(1):1–13 and 17.

Florian, M.-L. E. 1988. Ethylene oxide fumigation, a literature review of the problems and interaction with materials and substances in artifacts. *In A Guide to Museum Pest Control*, Eds. L.A. Zycherman and J.R. Schrock. FAIC and Assoc. Systematics Collections, pp151–158.

Florian, M-L. 1989. Integrated system approach to insect pest control: an alternative to fumigation. In *Proceedings of the International Conservation in Archives, Ottawa, May 10–12, 1988*, pp253–262.

Florian, M-L.E. 1992. Saga of the saggy bag. *Leather Conservation News*, 8:1–11.

Gilberg, M. and Brokerhof. 1991. The control of insect pests in museum collections: The effects of low temperature on *Stegobium paniceum*

(Linnaeus), the drugstore beetle. *Journal of the American Institute of Conservation*, 30(2):197–201.

Hinton, H.E. 1960. A fly larvae that tolerates dehydration and temperatures of –270°C to +102°C. *Nature*, 188:336–337.

Howard, L.O. 1896. Some temperature effects on household insects. *US Bureau of Entomology Bull. Series 6*, pp13–17.

Karow, A.M. and W.R. Webb. 1965. Tissue freezing. *Cryobiology*, 2(3):99–108.

Ketcham-Troszak, J.K. 1984. Investigation into freezing as an alternative method of disinfesting proteinaceous artifacts: The effects of subfreezing temperatures on *Dermestes maculatus* Degeer (Coleoptera: Dermestidae). Queen's University M.A. Thesis. Nov. 26, 1984, Kingston, Ontario, Canada.

Lee, R.E. 1989. Insect cold-hardiness: to freeze or not to freeze. How insects survive low temperatures. *Bioscience*, 39(5):308–312.

Lee, R.E. 1991. Principles of insect low temperature tolerance. In *Insects at Low Temperature*, Eds R.E. Lee and D.L. Denlinger. Chapman and Hall, New York, pp17–46.

Lee, R.E. and D. Denlinger. 1985. Cold tolerance in diapausing and non-diapausing stages of the flesh fly, *Sarcophaga crassipalpis*. *Physiological Entomology*, 10:309–315.

Lee, R.E., C. Chen and D.L. Denlinger. 1987. A rapid cold-hardening process in insects. *Science*, Dec. 4, 238:1415–1417.

Lindelv, F. 1976. Reactions in frozen foods. *In Towards an Ideal Refrigerated Food Chain.* International Institute of Refrigeration, Paris.

Luyet, B.J. 1960. Anatomy of the freezing process in physical systems. *Annals of the New York Academy of Sciences*, 85(2):115–138.

Luyet, B.J. 1970. Physical changes occurring in frozen solutions during rewarming and melting. In *The Frozen Cell*, Eds, G.E.W. Wolstenholme and M. O'Conner, J.A. Churchill Publishers, London, pp27–43.

Luyet, B.J. and P.M. Gehenio. 1952. Effect of glycerol in limiting ice formation in tissues subjected to low temperatures. *Biodynamica*, 7(38):107–118.

Mazur, P. 1965. Causes of injury in frozen and thawed cells. *Federation of American Society of Experimental Biology, Cryobiology*, 24(2) Part III Suppl.15:S175–182.

Meryman, H.T. 1966. Review of biological freezing. In *Cryobiology*, Ed. H.T. Meryman, Academic Press, London, UK, pp2–114.

Meyer, S. G. E. 1978. Effects of heat, cold, anaerobiosis inhibitors on metabolite concentrations in larvae of *Callitroga macellaria. Insect Biochemistry*, 8:471–477.

Mullen, M.A. and R.T. Arbogast. 1979. Time–temperature–mortality relationships for various stored-product insect eggs and chilling times for selected commodities. *Journal of Economic Entomology*, 72(4):476–478.

Mullen, M.A. and R.T. Arbogast. 1984. Low temperature to control stored-product insects. In *Insect Management for Food Storage and Processing*, Ed. F.J. Baur. American Association of Cereal Chemists, pp257–265.

Nesheim, K. 1984. The Yale non-toxic method of eradicating book-eating insects by deep-freezing. *Restaurator*, 6(3–4):147–164.

Rasie, L.B. 1977. Yale battles book-eating beetles. In *The Hartford Courant*, Boston Dec.4, p30.

Remmington, C.L. 1983. Correspondence. Division of Entomology, Peabody Museum, New Haven, Connecticut

Ring, R.A. 1982. Freezing-tolerant insects with low super-cooling points. *Comparative Biochemistry and Physiology* A, 73:605–612.

Ring, R.A. 1996. Personal communication. Professor, Biology Department, University of Victoria, British Columbia, Canada.

Salt, R.W. 1950. Time as a factor in freezing of undercooled insects. *Canadian Journal of Research, Section D, Zoological Science* 28(D):285–291

Salt, R.W. 1956. Freezing and melting points of insect tissues. *Canadian Journal of Zoology*, 34(1):1–5.

Salt, R.W. 1961. Principles of insect cold-hardiness. *Annual Review of Entomology*, 6:55–74.

Shchepanek, M.J. 1996. Observations of temperature and relative humidity during the cooling and warming of botanical specimens for insect pest control. *Collection Forum*, 12(1:)1–7.

Sinanoglu, O. and S. Abdulnor. 1965. Effect of water and other solvents on the structure of biopolymers. *Federation of American Society for Experimental Biological Proceedings*, 24:512–523.

Strang, T.J.K. 1992. A review of published temperatures for the control of pest insects in museums. *Collection Forum*, 8(2):41–67.

Strang, T.J.K. 1995. The effects of thermal methods of pest control on museum collections. *3rd International Conference on Biodeterioration of Cultural Property, Bangkok, Thailand, July 4–7*, pp199–212.

Strong-Gunderson, J.M. and R.A. Leopold. 1989. Cryobiology of *Musca domestica*: supercooling capacity and low-temperature tolerance. *Environmental Entomology*, 18:756–762.

Uvarov, B.P. 1931. Insects and climate. *Transactions of the Royal Entomological Society of London*, 79:1–247.

Wigglesworth, V.B. 1972. *The Principles of Insect Physiology*. Chapman and Hall, London.

Zachariassen, K.E. 1985. Physiology of cold tolerance in insects. *Physiological Reviews*, 65(4):799–832.

References for *The freezing process: its effect on dry materials of heritage objects*

Antonsson, M. and M.L. Samuelsson. 1996. Effects of Repeated Freezing on Paper Strength. Swedish National Testing and Research Institute, Materials Technology, SP Report 1996 : 19, Boras Sweden.

Beall, F.C. 1982. Effect of temperature on the structural uses of wood and wood products. In *Structural Use of Wood in Adverse Environments*, Eds R.W. Meyer and R.M. Kellogg. Society of Wood Science Technology, pp9–19.

Comben, A.J. 1964. The effect of low temperatures on the strength and elastic properties of timber. *Institute of Wood Science Journal*, 13:44–55.

Dawley, C.A. 1993. *The Effect of Conservation Freezing Treatments on Selected Properties of Wool.* M.A. Thesis, University of Alberta, Department of Human Ecology, Edmonton, Alberta, Canada.

Dehl, R.E. 1970. Collagen: mobile water content on frozen fibres. *Science*,170(3959):738–739.

Fisher, E.A. 1924. The freezing of water in capillary systems: a critical discussion. *Journal of Physics and Chemistry*, 28(194):360–367

Flanders, S.W. and W.N. Tobiasson. 1982. Designing with wood for lightweight air-transportable arctic shelter. How the materials were tested and chosen for design. In *Structural Use of Wood in Adverse Environments*, Eds R.W. Meyer and R.M. Kellogg. Society of Wood Science and Technology, pp385–397, Van Nostrand Reinhold, New York.

Florian, M-L.E. 1984. Conservation implications of structure, reactivity, deterioration and modification of proteinaceous artifact material. In *Protein Chemistry for Conservators*, Ed. C.L. Rose and D.W. Von Endt. American Institute of Conservation, May 15, 1984, pp61–88.

Florian, M-L.E. 1992. Saga of the saggy bag. *Leather Conservation News*, 8:1–11.

Hartwig, G. 1978. Mechanical and electrical low temperature properties of high polymers. In *Non-metallic Materials and Composites at Low Temperatures*, Eds A.F. Clark and R.P. Reed. Plenum Press, pp33–50.

Hendricks, K.B. and G. Morrow. 1985. *Recommended Storage Conditions for Holdings in Archives and Libraries*. Public Archives of Canada, Ottawa.

Hoadley, R.B. 1980. *Understanding Wood*. The Taunton Press.

Kite, M. 1992. Freezing test of leather repair adhesives. *Leather Conservation News*, 7(2):18–19.

Kreibich, U.T., F. Lohse and R. Schmid. 1979. Polymers in low temperature technology. *In Non-metallic Materials and Composites at Low Temperatures*, Eds A.F. Clark and R.P. Reed, Plenum Press, pp1–33.

Kubler, H. 1962. Shrinkage and swelling of wood by coldness. *Holz als Rohund Werkstoff*, 20(9):364–368.

La Fointain, R. 1984. *Silica Gel.* C.C.I. Tech. Bull. No.10

MacKenzie, A.P. 1966. Basic principles of freeze-drying for pharmaceuticals. *Bulletin of the Parenteral Drug Association*, 20(1):101–129.

Michalski, S. 1991. Paintings – their response to temperature, relative humidity, shock, and vibration. In *Art in Transit: Studies in the Transportation of Paintings*, Ed. M.F. Mecklen, Washington National Gallery, pp223–248.

Okuma, T., M. Miyama and T. Yasuda. 1991. Change in mechanical properties of textiles under extremely cold conditions. *Journal of the Society of Fibre and Technology*, 47(5):248–254.

Schirp, M. and H. Kubler. 1968. Investigations on dimensional changes of small wood samples during cooling. *Holz als Rohund Werkstoff*, 26(9):335–341.

Scott W. 1923. What is the relationship between the moisture content and viabilityof seed corn when subjected to low temperatures? *Proceedings of the Iowa Academy of Science*, 30:254–262.

Sehgal, S.D. and R.A. Lindberg. 1973. *Materials – Their Nature Properties and Fabrication.* Kailash Editions, Paris, France.

Strang, T. 1995. The effect of thermal methods of pest control on museum objects. Preprints, *3rd International Conference on Biodeterioration of Cultural Property, Bangkok, Thailand, July 4-7*, pp199–212.

Street, K.N. 1977. Fibre composite materials in an arctic environment. In *Materials Engineering in the Arctic.* American Society for Metals, Metals Park, Ohio, pp7–10.

Sulzberger, P.H. 1953. The effect of temperature on the strength of wood, plywood and glued joints. *Aeronautical Research Consultative Committee*, Dept. of Supply, Australia. Report ACA-46.

Taylor, M.A. 1978. *Textile Properties.* Forbes Publications, London.

Thomson, G. 1986. *The Museum Environment*, 2nd Edn. Buttersworth, London, UK.

References for *Heat treatment*

Chen C., R.E. Lee and D. Denlinger. 1991. Cold shock and heat shock: comparison of the protection generated by brief pretreatment at less severe temperatures. *Physiological Entomology*, 16:19–26.

Denlinger, D.L., K.H. Joplin, C-P Chen and R.E. Lee. 1991. Cold shock and heat shock. In *Insects at Low Temperatures*, Eds R.E. Lee and D.L. Denlinger. Chapman and Hall, New York, pp131–148.

Michalski, S. 1991. Paintings – their response to temperature, relative humidity, shock and vibration. In *Art in Transit, Studies in the Transport of Paintings*, Ed. M.F. Mecklenburg. National Gallery of Art, Washington, pp223–248.

Strang, T.J.K. 1992. A review of published temperatures for the control of pest insects in museums. *Collection Forum*, 8(2):41–67.

Strang, T.J.K. 1995. The effects of thermal control of insects. *3rd International Conference on Biodeterioration of Cultural Property, Bangkok, Thailand, July 4–7*, pp199–212.

Vannier, G. 1994. The thermobiological limits of some freezing intolerant insects: The supercooling and thermostupor points. *Acta Oecologica*, 15(1):31–42.

Vannier, G. and M. Canard. 1989. Coldhardiness and heat tolerance in the early larval instars of *Nineta pallida* (Schneider) (Neuroptera: Chrysopidae). *Neuroptera International*, 5(4):231–238.

Vannier, G. and J. Najt. 1991. Étudé écophysiologique du Collembole mélanésien 'Caledonimeria mirabilis': transpiration, thermotorpeur, cryorésistance. *Review of Ecological Biology*, 28(2):175–187.

References for *Anoxic atmosphere for the eradication of insect heritage eaters*

Bailey, S.W.and H.J. Banks. 1980. A review of recent studies of the effects of controlled atmospheres on stored product pests. In *Controlled Atmosphere Storage of Grain*, Ed. J.Shebjal. Elsevier Scientific Publishing, New York, pp101–118.

Burke, J. 1992. Vapor barrier films. *Newsletter, Western Association for Art Conservation*, 14(2):13–17.

Burke, J. 1993. Current research into control of biodeterioration through the use of thermal or suffocant conditions. *American Institute of Conservation News*, 18(2):1–4.

Bursell, E. 1970. *An Introduction to Insect Physiology*. Academic Press, New York.

Busta F.F., L.B. Smith and C.M. Christensen. 1980. Microbiology of controlled atmosphere storage of grains – an overview. In *Controlled Atmosphere Storage of Grains*, Ed. J. Shejbal. Elsevier Scientific Publishing, New York, pp121–131.

Calderon, M.and S. Navarro. 1980. Synergistic effect of CO_2 and O_2 mixtures on two stored grain insect pests. In *Controlled Atmosphere Storage of Grains*, Ed. J.Shebjal. Elsevier Scientific Publishing, New York, pp79–84.

Daniel V. and G. Hanlon. 1995. Non-toxic methods for pest control in museums. *3rd International Conference on Biodeterioration of Cultural Property, Bangkok, Thailand, July 4–7*, Preprint pp213–221.

Daniel, V., G. Hanlon, S. Maekawa and F. Preusser. 1993. Nitrogen fumigation: a viable alternative. *ICOM Committee for Conservation 14th Triennial Meetings, Washington, D.C.*

Daniel, V., G. Hanlon and S. Maekawa. 1992. Eradication of insect pests in museums using nitrogen. *WAAC Newsletter*, 15(3):15–19.

Denlinger, D.L. 1996. Personal communication. Professor, Department of Entomology, Ohio State University, Columbus, Ohio.

Di Maggio, D. 1980. Effect of nitrogen storage on the fungal contamination of cereal grains. In *Controlled Atmosphere Storage of Grains*, Ed. J. Shejbal. Elsevier Scientific Publishing, New York, pp147--155.

Friedlander, A. and D.L. Silhacek. 1983. *Biochemical aspects of the effects of altered compositions of atmospheric gases on stored product insects and the role of carbon dioxide in enhancing the activity of some conventional insecticides. Final Report I–56-79.* BARD, P.O.B. 6, Bet Dagan 50250, Israel.

Gilberg, M. 1989. Inert atmosphere fumigation of museum objects. *Studies in Conservation*, 34(2):80–84.

Gilberg, M. 1990. Inert atmospheres disinfestation using Ageless oxygen scavenger. *ICOM Committee for Conservation, 9th Triennial Meeting, Dresden, GDR, August 26–31*, Preprint II:812–816.

Gilberg, M. 1991. The effects of low oxygen atmospheres on museum pests. *Studies in Conservation*, 36:93–98.

Gilberg, M. 1993. Inert atmosphere disinfestation of museum objects using Ageless oxygen absorber. *2nd International Conference on Biodeterioration of Cultural Property, Yokohama, Japan*, pp397–406.

Gilberg, M. and A. Roach. 1993. The effects of low atmospheres on the powder-post beetle, *Lyctus brunneus* (Stephens). *Studies in Conservation*, 38:128–132.

Grattan, D.W. and M. Gilberg. 1996. Ageless oxygen absorber: chemical and physical properties. *Studies in Conservation*, 39(3):210–214.

Hanlon, G., V. Daniel, N. Ravenel and S. Maekawa. 1992. Dynamic system for nitrogen anoxia of large museum objects: a pest eradication case study. *2nd International Conference on Biodeterioration of Cultural Property*, Yokohama, Japan, pp 387–396.

Jay, E.G. and W. Cuff. 1981. Weight loss and mortality of three life stages of *Tribolium castaneum* (Herbst) when exposed to four modified atmospheres. *Journal of Stored Products Research*, 17:117–124.

Jay, E.G., R.T. Arbogast and G.C. Pearman. 1971. Relative humidity: Its importance in the control of stored-product insects with modified atmospheric gas concentrations. *Journal of Stored Products Research*, 6:325–329.

Koestler, R.J. 1992. Practical application of nitrogen and argon fumigation procedures for insect control in museums objects. *2nd International Conference on Biodeterioration of Cultural Property, Yokohama, Japan*, pp96–98.

Koestler, R.J. 1993. Insect eradication using controlled atmospheres and FTIR measurements for insect activity. *ICOM Committee for Conservation 10th Triennial Meetings, Washington, D.C.*, pp882–886.

Koestler, R.J. 1995. Methods of controlling biodeterioration in fine art: an overview. *Kulturguterhaltung: Problemdefinition und Losungsmoglichkeiten. Beitrage eines Workshop. Oktober in Wein, Veranstalted vom osterreichischen EUROCARE Sekretariat.* BIT-EUROCARE Sekretariat, Wiedner Haupstrasse 76, A-1040 Wein, pp7–14.

Koestler, R.J. and T.F. Mathews, 1994. Application of anoxic treatment for insect control in manuscripts of the Library of Megisti Laura, Mount Athos, Greece. Environment and Conservation of Writing Images and Sound: Proceedings of Association pour la Recherche Scientifique sur les Arts Graphiques, May 16–20, pp59–62.

Kukal, O., D.L. Denlinger and R.E. Lee. 1991. Developmental and metabolic changes induced by anoxia in diapausing and non-diapausing flesh fly pupae. *Journal of Comparative Physiology* B, 160:683–689.

Navarro, S. and M. Calderon. 1980. Integrated approach to the use of controlled atmospheres for insect control in grain storage. In *Controlled Atmosphere Storage of Grains*, Ed. J. Shejbal. Elsevier Scientific Publishing, New York, pp73–78.

Nikam, T.B. and V.V. Khole. 1989. *Insect Spiracular Systems*. Ellis Horwood, Chichester, p136.

Pelhate, J. 1980. Oxygen depletion as a method in grain storage: microbiological basis. In *Controlled Atmosphere Storage of Grains*, Ed. J. Shejbal. Elsevier Scientific Publishing, New York, pp133–146.

Richard-Molard, D., B. Cahagnier and J. Poisson. 1980. Wet grains storages under modified atmospheres, microbiological aspects. In *Controlled Atmosphere Storage of Grains*, Ed. J. Shejbal. Elsevier Scientific Publishing, New York, pp173–182.

Rust, M.K and J.M. Kennedy. 1993. The feasibility of using modified atmospheres to control insect pests in museums. *Getty Conservation Institute Scientific Program Report*, March.

Serafini, M., A.A. Fabbri, J. Shejbal, C. Fanelli, D. Di Maggio and A. Rambelli.1980. Influence of nitrogen on the growth of some storage fungi on moist wheat. In *Controlled Atmosphere Storage of Grains*, Ed. J. Shejbal. Elsevier Scientific Publishing, New York, pp157–171.

Shejbal, J. 1980. Storability of cereal grains and oil seeds in nitrogen. In *Controlled Atmosphere Storage of Grains*, Ed. J. Shejbal. Elsevier Scientific Publishing, New York, pp185–205.

Soderstrom, E.L. and D.G. Brandl. 1982. Antifeeding effect of modified atmospheres on larvae of the Navel orange worm and Indian meal moth (Lepidoptera: Pyralidae). Journal of Economic Entomology, 75A:704–705.

Storey, C.L. 1980. Functional and end-use properties of various commodities stored in a low oxygen atmosphere. In *Controlled Atmosphere Storage of Grains*, Ed. J. Shejbal. Elsevier Scientific Publishing, New York, pp311–319.

Valentin, N. 1990. Insect eradication in museums and archives by oxygen replacement, a pilot project. *ICOM Committee for Conservation, 9th Triennial Meeting, Dresden, GDR, August 26–31*, Preprints II: 821–823.

Valentin, N. and F. Preusser. 1990a. Insect control by inert gases in museums, archives and libraries. *Restaurator*, 11:22–33.

Valentin, N. and F. Preusser. 1990b. Nitrogen for biodeterioration control on museum collections. In *Biodeterioration Research*, Vol. 3, Eds G.C. Llewellyn and C.E. O'Rear. Plenum Press, New York, pp511–523.

Valentin, N., M. Alguero and C. Martin de Hijas. 1992. Evaluation of disinfection techniques for the conservation of polychrome sculpture in Iberian museums. In *Conservation of Iberian and Latin American Cultural Heritage, International Institute for Conservation, Madrid, September 9–12*, pp165–167.

Yamamoto, A. and H. Mitsuda. 1980. Characteristics of carbon dioxide gas adsorption by grain and its components. In *Controlled Atmosphere Storage of Grains*, Ed. J. Shejbal. Elsevier Scientific Publishing, New York, pp247–258.

13

Integrated Insect Pest Control (IIPC) Programme

13.1 YOUR IIPC PROGRAMME

IIPC is similar to the commonly used acronym IPM (Integrated Pest Management) but is specifically for insect pests and their complete elimination.

Integrated refers to the involvement of conservators, collection managers, maintenance personnel, landlords, entomologists and building engineers contributing to the insect pest control programme. The programme is also integrated in that it uses information on all aspects of the insect, the collection and the building and its environment. The key to 'zero point' insect activity in heritage objects, whether stored in a drawer or in a high-technology mobile storage unit, or displayed in a cupboard or positive-pressure display case, is in your integrated insect pest control programme. The programme determines if there is a problem, assesses that problem, eliminates it and prevents it from happening again. It may seem like a gigantic endeavour and initially it is labour-intensive, but once a zero point is reached and the programme is in place it is very simple. It is impossible to design a generalized IIPC programme that suits all of the variety of museums, storage areas, homes, etc. This is because of the different sizes of the collections, materials of the heritage objects, insect problems, environments, budgets, number of staff, etc. However, it is possible to review the goals of such a programme and the methods used to reach those goals. The following example of accessing the problem designing and establishing an IIPC programme in a large museum, as well as other information you have gleaned from the book, should help you design a programme to suit your needs.

For further information, see Florian (1986, 1987, 1989) and Osmun (1984).

13.2 AN EXAMPLE OF AN ASSESSMENT AND IIPC: THE ROYAL BRITISH COLUMBIA MUSEUM (RBCM) COLLECTIONS AND BUILDINGS

13.2.1 Each museum is unique

The project was undertaken to determine the presence or extent of an insect problem in the museum buildings and to suggest a management programme for preventative insect pest control. The buildings included the Curatorial (collections) building with 13 floors, each of approximately 3,300 square meters, and the outer stairwells, which are not heated; the Ellery Street Warehouse (approximately 6,600 square meters) and parts of the Exhibits building. The final report was an 80 page document.

Prior to this project, which started January 27, 1986, insect pest control had been undertaken on a passive level, waiting for the insect to appear and then responding. The need for the assessment of the insect pest problem became apparent when a minor insect outbreak occurred, and in response, because of the lack of a thorough knowledge of the problem, staff activities and the method of control were inappropriate.

13.2.2 First steps first

To devise an insect pest control programme requires first to define the problem and then to establish methods to solve the problem. This requires information about the presence and type of insect; the type, care, storage and use procedures of collections; the building workings and environment, etc. The first step was to discuss the problem with supervisors, conservators and collections management staff, and designate one person to undertake or coordinate activities. Cooperation such as entry to collection areas and discussions with collection management regarding procedures was assured. An informal discussion was given at a general staff meeting of all collections, curatorial and conservation staff to explain the activities that would be going on, their goals and the need for cooperation and assistance.

13.2.3 Survey of the Curatorial (collections) building

Because there had never been an inspection for insect activity of the collections areas in the Curatorial building, the first job was to look at suspect places. After discussions, many staff provided anecdotal information that helped locate infestations. Thus this project began by eradication of a few active insect infestations, and establishment of a diary of events.

These activities helped to collect information about the insect species and the type of materials infested, and to become familiar with the collection areas and staff. Many non-active infestations were located. In the past, infestations had been fumigated but the remains of the infestation were not removed. Because of this there was no way of knowing when the infestation had occurred.

At the same time, insect surveys of the main collection areas in the Curatorial building and outer stairwells, as well as the warehouse and parts of the Exhibits building were undertaken by the coordinator. In the initial survey a diary was kept for recording occurrence, location, species, etc. of the insects and insect remains in the collection areas and on the window sills of the building. The insects were placed in glassine envelopes on which was marked the location and date, and immediately frozen for at least 48 hours at −20°C. They were then identified. The diary was later shown to be cumbersome and was replaced by simple forms and computer storage of the data.

In some cases large numbers of dead insects were found, but there was no way of knowing how long they had been there. This initial collection of insects assisted in assessing the insect problem, and establishing methodology and staff involvement for future monitoring and collection inspections.

13.2.3.1 A ZERO POINT IS ESSENTIAL FOR MONITORING INSECT ACTIVITY

It was then decided that every insect should be collected and its location recorded, and at the same time all window sills would be cleaned to ensure that the insects collected on the next inspection were new arrivals, thus establishing a zero reference point. Simple floor plans of the collection areas were made and the location of the insect marked on the floor plan. The insects were attached to the form with adhesive tape. It became apparent from this survey that the banks of windows on three sides of the building adjacent to the collection areas were acting as light traps. Most insects collected were from these windows.

The number of insects was not important at this time. The main value of collecting all the insects was to have a zero point for future surveys.

13.2.3.2 WEEKLY MONITORING AND EXACT LOCATION ARE ESSENTIAL FOR DATA INTERPRETATION

a Monitoring using the windows as light traps

It was then decided to number the windows on the floor plan and collect all the insects weekly. Floor plans, with all the windows numbered for each area, were photocopied and given to the appropriate staff. The window number was consistent for each floor so information, for example of all the south-east windows of the building, could be correlated. The forms required the usual information, such as date, location, insect number, living or dead, and one form a week was required from each collection area. The survey was done on the same day each week and was returned on that day to the coordinator. The information was eventually put into a computer software data filing program for reference. The raw data was tabulated to show the population and species distribution by floor, window and floor/window. The distribution, concentration and fluctuation of the insects was analysed, and the biology of the specific insects in reference to food habits, environmental indicators and insect relationships was studied.

Today there are many software programs designed specifically for insect pest control management which can generate wonderful graphs, charts, etc., but 10 years ago we felt fortunate to be able to just store the information in a retrievable form.

Some results and interpretations of the monitoring are presented under light traps in chapter 10, and in Florian (1987).

b Monitoring insects which do not respond to sunlight

The limitation of this window light trap method of monitoring is that it is monitoring only those insects that respond to daylight and fly to the windows. The absence of moths was apparent.

Tests were run in all collection areas using yellow sticky traps, installed hanging from every red exit light or attached to a blue 4 watt night-light that plugs directly into the electrical receptacle at baseboard level. Yellow sticky traps or plastic strips are universally available. They are plastic strips coated with a tacky polyethylene glue.

All the traps were professionally labelled showing that they were put in place by the Conservation Section. The only insects trapped were adjacent to mountain sheep skulls which were inspected and shown to have a webbing clothes moth infestation. This is described in detail under finding the pupae in chapter 10.

In one situation when *Reesa vespulae* beetle numbers were abnormally high on specific windows in the herbarium, stick traps were set up. Goose neck lamps with the sticky tape hanging from them were placed on small tables located between the herbarium cabinets adjacent to the specific windows. Adult beetles were trapped in one location and inspection of the collection found an isolated infestation in some duplicate specimens that had been temporarily stored without the usual heat and freezing treatment.

Yellow sticky traps attached to the 4 watt night-light are used in a heritage house which has an endemic problem of white shouldered moths and this method is most successful. (See 10.2.4 for method details).

It is important to remove the trapped insects immediately because they attract insect-eating insects, such as the varied carpet beetle.

13.2.4 Survey of the Ellery Street Warehouse

The large size of the warehouse (approximately 6,600 square meters) and complexity of the storage of artifacts on pallets placed on high shelving made the inspection of the artifacts impossible. It was decided to collect cobwebs and dust and examine these for evidence of insects. Even though the maintenance of the floor was good, there were still fragments of cobwebs at the base of the shelving framework and in cracks of the cement floor. Fragments of the exoskeletons of insects were used for identification. A floor plan showing the location of the sample is necessary. This method proved adequate and fortuitously allowed us to locate a cigarette beetle infestation in an herbal collection.

For continued success of this method of monitoring, it is essential that the floor areas are vacuumed clean after collection of the samples so as to have a zero reference point for the next survey.

13.2.5 Survey of Curatorial Building stairwells

The unheated stairwells at the north-east and north-west ends of the Curatorial Building have windows on the east and west side of each stairwell. Alternate windows are set at floor and waist level. Dust had accumulated in the floor level windows where the caulking was absent or incomplete. Dust samples were removed and examined under the dissecting microscope. After collection they were frozen for 48 hours as a precaution against live insects. Analysis showed very few insect remains: 2 varied carpet beetles, 9 *Reesa* beetles, 11 webbing clothes moths, 30 flies and 16 mosquitoes. These insect species were also found in the Tower. In addition, remnants of 1 larder beetle were found in the penthouse on the 8th floor where a dermestid colony was housed several years before. The dust was an accumulation over the years. The only living insects were 6 flies.

The purpose of the analysis was to determine if there was a significant number of insects which would indicate a source or a problem.

The stairwells have open venting to the outside at the main floor level and on the ceiling of the top floor. The presence of mosquitoes indicates that these insects were coming in through these vents. Flies may also come in this way.

It was reported in April that clothes moths were seen in the stairwell between 3 and 3M, and some were captured in the front office on the 3rd floor (north-west corner adjacent to the stairwell). The presence of insect remains and a large number of larval moults in the west stairwell windows adjacent to 3 and 3M suggested an active infestation at one time. It would be a restricted colony but was obviously the source of the moths seen in April.

The analysis of the dust was an adequate method of survey.

13.2.6 Summary of project

The project was extensive, lasting a year and covering large areas as described above. It not only included the development of monitoring for insects but all aspects related to obtaining an insect free collection. The overall summary of the report was as follows:

1 THE INSECT PROBLEM:
- There is no major insect problem in the Museum buildings
- The active insect infestations have been eradicated
- The source of the diffuse populations of insects has not been definitively shown, but building problems are suspected.

The potential insect problem is possible because of:

2 THE BUILDING PROBLEM:
- Lack of insect-tightness; cracks at the beginning of windows on east and west sides (repairs required)
- Open air vents in stairwells (screens required)
- Large space under doors between stairwells and tower (weather stripping required).

3 MAINTENANCE PROBLEM:
- Inappropriate methods (vacuuming, not feather dusting or mopping, is required)
- Inaccessible areas because of empty box storage, books and uncurated materials, etc. on floor
- Inadequate inspection of artifacts and other materials coming into the museum
- Holding room for artifacts is required
- Need for examination of non-artifact materials entering tower
- Potted plants and flowers should not be allowed into buildings.

4 COLLECTIONS PROBLEM:
- Lack of active monitoring of insect activity, need for continuous inspection of collection
- Compactness of storage makes inspection and monitoring impossible
- Inaccessible floor areas under rolling storage makes maintenance impossible
- Lack of clarification of responsibility to care for and curate artifacts.

5 STAFF PROBLEM:
- Need for clarification of responsibility
- Need for permanent recording
- Need for communication through coordinator to all involved in insect control
- Need for manual with procedures and pertinent information
- Need for coordination of all activities related to insect control.

6 INFORMATION PROBLEM:
- Need for manual as above
- Need for training, i.e. insect remains identification, procedures, etc.

The final recommendations were to implement an integrated systems approach to insect pest control to address the above problems and to develop a manual with pertinent information on procedures for surveys, monitoring, isolation of infestations, eradication treatments and salient information on the identification and biology of the significant insect pests. Unfortunately, this manual is still unwritten. But the IIPC programme is active and the museum has no insect problems. There is a small endemic population of insects which seem to be interrelated and involved in their own ecosystem. Continual monitoring and inspection gives information on the status of this population and will show if they encroach on the collections and present a problem.

For further information, see Florian (1986).

13.3 AN IIPC PROGRAMME

The following is an outline of an IIPC programme. It may, initially, seem complicated and unwieldy but familiarization of it will make it seem almost too simplistic.

1 BUILDING

Location and structure:

- Designed for ease of cleaning and general maintenance with minimal cracks and crevices, and smooth wall and floor surfaces
- Location should not be near or adjacent to buildings with food services
- Plumbing system should be visible or easily accessible for inspection for small leaks.

Maintenance:

- Regular maintenance schedule is required.
- Vacuuming must be done, not mopping or feather dusting. Disposable vacuum bags must be used. When full they must be placed in a plastic refuse bag and sealed, before destroying. Contents of vacuum bags should be examined periodically for presence of insects as prescribed by the coordinator.

Building environment:

- Record environmental parameters
- Maintain constant acceptable environmental parameters according to conservation standards

2 COLLECTION STORAGE AND EXHIBIT AREAS

Design:

- Accessibility for maintenance and inspection
- Visibility of collections for inspections
- Use of insect-proof cabinets, when possible
- Use of non-adsorptive materials, when possible

Location:

- Off floor with space underneath accessible for maintenance, or sealed to floor.

Maintenance:

- Design a continuous cleaning or maintenance programme
- Vacuum floors. Use a built-in central vacuum system or normal vacuum with an extension tube from vacuum machine to an exhaust outside the storage area. Use hepa filters in vacuum. Vacuum areas whenever artifacts have been removed. Use disposable vacuum bags and when full, seal in plastic garbage bag and destroy. The contents of the vacuum bags should be examined periodically for insects by coordinator on a continual basis.

Environment:

- Record environmental parameters
- Maintain constant acceptable environmental parameters according to conservation standards.

3 ENVIRONMENTAL INFORMATION DOCUMENTATION

- Collate collection area environmental records and be aware of any environmental changes which may impact on insect pest activity
- Advise as to procedures when environmental change or control is prescribed
- Establish a liaison with power plant staff so they will inform coordinator of any environmental changes that they will be making.

4 PREVENT INTRODUCTION OF INSECTS INTO THE BUILDING

- Maintain tightness of building
- Prevent food in collection areas
- Prevent plants in collection areas or where artifacts are temporarily stored, i.e. offices used for research, documentation. Ideally outdoor clothing should be kept in a cloakroom away from collections
- Maintain inspection room for all incoming artifacts and have an inspection system for checking other raw materials, i.e. working materials, packing materials. Suspect artifacts or materials should be treated according to specified procedures.

5 MONITORING AND INSPECTION

- Design and test monitoring methodology
- Make floor plan of building or storage area to record insect trap information and inspection logistics
- Use checklists: where, what and when found
- Coordinate continuous collection inspections with collection managers.

6 ASSESSMENT OF PROBLEM

a Insect:

Establish a liaison with an entomologist to assist in difficult problems of identification, ecology, behaviour, etc.

i Insect identification
- potential damaging or harmless insect.

ii Behaviour/habits of insect
- procedural models are based on insect behaviour and biology in specific environment.

iii Insect ecology
- insect may be environmental indicator
- insect's environmental requirements may indicate a change in museum/storage environment
- insect interrelationships may explain presence of specific species.

b Artifact materials and documentation:

i Identify materials and determine vulnerability to insect

ii Examine documentation of artifact to determine possible source of infestation and previous history of infestation or treatments (freezing, fumigation, moth proofing)

c Define magnitude of problem — species, numbers, location:

i Determine source of infestation

ii Locate all stages of the life cycle; larvae may move to another area to pupate
iii Determine extent of infestation
iv Determine vulnerability of artifacts/materials, etc.
v From above determine need for control measures

7 ERADICATION AND CLEAN-UP PROCEDURES
- Decide on eradication treatment, regarding material interaction, health hazards, insect biology, legal aspects
- Ensure that the insect remains have been removed after treatment to establish a zero point for future reference
- Emergency measures may be needed; have materials, facilities and personnel organized in case of emergency.

8 DOCUMENTATION OF ALL PROCEDURES AND RESULTS
- Document completely all treatment in conservation treatment report
- Record information on insects collected from surveys, monitoring and collection inspections, as to identification, location, numbers and biology and interpret results.

9 EVALUATION
- Evaluate success of treatment; ease of conduction of procedures; people problems; logical sequence.

10 INFORM AND EDUCATE STAFF
- Coordinate all procedures and inform and educate personnel as to reasons for procedures
- Inform staff on a regular basis about results of their efforts
- For each specific collection there needs to be one person responsible and trained in procedures: surveys, collection inspection, treatment, clean-up and documentation.

REFERENCES

Florian, M-L.E. 1986. *Assessment of the insect pest problem in B.C.P.M. collections and buildings and an integrated insect pest control management program.* Conservation Section, B.C.Provincial Museum, Victoria, B.C. October, unpublished in-house report, 80pp.

Florian, M-L.E. 1987. Methodology used in insect pest survey in museum buildings: a case history. *8th Triennial ICOM Meeting, Biodeterioration Working Group, Sydney, Australia, September*, pp1169–1174.

Florian, M-L.E. 1989. Integrated systems approach to insect pest control: an alternative to fumigation. In *Proceedings of the International Symposium, Conservation in Archives, Ottawa, Canada, May 10–12, 1988*, pp253–262.

Osmun, J.V. 1984. Insect pest management control. In *Insect Management for Food Storage and Processing*, Ed. F.J. Baur. American Association of Cereal Chemists, St. Paul, Minn, pp15–24.

14

Life Cycle of Conidial Fungi

The majority of fungi that grow on the surfaces of heritage objects and produce surface mould or mildew are conidial fungi. The life cycle of the conidial fungi (Figure 14.1) starts with a conidium (an asexual spore) which germinates on the surface of materials and produces a vegetative stage. This in turn produces masses of conidia which become airborne. Under adverse environmental conditions the fungus may produce a few sexual spores in materials on special structures.

Asexual spores are produced without cell fusion and are thus genetically identical. They are usually formed on the surface of the mycelium and are seen as a dusty circle of fungus growth on a substrate such as an orange. The conidia are dispersed by air and fall on and initiate growth on surfaces such as damp or wet artifacts. The majority of fungi which grow on artifact surfaces and cause mould or mildew are called conidial fungi because their growth is initiated by an airborne conidium.

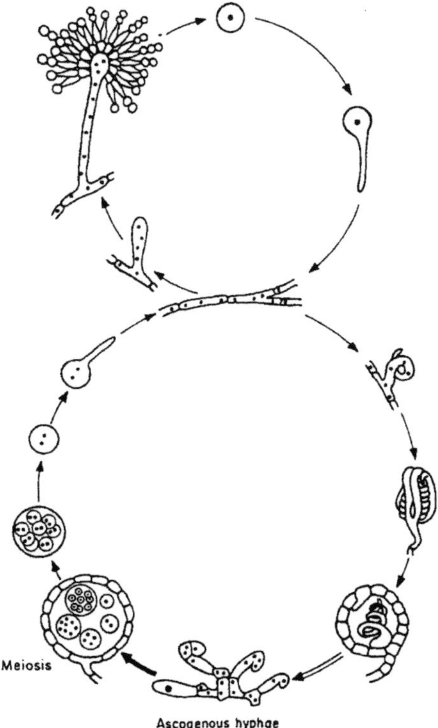

Figure 14.1. The life cycle of an Aspergillus *sp. The top cycle illustrates the asexual phase and the bottom the sexual phase. The conidia, shown as chains on the conidiophore (top left) are airborne. The conidia land on a material, germinate and produces a germ tube. This grows into a mycelium which may form conidiophores to repeat the cycle. Under adverse conditions ascogenous hyphae may pair and nuclei may fuse to start the sexual phase. The nucleus divides by meiosis to form sexual ascospores which when freed start a new generation (from Burnett, 1976).*

Conidia are usually spherical structures of about 5–50mm in diameter. There may be a single cell or a group of cells of low metabolic activity. They have a reproductive and survival function and are the main unit of dispersal.

Sexual spores are produced, usually under adverse growing conditions, by cell fusion followed by cell division, which allows genetic variability. They are commonly formed in the body of the thallus and are rarely airborne. Those that are airborne are plant pathogens that require a specific plant host (e.g rusts) or fungi that require a specific substrate (e.g. mushrooms) for development. The sexual spores are named according to the fungus class to which they belong: ascospores, phycospores and basidiospores.

The basic unit of vegetative growth of a fungus is the hypha. Germinating conidia produce a germination tube (Figure 14.2) that develops into a hypha which initiates vegetative growth. Hyphae in conidial fungi are thread-like

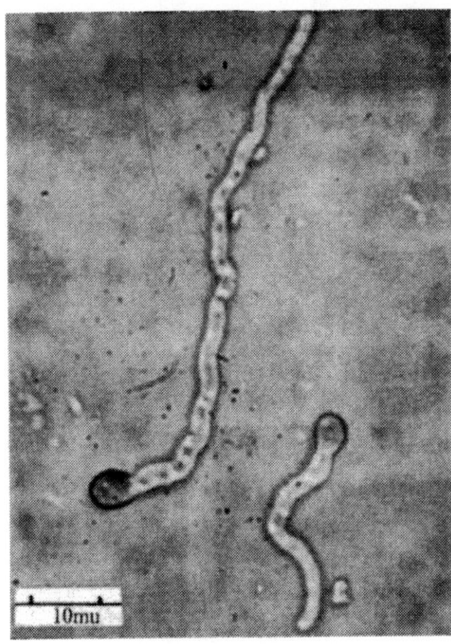

Figure 14.2. A germinating conidium with a germ tube which is about 24 hours old (micrograph by M-L. Florian).

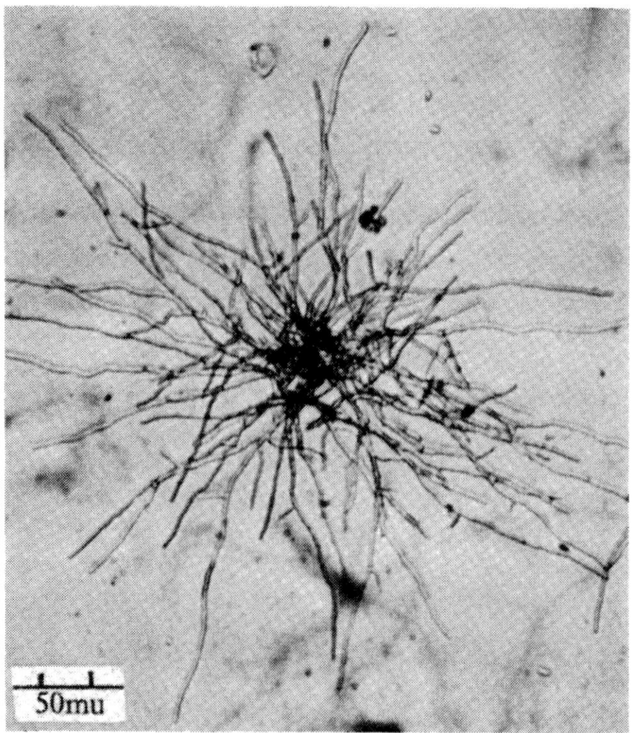

Figure 14.3. A circular colony of hyphae is called a mycelium (micrograph by M-L. Florian).

(average 5mm in thickness), multi-cellular structures which grow by tip elongation and profuse branching. A group or mass of hyphae is called the mycelium (pl. mycelia) (Figure 14.3). In conidial fungi the mycelium may take the form of a diffuse, felted network in a substrate, like a mouldy spot on jam. The substrate is any material on which the fungus grows, e.g. jam, orange skin, paper, leather, textile.

The hyphae secrete enzymes that digest the complex proteins, carbohydrates and fats of the dead organic substrates into simple amino acids, simple sugars and fatty acids. These nutrients are absorbed into the hyphae along with substrate water. The moulds or mildews which live on dead organic material are called saprophytes, in contrast to parasitic fungi which survive only on a living host.

The process of differentiation of hyphae into asexual conidia is called conidiation. Sporulation is used as a general term including the formation of both conidia and sexual spores.

The circular shape of a fungus spot is due to the concentric growth of the hyphae outwards from the central germinated spore or conidia. Growth may also occur downwards into the substrate. Hyphae may force themselves between fibres by secreting enzymes which digest the amorphous material between fibres, such as the grounds in paper, or digest the fibres themselves and then absorb the digested substrate. Informative illustrations are shown in the article by Szczepanowska (1986).

Under adverse environmental conditions some fungi species produce sclerotia which look like black fly spots in the fungal stain. Sclerotia are made up of an organized mass of pigmented hyphae and stored nutrients. They function in vegetative propagation.

For further information, see Cole and Kendrick (1981) and Smith and Berry (1975).

REFERENCES

Burnett, J.H. 1976. *Fundamentals in Mycology*, 2nd edition, Edward Arnold (Publishers) Ltd, London.

Cole, G.T. and B. Kendrick. 1981. *Biology of Conidial Fungi*, Vol. 1. Academic Press, New York.

Smith, J.E. and D.R. Berry. 1975. *Filamentous Fungi.* Vols 1, 2 and 3. Wiley, New York.

Szczepanowska, H. 1986. Biodeterioration of art objects on paper. *The Paper Conservator*, 10:31–39.

15

The Sources of Fungal Conidia Contamination on Artifact Materials

The powdery fungal growth on the surfaces of materials, which we call mould or mildew, is the type of fungal growth that develops from a conidium (pl. conidia).

The source of the conidia may be from:

- airspora
- contact from adjacent mouldy materials
- contaminated solutions or materials used for surface treatment or during fabrication.

Contaminated solutions may be, for example, cleaning solutions, protein or starch adhesives or grounds, and the contaminated storage materials may be reused plastics, papers or textiles.

15.1 AIRSPORA

Air is full of particulate material, for example pollen grains, textile fibres, skin cells, starch grains, inorganic particles, fungal spores and conidia. The size of airborne particulate materials varies from 0.1mm to 1cm (Table 15.1). They are carried passively in the air and eventually settle on surfaces; every object which has dust on it will have some conidia in the dust.

The multitude of airborne spores and conidia is called the *airspora*. The fungal structures in airspora are mainly airborne basidiospores, and conidia of ascomycetes and the fungi imperfecti. The properties of conidia which affect dispersal are shape, size, surface roughness, density, pigmentation and possibly electrostatic charge.

The sources of these conidia are deteriorating vegetation, litter, straw and compost. Airspora composition is analysed by first trapping the conidia and spores and then identifying them (Bassett *et al.*, 1978; Lacey, 1981; Nilsson, 1983). The main interest in airspora is in monitoring for pollen allergy and hayfever studies.

Table 15.1. Types and sizes of airborne particulate material

Type	Diameter (mm)
Viruses	0.015–0.45
Bacteria	0.3–10.0
Fungus spores or conidia	1.00–100.00
Algae	0.5–1cm
Milled flour	3.0–70.0
Moss spores	6.0–30.00
Fern spores	20.0–60.00
Pollen	10.00–100.00
Textile fibres, cotton, synthetics, wool, etc.	0.1–1cm
Skin cells	20–60.00
Plant fragments, minute seeds, mites, insects, spiders	Greater than 100
Inorganic particles (glass, calcium carbonate, soil, etc.)	Less than 1

15.2 THE GENERA OF CONIDIAL FUNGI IN AIRSPORA

15.2.1 Airspora outdoors

The conidia of conidial fungi form a dominant part of the airspora. Some species are ubiquitous and make up the predominant fungal species, while other species are characteristic of a particular climatic region and are often present in relatively small numbers. In outdoor airspora worldwide, the most common conidial fungus genus (pl. genera) is *Cladosporium*, which accounts for more than half of the airspora. The next most abundant, *Alternaria. Aspergillus* and *Penicillium* conidia make up a small part of airspora, but are widely spread. Of the two genera, *Penicillium* predominates in most temperate regions but is replaced by *Aspergillus* in the humid tropics. The relative amounts of different genera vary with the geography, seasons and local weather conditions, but the important information is that they are everywhere.

Table 15.2 shows that in two geographically different locations there are many genera in common. It also shows that

Table 15.2. Comparative counts of airborne conidia indoors and outdoors

	Tulsa, Oklahoma (% of plates)		Cardiff, Wales (% colonies on total plates)	
Colony type	Outdoors	Indoors	Outdoors	Indoors
Alternaria	75.8	43.7	0.6	–
Arthrinium	13.8	7.2	0.02	0.08
Aspergillus	6.3	5.6	2.8	4.57
Aureobasidium	68.0	29.00	8.2	2.15
Botrytis	1.1	–	2.2	2.5
Chrysosporium	–	1.4	1.46	2.07
Cladosporium	78.3	41.9	54.00	39.00
Epicoccum	38.1	20.5	1.5	0.7
Fusarium	3.1	1.4	0.12	0.4
Helminthosporium	21.8	11.6	–	–
Penicillium	18.9	21.1	9.34	16.00
Phoma	17.7	3.3	2.78	0.5
Sterile mycelia	30.7	20.7	16.3	30.00

After Lacey, 1981

many of these species are found indoors and outdoors, but at different relative amounts. The airspora quantity varies according to weather, locality, season and time of day. The viability of freshly deposited conidia varies greatly (Pathak and Pady, 1965). On average 40% of the airborne conidia are viable.

15.2.2 Airspora indoors

The indoor airspora (Table 15.2) will reflect the outdoor airspora, but their numbers are usually smaller. Often *Aspergillus* and *Penicillium* conidia are in greater numbers indoors because additional sources may come from humidifiers, humidified heating ducts, pets, wool carpets, deteriorated food products or plant material (Gregory, 1973; Lehtonen and Reponen, 1993). The numbers will vary according to the activity in the rooms (Gallo, 1993). For example, basements and rooms where vegetables are stored usually have a higher *Penicillium* count than cleaner and better environmentally controlled rooms.

15.3 THE FUNGI RELATED TO HERITAGE ARTIFACTS

The studies of Kowalik and Sadurska (1957) and Gallo (1993) compared the airspora of air with that which developed on old books and prints. They found that the fungi growing on the materials were in the air but not all of the fungi in the air grew on these materials.

Florian and Dudley (1976) showed that for a variety of 12 papers commonly used in paper conservation, each had a unique fungal population in terms of species and quantities.

The fungi identified were common airborne fungi or those commonly found in pulp, and pulp mill slime (Appling, 1955). Valentin (1986) found a similar fungi population isolated from paper and parchment.

The fungi could have come from contamination during paper fabrication, airborne conidia or from adjacent contaminated materials. Aqueous solutions used for conservation treatments, such as starch or protein grounds or adhesives, are also sources of fungi unless sterilized.

Strzelczyk (1981) reported that the most common fungi found on paintings on canvas were *Penicillium* and *Aspergillus*. She listed other researchers' findings which varied from her's and stated that the species of fungus present are dependent on the climatic zone in which they occur.

Strzelczyk (1981) also listed micro-organisms that destroy mural paintings. The list showed that murals in Rome, Poland, Florence, the former USSR and Munich have similar species associated with the deterioration.

Gargani (1968) reported similar results for frescoes. The common fungus on the frescoes in Florence after the 1966 flood was *Penicillium*.

Florian (1976) isolated fungi from Inuit garments and footwear that had become mouldy because of a refrigeration breakdown. Ninety per cent of the fungus population was *Penicillium cyclopium* Westling as would be expected from this temperate climate. The other species are those found ubiquitously all over the world. *Rhodotorula* sp., a yeast which is commonly associated with leather fabrication, was present.

Table 15.3. Summary of fungi isolated from different heritage objects reported in conservation-related reference papers.

Fungus	Paper	Oil canvas	Water colour	Fresco	Leather
Alternaria	♦	♦	♦	♦	♦
Aspergillus	♦	♦	♦	♦	♦
Aureobasidium	♦	♦		♦	
Botrytis		♦	♦	♦	
Cephalosporium			♦	♦	
Chaetomium	♦	♦		♦	
Cladosporium	♦	♦	♦	♦	♦
Fusarium			♦	♦	
Geotrichum		♦			
Monilia	♦				
Mucor	♦	♦	♦	♦	
Neurospora	♦				
Papularia		♦	♦	♦	
Penicillium	♦	♦	♦	♦	♦
Rhizopus		♦	♦	♦	♦
Rhodotorula					♦
Sepedonium			♦	♦	
Stachybotrys	♦				
Stemphylium		♦	♦	♦	
Trichoderma	♦				♦
Trichothecium		♦	♦	♦	
Verticillium		♦	♦	♦	

References: Florian (1976); Florian and Dudley (1976); Gargani (1968); Strzelczyk (1981); Valentin (1986); and Zainal *et al.* (1981).

Zainal *et al.* (1981), in Kuwait, isolated fungi from various leather objects (saddle, water sack, howdah, wallet and book-binding). The commonest fungus was *Aspergillus*, as would be expected in this warm climate.

A summary of the above reports is shown in Table 15.3. The summary shows that different objects from all over the world have many fungal species in common. Many of these species are also shown in Table 15.2, which illustrates their cosmopolitan nature (Florian, 1993). The four main genera (*Alternaria*, *Aspergillus*, *Cladosporium* and *Penicillium*) found in airspora worldwide were found on all types of heritage objects. *Aspergillus* and *Penicillium* are considered the most widespread and destructive agents of decay on earth and were isolated from all objects.

This supports the common origin of the fungi on heritage objects as coming from airborne conidia during fabrication or during use.

These fungi species are rarely substrate specific, meaning that they are not found only on one type of substrate, such as frescoes or leather. The presence of a particular species on a specific material does not mean that it needs that specific substrate to grow on. It is usually just by chance that a conidium of one species landed on that spot and was isolated and identified. Oil-digesting fungi have been isolated from oil used as a surface treatment, but these species, most probably, were incorporated with contaminated oil and are not specific to the material treated with the oil.

There is always a real problem determining whether or not the isolate was a causative organism, i.e. it caused the discoloration or damage, or whether it came by chance after the fact and was subsequently isolated. The isolate could be a conidium that just recently landed on an object and has nothing to do with the deterioration that occurred years ago. Current information on the longevity of conidia suggests that they remain viable only under special storage conditions and for much less than a hundred years. (See section on conidia longevity in chapter 16.)

The deposition of the conidia is influenced by the condition of the surface of the materials and by air currents. Sticky, irregular surfaces capture more conidia than smooth, dry surfaces and surfaces under constant ventilation collect fewer conidia than those in still areas.

15.4 IS THERE A NEED FOR IDENTIFICATION OF THE SPECIES OF FUNGI?

Identification of the species of conidia fungi involves extensive mycological research: isolating the conidia, growing them under sterile conditions on various specially prepared nutrients, observations of the growth pattern, and microscopic analyses of the conidia formation and markings. The identification of some species of *Penicillium* or *Aspergillus* often requires extensive comparative growth tests.

Thus requesting an identification of a fungus species must be done for a very specific reason. This often is considered when there is concern of a health hazard.

15.5 IS THERE A HEALTH HAZARD?

Every museum or institute should have written procedures for protective measures to be followed in the event of a fungal infestation in their collection. These procedures should be written with the cooperation of the local health officials. One should always presume that there is a health hazard. By using the procedures outlined in chapter 20 the main health hazards can be eliminated. These procedures will protect the staff and the public, as well as the heritage objects.

First and foremost, people with an allergic history or who are asthmatic should not be involved with any project involving fungi.

There are some fungal species that trigger allergic responses more than others and there are species which can cause toxic and pathological diseases. Toxins do not present a hazard as they must be ingested. Diseases caused by fungi occur only after prolonged exposure to specific airborne fungal conidia, for example *Aspergillus fumigatus* can cause lung disease in people who work in mills or processing plants associated with cereals and grains where the organism is prevalent.

Protective measures outlined in chapter 20 can usually give adequate protection against conidia of fungi, but if there is a health hazard concern, the species should be identified. Most government microbiology systematics laboratories or health ministries can advise you as to where this identification can be done. A mycology laboratory at a university may also be of assistance.

15.6 SPECIES IDENTIFICATION IS ONLY ONE STEP IN HELPING TO DETERMINE THE CAUSE OF AN INFESTATION

If there is a major infestation and it has been decided to analyse it, just the identification of the fungal species is not enough. Various factors related to the infestation need to be examined:

- Most infestations will include an array of fungal species reflecting the airspora.
- The relative amounts of the species should be determined, as well as species identification.
- If one species is prevalent, the source of this species should be perused.
- The shape of the fungal growth should help to determine the method of contamination (air, contact, treatment) (see chapter 18).
- An analysis of the conidia load in the air should be undertaken.
- Identification of the fungal species would show if they are hyperallergenic, and if this is the case the source of these species should be perused

15.7 MONITORING CONIDIA LOADS AS A PREVENTION IN STORAGE AREAS OR ROOMS

Monitoring conidia loads in storage areas or homes can be done with simple swab test kits to monitor the dust, or with centrifugal air samplers to test the air. The monitoring of the conidia load is meaningful only if there has been contamination of the area and there is a need to determine if clean-up procedures have been successful, or if a fungus problem needs to be assessed. The reason for this is that whether or not you have a problem, there will always be some viable conidia in the air or dust and therefore positive results do not mean there is a problem.

The testing of air or dust for viable conidia can be related to answering a specific question. For example, if a display of some heritage textiles was to be placed in a heritage site, such as a flour mill, which is notorious for high numbers of conidia from the grain, analysis of the dust and air (in this site) would be logical. The results would determine if there was an unusually high concentration of viable conidia. The conidia could present a potential fungal problem if the displayed objects became damp or wet. If there is a problem the display method could be designed to protect them from airborne contamination. Such a display method is a positive-pressure show case, where air is filtered through a hepa filter and actively brought into the show case, resulting in air always leaking out of the show case (Byers and Thorp, 1990).

15.8 PARTICULATE FILTERS AND DUST

The use of normal particulate filters in air-conditioning systems will usually take out the large particles and most of the conidia from intake air. Finer filters are of little use because there will always be conidia in storage rooms and exhibit areas. Every person who enters comes in with some airspora on them, and every open outside door allows conidia to fly in; this cannot be avoided. The best approach is to remove the dust, according to conservation standards, from the heritage objects and then to cover them to prevent further dust accumulation on their surfaces.

15.9 VACUUMS USED IN MAINTENANCE AND CLEANING UP A FUNGAL INFESTATION

Vacuums used for maintenance in storage areas should have hepa filters which ensure that the conidia are captured. The exhaust of the vacuum should be outside the room; this can be done by using a central vacuum unit in an adjacent room with outlets in the room, or by using extensions of long vacuum hoses. Vacuum bags that have been used for removing fungi should be incinerated.

REFERENCES

Appling, J.W. *et al.* 1955. *Microbiology of Pulp and Paper.* Tappi Monograph Series, No. 15. Tappi, New York.

Bassett, I.J., C.W. Crompton and J.A. Parmelee. 1978. *An Atlas of Airborne Pollen Grains and Common Fungus Spores of Canada.* Research Branch, Canada Department of Agriculture. Monograph No. 18. Ottawa, Ont.

Byers, R. and V. Thorp. 1990. Positive pressurized display cases. *International Institute of Conservation - Canadian Group, Preprints, 16th Annual Conference, Quebec City, May 25–27,* p34.

Florian, M-L.E. 1976. Fungicide treatment of eskimo skin and fur artifacts. *Journal of International Institute of Conservation,* 2(1):10–17.

Florian, M-L.E. 1993. Conidial fungi (mould) activity on artifact materials. A new look at prevention, control and eradication. *International Committee of Museums 10th Triennial Meeting, June,* Preprints 2:868–874.

Florian, M-L.E. and D. Dudley. 1976. The inherent biocidal features of some paper conservation processes. *American Institute of Conservation preprint,* pp41–47.

Gallo, F. 1993. Aerobiological research and problems in libraries. *Aerobiologia,* 9:117–130.

Gargani, G. 1968. Fungus contamination of Florence art-masterpieces before and after the 1966 disaster. In *Biodeterioration of Materials, Microbiological and Allied Aspects,* Eds A.H. Walters and J.J. Elphick. Elsevier Publishing, New York, pp252–257.

Gregory, P.H. 1973. *Microbiology of the Atmosphere,* 2nd Ed. Leonard Hill, Aylesbury.

Kowalik, R. and I. Sadurska. 1956. Microorganisms destroying paper, leather and wax seals present in the air of archives. *Acta Microbiologica Polonica,* 5:277–284.

Lacey, J. 1981. The aerobiology of conidial fungi. In *Biology of Conidial Fungi,* Vol. 1, Eds G.T. Cole and B. Kendrick. Academic Press, New York, pp373–416.

Lehtonen, M. and T. Reponen. 1993. Everyday activities and variation of fungal spore concentration in indoor air. *International Biodeterioration and Biodegradation,* 31:35–39.

Nilsson, S. 1983. *Atlas of Airborne Fungal Spores in Europe.* Springer-Verlag, New York.

Pathak, V.K. and S.M. Pady. 1965. Numbers and viability of certain airborne fungus spores. *Mycologia,* 57:301–310.

Strzelczyk, A.B. 1981. Painting and sculptures. In *Economic Microbiology, Vol. 6. Microbial Biodeterioration,* Ed. A.H. Rose. Academic Press, London, New York.

Valentin, N. 1986. Biodeterioration of library materials, disinfection methods and new alternatives. *The Paper Conservator,* 10:40–45.

Zainal, A.S., M.A. Ghannoum and A. K. Sallal. 1981. Microbial biodeterioration of leather and leather-containing exhibits in Kuwait national museum. *Biodeterioration,* 5:416–426.

16

The Conidium

16.1 THE BIOLOGY OF THE CONIDIUM

The majority of fungi that grow on the surfaces of the materials of heritage objects and cause surface mould or mildew, are the conidial fungi. These fungi produce conidia that are airborne, land on surfaces, and initiate the surface growth.

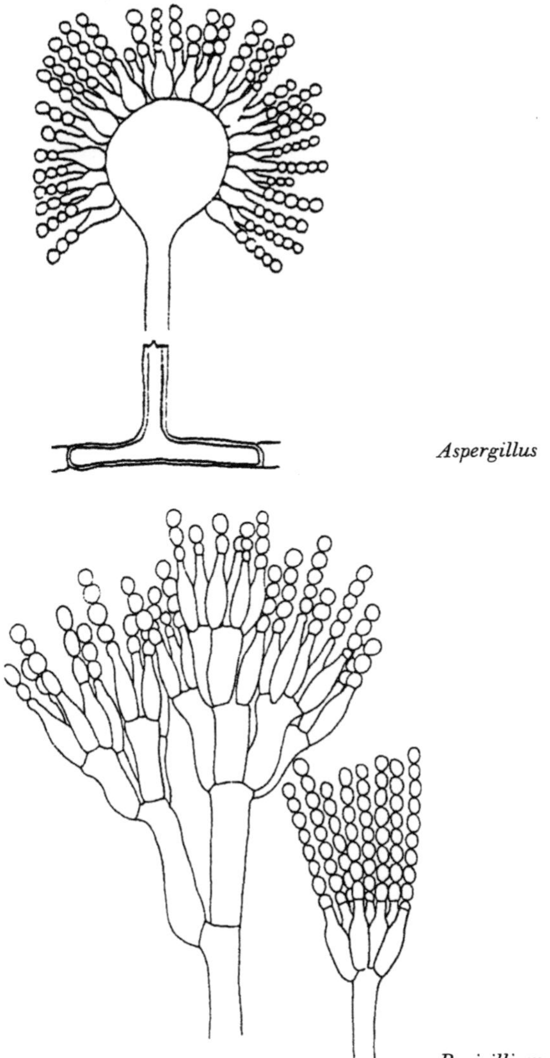

Figure 16.1. Diagrams showing the variation of conidiophore structure and surface attachment of conidia in Aspergillus *and* Penicillium *spp. The conidia are in chain-like formation on the finger-like sterigma (from Malloch, 1981).*

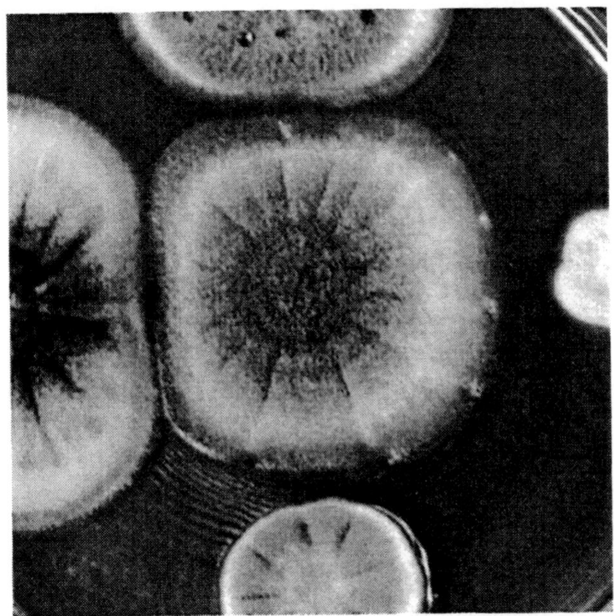

Figure 16.2. Vegetative growth (mycelia) of different species of fungi growing on a nutrient agar substrate.

The life cycle of the conidial fungi (see Figure 14.1) starts with a conidium that germinates and produces a vegetative stage on which are produced hundreds of new conidia, which completes the cycle. The conidium is often called a spore. Figure 16.1 shows the formation of conidia from the vegetative growth of some common conidial fungi. Conidia are formed on the surface of the mycelium and are seen as a dusty, powdery surface on the fungus growth (Figure 16.2). We have all seen this as the green, powdery, rotten spot on an orange. The conidia are picked up by air currents and may eventually fall on surfaces of heritage objects; if these are damp or wet they may initiate vegetative growth. Heritage objects may also be contaminated with conidia which come from contaminated materials that were used in making the object, e.g. protein and starch glues or paper.

The majority of surface, powdery mould that develops on heritage objects originates from airborne conidia or conidia from adjacent mouldy materials. Thus, it is the conidium that is the culprit, and it is obvious that an understanding of the conidium is needed to make a logical decision about prevention and eradication of fungal infestations. Whether they are in your home or in a museum, the problems are the same.

For further information, see Cole and Kendrick (1981).

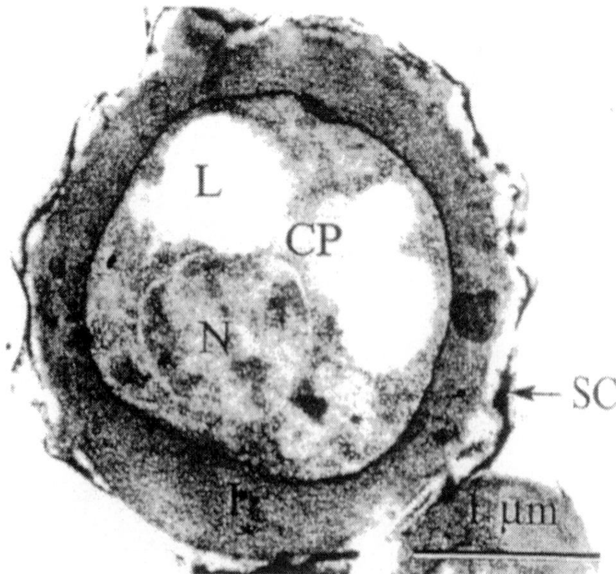

Figure 16.3. Transmission electron micrograph of cross-section of Aspergillus niger *conidium. CP =cytoplasm, N = nucleus, SC = surface coating of cell wall, L = lipid in vacuoles, I = inner osmophilic layer of cell wall (from Tiedt, 1993).*

a

b

c

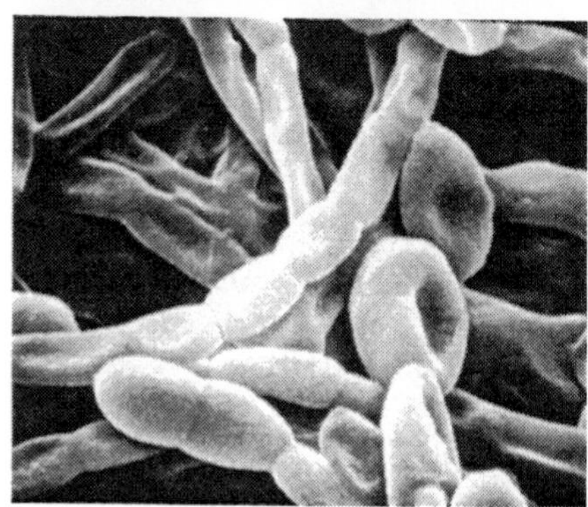

d e

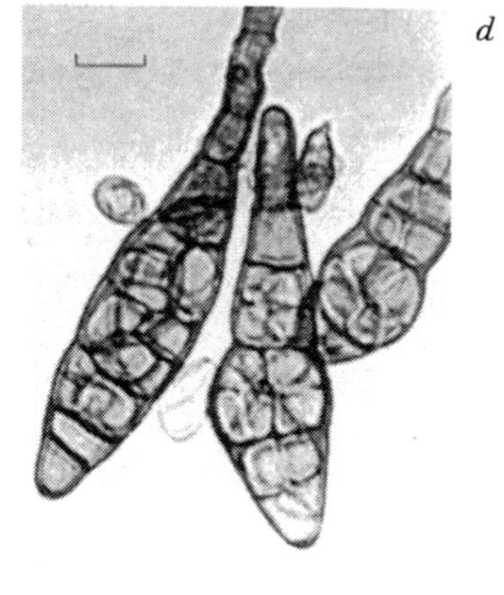

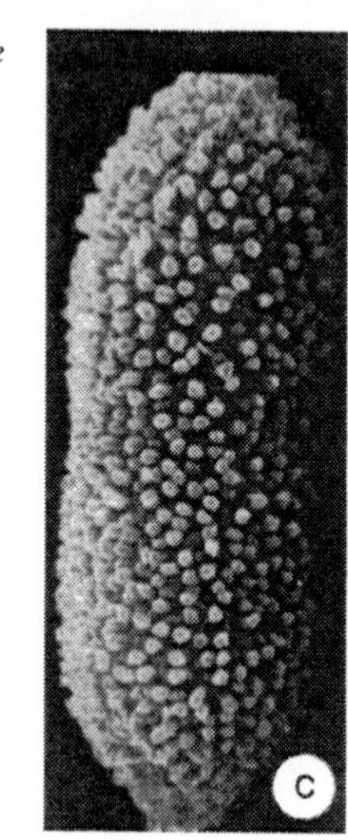

Figure 16.4. Characteristic cell wall markings of some fungal conidia. The conidia diameters vary from 5–10mm. a, Conidia (unidentified) in a fox spot on 150-year-old paper; b, conidia (unidentified) on bond paper of today; c, Aureobasidium pullulans, *yeast-like cells; d,* Alternaria alternata, *common airborne conidia; e,* Cladosporium herbarum, *common airborne conidia. (a and b, Micrographs taken in Scanning Electron Microscopy Laboratory, Pacific Forest Centre, Canada Forest Centre by Lesley Manning, Microtechnique Biologist; and c to e, from Basset* et al., *1978, with permission.)*

16.2 STRUCTURE OF THE CONIDIUM

The conidia of the different fungal species that cause problems on heritage objects have a similar structure and composition.

Conidia are usually spherical structures of about 5–50mm in diameter. They may be a single cell, or a group of cells, of low metabolic activity. They have a reproductive and survival function and are the main unit of dispersal.

The conidium has a rigid, non-living, protective, outer cell wall which surrounds the living membrane-bound cytoplasm (Figure 16.3).

The cytoplasm contains the organelles (i.e. nucleus, mitochondria, and endoplasmic reticulum) required to run the metabolism of the cell. The cytoplasm also contains all the materials needed for its initial development: genetic material, food (as lipid droplets, carbohydrates, minerals and protein) and a watery solution, consisting largely of enzymes.

The cell wall has characteristic markings (Basset, 1978; Nilsson, 1983) (Figure 16.4) which are often species-specific and aid in the identification of the fungus species. The conidial wall is composed of glucose-based carbohydrates called glucans, and chitin. Chitin is water impermeable and protects the conidium from chemical and biological deterioration.

In some powdery moulds, the powder, or mass of conidia, may be coloured green, black or pink. The colour of the powdery conidia does not stain the materials of heritage objects. When the object's surface is dry the conidia can be removed mechanically and no stain remains. It is the pigments secreted by the actively growing hyphae of the fungus and/or pigment in the hyphae that cause the coloured spot in the materials.

The amount of water in dormant conidia varies in the different species. There are two groups, one with low water content ranging from 6–25% of fresh weight, and the other group has higher water contents ranging from 52–75% of fresh weight. Conidia of the latter fungi can germinate even when the ambient air humidity is low, below 60% relative humidity (RH), and are thus called xerophylic (dry-loving) fungi (Arai, 1987; Griffin, 1981). The ability of the conidium to germinate under low humidity is attributed to polyols, such as glycerol, which are stored in the conidium of the xerophylic fungus and act as water regulators (Griffin, 1981). The significance of these xerophylic fungi is that they may germinate unexpectedly in low environmental humidity.

For further information, see Latge et al. (1988), Turian and Hohl (1981) and Weber and Hess (1976).

16.3 THE CONIDIAL DEVELOPMENTAL STAGES

The conidium does not simply germinate when it lands on a surface, there are a number of specific sequential stages it goes through before this happens: conidia formation, maturation, dormancy, activation and germination.

When the conidium becomes airborne it may or may not be mature:

- *Conidial maturation* is the internal development required to become morphologically and physiologically complete, which includes dehydration. It may mature when it lands on some substrate and then become dormant.
- *Conidial dormancy* is the inherent low metabolic state which prevents germination even under conducive environmental conditions. Dormancy may be caused by an internal self-inhibitor, membrane impermeability or some chemical metabolic block.
- *Conidial activation* is a treatment which breaks the dormancy of the conidia by counteracting the causes of dormancy, preparing the conidia for germination. The activator may be some physical or chemical factor or a combination of factors. The are no observable morphological changes in activated conidia.
- *Conidial germination* is an irreversible change which means that the germinating conidia cannot revert to an inactive state. It includes: swelling of the conidium, germ tube and hyphae formation and an increase in metabolic activity indicated by an increase in oxygen requirement.

16.4 DORMANCY OF CONIDIA

16.4.1 Dormancy and activation are survival mechanisms

Dormancy and activation in conidia are survival mechanisms. Conidial germination is the critical event in the propagation of the species. Logically, the conidia should not be committed to germination unless the environment will provide a favourable opportunity for continued growth and development. Dormancy and activation prevent this from happening. The thousands of conidia produced also help to increase the fungi's chance of survival.

Conidial dormancy and activation are probably the most important aspects of prevention and control of fungal activity on heritage objects, but have been completely overlooked in our present control approaches, which are based on the parameters of growth of the vegetative stage of the fungus.

All we have to do to convince ourselves of the importance of dormancy and activation is to look outside on a warm rainy day. As always, everything is covered with airborne conidia and is wet and warm, and according to our simplistic understanding of fungi, all of the conidia should germinate and everything should be covered with fungal growth, but this is not the case. The reason there is no fungal growth is because the dormant conidia have not been activated for germination.

For further information, see Sussman (1966a).

16.4.2 Causes of dormancy in conidia

Dormancy is any low metabolic state or reversible cessation of the development of an organism. We are familiar with dormancy in seeds and insects, the process is similar with fungal conidia. Dormant conidia cannot germinate unless the dormancy is broken by some activation treatment.

Dormant conidia can survive adverse environmental conditions such as freezing, dehydration, extreme temperatures and osmotic pressure changes, but this resistance is lost once dormancy is broken. Once the conidia have become activated, germination can proceed if there are conducive environmental conditions. Deactivation can also occur if conducive environmental conditions are withdrawn, but when they return, germination starts immediately.

Conidial dormancy may be caused by internal and external factors.

16.4.3 Internal dormancy

Internal dormancy is controlled by self-inhibitors, conidia wall impermeability or inherent chemicals which prevent metabolic activity and act as a metabolic block.

SELF-INHIBITORS

Self-inhibitors may be metabolic products in the parent colony that act to prevent germination of their own conidia while they are still attached to the parent colony. Rarely do we see new fungal growth on top of old fungal growth. These same self-inhibitors may be within the conidia themselves because large aggregations of conidia do not germinate. Once the conidia are well separated, germination can occur. This is indeed an ecological adaptation that ensures distribution of the species.

The mode of action of self-inhibitors (Allen, 1976; Macko, 1981) is not well defined. These biologically active substances may aid in the future development of biodeterioration control and fungistats (Lax *et al.* 1985).

CELL WALL IMPERMEABILITY

When first formed the cell wall of the conidium is usually impermeable to water. Water is required before germination can begin, thus the cell wall must become permeable through activation treatments.

METABOLIC BLOCKS

Metabolic blocks are caused by inherent chemicals that have to be removed or altered to allow activation.

16.4.4 External dormancy

External or exogenous dormancy is the result of unfavourable chemical or physical conditions outside the conidia in the substrate or environment.

The substrate may have:

- a low water activity
- a lack of external nutrients
- extreme pH
- toxic chemicals
- inhibitors.

The environment may have unsuitable parameters:

- extreme temperatures
- low RH
- pollutant gases, etc.

16.5 ACTIVATION OF CONIDIA

16.5.1 Introduction

Activation is a treatment which breaks the dormancy of the conidia by counteracting the internal self-inhibitor, membrane impermeability, or metabolic block, to prepare the conidia for germination. The activator may be some physical or chemical factor or a combination of factors.

Activation does not initiate germination. Conidia that are activated do not germinate unless appropriate environmental and substrate parameters are present. Activation may be reversed and activated conidia may remain activated for long periods of time. There is no apparent morphological change accompanying activation.

Unlike dormant conidia, activated or germinating conidia can be killed by freezing or extremes in temperature.

In mycological research there is a great deal of literature on the activation of the conidia which cause horticultural or agricultural problems. However, growth of fungi on materials and biodeterioration of material, especially materials of heritage objects, are rarely mentioned in the literature.

For further information, see Cotter (1981), Schmit and Brody (1976) and Sussman (1976).

16.5.2 Activation treatments against self-inhibitors

16.5.2.1 Dilution

Most self-inhibitors are diffusible and can be diluted, or are reversible, which is essential to their role of imposing a reversible block to development.

Water leaching or physical separation of conidia counteracts the self-inhibiters. Often water leaching is all that is required; but this can only occur when the cell wall is permeable.

16.5.2.2 Ultraviolet light

Ultraviolet light can cause a reversal in the action of some self-inhibitors. Ultraviolet light is known to cause a conversion of the self-inhibitor *cis*-cinnamates of rust fungi leading to the inactive *trans*-isomers.

16.5.3 Activation treatments against impermeable cell walls

16.5.3.1 Heat treatment

Mild heat treatment may activate dormant conidia. Heat activation requires temperatures which range from 40 to 75°C for varying lengths of time from 5 minutes to 5 hours. Different species require a different durations and temperatures.

There are lipids in the conidial cell wall that give it hydrophobic characteristics which are altered by heating and make the cell wall permeable to water.

It has been suggested that heat activation may also be related to protein denaturation. Protein denaturation may result in amino acid accumulation or a relaxed state that results in full respiratory phosphorylation capacity and subsequent germination.

Heat-activated conidia remain activated even if they are dried or frozen before being exposed to a conducive environment for germination.

16.5.3.2 Alternating humid/dry or hot/cold cycles

In nature, conidia are normally exposed to alternating humid and dry air, and high and low temperature. These fluctuations increase the water permeability of their cell wall allowing activation in preparation for germination. These fluctuations occur commonly in nature and to some extent in homes and museums which do not have controlled air-conditioning.

16.5.3.3 Chemicals as activators

Some chemicals which have been shown to be conidial activators of specific fungi are:

- acetone, which is a lipid solvent
- alcohols (methanol, ethanol), which act as wetting agents
- ethylene glycol and glycerol, which act as water regulators and plasmolysis controllers
- detergents, e.g. Tween-20, which act as wetting agents and surfactants
- nutrients in the substrate (casein, yeast extract, the amino acid proline and amino acid mixtures)
- acid and alkaline treatments.

Chemicals that do not penetrate the cell wall do not cause activation.

16.5.4 Conservation implications of activation

16.5.4.1 Nutrients may be present on deteriorated surfaces of heritage objects

Many of the above nutrients may be inherently present on the surfaces of heritage objects. We would expect to find amino acids and peptides on the deteriorated surface of leather, where they can act as activators or stimulants of fungal growth.

16.5.4.2 Are herbarium collections in jeopardy?

The implications of heat activation, in reference to care of heritage objects, relate specifically to those collections which are subjected to heat treatment. Herbarium specimens are commonly dried by heat, and some conservation treatments on artifacts and archival paper require heat for surface or adhesive drying. It is possible that short-term heating may activate fungal conidia on these objects or specimens, and if by accident the activated conidia are later exposed to water or high RH they could germinate immediately. Remember conidia are everywhere and on all surfaces.

Heat treatments are now being considered in insect eradication methods. Certainly, the potential of increasing the amount of germination of the ubiquitous surface conidia on treated objects must be tested if this eradication method is recommended. This is an example of the complex interaction of any treatment on our precious heritage objects. Our ethical responsibility requires that we look at all aspects of interventive treatment.

16.5.4.3 CHEMICALS USED IN CONSERVATION TREATMENTS MAY BE ACTIVATORS

Many conservation treatments of leather, textiles and paper, which are prone to mould, involve the use of some of the chemical activators listed above.

For example, parchments treated with ethylene oxide for insect pest eradication, were shown to be more prone to fungal activity subsequently. The increased susceptibility may be due to small amounts of ethylene glycol, a by-product of fumigation, which could act as an activator on conidia which have fallen on the books after fumigation.

Empirical remarks such as 'leather treated with polyethylene glycol (PEG) supports fungus growth', may be related to the role of PEG in conidial activation or just that the sticky surface traps conidia.

Many conservation treatments use ethyl alcohol and acetone. In all likelihood, they are used in such high concentrations that they act as biocides rather than conidial activators. But the presence of protein grounds, alkaline treatment, humectants, surfactants, or detergents may cause conidial activation which could lead to excessive germination in the event of accidental high humidity or wetting.

When a fungal problem occurs, it is essential to look at conservation treatment reports to determine if treated objects were more prone to fungal activity.

16.5.4.4 WHY ARE SOME OBJECTS OR PARTS OF OBJECTS MORE PRONE TO SURFACE MOULD?

Often when a group of heritage objects have become, by accident, damp or wet only some parts of the object or specific objects become mouldy. This could be due to a number of things, one being previous activation of conidia. Parts of an object may have deteriorated more than others. The deteriorated surfaces may have surface metabolites which could trigger activation. Another reason could be that the mouldy surface may be more adsorbent than less deteriorated areas and be a more conducive environment for germination.

For further information, see Florian (1993, 1994).

16.6 DEACTIVATION

Virtually all of the activation treatments are reversible when conidia are incubated under non-permissive germinating conditions. Deactivation can only occur *before* the conidium begins to swell. Once swelling starts, the conidium is on the irreversible road to germination.

Deactivation may occur with partial dehydration, low oxygen tension (less than 2%) within 6 hours of activation, low or high pH, or low or high temperatures. Incubation at 0°C results in effective deactivation. If the deactivated conidia are returned to permissive conditions, swelling of conidia, the first step in germination, occurs within 10–20 minutes.

This is significant in reference to heritage objects that have accidentally become damp or wet and are stored temporarily under refrigeration prior to salvage treatments. Microscopic examination of the conidia will show that swelling or germ tube emergence has occurred, and this information can be used as a guide to logical treatment. If germination starts after removal from the low temperature, the material must be dehydrated rapidly.

16.7 GERMINATION

Once dormancy is broken, germination begins if conducive environmental conditions are present. These environmental conditions are discussed in chapter 17.

The germination process of conidia, like activation, is not addressed in our present preventative and eradication methods. We usually think only of fungus vegetative growth and look at environmental parameters that influence this growth.

Conidial germination is the greatest problem with fungal activity. It often goes unseen and only when it appears as mouldy spots on leather, mildew on textiles, and red-brown fox spots on paper are we aware that it has occurred.

The process of germination includes conidial swelling, the rupture of cell walls, formation and emergence of the germ tube and an increased rate of metabolic activity.

Swelling is the first activity in the germination process and is caused by the imbibition of water. It does not require energy and acts to remove the hydrophobic surface layer, and to solubilize secreted enzymes.

Structural changes during germination consist of rupture of the conidial wall, and germ tube emergence and elongation. These changes can be observed under light microscopy. All these activities require metabolic energy which can be derived from external or internal energy sources. The oil droplets inherent in conidia appear to coalesce when germination occurs. There is also synthesis of new cell wall material and changes on the ultrastructural level.

Exogenous nutrients may not always be required for conidial germination, but are required for subsequent continued growth; if they are not present the germinated conidia will die. One major group of fox spots on old paper in books is caused by germinated conidia which have died before vegetative growth has occurred. If growth continues, the vegetative colony develops and produces conidia.

For further information, see Gottlieb (1978), and Schmit and Brody (1976).

16.8 HOW LONG DO CONIDIA SURVIVE?

16.8.1 Survivability

How long do conidia remain viable? Will the conidia from old infestations cause problems in the future? There are so many variables that it is difficult to answer these questions.

Survivability in nature, as well as indoors, depends on resistance to deleterious agents, temperature extremes, chemicals, radiation, desiccation, competitive saprophytic ability and mutational capacity.

Conidia with low moisture content remain viable longer than those with higher moisture content.

It is important not to confuse survivability under natural conditions with special culture techniques designed for long-term storage of fungi, e.g. freeze-drying, freezing under nitrogen, and spray-drying. The conditions required in these methods never occur naturally.

Tests using closed sterile cultures give direct evidence of survivability of conidia in these conditions.

Table 16.1 gives a summary of the longevity of conidia and laboratory storage conditions for different fungal species (Sussman, 1966b). The two most common fungi found on heritage objects are *Aspergillus* and *Penicillium species. Aspergillus* spp. can survive for up to 22 years, and *Penicillium* spp. for up to 10 years. The table also shows that the temperature and humidity of storage influence conidial survival.

16.8.2 Are the conidia we isolate from our heritage objects those of today's dust or from fungal problems of the past?

Isolation of conidia from old heritage objects cannot always produce meaningful results. There is no way of telling when the conidia landed on the heritage object, unless it too has been sealed and kept in a sterile condition for centuries.

The above does not give any information that helps determine the viability of conidia in an infestation. If an old infestation is located, a viable conidia count could be done by a microbiologist. If the infestation showed a large percentage of viable conidia, this information would guide one on precautionary handling methods to prevent cross-contamination of adjacent materials in close proximity to the infestation. However, the health hazard for allergic people is the same from dead or viable conidia.

In a library that was water damaged (Rebrikova, 1993), it was impossible to disinfest the massive amounts of mouldy paper The viability of the conidia produced on the books was monitored. There was a 10% loss of viability over a period of 40 months. The loss of viability was attributed to the storage environment. Even if the viability decreases dramatically, it is necessary to remove the masses of conidia from the books.

Table 16.1 Summary of longevity of conidia and conditions of storage (after Sussman, 1966b). A. = Aspergillus

Organism	Longevity	Conditions of storage
Mucor sp.	8–10 years	Unsealed test tubes
Rhizopus nigricans (*R. stolonifer*)	22 years	Dried in sealed tubes
A. oryzae	>22 years	" "
Aspergillus sp., *Penicillium* sp., *Fusarium* sp.	8–10 years	" "
	Average of 5 species	
Erysiphe graminis,	40 days	-10 to 0°C
E. cichoracearum,	20 days	0 to 10°C
Podosphaera leucotricha,	8 days	10 to 20°C
Sphaerotheca pannosa,	4 days	20 to 30°C
S. fuligenea	1 day	30 to 40°C
Neurospora crassa	2–3 years	5°C, on agar
Aspergillus niger	>2 years, 8 mo	7°C, on agar
A. wentii	"	"
A. flavus-oryzae	"	"
A. fumigatus	"	"
A. fischeri	"	"
A. versicolor	"	"
Rhizopus sp.	"	"
Penicillium sp.	"	"
Alternaria sp.	"	"
Chaetomium sp.	"	"
Trichoderma sp.	"	"
A. niger	12 years	Covered test tubes, room temperature
A. flavus	>12 years	"
A. fumigatus	>15 years	"
A. fischeri	>10 years	"
A. ficuum	>12 years	"
A. glaucus	>15 years	"
A. nidulans	>12 years	"

REFERENCES

Allen, P.J. 1976. Control of conidia germination and infection structure formation in the fungi. In *Physiological Plant Pathology*, Eds R Heitefuss and P.H. Williams, Springer-Verlag, Berlin, New York, pp51–85.

Arai, H. 1987. On the foxing-causing fungi. *ICOM Committee for Conservation, 8th Triennial Meeting, Sydney, Australia, September 6–11*, pp1165–1167.

Basset, I.J., C.W. Crompton and J.A. Parmelee. 1978. *An Atlas of Airborne Pollen Grains and Common Fungus Spores of Canada*. Research Branch, Canada Department of Agriculture, Monograph No. 18. Ottawa, Ont.

Cole, G. T. and B. Kendrick. 1981. *Biology of Conidial Fungi*, Vol. 2. Academic Press, New York.

Cotter, D. A. 1981. Spore activation. In *The Fungal Spore*, Eds G.Turian and H. R. Hohl. Academic Press, New York, pp385–411.

Florian, M-L.E. 1993. Conidial fungi (mould) activity on artifact materials. A new look at prevention, control and eradication. *International Council of Museums 10th Triennial Meeting*, August, Washington D.C. Preprints, 2:868–874.

Florian, M-L.E. 1994. Conidial fungi (mould, mildew) biology: a basis for logical prevention, eradication and treatment for museum and archival collections. *Leather Conservation News*, 10:1–26.

Gottlieb, D. 1978. *The Germination of Fungus Spores*. Meadowfield Press, Durham, England.

Griffin, D.H. 1981. *Fungal Physiology*. Wiley-Interscience publication, New York.

Latge, J.-P., H. Bouziane and M. Diaquin. 1988. Ultrastructure and composition of the conidial wall of *Cladosporiuum cladosporioides*. *Canadian Journal of Microbiology*, 34:1325–1329.

Lax, A. R., G. E. Templeton and W. L. Meyer. 1985. The identification of a self-inhibitor from *Colletotrichum gloeosporioides*. *Phytopathology*, 75(4):386–389.

Macko, V. 1981. Inhibitors and stimulants of conidia germination and infection structure formation in fungi. In *The Fungal Spore Morphogenetic Controls*, Eds. G. Turian and H. R. Hohl. Wiley, New York, pp55–84.

Malloch, D. 1981. *Moulds. Their Isolation, Cultivation and Identification*. University of Toronto Press, Canada.

Nilsson, S. 1983. *Atlas of Airborne Fungal Spores in Europe*. Springer-Verlag, New York.

Rebrikova, N.L. and N.V. Manturovskaya. 1993. Studies of factors facilitating the loss of viability of microscopic fungi in library and museum collections. *International Council of Museums, 10th Triennial Meeting*, August, Washington D.C. Vol. II, pp887–890.

Schmit, J.C. and S. Brody. 1976. Biochemical genetics of *Neurospora crassa* conidial germination. *Bacteriological Reviews*, 40(1):1–41.

Sussman, A.S. 1966a. Dormancy and conidia germination. In *The Fungi: An Advanced Treatise, Vol. II The Fungal Organism*, Eds G.C. Ainsworth and A.S. Sussman. Academic Press, New York, pp733–760.

Sussman, A. S. 1966b. Longevity and survivability of fungi. In *The Fungi: An Advanced Treatise, Vol. II The Fungal Population*, Eds G.C. Ainsworth and A.S. Sussman. Academic Press, New York, pp477–486.

Sussman, A.S. 1976. Activators of fungal conidia germination. *In The Fungal Spore. Form and Function*, Eds D.J. Weber and W.M. Hess. Wiley-Interscience Publication, New York, pp101–139.

Tiedt, L.R. 1993. An electron microscope study of conidiogenesis and cell wall formation of conidia of *Aspergillus niger*. *Mycological Research*, 97 (12): 1459–1462.

Turian, G. and H. R. Hohl. 1981. *The Fungal Spore*. Academic Press, New York.

Weber, D.J. and W.M. Hess. 1976. *The Fungal Spore. Form and Function*. Wiley-Interscience Publication, New York.

17

Environmental Factors in Museums and Homes which Influence Germination and Vegetative Growth of Fungi

There is no definitive transition between germination and vegetative growth of fungi. It is a continuous process.

The environmental factors which influence conidial germination and subsequent hyphal growth are the same. These factors are many and often interrelated and include water relationships, temperature, oxygen and carbon dioxide, pH, light and toxic characteristics of the substrate.

17.1 WATER RELATIONSHIPS

In museums and homes most fungal problems occur at normal temperatures and amounts of oxygen, at near neutral pH and in the absence of toxic chemicals, but there is always some excess water. The excess water may come from disasters such as floods or water used for extinguishing fire, fluctuating environmental relative humidity, microenvironments such as window sills or basement floors or even from aqueous conservation treatments. Because excess water is the predominant factor affecting fungal activity it is essential to understand the water relationships of the fungus with the materials and the environment. The information is necessary in devising logical methods for recovery of the mouldy object and for eradication and prevention of fungal activity.

There are three aspects to water relationships:

- the water vapour in the air
- the equilibrium water content and its activity in the substrate, the materials of the heritage object
- the water content of the conidia and hyphae.

The amount of water in fungus and substrate is influenced by the interrelationships of fungus, substrate, air and temperature. From the discussion on environmental parameters (chapter 2) it is shown that temperature influences all aspects of water relationships.

17.1.1 Water vapour: relative humidity (RH)

The physical aspects of RH are explained in chapter 2 on environmental parameters, and in Thomson (1986).

Water vapour in air is measured as relative humidity. It is used to record the amount of water in a given volume of air at a specific temperature and pressure. It is measured as a percentage of the total amount of water which that volume of air can hold; that is a percentage of its holding capacity. For example, at sea level $1m^3$ of air at 20°C has a holding capacity of 20g of water, but it only contains 10g if the relative humidity of that air is 50%, or 50% of its holding capacity.

Temperature influences the RH of air directly, increasing the temperature lowers the RH and vice versa.

Most information about fungal problems in museums or homes suggests that to prevent fungal growth the RH should be below 70%. In many cases this is adequate, but fungal growth does occur below ambient 70% RH. This can occur in microenvironments with a high RH, or in specific materials which have an EMC or water activity that can support fungal growth, or by fungal species with low water tolerance. Control of RH alone does not necessarily solve all the fungal problems.

17.1.2 Equilibrium moisture content (EMC) and water activity (a_w) of materials; moisture content (MC) of organisms

17.1.2.1 Introduction

Water in the substrates (materials of heritage objects) is expressed either as a quantitative amount, called the *equilibrium moisture content* (EMC), or according to the water's physical characteristic, called the *water activity* (a_w).

EMC is calculated as the percentage of weight loss when materials are dried. Percentage EMC equals wet weight, minus oven dry weight, divided by dry wet weight, multiplied by 100 (see also 2.4).

Water activity is a thermodynamic description of the water in materials. Water activity is based on the ratio of the vapour pressure of the water in substrate (p) and the vapour pressure of pure water (p_o), at the same temperature and RH, therefore:

$$a_w = p/p_o$$

The water activity of pure water is a_w 1. If solutes such as salt, glycerol or protein are added to pure water, the vapour pressure of the water solution water and the a_w are decreased. The range of a_w is 1 to 0.01. Water with a_w 1 is more volatile than a solution with a_w 0.5.

Life exists over the range of a_w 0.99+ to 0.60. Growth of animals needs a_w 0.99+, and most micro-organisms need a range between a_w 0.85 and 0.95. Growth cannot occur at a_w 1.00, which would be pure water without nutrients. Growth does not occur below a_w 0.7 because enzymes and proteins are altered and at a_w 0.55 DNA becomes denatured.

The amount of water in fungi is expressed as the *moisture content* (MC). It is calculated as a percentage of body or wet weight. When fungi are metabolically active they require substrate water of a specific a_w so as to maintain a cellular water content of 80 to 90%.

17.1.2.2 SUBSTRATE EMC AND WATER ACTIVITY

a Location of water in materials

The actual amount of the EMC in a material at a given temperature and RH is determined by the a_w and the nature of the material; the amount of free surfaces and of hydrophilic bonds. The surfaces are on the fibres, structural chemicals and their water surfaces. The bonds are on chemicals in solution and within and outside of the structural chemicals.

The water in materials has different water activities according to its location and the bond strength, e.g. *bound (monomolecular), multi-layered, or free.* This is shown in Figure 17.1.

Bound water is bonded to molecules by strong covalent bonds. It has an a_w of less than 0.2, and it does not have solvent ability nor can it freeze.

Water in the *multi-layer* region is weakly bonded to molecule surfaces and water layers, and is located in capillaries less than 30mm in diameter. It has an a_w of 0.2–0.7. It is similar to bound water in that it does not have solvent power and rarely freezes. It varies from bound water by having a different vapour pressure because of the weaker bond strength and greater thermal expansion. Most of this water moves in and out of dry heritage objects as water vapour with RH and temperature changes. It is the loss and gain of this water which causes dimensional changes in materials of objects.

Free water is water in capillaries greater than 30mm in diameter. It has an a_w above 0.7. Free water is involved as a solvent, it readily freezes, and is quickly lost on drying. This is the water that is readily available for micro-organism activity.

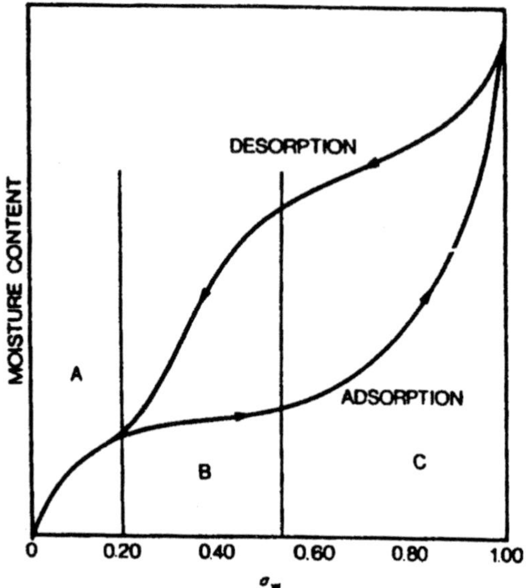

Figure 17.1. General adsorption and desorption curves of organic material over the range of 0 to 1.00 a_w. Water below 0.2 a_w is bound water, from 0.2 to about 0.55 a_w is multi-layered water, and above 0.55 is condensed water. The graphs shows the different amounts of each type of water and the different rates of adsorption and desorption (from Troller and Christian, 1978).

In the process of drying materials, the condensed water evaporates rapidly, but it takes heat (energy) to remove the molecularly bonded water. This reflects the varying bond strength of the water in the different locations.

It is also the bond strengths which determine the availability of the water for fungal activity.

b Movement of water vapour in and out of materials

Water vapour moves in and out of materials according to a diffusion or vapour pressure gradient, that is from a higher to a lower RH, or from a higher to a lower vapour pressure, to bring about equilibrium. The ability of materials to adsorb water vapour is called the *regain ability*. Often very old materials that are brittle and dry have lost bonding sites for water and thus have lost their regain ability.

The actual amount of the EMC is determined by the nature of the material, but this amount fluctuates with changes in temperature and in RH. At a constant RH, an increase in temperature will decrease the EMC and vice versa. At a constant temperature but with a reduction in RH the EMC will also reduce and vice versa.

If the RH is near 100% the EMC will reach the material saturation point; the material will feel damp but not wet. Water adsorbed above the saturation point makes materials wet. We are familiar with the fibre saturation point of wood of 28%; above 28% the wood contains free water in the cell lumens, which is readily available for fungal activity.

The diffusion of water vapour from a wet material to drier air, if the temperatures are the same in the air and material, is a very passive process and it takes a long time, but if the wet object is heated the loss of water is rapidly increased. This is because the temperature increases the volatility or vapour pressure of the water and also because of an increase in molecular movement.

The vapour pressure of water in materials can also be altered by adding solutes to the water. Adding a humectant such as glycerol (solute) will decrease the vapour pressure and cause more water vapour to move into the material against the RH or temperature gradient.

17.1.3 Conidia and hyphae: MC and a_w

17.1.3.1 MOISTURE CONTENT

Water is essential for life, thus organisms have many methods of preventing body water loss by water-impermeable, extracellular, waxy surfaces, such as the insect exoskeleton and conidial cell wall. Living organisms control the movement of water in and out of cells by the process called osmosis. Thus the MC is rarely directly influenced by RH or temperature.

The MC range of most dormant conidia is 6–25% of fresh weight; some conidia from xerophylic (dry-loving) fungi species have higher water contents ranging from 52–75% of fresh weight. These latter conidia have glycerol or another polyol in the cell which acts as a humectant and traps the water. The presence of this greater amount of internal water allows these conidia to germinate at a lower a_w in the substrate than those conidia with a lower MC.

Water activity is not a new concept, but only recently has it been considered in conservation. Arai (1987) isolated fungi from infested hemp paper which he considered as xerophylic (tonophilic) because of their ability to germinate in substrates with a low a_w. Florian (1991, 1993, 1994) reviewed the significance of a_w in fungal infestations of museum objects. Gallo *et al.* (1994) selected a number of species of fungi commonly associated with foxing on paper and studied the relationship between the water activity in the various types of paper and its influence on the ability of conidia to germinate.

17.1.3.2 Maintenance of water levels in living fungal structures

As germination of the conidia proceeds the internal moisture content increases until a stable amount, around 80% water, is reached. This is the normal amount of water found in most living, metabolizing cells and this amount remains constant during life. Even if the relative humidity or substrate EMC varies (within limits), the fungi can retain this same amount of water by producing polyols to alter its own internal water vapour pressure to allow passive diffusion, or by active osmosis against the diffusion gradient across semipermeable membranes. Death due to dehydration occurs if the limits of their ability to control this cell water are reached.

Water from the hyphal tips is secreted with enzymes into the substrate and is reabsorbed with digested nutrients. It is not clear if fungi can adsorb water vapour from the air or if they are solely dependent on the moisture in materials. Fungal conidia and hyphae are often covered by a mucopolysaccharide, a slimy substance, which acts as an external reserve of water. Fungi also secrete glycerol into the substrate, which must act as a humectant and capture water from the air for reabsorption.

17.1.3.3 Categories of fungi related to moisture requirements

Fungi are often categorized according to their water requirements, hydrophilic (loving water) and xerophilic (loving dry conditions). There is a lot of confusion in the literature with these terms. Griffin (1981) discussed the problem of categorizing fungi according to their water requirements, and suggested the terms, xerophilic fungi for those that require a low water activity for optimum growth and xerotolerant fungi for those which can grow at low a_w but optimum growth requires a higher a_w. Xerophilic fungi cannot grow at a water activity of above 0.98, and minimum growth occurs at 0.90. Xerotolerant fungi have minimum growth at about 0.97 a_w.

Pitt (1975, 1981) defines a xerophylic fungus as a fungus which is capable of growth at a water activity below 0.85 and states that the limit 0.85 has been chosen as an empirical but practical value in food technology. In defining xerophylic fungi he suggests that halophilic (lovers of salt), osmophilic (lovers of high osmotic pressure) and xerophylic (lovers of dryness) are overlapping and imprecise terms. The interest in xerophilic fungi is because they are considered to be the cause of fox spots (Arai, 1987). In his list of 44 known xerophylic fungi, 12 were genus *Aspergillus*, 14 *Penicillium* and 7 *Eurotium*, all common, cosmopolitan species. The remaining 11 included 7 different rare species. The *Aspergillus* spp. had a lower minimum water activity requirement than the *Penicillium* spp. The prevalence of these species on archival and artifact materials (Arai, 1987; Florian, 1976; Florian and Dudley, 1976; Valentin, 1986) suggests that they may be present because of their xerophylic nature.

Griffin (1981) suggested that the mechanism of tolerance to low water activity is due to the production of polyols, such as glycerol, which act as osmoregulators in xerophylic fungi conidia. Hocking (1986) reported that high concentrations of sugars and polyethylene glycol in the growth medium increases glycerol amounts in the fungal cells. This suggests a feedback mechanism for survival in adverse environments.

17.1.4 Controlling fungal activity by water relationships

17.1.4.1 Lowering the a_w in the substrate as a means of controlling fungal activity

We normally think of EMC and RH as the means of controlling fungal activity. In the food industry, moist foods are preserved by lowering the water activity (Griffin, 1981; Labuza, 1975; Rockland and Stewart, 1981; Scott, 1957; Troller and Christian, 1978). Variations in water activity are the main reasons that some materials (without toxic chemicals), held at the same RH and temperature, are more prone to fungal attack than others. Some materials may have a low EMC but high a_w, which does not protect them from biodeterioration, whereas others may have a high EMC but, because of solutes present, the low water activity makes the water unavailable for fungal activity.

Foods which have a moisture content near 30% EMC would normally support fungal activity, but they can be preserved by reducing the a_w below 0.7. This is done by increasing the amount of salt or sugars or by using a humectant such as sorbitol in the food. The food is still moist but the water is bonded to the additive and is not available for fungal growth.

It does not seem possible to use this as a method for preventing fungal activity on heritage objects, but it helps us to understand why some materials do not support growth and other materials easily become mouldy (Florian, 1993, 1994).

Scott (1957) summarized the water relations of microorganisms in reference to food preservation. They are still valid today:

1. *Water activity, rather than water content, determines the lower limits of water availability to microbial growth. Most bacteria do not grow below a_w = 0.91, most moulds cease to grow below a_w = 0.8. Some xerophilic fungi were reported to grow at activities of a_w 0.65, but the range of 0.70–0.75 are generally considered their lower limits.*
2. *Environmental factors affect the level of water activity required by microbial growth. The general principle which seems usually to apply is the less favourable are the other environmental factors (nutritional adequacy, pH, oxygen pressure, temperature) the higher the minimum water activity at which microorganisms will grow ...*
3. *When water activity is depressed by solutes, the solutes themselves may have effects which complicate the effect of water activity* per se.

The concept of a_w may seem complex, but it is a common feature of many materials. There can be a number of reasons for the reduction of a_w in materials:

- During manufacturing of materials, water soluble chemicals are added which will lower the a_w, e.g. in archival paper – soluble grounds, fillers, whiteners, etc.; in leather – soluble tannage chemicals, whiteners, chelators, antioxidants, etc.
- Over time, chemical alteration due to oxidation may produce soluble products which lower the a_w.
- Some conservation treatments, such as humectants and impregnants, can lower the a_w.

We have not intentionally used decrease of water activity to control fungal activity on heritage objects but many of the common conservation treatments, such as humectants, deacidification, and polyethylene glycol impregnation, must change the water activity. Many of these are mass treatments, thus it seems ethical that research should be done to determine their influence on fungal activity before they are used. Addition of any water soluble chemical must alter the a_w, which could influence (increase or decrease) the material's protection against fungal activity. This is another example of how important it is to know the whole picture. Research is needed on this subject.

17.1.4.2 Temperature and water activity are interrelated
Scott (1957) reported that at a given temperature, a reduction in water activity causes a fall in germination rate, an extension of the latent period and a reduction of the rate of germ tube extension. At optimum temperatures the range of water activities supporting germination was greatest.

17.1.4.3 Lowering the EMC as a means of preservation
EMC in materials is reduced by loss of water bonding sites. We are familiar with the process of leather tannage which decreases the available water sites by cross-linking collagen, thus making it resistant to biological deterioration. This is preservation due to reduced EMC.

Over time, water sites are lost, resulting in a decrease in EMC that in turn increases the concentration of chemicals in the material, lowering the a_w; both of which prevent fungal activity.

17.1.4.4 Beware of microenvironments and dust
Microenvironments which increase the EMC in materials are often the cause of fungal activity. Some examples of common microenvironments are that mouldy piece of paper at the bottom of a pile on a cold floor, or the mouldy piece of paper on the window sill or next to a metal window frame. The most prevalent microenvironment that supports fungal activity is in the dust on the surface of materials. This is where most of the surface fungi are growing. They are growing there because the dust captures the conidia and the other particles (plant and animal fibre, skin cells, pollen cells, starch grains), which adsorb enough moisture to allow the conidia to germinate and possibly support limited growth.

17.2 TEMPERATURE, GASES, pH AND LIGHT

17.2.1 Introduction

In the past, simply lowering the RH and temperature was thought to be the way to control fungal activity.

Lowering the RH sometimes has some merit. Certainly, water vapour is important, but the control of fungal activity depends on the ability of the substrate to adsorb the water vapour. At a given RH and temperature, some materials cannot adsorb water vapour and thus do not support fungal activities, whereas others can adsorb enough water vapour to support luxurious fungal growth. Thus it is the regain ability of the material which is the limiting factor, not RH. The role of RH in the EMC of the material of heritage objects, the substrate for fungal activity, is discussed in section 17.1 above.

Lowering the temperature sometimes has some merit. We are familiar with temperature growth curves which show slow growth rates at the temperature extremes and rapid growth rates at the optimum temperature. What this tells us is that growth can occur over a wide range of temperatures, but the growth rates are different. The organism is viable at the extremes, until lethal temperatures are reached. Temperature influences the rate of metabolic activity, thus the rate of growth.

Fungal responses to temperature are a result of the interaction of temperature with other factors (such as RH, nutritional state, age of organism, species), thus the optimum temperature and ranges reported are valid only under specific conditions. But to generalize, germination or growth is limited by minimum temperatures between 0 and 10°C and maximum between 34 and 36°C, with the optimum temperature range being 20–26°C.

17.2.2 Lethal high temperature

The moisture content of conidia and temperature are interconnected. Dry conidia have a longer viability and are more heat resistant than swollen hydrated conidia. During germination, heat resistance is lost. Swollen conidia of *Aspergillus niger* incubated at a temperature of 41°C had abnormal germ tube formation, and at 44°C, germ tube emergence was prevented. At the maximum temperatures the swollen conidia can remain viable for only a few hours. This information is relevant to control or prevention of conidial germination.

The conservation implications of this relate to treatments that involve heat. Herbarium specimens are usually dried at temperatures much above the maximum of 36°C, thus germinating conidia on the specimens related to plant pathogens and airspora will be killed during preparation, but dried conidia may be activated.

This information also suggests that drying at 34–36°C has the advantage of not only drying immediately, but also killing, the germinated conidia and vegetative growth.

Temperature tolerances are also influenced by the type of media (nutrients) available.

17.2.3 Low temperatures and the freezing process

17.2.3.1 *Effects of refrigeration at 4°C*

To prevent fungal activity, a low temperature (above freezing) alone is not logical. We use refrigeration for preserving food, not to kill fungi, but to simply slow down the rate, or limit, of growth. At the minimum temperature extremes, growth occurs. Often the fungal growth that occurs under stress results in the production of melanin-pigmented hyphae and polyols that present future conservation problems. At low temperatures materials have a higher moisture content than at higher temperatures, which is an advantage for the fungal growth.

17.2.3.2 *Effect of freezing on micro-organisms*

The effect of freezing on bacteria, yeasts and moulds in frozen food shows that the numbers decrease with an increase in freezing period, but a few will survive for several years.

There is extensive literature on the effects of freezing on micro-organisms in reference to freezing of viable stock cultures for long-term storage, and storage of frozen viable animal cells and tissue (Churchill, 1970; Meryman, 1966). The procedures are very specific and not comparable to putting wet mouldy materials in a freezer, but there are some basic phenomena which help us understand what happens and what is to our advantage or disadvantage when we do this.

In a review (Calcott, 1978) of the literature on the survival of micro-organisms in freezing temperatures, the following generalizations are apparent:

- there is species difference in survival
- the lethal aspects of low temperature are time and temperature dependent;
- the media is an important factor, e.g. water is moderately lethal whereas saline or a nutrient medium are more lethal
- the age and density of the population is significant; the older and denser, the better the survival
- storage death and thawing death are different.

The papers by Mazur, 1956, 1960 and 1965, review the significant aspects of freezing temperatures on bacteria and fungal survival. The rates of cooling and thawing are significant. For example, cooling yeast cells and *Escherichia coli* at 7°C per minute gave optimum survival; as the rate increased or decreased, the survival rate was reduced; the rate of 1°C per minute and 100°C per minute gave maximum kills (Mazur, 1965).

In general organisms succumb to freezing and thawing more quickly when held at or near their freezing temperatures, and slow thawing is more lethal than fast.

Hydrated spores are more vulnerable to freezing than dry spores. Mazur (1956) reported that frozen, hydrated spores had low survival and dry fungal spores frozen in air are hyperresistant to freezing because of their low water content (6–25%).

Mazur (1960) reported that vegetative yeast cells and fungal hyphae are vulnerable to the freezing of water. Spores are more resistant but few survive –40°C, and survival is time dependent; the longer at the minimum temperature, the fewer survive. In all organisms and stages (e.g. vegetative), the rate of freezing and thawing is critical for survival. The slower the freezing and thawing, the fewer survivals.

Some cells which may escape death on the first freezing will not survive a second freezing. The resistance to the first freezing is not due to an individual selective advantage, but to some physiological state that may be altered on the second freezing.

Haines (1934) reports that even at below 0°C micro-organisms will grow. Experimentation on frozen food showed that growth of some bacteria did occur at –5°C on unfrozen medium, but it took several months to show visible increases. Also some fungi were reported to grow at –7°C as long as the substrate was not frozen.

17.2.3.3 *The limiting factor for growth is the water activity (a_w)*

Water, only in the free or condensed state, at a water activity above approximately 0.75a_w is available for fungal growth.

Lowering the temperature lowers the water activity and thus limits growth. Also ice formation, withdrawing free water and increasing the solute concentration will lower the water activity and limit growth.

Free water in materials at just below 0°C may not be frozen because it may be held in capillaries in the condensed state, or because the solutes present will lower the freezing point of the solution.

The significance of this in reference to micro-organism growth is that if wet materials are stored at below 0°C for a prolonged period the temperature must be low enough to stop the growth. Certainly the rate of growth and metabolic activity is reduced by low temperature, and maybe this is all we have been striving for in the past, but the goal should be to stop growth. Growth can be stopped in storage at –20°C, which is a common storage temperature for frozen foods. But at this temperature ice damage of the water-soaked materials may occur (see chapter 19).

17.2.3.4 *Summary of the effect of freezing on micro-organisms*

1. Growth can occur below freezing temperatures as long as there is unfrozen water.
2. The cause of death may be due to dehydration, internal ice, or concentration effects.
3. During the freezing process, the slower the rate of cooling and thawing and the longer the time at the minimum temperature, the less survival.
4. The minimum temperature for microorganism control should be –20°C.
5. There are differences in species response to resistance to freezing.
6. Dry conidia are more resistant than hydrated conidia.
7. The initial freezing of the micro-organisms can reduce the viable population size dramatically if the rate of freezing and the low temperature reached are controlled. If micro-organisms are a major threat, repeated freezing can almost eliminate the population.

8 Growth at low temperatures is slow. A few conidial fungi can grow at near freezing point or even below the freezing point.
9 Scott (1957) discussed the growth of fungi in frozen food. As food is frozen a concentrated unfrozen solution may form in which fungi may grow down to −8°C.
10 Dormant conidia can survive storage in cold water and will survive freeze–thaw cycles.
11 Death is caused in the freezing process by physical damage by ice crystals, i.e. rupture of membranes and organelles, and the concentration effect. The concentration effect is a result of water removal by ice formation and the subsequent increase in concentration of the metabolic acids and enzymes causing lethal pH and ionic changes.
12 In the preservation of fungi for systematic research, methods of freezing have been perfected to allow long-term storage of fungi cultures. These methods prevent ice formation and concentration effects.
13 Mazur (1968) reviewed the subject of the effects of freezing on fungi in detail.
14 The freezing of cultures for preservation requires that only enough viability remains in a culture to initiate a new culture, a very low proportion of viable cells actually survive. The optimum procedures for preservation include slow cooling (1–10°C/minute) to prevent intracellular freezing and thermal shock, suspension in a medium such as glycerine or sucrose to cause supercooling, flash freezing to and storage at −130°C, and rapid thawing. Slower thawing is lethal (1°C/minute or slower).
15 These conditions do not occur in nature or when materials are placed in a freezing chest and allowed to thaw in the refrigerator.

17.2.3.5 Freezing or refrigeration for temporary storage of wet materials

The greatest threat of potential fungal growth comes when artifacts become wet or very moist due to flooding or accidental wetting.

If water-soaked materials are placed in freezing conditions and then removed to thaw slowly in a refrigerator, this should kill most of the vegetative growth of the germinated fungi, and a large percentage of hydrated conidia.

Air-dry conidia are more resistant to freezing than hydrated conidia and hyphae, which are vulnerable to freezing because of their high content of free water.

Refrigeration (4°C) of wet materials is often recommended to save time in preparation for treatment. Refrigeration storage at low, but not freezing, temperatures will slow down metabolic activity and may prevent additional conidial germination, but maintains a high moisture content in materials. On removal from the low temperature, germination proceeds rapidly and materials still need to be dried. However, storage at temperatures around 36°C not only dries the materials initially but will slow down the growth rate, reduce the conidial germination and kill many germinating conidia. We should consider using immediate drying rather than cold storage for water-damaged materials. Of course there is always the problem that some materials may distort by rapid drying, but methods of slow drying or drying under constraint may be acceptable.

Dehydration *in situ* is the most logical approach. By using large industrial dehumidifiers, large rooms can be treated rapidly. This prevents handling, eliminates the need for freezing/refrigeration space and reduces cross-contamination.

17.2.4 **Oxygen and carbon dioxide**

Griffin (1981) stated that oxygen and water are universal requirements for germination. He suggested that carbon dioxide may also be a universal requirement.

Oxygen is required for oxidative respiration, essential for germination and growth of conidia. Conidia submerged in water under anaerobic conditions rarely germinate. But anaerobic respiration does occur in fungi, resulting in the formation of the fermentation products such as lactic acid or alcohol.

The literature (Hall, 1981; Nakamura and Hoshino, 1983; Pitt 1981) reports that many fungal conidia germinate or produce normal growth at oxygen concentrations as low as 0.25%. An oxygen concentration of 0.2% is suggested as the maintenance level required for dormant conidia.

The use of controlled atmospheric gases for insect and fungi control is widely used in the storage of cereals in granaries. This research has shown that the effects of controlled atmospheric gas on fungal activity are significant. Under anoxic conditions some fungi do not produce spores, conidia, toxins or pigments and vegetative growth is dramatically reduced. Of all the gases tested, 100% nitrogen gave the most significant results (Di Maggio, 1980; Serafini *et al.* 1980).

In the food industry the prevention of fungal activity, growth and toxin production has been accomplished by using controlled atmospheres in storage and packaging, e.g. an increase in carbon dioxide (above 10%) and a decrease in oxygen (2%), and exclusion of oxygen by vacuum packaging (Northolt and Bullerman, 1982). Wellheiser (1992) made a thorough review of the subject of altered atmospheric gases (carbon dioxide, carbon dioxide/nitrogen, and reduced oxygen) used for disinfestation of artifact materials. In the results she reported that: 'While growth may be arrested, suppressed ... the spores of fungi can survive the unfavourable conditions in a state of rest and can remain viable for many years (Brokerhof, 1989). However, recent studies into microbial control by low oxygen and low RH environment show considerable promise (Valentin, Lidstrom, Preusser 1990)'. She further reported: 'It was also found that almost all moulds cannot grow under the oxygen-free conditions created by oxygen absorbers'.

The use of controlled atmospheric gases has been suggested for control of fungi growth on artifacts. Valentin *et al.* (1990) tested the effect of different environments with varying relative humidity, and oxygen and nitrogen concentrations on the respiration rate of fungi on parchment. They found that reduction in RH was more significant in reducing the respiration rate than low oxygen concentrations. Significant reductions of respiration did occur at 1% and 0.1% oxygen concentrations but the fungi were still viable after 3 weeks.

It has been demonstrated that carbon dioxide is required for germination of a number of fungi, but is inhibitory to others. Pitt (1981) reported that the growth rate is increased with increased levels up to 15% carbon dioxide and is reduced if the concentration is higher. Carbon dioxide is used as a carbon source for carbon fixation in very few fungi.

Pitt (1981) reported that the effect of oxygen and carbon dioxide is dependent on the concentration dissolved in the substrate, not in the air. Fungi are also considered as sequesters of oxygen. Thus experiments using specific concentrations of the gases in the air may be influenced by substrate and fungal absorption.

Research is needed to determine if the use of altered atmospheric gases as a control measure fungi in the museum is effective.

17.2.5 Hydrogen ion (pH) and osmotic forces of substrate

The hydrogen ion concentration of the substrate influences the germination of conidia. Generally, the optimum is in the acid range from pH 3.0 or 4.0 to pH 7.00, and the full range is pH 2.0–9.0.

Griffin (1981) pointed out that most research on the effect of pH on the growth of fungi is not conclusive, but most fungi grow in a substrate initially of pH 4–7.

Extracellular pH of the substrate has no influence on the cytoplasmic pH, thus the effects of pH are indirect effects on the ionization of weak acids and bases in the medium. Fungi often change the pH of the medium by production of secreted metabolic products such as organic acids, e.g. citric acid.

17.2.6 Light

The role of light in germination is not clearly established. In some experiments it acts as a stimulator and in others as an inhibitor of growth regulation, conidiation or sporulation and pigmentation. It is often difficult to separate heat from the light effect.

The fungicidal effect of ultraviolet light at the wavelength that occurs in natural sunlight (above 290nm) has less effect than that used for germicidal purposes in laboratories (250–270nm).

The ultraviolet levels required to kill fungi cause ageing of papers. Melanin, caratenoids and pigments in conidia may give some protection against ultraviolet.

For further information, see Cole and Kendrick (1981) and Sussman (1976).

17.2.7 Nutrients

Germination and growth require a balance of many substances, water, ions, enzymes, inhibitors and stimulants, and endogenous features.

Ions are required for normal development and as germination stimulators. The role of calcium ions in germination (Rivera-Rodriquez and del Valle, 1992) and in enhancing the enzyme protease and magnesium that regulate germ tube formation (Walker *et al.* 1984) have been reported.

Conidia may contain sufficient carbon reserves to allow respiration to start, but in some species it is insufficient to allow germination to proceed to the formation of the germ tubes.

Common nutrients are carbohydrates (glucose, fructose, glycogen, sucrose), amino acids and polyalcohols, which are normally found in the soil and on plant parts (Anderson and Smith 1976; Griffin, 1981).

For further information, see Cole and Kendrick (1981).

REFERENCES

References for *Water relationships*

Arai, H. 1987. On the foxing-causing fungi. *ICOM Committee for Conservation, 8th Triennial Meeting, Sydney, Australia, September 6–11*, 3:1165–1167.

Gallo, F., C. Marconi, P. Valenti, P. Colaizzi, G. Pasquariello, M. Scorrano, O. Maggi and A.M. Persiani. 1994. Research on some key factors involved in the biodeterioration of books and documents. *Environment and Conservation of Writing, Images, and Sound, Proceedings of ARSAG's 2nd International Study Days*, May 16–20, pp63–71.

Griffin, D.H. 1981. *Fungal Physiology*. Wiley-Interscience publication, New York.

Florian, M-L.E. 1976. Fungicide treatment of eskimo skin and fur artifacts. *Journal, International Institute of Conservation*, 2(1):10–17.

Florian, M-L.E. 1991. Per Guldbeck Memorial Lecture: About time. - *International Institute of Conservation - Canadian Group* Annual Meeting, May 25. *IIC-CG Newsletter*, Autumn, 1991.

Florian, M-L.E. 1993. Conidial fungi (mould) activity on artifact materials. A new look at prevention, control and eradication. *International Council of Museums 10th Triennial Meeting*, August, Preprints, Washington D.C., Dearborn, Mich, 2:868–874.

Florian, M-L.E. 1994. Conidial fungi (mould, mildew) biology: a basis for logical prevention, eradiation and treatment for museum and archival collections. *Leather Conservation News*, 10:1–29.

Florian, M-L.E. and D. Dudley. 1976. The inherent biocidal features of some paper conservation processes. *American Institute of Conservation 4th annual meeting* preprint, pp41–47.

Hocking, A.D. 1986. Effects of water activity and cultural age on the glycerol accumulation of five fungi. *Journal of General Microbiology*, 132:269–275.

Labuza, T.P. 1975. Interpretation of sorption data in relation to the state of constituent water. In *Water Relations of Food*, Ed. R.B. Duckworth, Academic Press, London, pp155–172.

Pitt, J.I. 1975. Xerophylic fungi and the spoilage of food of plant origin. In *Water Relations of Food*, Ed. R.B. Duckworth, Academic Press, London, pp273–307.

Pitt, J.I. 1981. Food spoilage and biodeterioration. In *Biology of Conidial Fungi*, Vol. 2, Eds G.T. Cole and B. Kendrick, Academic Press, New York, pp111–142.

Rockland L.B. and G.F. Stewart. 1981. *Water Activity: Influences on Food Quality*, Academic Press.

Scott, W.J. 1957. Water relations of food spoilage microorganisms. *Advances in Food Research*, New York, 7:83–127.

Thomson, G. 1986. *The Museum Environment*, 2nd Edn. Butterworths, Boston, Mass.

Troller, J.A. and J.H.B. Christian, 1978. *Water Activity in Food.* Academic Press, New York.

Valentin, N. 1986. Biodeterioration of library materials, disinfection methods and new alternatives. *The Paper Conservator*, 10:40–45.

References for *Temperature, gases, pH and light*

Anderson, J.G. and J.E. Smith. 1976. Effects of temperature on filamentous fungi. In *Inhibition and Inactivation of Vegetative*

Microbes, Eds F.A. Skinner and W.B. Hogo. American Press, London : New York, pp191–217.

Brokerhof, A.W. 1989. *Control of Fungi and Insects in Objects and Collections of Cultural Value: 'State of the Art'.* Central Laboratory for Objects of Art and Science, Amsterdam.

Calcott, P.H. 1978. *Freezing and Thawing Microbes.* Meadowfield Press, England.

Churchill, J.A., G.E.W. Wolstenholme & M. O'Conner. 1970. *The Frozen Cell*, J.A. Churchill Publishers, London.

Cole, G.T. and B. Kendrick. 1981. *Biology of Conidial Fungi*, Vol. 2. Academic Press, New York.

Di Maggio, D. 1980. Effect of nitrogen storage on the fungal contamination of cereal grains. In *Controlled Atmosphere Storage of Grains*, Ed. J. Shejbal, Elsevier Scientific Publishing, New York, pp147–155.

Griffin, D.H. 1981. *Fungal Physiology*. Wiley-Interscience publication, New York.

Haines, R.B. 1934. The minimum temperature of growth of some bacteria. *Biological Applications of Freeze-drying*, 34:277–282.

Hall, R. 1981. Physiology of Conidial Fungi. In *Biology of Conidial Fungi*, Vol. 2, Eds G.T. Cole and B. Kendrick, Academic Press, New York, pp417–457.

Mazur, P. 1956. Studies on the effects of sub-zero temperatures on the viability of spores of *Aspergillus flavus.* 1. The effect of rate of warming. *Journal of General Physiology*, 39:869–888.

Mazur, P. 1960. Physical factors implicated in the death of microorganisms at sub-zero temperatures. *Annuals of the New York Academy of Science*, 85:610–629.

Mazur, P. 1965. Causes of injury in frozen and thawed cells. *Federal of the American Societies for Experimental Biology Cryobiology*, 24(2) Part III, Suppl. 15:S175–182.

Mazur, P. 1968. Survival of fungi after freezing and desiccation. In *The Fungi An Advanced Treatise, Vol III, The Fungal Population*, Eds C. Ainsworth and A.S. Sussman. Academic Press, New York, pp325–394.

Meryman, H.T. 1966. Review of biological freezing. In *Cryobiology*, Ed. H.T. Meryman, Academic Press, London, UK, pp2–114.

Nakamura, H. and J. Hoshino. 1983. Techniques for the preservation of food by employment of oxygen absorber. In *Sanitation Control for Food Sterilizing Techniques*, Sanyu Publishing Co, Tokyo, pp1–44.

Northolt, M.D. and L.B. Bullerman. 1982. Prevention of mould and toxin production through control of environmental conditions. *Journal of Food Protection*, 45(6):519–526.

Pitt. J.I. 1981. Food spoilage and biodeterioration. In *Biology of Conidial Fungi*, Vol. 2, Eds. G.T. Cole and B. Kendrick. Academic Press, New York, pp111–142.

Rivera-Rodriguez, N., and N. R. del Valle. 1992. Effects of calcium ions on the germination of *Sporothrix schenckii* conidia. *Journal of Medical and Veterinary Mycology*, 30:185–195.

Scott, W.J. 1957. Water relations of food spoilage microorganisms. *Advances in Food Research*,7:83–127.

Serafini, M., A.A. Fabbri, J. Shejbal, C. Fanelli, D. Di Maggio and A. Rambelli. 1980. Influence of nitrogen on the growth of some storage fungi on moist wheat. In *Controlled Atmosphere Storage of Grains*, Ed. J. Shejbal, Elsevier Scientific Publishing, New York, pp157–171.

Sussman, A.S. 1976. Activators of fungal conidia germination. In *The Fungal Spore. Form and Function*, Eds. D.J. Weber and W.M. Hess. Wiley-Interscience Publication, New York, pp101–139.

Valentin, N., M. Lidstrom and F. Preusser. 1990. Microbial control by low oxygen and low relative humidity environment. *Studies in Conservation*, 35:222–230.

Walker, G.M., P.A. Sullivan and M.G. Shepherd. 1984. Magnesium and the regulation of germ tube formation in *Candida albicans. Journal of General Microbiology*, 130:1941–1945.

Wellheiser, J.G. 1992. *Non-chemical Treatment Processes for Disinfestation of Insects and Fungi in Library Collections, 60.* K.G. Saur, Munich.

18

The Fungal Infestation

18.1 MANIFESTATION OF FUNGAL GROWTH

18.1.1 Fungal growth may be in or on materials

Active fungal growth *in* materials of heritage objects is rare. When it occurs it may be the result of growth of conidia which have been incorporated into the materials during fabrication (paper making), or by some cleaning or conservation treatment (contaminated protein glue) or of a fungus which was already growing in the material (e.g. in wood or hair) before it was used to make the heritage object.

The majority of fungal infestations are *on* surfaces of heritage objects. The surfaces have been contaminated with conidia which came from airspora and landed and germinated on the surface of the object material. The airborne conidia could come from outside air or from indoor mouldy surfaces, such as humidifiers, fruit, mouldy artifacts. (See airspora section in chapter 16 for more detail.)

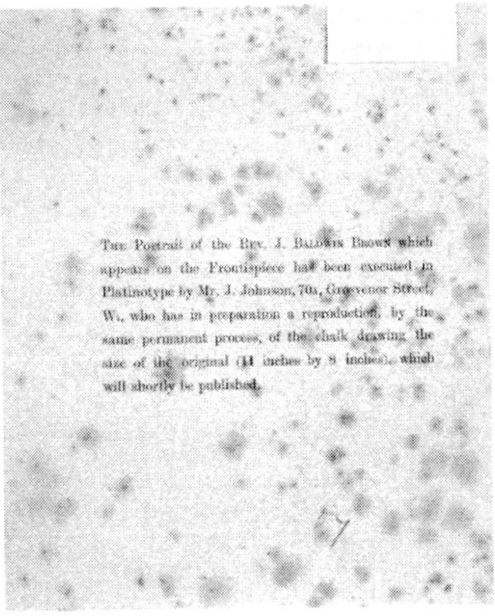

THE Portrait of the REV. J. BALDWIN BROWN which appears on the Frontispiece has been executed in Platinotype by Mr. J. Johnson, 70a, Grosvenor Street, W., who has in preparation a reproduction, by the same permanent process, of the chalk drawing the size of the original (14 inches by 8 inches), which will shortly be published.

Figure 18.1. Fungal growth on a 19th-century book. The circular nature of the spots suggest that they are a result of growth of airborne fungi which landed on the page and because of a conducive environment were able to germinate and develop circular colonies (by M-L. Florian).

18.1.2 The origin of the contamination influences the fungal growth patterns

Single conidia, from airspora, which germinate on surfaces with limited water or nutrients can develop into a small circular colony (Figures 18.1 (6204, 6205), 14.3 and 16.2). If environmental conditions become conducive for growth, a luxuriant colony, dusty from conidiation, can develop. Depending on the nature of the substrate, fungal hyphae may penetrate the substrate or be restricted to the surface.

Besides airspora, the conidia could come from physical contact with mouldy materials, which may result in the transfer of large numbers of conidia to the heritage object surface. If only a small group of the conidia (Figure 18.2 – 9701 and 9711 – overleaf) was transferred, germinated and then died, an irregularly shaped spot is formed. Florian (1996a, b) has shown this to be the cause of irregularly shaped fox spots on 18th- and 19th-century paper.

If the surface is extensively contaminated with conidia it will be completely covered with a uniform fungal growth. This would also occur if a contaminated solution was applied to the surface. An example of a stone sculpture of a lion illustrates this point. On the surface of the sculpture were a few isolated fungal spots. The surface of the sculpture was washed all over with a non-ionic detergent solution. Within a few weeks the complete surface of the sculpture was covered with fungal growth. This occurred because the washing solution had become contaminated with the conidia and they were spread all over the surface during the washing process. It is likely that the detergent acted as an activator for germinated conidia.

Florian and Dudley (1976) showed that papers used in paper conservation treatments were often contaminated with conidia. Samples of 12 different types of paper were placed on sterile culture media in petri plates and the surface conidia on the paper samples germinated and produced growth. The results showed that each paper had a specific pattern of fungal growth. Some papers were covered with only one species of fungus, which suggested contamination during manufacturing or contact with mouldy materials. Some papers developed a few circular colonies, of different colours, from a variety of fungal species, which suggested normal surface contamination from airspora. One paper which had been treated to prevent water adsorption did not support any fungal growth, illustrating the influence of the microenvironment of the paper on fungal growth.

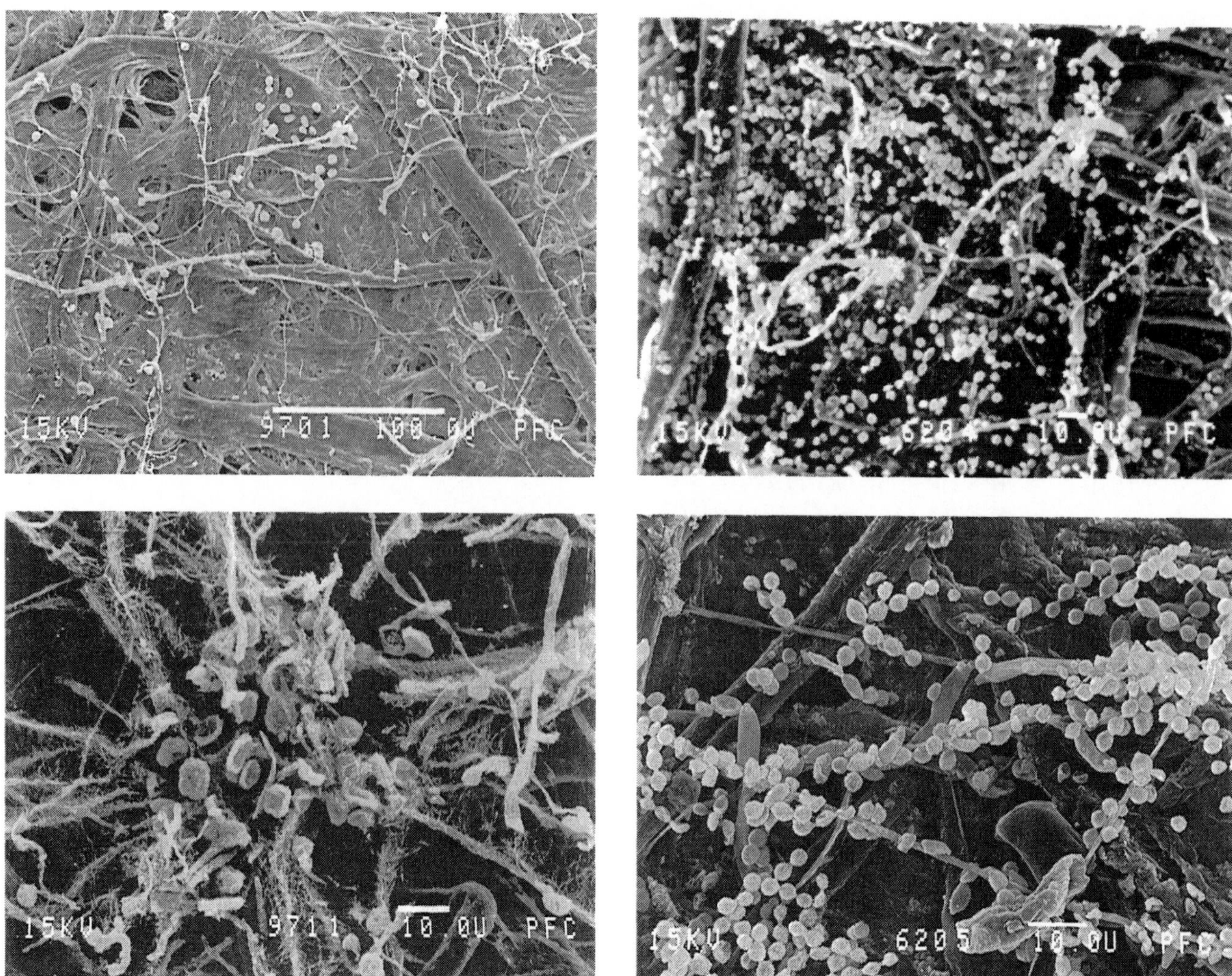

Figure 18.2. Scanning electron micrographs of old and contemporary fungal spots on paper. Micrographs 9701 and 9711 (top and bottom left) are of old fungal spots, caused by surface contamination during the fabrication of the book. Micrographs 6204 and 6205 (top and bottom right) are contemporary fungal spots which grew on paper from airborne conidia. 9701 shows the sparse growth on a true fox spot. The details of the old conidia in 9711 show their dehydrated forms and separation of the paper fibres. The contemporary spots show a profuse growth and conidiation (formation of conidia). The newly formed conidia are still in chains (by Lesley Manning, Microtechnique Biologist, Scanning Electron Microscopy Laboratory, Pacific Forest Centre, Canada Forest Centre).

18.1.3 What are they feeding on?

Conidia contain a small amount of endogenous nutrients that can only support germination. Conidia can germinate with just water, but cannot develop mycelia without absorbing exogenous nutrients, such as simple sugars, amino acids and fatty acids. If these are not present in the substrate, the fungi can enzymatically break down complex biochemicals in the substrate, for example carbohydrates, proteins and fats, into absorbable forms. Only a few specific fungi have the ability to attack the structural chemicals, cellulose, collagen and keratin.

Dust on the surfaces of materials may contain starch grains, oil, plant and animal cells, fibres of all sorts and particulate material. It traps conidia and because of the extensive fibre surfaces can be a moist microenvironment which may support some conidial germination but little, if any, mycelium growth.

Sometimes the simple organic nutrients needed for fungal activity are on surfaces of heritage objects that have been exposed to deteriorating environments during use. An example would be the presence of free amino acids from the breakdown of collagen on the surface of the weathered leather of a purse, saddle, etc. Some surfaces of textiles and paper are treated with grounds or sizes that contain free amino acids and simple sugars. These nutrients increase the moisture content of the material. The surface would then have a unique microenvironment with its readily absorbable nutrients and extra moisture. For the lucky conidia that land there, germination and some mycelial growth are assured.

All surfaces have conidia from airspora, but only some surfaces support their development. Deteriorated surfaces with nutrients and moisture, and surfaces which are rough, electrostatically charged or sticky and capture conidia are prone to fungal growth. Materials that have lost their regain ability and have a low moisture content or are impregnated with solutes (such as salt or glycerol) that lower the water activity, rarely support fungal activity. This is discussed in detail under water relationships of fungi in section 17.1.

Once the easily digested nutrients in the substrate are utilized, some fungi, by a feedback mechanism, may respond to the presence of the structural organic materials, cellulose, collagen, and keratin, and produce specific enzymes to digest them. Only a few species of fungi are specialized to produce these specific enzymes. Such is the case with the wood infesting fungi. Some can produce only cellulase and digest cellulose and some can only produce lignase which digests lignin, thus respectively the brown and white rot fungi.

There is only a small group of fungal species which can digest collagen and keratin but a larger group which can digest cellulose. In nature, it is usually bacteria which break down these structural chemicals.

It is important to realize that the manifestation of fungal activity on surfaces of heritage objects is dependent on the material of the object, the fungal species, method of contamination and density and age of the growth, as well as the environmental conditions during growth.

18.1.4 Determination of the location of the discolouration and presence of fungal structures in infested material

There are many papers that describe and illustrate the fungal structures on all types of heritage objects (Aranyanak, 1995; Beckwith *et al.* 1940; Daniel, 1988; Florian, 1994, 1996a; Gallo and Hey, 1986; Gallo and Pasquariello, 1989; Kowalik *et al.*, 1962; Nyuksha, 1960; Szczepanowska, 1986; Szczepanowska and Lovett, 1992; Valentin, 1986).

Near ultraviolet black light has been used to highlight fox spots on paper (Bertalan, 1994; Gallo and Pasquariello, 1991). The fox spots appear as yellowish or white fluorescent spots against a black background. But, unfortunately, it has not been verified if all the fluorescent spots contain fungal structures.

By using a dissecting light microscope (10–20x magnification), it is possible to view pigmented fungal structures directly on the paper or textile without any pretreatment or sampling. Determining the presence of non-pigmented hyphae in the substrate is not always possible, but because of the abnormal direction of the hyphae and different size in relationship to the substrate fibres they may be obvious.

If verification has not been accomplished by this method, when ethically possible, minute samples taken from one of the spots can be stained with histological stains. Many stains are recommended in the literature to stain the fungal structures. A simple non-toxic solution can be made from 0.5% of aniline blue, or 0.5% cotton blue, or 0.5% toluidine blue in a 20% aqueous solution of glycerol. The fungal hyphae will stain blue. The minute samples are placed directly into a small drop of the chosen stain solution on the microscope slide and then covered with a glass cover slip for microscope viewing.

18.1.5 Contemporary and aged fungal spots

18.1.5.1 Introduction

Surface fungal activity may have occurred within a few months or hundreds of years ago; for convenience they are called contemporary or aged fungal spots (Figure 18.2).

Aged spots started out just like contemporary spots but because of the ravages of time, photo-oxidation and hydrolysis, etc., they have become rusty brown in colour. Contemporary spots, which have occurred within the last few years, still have the inherent colour of the fungal structures and pigments with no discoloration in the substrate fibres. As fungal spots age, the fungal structures change to a rusty brown colour and there may also be a colour change in the substrate fibres. It is a universal phenomenon. In the paper and archival world these aged spots are called fox spots because of the similarity in colour to the rusty brown of fox fur. The possible causes of the colour are discussed under fungal metabolic products in section 18.2.

The shapes of the contemporary and aged spots show common causes. Irregular, diffuse, aged and contemporary spots may have originated from surface contamination by a few conidia, as described above. The contemporary spots are often overlooked because they are not easily seen. They are just germinated conidia and appear only as wisps of fluff in raking (horizontal) light. Aged, irregular spots are easily observed because of their rusty brown colour.

Circular spots with a dusty surface are commonly caused by single conidia that have developed to form a mycelium and produce new conidia. If these spots are old they will have the rusty brown colour (Figure 18.1), but if they are contemporary they will have the green or black colour of the conidia. In both spots the conidiophore, structures on which the conidia develop, will be present (Figure 16.2).

18.1.5.2 Contemporary spots: evidence of fungal activity

Surface growth on materials can vary from minute spots to confluent growth with or without dusty conidia. The effects on the material may vary from slight discoloration to complete enzymatic solublization, depending on the species of the fungus.

In most cases the fungus is only growing in the dust and deterioration products on the surface of the materials. In these cases, in a recent infestation, when the fungus is removed mechanically (vacuum, dry swabs, electrostatically) the cleaned surface may or may not show evidence of fungal activity. If there still is discoloration, it can be due to the presence of coloured conidia trapped between fibres or pigmented hyphae, sclerotia, or secreted pigments in the substrate.

In fibrous materials (paper, textiles), if the growth has penetrated the surface and has digested some of the additives (sizes, grounds) between the fibres, the spots will appear as depressions that will have greater light penetration and wettability.

If the fibrous material (wood cells, collagen bundles, hairs) is enzymatically attacked, pitting and lytic troughs may be apparent along the length of the fibres. Pitting has been observed in hairs of natural history specimens in storage and reported to be caused by fungal activity (Hawks and Rowe, 1988; Nygam, 1995). A lytic trough is made by the fungal hyphae digesting a pathway along the fibre on which it lies. An example is the soft rot fungi of wood which attack the cellulose in cells of wet wood surfaces in outdoor environments. Their activity is seen by characteristic lytic troughs which follow the cellulose spiral alignment in the cell wall.

A few fungi (e.g. *Chaetomium globosum*) which can digest the cellulose in cotton and linen fibres in paper or textiles may cause a complete loss of the fibres in the area of infestation. In such extreme cases the fungal hyphae may be felting the damaged area giving it its only strength.

Different types of fungal growth patterns on contemporary surface will be observed depending on the amount of growth, restrictive nature of the substrate (material) and the fungal species. Some examples are shown in Figures 18.2–18.5.

Spots of surface growth on a layered paper card with an aluminium silicate ground (Figure 18.3) show the pigmented fungal hyphae lying in lytic troughs or depressions caused by digestion of the ground or binder.

Spots of surface growth on a bond paper showed discoloration of the amorphous ground with no visually observable damage to fibres. The hyphae (pigmented or unpigmented) were loosely attached on the surface and between fibres.

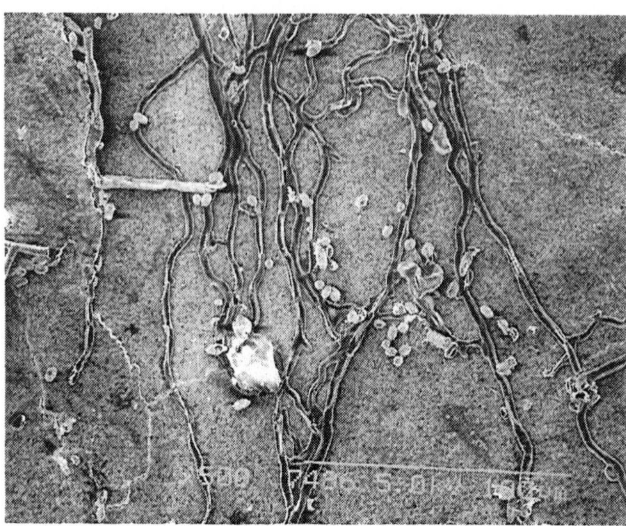

Figure 18.3. Spots of surface growth on a layered paper card with an aluminum silicate ground show the pigmented fungal hyphae lying lytic troughs or depressions caused by digestion of the ground or binder (by Mary Mager, SEM Microscopist, Scanning Electron Microscope Laboratory, Metallurgical Engineering, University of British Columbia).

Figure 18.4. Circular black spots on cotton textile showed pigmented hyphae entwined between the ultimates of the threads with little or no evidence of damage or discoloration of the fibres. The hyphae were pigmented (by Mary Mager, SEM Microscopist, Scanning Electron Microscope Laboratory, Metallurgical Engineering, University of British Columbia).

Conidiation had occurred and the conidia were black and loose on the surface.

Circular black spots on cotton textile (Figure 18.4) showed pigmented hyphae entwined between the ultimates (single fibres) of the threads with little or no evidence of damage or discoloration of the fibres. The hyphae were pigmented.

Spots on a plastic felted tyvec (Figure 18.5) showed pigmented hyphae and sclerotia confluent with the substrate fibres.

Spots on kraft cardboard show hyphae throughout the thickness of the paper and surface-pigmented conidia with little or no discoloration of the substrate.

18.1.5.3 Aged Fungal Infestations – Fox Spots

There is extensive conservation literature that describes fox spots on paper. This literature is thoroughly reviewed in the *Paper Conservation Catalog* (Bertalan, 1994). There is agreement that there is a need for a better description of these disfiguring and damaging spots. The general understanding is that they are discrete spots which are darker than the normal substrate, e.g. paper. Confusion sets in when large diffuse offprints, margin shadows and tide lines are also called foxing. Some spots may be caused by accidental aerosol spray of cleaning solutions, sneezes, rain, food, etc. These liquid splashes can be identified by their characteristic tide margin or water front.

The literature review (Bertalan, 1994) suggests that there are different causes for the spots on paper. The discoloration in paper could be due to (i) photo-oxidation of lignin, grounds, fillers, or cellulose, (ii) inherent particulate iron, copper or iron sulphide incorporated during manufacturing, (iii) fungal metabolic products which interact with themselves (glucose and amino acids), (iv) fungal metabolic products which interact with the substrate, (v) free fungal pigments in the substrate; and (vi) pigmented fungal structures.

Cain and Miller (1984) have classified various fox spots: *bullseyes* with a dark centre and concentric rings; *snowflakes* with light brown areas having scalloped edges and without a central spot, *offprints* and *shadows*. The latter two are related

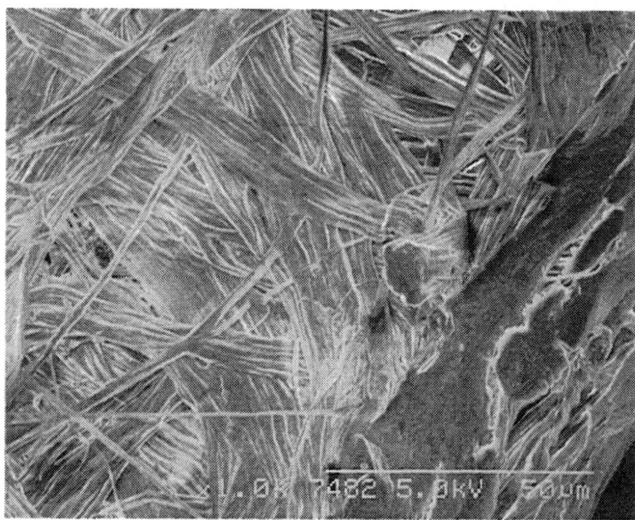

Figure 18.5. Spots on a plastic felted paper tyvec showed a mass of pigmented hyphae, a sclerotia, confluent with the substrate fibres (by Mary Mager, SEM Microscopist, Scanning Electron Microscope Laboratory, Metallurgical Engineering, University of British Columbia).

to the print on a page. The bullseye spots are associated with a central iron fragment, and most of the snowflakes have a small increase of iron concentration, within 10% over the background. In this latter class, fungal hyphae were noted in a few spots and the spots showed variable responses to ultraviolet absorbancy.

Meynell and Newsan (1978) examined fox spots which they described as irregular, yellowish-brown patches that did not appear mouldy to the eye and where the paper was intact. They examined the fox spots using a histological technique for staining fungal structures and showed the presence of fungal hyphae. Gallo and Pasquariello (1991) have carried out extensive work over the years showing the presence of fungi in fox spots. Gallo and Hey (1986) have observed fungal structures in fox spots and have tried to duplicate the stains by using fungi isolated from these spots, but without success.

Linterink *et al.* (1991) after discovering the repetition of identically shaped foxed areas on pages in different parts of a book and in other books of the same title, realized that these were papers which had been stacked and dried together at one time and then separated prior to bookbinding. The stain had migrated through the sheets of paper in the stack, leading to the conclusion that foxing stains are three-dimensional stain structures which are generated in stacks of paper either during the production process or in the book itself. The study did not undertake any microscopic examination of the paper to determine what had migrated but suggested that foxing may be due to moisture condensation processes.

Strzelczyk and Pronobis-Bobowska (1993) analysed rusty-red irregularly shaped fox spots and reported: (i) they are not associated with iron, (ii) they are found on ancient and modern papers but are more abundant on 19th-century papers, (iii) they show fluorescence under ultraviolet light, (iv) they are more acidic than adjacent unfoxed paper and (v) they contain amino acids. They did not examine the spots for the presence of fungal structures.

Arai (1993) considered fungi as the causative agents for brown fox spots on hemp paper and demonstrated the presence of fungal metabolic products in these spots.

Florian (1996a) reported on the commonest rusty-brown, irregular spots on 18th- and 19th-century books and showed that they contain a small group of fungal conidia, some of which have germinated and produced only limited hyphal growth (Figure 18.2 – 9701 and 9711). Some of the fox spots which showed migration of the colour through 3 or 4 pages, contained a group of conidia in the spot only on one side of one of the pages involved. The origin of the contamination is suggested to be during the paper-making process. Papermakers' felts were suggested as the origin of the contamination (Sharpely and King, 1972).

Florian (1996b) reported on analyses of different coloured, not rusty-brown, spots which showed particles of iron, calcium, bronze and protein. There was no evidence of fungi in these spots.

Our present knowledge shows that there are different colours and causes of spots which we clump together as fox spots. It seems logical at this stage to call only the rusty-brown spots 'fox spots', because of their colour. These spots appear to have all been caused by fungal activity. The shapes vary, which suggests different methods of initial contamination of these spots.

The irregular, diffusely shaped fox spots are caused by contamination during fabrication of the paper. Circular, fluffy fox spots, which are often located toward the outsides of the pages and on the sides of the book, originated from contamination during use.

At the moment, fox spot seems to be a useful term but in the near future, when we are able to describe the stains better, we should use a specific terms such as conidial spot, fungal growth spot, iron stain, water stain, etc.

18.1.6 The colour in fox spots

18.1.6.1 The source of the colour

It must be determined what type of spot is under discussion. There are several types of spot: (i) those that originated from a group of conidia, some of which germinated and produced minimal hyphal growth, (ii) those that developed mycelia and (iii) those that developed along with mycelium conidiophores and new conidia. Each one will leave in the substrate a different group of products. The conidia will leave their structures and minimal amounts, if any, of metabolic product and products of substrate hydrolysis. The mycelia will leave an array of metabolic products and their structural chemicals, and breakdown products of the substrate. The final stages will be rich in metabolic products (mainly organic acids and products of their structures), new conidia and minimal breakdown products of the substrate. The most important point is that all colonies, on ageing, form rusty-red fox spots.

Thus the system with the conidia with the least amount of materials holds the key to the cause of the discoloration. What is there is basically the structural components of the fungus. The major chemicals of these structures are lipids and proteins. In these spots the colour comes from two sources: a rusty-red, alkaline-soluble material and an alkaline-insoluble, straw-coloured stain in the paper fibres. When the contaminated page was new, there was no obvious discoloration in the spot, but the fungal structures or products have formed a unique chemical environment which, over time, has caused the discoloration in the structures, as well as in the paper fibres.

Discoloration of the paper fibres in unfoxed, sized paper has been attributed to acid damage. Bertalan (1994) and Strzelczyk and Pronobis-Bobowska (1993) reported that the acidity of fox spots is higher than the native paper. Considering these two points, because of the similarity in colour of the paper fibres in the fox spots on unsized paper and in unfoxed, sized paper, this paper fibre discoloration may also be due to acid damage.

The question of the role of iron in enhancing the chemical activity and discoloration in the spots is still an issue (Cain, 1993; Cain and Miller, 1984; Tang, 1978). There may be a slight increase of iron, above the background, in snowflake spots (Cain and Miller, 1984) associated with fungi. Florian (1996b), reported that Electron Dense X-ray analyses did not show iron levels above the background in the rusty-brown fox spots (the same as snowflake spots). Hyphae of fungi have a strong chelation ability for iron and many other metals. Mycelium globs mixed with the slurry of paper fibres in iron vats could possibly chelate iron and if these mycelium globs were incorporated into the paper they could show an increase in iron. Mycelium globs were observed (Florian, 1996b) in grey spots with a smooth depressed surface, thus were not considered as fox spots, and there was no increase in iron in these spots.

Arai *et al.* (1988) reported that fungal amino acids, metabolic acids and sugars are present in extracts of fox spots. They hypothesized that the colour in fox spots could be caused by the formation of the red-yellow to red-brown melanoidin which could be formed in the paper by the interaction of the amino acids and sugars. This reaction is called the Maillard browning reaction (Hayashi and Namiki, 1986). It is a very common heat-initiated reaction which we observe every day in the brown crusts of our bread. The Maillard reaction and melanoidin colour is influenced by the type of amino compound and reducing sugar. More melanoidin is formed and the colour is redder under alkaline conditions than under acidic conditions.

Arai *et al.* (1990), in an effort to induce fox spots artificially by the formation of melanoidins, tested a number of amino acids and sugar combinations. α–Aminobutyric acid in combination with glucose gave the most obvious fox-coloured spot, which was fluorescent, and they stated that α–aminobutyric acid along with L-malic acid and glucose are the main causes of fox spots.

Florian (1996a,b) suggested that the fungal structures play a major role in the colour formation in the fox spots. The chemical composition of conidia varies with species and nutritional state, but on average the main components are nearly 50% proteins, up to 50% lipids and 5% trehalose (sugar) of the dry weight.

Conidia of ascomycetes and fungi imperfecti are reported (Schmit and Brody, 1976; Weete, 1980) with lipid amounts of up to 50% dry weight. The lipid composition in conidia is reported to be similar to mycelia. The oxidation of polyunsaturated fatty acids forms lipid hydroperoxides which are strong oxidizing agents.

In the food industry, lipid auto-oxidation, which forms very destructive high-energy free radicals and peroxides, is a major problem in the browning of food and the breakdown of proteins during food storage (Karel, 1978). Lipid auto-oxidation increases with a decrease of water and is accompanied by a fluorescent lipoprotein that in the food industry is called an ageing protein.

Considering that the auto-oxidative reactions of lipids are not heat initiated, are accompanied by a fluorescent product, occur under low water and occur commonly, it could be hypothesized that lipid auto-oxidation alone could cause the browning of the fungal structures and the paper fibres, in fox spots. Lipid auto-oxidation could also cause the observed breakdown of the fungal proteins to soluble amino acids, as well as the discoloration in the paper fibres.

Peroxides and fluorescence which are observed in tidelines (Eusman, 1995) of old paper could also be the result of lipid auto-oxidation, and the lipids could come from conidial and mycelial fragments which must be present in all handmade papers.

Analyses of water and alkaline extracts from the fox spots are ongoing (Florian, 1996a).

18.1.6.2 *Conservation efforts to remove the colour in fox spots*

In the conservation treatment literature (Bertalan, 1994) many methods for fox spot removal from paper have been suggested. It has been a difficult task. Most of the treatments give only partial reduction of the discoloration or a temporary improvement. Bleaching is the most common treatment. Bleaching is not a stabilizing treatment and may be damaging, thus it can only be used after careful consideration of preservation and aesthetic concerns. Chelating agents have been used to remove the iron, but without determining if iron is really present or is the cause of discoloration. The majority of these papers do not identify the cause or type of stain.

There are a few papers (Gallo and Hey, 1986; Szczepanowska, 1986; Szczepanowska and Lovett, 1992; Wojtczak, 1990) which report on treatments specifically for fungal spots, e.g. organic solvents have shown some success in the removal of fungal pigments. Fluffy, surface fungal growth has been removed mechanically and by vacuum aspiration (Lee, 1988; Szszepanowska and Lovett, 1992). Lasers have been tried (Asmus, 1986; Szczepanowska and Lovett, 1992;), but potential substrate damage needs to be determined.

18.2 THE COMPOSITION OF FUNGAL STRUCTURES AND PRODUCTS IN FUNGAL INFESTATIONS

18.2.1 Introduction

The fungal colony, whether a minute spot or profuse colony, may contain: hyphae and other fungal structures; secreted and internal metabolic products (enzymes, amino acids, organic acids, pigments, proteins); chelated metals and oxygen. Other fungal structures such as conidia, spores and sclerotia may also be present.

The following literature review includes relevant information about the fungal structures and products present in an infestation. The information pertains to the group of filamentous conidial fungi which are the common surface fungi.

One of the greatest problems in conservation of paper and textiles is the removal of fungal spots. The literature is reviewed in reference to this problem: what's there and how can it be removed.

18.2.2 The structure and chemistry of fungal structures and metabolic products

18.2.2.1 *Hyphal cell wall structure and chemistry*

The cell walls of fungal hyphae are similar in structure to the cellulose walls of plant cells, but differ chemically. The cell walls are composed of four layers of different thicknesses with different amounts of amorphous glucans in which are embedded chitin micrifibrils at different angles (Figure 18.6). The conidia have a similar cell wall.

The outside layer, which may be covered with a polysaccharide mucus, contains a mixture of glucans and mannose, which are water or alkaline soluble. Next is a layer of glucans complexed with proteins. This layer is separated from the innermost layer by a protein layer. The inside layer, which may make up to about two-thirds of the wall, is a layer of chitin microfibrils embedded in a matrix of glucans associated with a protein in the form of a glycoprotein.

It is an incredibly strong and insoluble structure. It is ironic that the mycelial wastes from the lemonade citric acid industry

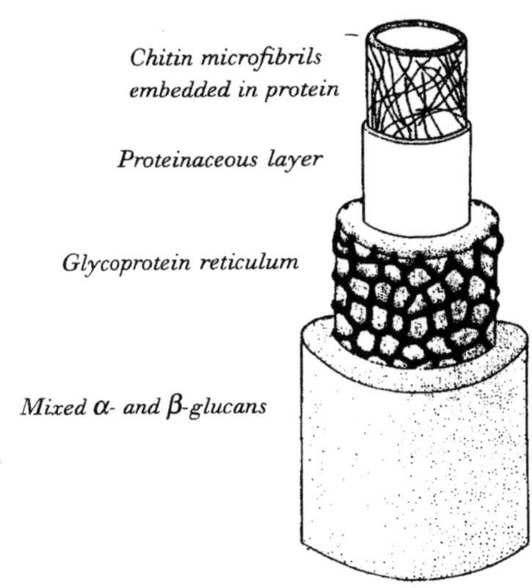

Figure 18.6. Details of the structure of the cell wall of hyphae of Neurospora crassa, *a common conidial fungus. The cell walls are composed of four layers of different thicknesses with different amounts of amorphous glucans in which are embedded chitin micrifibrils at different angles (from Burnett, 1976).*

and others are used in the pulp used to make wet-laid papers (used for water filters) to increase wet strength and metal adsorption (Wales and Sagar, 1990). Maybe this mycelial waste will be used for paper conservation repairs and metal chelation in the future.

Sclerotia (Willetts and Bullock, 1992) are hard, tuber-like, minute masses of organized hyphae formed when the fungus is stressed by an adverse environment. The sclerotia has a melanin-pigmented outer rind, middle cortex and internal medulla. The function of the sclerotia is to store glycogen, fats and proteins for growth of the hyphae when conducive growth parameters return. Sclerotia are commonly present in fungal spots in natural and synthetic textiles (Figure 18.5).

The amounts of the chemicals in the hyphal cell wall vary with species. One example is an albino strain of *Aspergillus nidulans*, which contains 55.1% glucans, 14.3% chitin, 10.8% galactosamine, 10.6% protein and 9.0% lipid (Kuo and Alexander, 1967). In brown-pigmented hyphae the pigment *melanin* may be in amounts of up to 50%, but this varies with the age of cultures, light, stress and species. Melanin is embedded in the outer layers, usually in the form of small particles 30–150nm in size.

Chitin, an insoluble linear β–(1,4)-linked polymer of *N*-acetylglucoseamine (GlcNAc), is one of the most abundant polysaccharides in nature. Bartnicki-Garcia (1968) has shown that there are eight chemical taxonomic categories of the cell wall into which fungi can be placed. The taxonomic groups of fungi, *Ascomycetes* and *Deuteromycetes*, contain the conidial fungi which cause surface growth or spots on damp textiles, paper or leather, and have the cell wall chemical category of chitin–glucans complex. The glucans are non-cellulosic glucans with β–(1,3)-linked glucose residues.

The solubility of the glucan–chitin complex is important if hyphae have to be removed from infested artifact materials (Florian and Purinton, 1995). The variation and complexity in the glucan–chitin complex, with glucans, glycoproteins and chitin, makes the solubility complicated. Chemical solvents for chitin are given in the literature (Burnett and Trinci, 1975; Muzzarelli, 1977) but the solvents are extremely toxic and/or not suitable for conservation treatment, e.g. hexafluoro-isopropanol, hexafluoroacetone sesquihydrate, 2-chloroethanol, 1-chloro-2-propanol, 40% trichloroacetic acid, 40% chloral hydrate and 20% methylene chloride, *N,N*-dimethylacetamide and a lithium chloride mixture.

For further information, see Bartnicki-Garcia (1968), Burnett and Trinci (1979), Muzzarelli (1977) and Zikakis (1984).

18.2.2.2 THE ENZYMES USED FOR HYDROLYSES OF CHITIN-GLUCAN COMPLEX

The enzyme mixture of a glucanase and chitinase has been used to remove insoluble hyphal cell walls. The choice of a specific enzyme is not as easy as just purchasing a protease for protein hydrolysis. There are different chitinases and glucanases which are commercially prepared from different micro-organism sources and each acts a little differently. For example, in the literature the following glucanases have been used: Exo-**B**–D-(1-3) glucanase, β–glucosidase (E.C.3.2.1.21), chitobiase (E.C.3.2.1.29) and chitinase (E.C.3.2.1.14). Enzymes are described by the Enzyme Commission (EC) system of classification according to the position of chemical bonds they lyse. The commercially available enzymes, because they originate from micro-organisms, have the specified enzyme and often contain smaller amounts of other enzymes, such as cellulase.

The enzyme mixture of a glucanase and chitinase has been used to remove the insoluble fraction of the cell wall (Kuo and Alexander, 1967). It was shown that the higher the melanin content the less effective were the enzymes, which supports the role of melanin in protection against biodegradation. Potgieter and Alexander (1966) showed that some bacteria can digest the hyphal walls of specific fungal species, but the sclerotia of *Rhizoctonia solani*, which contain 8.5% melanin-like material, are resistant. This suggests the role of melanin in protection from microbial lysis. On the other hand, in soil the fungus *Trichoderma harzianum* excretes β–glucosase and chitinase which can dissolve melanin-containing sclerotia of *Rhizoctonia solani* and *Pythium aphanidermatum*. This suggests that secretions from *T. harzianum* could be used to degrade black hyphae in paper biologically, but, unfortunately, it also produces cellulase.

This enzyme treatment seems a logical conservation treatment for removal of pigmented hyphae, but there are problems. Edmond and Horton-James (1991) used this method to try to remove black hyphae from modern acrylic paint on wooden Australian aboriginal objects. They were unsuccessful and attributed the failure to the inability to control the appropriate enzyme concentrations. Florian and Purinton (1995) tried the above enzymes in various sequences and were not able to digest black, melanin-containing hyphae from paper, tyvec or cotton. They attributed the poor results to inhibition of enzymes by melanin.

Sporopollen is another structural chemical found in some fungi (Gooday, 1981) which is insoluble. We are familiar with this in pollen grains. It is the resistance of sporopollen that has allowed the ancient pollen grains to survive for eons. It is resistant to strong acids and alkalis but can be degraded by using a strong oxidizing agent followed by concentrated strong acids. This is not the sort of treatment recommended in conservation.

Florian (1996a) reported that fungal structures in fox spots, approximately 150 years old, were soluble in alkaline solutions, which suggests that the insoluble cell wall had been attacked by the chemical environment in the fox spot over the years.

For further information, see Bloomfield and Alexander (1967), Kuo and Alexander (1967), Muzzarelli (1977) and Zomer *et al.* (1985).

18.2.3 **Pigments**

18.2.3.1 Melanin and other brown pigments

Melanins are a group of chemically similar, brown or black pigments. The role of melanins in fungi is for survival through protection from ultraviolet light, soil degradation and biodeterioration, and for structural rigidity and ion binding. Melanin has a great biosorption ability for copper, cobalt, cadmium and an organotin (Gadd *et al.* 1990).

Melanins are formed by oxidative polymerization of non-nitrogenous phenolics called polymeric quinoid pigments. They are found in the cell wall and free in the substrate from secreted phenols. Melanin confined to the cell wall may be in granules or amorphous. The insoluble melanin in the soil is the main component of humic acid.

There are also brown pigments formed in culture media from the hydrolysis of the amino acid tyrosine by secreted tyrosinase. The slowing or stopping of growth often induces the formation of tyrosinase which leads to the accumulation of melanin. Also, the amounts of tyrosine-based and melanin pigments in substrates increase with the age of the cultures.

Melanins are insoluble in water, mineral acids and the usual organic solvents, but soluble in alkali and are bleached by oxidizing agents.

Melanin inhibits lysis of fungi by a chitinase and β–(1-2)-glucanase mixture (Kuo and Alexander, 1967).

Melanin in *Aspergillus phoenicis* conidial walls, *Aspergillus nidulans* cell walls and sclerotia of *Cladosporium* and *Sclerotium rolfsii* was dissolved by 1N potassium hydroxide, and bleached by 5% sodium hypochlorite and 30% hydrogen peroxide, allowing lysis of the pigmented structures (Bloomfield and Alexander, 1967). Bleaching of melanin has also been accomplished by using hydrogen peroxide along with copper (II), ultraviolet A light and high pH (Korytowski and Sarna, 1990).

For further information, see Bell and Wheeler (1986) and Rast *et al.* (1981).

18.2.3.2 The colourful pigments

Pigments in fungi may accumulate in hyphae and conidia or diffuse into the substrate. The location of the pigment can be determined by simple light microscopy. The production of a pigment is species specific but the amount is influenced by nutrients and metals in the substrate, and light and adverse environmental factors which cause limiting growth.

There is a series of papers on the structure and physical characteristics of fungal pigments in the journals, *Acta Chemica Scandinavica* and *Zeitschrift für Naturforsch*, and volumes of reference books on plant pigments (Kost, 1989), some of which are found in fungi. It is an immense topic.

Our major interest in the pigments is their removal. Logical methods should be based on their specific solubility. It is not clear from the literature if extraction of the pigments in cells requires prior cell lysis or breakdown of the cell walls.

Different pigments are soluble in different solvents. For instance, anthraquinone (a red-brown pigment) and sclerotiorin (yellow), are soluble in alkali, carotenoids (yellow, orange) are soluble in fat solvents, chitin-bound carotenoids are soluble in warm ethanol or acetone (Muzzarelli, 1977) and red anthrocyanin and xanthene (a pH indicator) are water-soluble. The methods of identification of the pigments in the literature (i.e. thin layer chromatography) give a key to their solubility because of the solvents used in the chromatography.

Many of the water-soluble pigments are pH indicators and some contain copper, zinc or iron.

There have been many studies on the fungal pigments or stains in or on artifact materials (Breccia *et al.* 1972; Gallo and Hey, 1986; Szczepanowksa, 1986; Szczepanowksa and Lovett, 1992; Wojtczak, 1990).

Wojtczak (1990) described the difficulty in removing fungal stains from paper. Organic solvents gave poor results and acidified bleaching, no removal. Gallo and Hey (1986) isolated what they considered to be the causative fungal species of the stains in old paper and reinfested paper with these species to duplicate the stains, but without success. They also described methods of stain removal and mentioned that the stains return, even if they have been bleached. This can be explained by the reduction of a melanin pigment during bleaching which could convert back to a dark pigment after oxidation. There needs to be a method to remove the pigment, not just chemically alter it.

A review of the above illustrates the difficulty in removing stains or pigment with present treatments. These treatments are for pigments which are free in the substrate and do not take into consideration that the stains may be melanin or other pigments incorporated into chitinous cell walls. The initial step should be to determine where the pigment is located. As mentioned before, it may be secreted pigment in the substrate, pigment bound to the hyphal cell wall or inside the cell or pigment in conidia. This can be determined simply by light microscopy.

For further information, see Kost (1989) and Neil (1987).

18.2.4 **Organic acids, enzymes, amino acids, sugars, lipids and glycerol**

18.2.4.1 Organic acids

During germination, after the germ tube has emerged, metabolic products necessary for growth and development are produced. Enzymes necessary for substrate digestion are secreted, as well as products of oxidative respiration; the organic acids from the Krebs cycle, i.e. citric, oxalic, succinic, glutamic, fumaric, malic and acetic acids, may be secreted into the substrate. The organic acids are common products, for example the lemonade industry is dependent on citric acid secreted by fungi.

Arai (1987) and Arai *et al.* (1988, 1990) isolated some of these organic acids from induced fox spots and from old fox spots on oriental hemp paper, and suggested their possible role in the formation of the discoloration in the fox spots.

18.2.4.2 Enzymes, amino acids and sugars

Enzymes necessary for substrate digestion are also secreted into the fungal spots. Proteolytic enzymes have been isolated from leather bookbinding infested with fungi by Makes (1984). There will be some products of enzymatic digestion, such as free amino acids, simple sugars, glycerol and fatty acids, depending on the substrate composition. Szczepanowska (1986) discussed both enzymes and metabolic products in reference to fungal activity on archival paper.

The literature on a common filamentous fungus shows that the predominant amino acids would be phenylalanine, glycine, glutamic acid and aspartic acid (Schmit and Brody, 1976). These amino acids were shown to be present in analyses of some fox spots on 150-year-old paper (Florian, 1996), and the relative amounts suggested conidial germination rather than mycelial growth products. Strzelczyk and Probonis-Bobowska (1993) used ninhydrin, which is a colour indicator for proteins and amino acids, on fox spots on paper *in situ*, and demonstrated the presence of proteins or amino acids in the stains.

Arai *et al.* (1988), identified some amino acids in fungal spots from archival materials. They theorized that the brown fox colour could be due to the chemical reaction of amino acids with glucose (Maillard reaction) which forms red-brown melanoidins.

Melanoidins are extremely common: the brown on a crust of bread is due to melanoidins. Ashoor and Zent (1984) examined the Maillard reaction using different reducing sugars and amino acids. They used a pH between 6 and12 because below pH 6 they did not get any browning. Most papers on which foxing is present are acidic, which is the least effective pH for melanoidin production.

They also tested different sugars and amino acids with regard to the amount of browning. There were three groups of amino acids: (i) high browning: the L-amino acids lysine, glycine, tryptophan and tyrosine; (ii) intermediate browning: the L-amino acids proline, leucine, isoleucine, alanine, hydroxyproline, phenylalanine, methionine, valine, and the amides L-glutamine and L-asparagine; (iii) low browning: the L-amino acids histidine, threonine, aspartic acid, arginine, glutamic acid and cysteine. The efficiency of the sugars decreased respectively: α–lactose, D-ribose, D-fructose, D-glucose. Glucose would be the common sugar present from cellulose breakdown of paper fibres and is the least effective in melanoidin production.

Hayashi and Namiki (1986) also examined the mechanism of melanoidin formation in the Maillard reaction. They showed that the higher the pH, the greater the browning. High temperatures were used, i.e. boiling water, 90°C and 80°C and the sugar/β–alanine system.

Interestingly, Sirianuntapiboon *et al.* (1988) discussed the use of fungal mycelium to adsorb melanoidin from molasses waste water. The melanoidin is adsorbed to living mycelium. The mycelium was autoclaved, to kill the fungus, then washed with an alkaline solution to release the adsorbed melanoidin. Maximum adsorption occurred with pretreatments of 0.1 N sodium hydroxide or 0.1 M buffer (pH 7).

Arai *et al.* (1990) tested a number of amino acids and sugar combinations in an effort to induce fox spots artificially by the formation of melanoidins. α–Aminobutyric acid, in combination with glucose, gave the most obvious fox-coloured spot which was fluorescent. They hypothesized that α–aminobutyric acid along with L-malic acid and glucose could be the main cause of fox spots.

Florian and Prescott (1996) have not been able to demonstrate, by nuclear magnetic resonance (NMR) analysis, the presence of melanoidins in an alkaline extract from 150-year old-fox spots.

18.2.4.3 Lipids and glycerol

Lipids and their breakdown products, fatty acids and glycerol, must also be present in fox spots. Conidia may have up to 50% dry weight of lipids and hyphae may contain stored lipids in vacuoles (Schmidt and Brody, 1976).

Lipids easily undergo auto-oxidation and the effects of this have been discussed in section 18.1.6.1. This destructive auto-oxidation of lipids may be the cause of the discolouration of the fungal structures as well as the discolouration in cellulosic fibres of fox spots (Florian, 1996a).

Under stress and low a_w many xerophilic fungi may produce glycerol in their cells (Griffin 1981; Hocking, 1986; Nobre and Da Costa, 1985). On the death of the fungus this remains to act as a humectant in this spot. Glycerol may increase the moisture content of the spot and act as an activator for conidial germination, which would explain why new fungi often grow on old fox spots (Arai, 1987).

The role of some of these metabolic products in causing the discoloration in fox spots still needs to be researched. Florian (1996a) has shown that the discolouration in irregular fox spots is in the fungal materials and in associated paper fibres. The fungal discoloration is alkaline soluble, but the discoloration in the paper fibres is insoluble. Many of the metabolic products mentioned above are water soluble and could be removed by conservation washing treatments. Consideration should be given to removing these metabolic products from materials that have recently become infested by fungal vegetative growth.

The fungal infestations of today could be the fox spots of the future.

18.2.5 **Chelated metals**

Fungi require trace elements for growth and have the ability to chelate most metals (e.g. iron, copper and zinc), which may be stored as a reserve for future translocation or to alleviate a toxic environment (Hughes and Poole, 1989). The metals are bonded to the cell wall of the hyphae.

The chitin–glucan complex in the hyphal cell wall acts as a chelating polymer; the metal is bound by simple anionic processes. The presence of melanin increases the chelating ability of the polymer.

Melanin in hyphal cell walls chelates metals (Gadd *et al.* 1990), and other pigments also incorporate metals (copper, zinc) into their structure.

Dead hyphae retain their biosorption ability. Mycelium wastes from the lemonade industry (and others) are used for biosorption of metallic wastes in polluted effluents and recovery of useable metals (Fourest and Roux, 1992; Hughes and Poole, 1989; Luef *et al.* 1991; Wales and Sager, 1990). Ironically, mycelium wastes have been made into wet-laid papers for chelation uses.

Historically, fox spots on paper have been associated with iron because of the rusty colour of the discoloration. Tang (1978) and Cain and Miller (1982) reviewed this early literature. They both have undertaken metal analysis of fox spots and stains. Tang (1978) found increased amounts of copper and iron in fox spots compared with the controls. They attributed the paper deterioration to the iron. Cain and Miller (1982) classified the stains. One class showed fragments of iron in the paper, however there were other stains which had an increase in iron over the background but did not show iron particles. They suggested that these were related to fungi. In both research projects the fungal presence in the spots was not determined. Arai (1987) and Arai *et al.* (1988) reported that there was no metal in old fox spots on hemp paper but it was present in fungal-induced spots. Florian (1996b) reported that in irregularly shaped, fox-coloured fungal spots in 150-year-old paper, there was no increase in iron over the background in the paper using EDX analysis. If fungal structures chelate iron from the paper they are growing on, there would be a small increase in the hyphae above the background level, but EDX analysis of fungal cell walls showed no increase. On the other hand, there were black circular spots with a particle in the centre of the spot that was 100% iron. There were no fungal structures associated with these spots.

The above information shows clearly that iron is not associated with the commonest fox spots, the rusty red, irregular, fungal fox spots. The rusty red colour in fox spots and the association of rusty red of iron oxide is an example of a mindset. There is no basis for this except the colour association.

In summary, the occasional particles of iron could come from the manufacturing process but there does not appear to be any iron associated with fox-coloured spots caused by fungi.

REFERENCES

Arai, H. 1993. Relationship between fungi and brown spots found in various materials. *Biodeterioration of Cultural Property, Proceedings of the 2nd International Conference, Yokohama, Japan, October 5–8*, pp320–336.

Arai, H. 1987. On the foxing causing fungi. *International Council of Museums Committee for Conservation, 8th Triennial Meeting, Sydney, Australia, September 6–11*, pp1165–1167.

Arai, H., N. Matsui, N. Matsumura and H. Murakita. 1988. Biochemical investigations on the formation mechanisms of foxing. *International Institute for Conservation. The Conservation of Far Eastern Art, Kyoto Congress, Japan, September 19–23*, pp11–12.

Arai, H., N. Matsumura and H. Murakita. 1990. Induced foxing by components found in foxed areas. *ICOM Committee for Conservation, 9th Triennial Meeting, Dresden, Germany, August 26–31*, pp801–803.

Aranyanak, C. 1995. Microscopic study of fungal growth on paper and textiles. *3rd International Conference on Biodeterioration of Cultural Property, Bangkok, Thailand, July 4–7*, pp42–55.

Ashoor, S.H. and J.B. Zent. 1984. Maillard browning of common amino acids and sugars. *Journal of Food Science*, 49:1206–1207.

Asmus, J.F. 1986. More light for art conservation. *Circuits and Devices Magazine*, 2(2):6–15.

Bartnicki-Garcia, S.B. 1968. Cell wall chemistry, morphogenesis, and taxonomy of fungi. In *Annual Review of Microbiology* (Eds. C.E. Clifton, S. Raffel and M.P. Starr), 22:87–108.

Beckwith, T.D., W.H. Swanson and T.M. Iiams. 1940. Deterioration of paper: the cause and effect of foxing. University of California, (L.A.) *Biological Sciences Publication*, 1(13):299–356.

Bell, A.A. and M.H. Wheeler. 1986. Biosynthesis and functions of fungal melanins. *Annual Review of Phytopathology*, 24:411–451.

Bertalan, S. 1994. Foxing. In *Paper Conservation Catalog*, 9th edition, American Institute of Conservation,13:1–39.

Bloomfield, B.J. and M. Alexander. 1967. Melanins and resistance of fungi to lysis. *Journal of Bacteriology*, 93(4):1276–1280.

Breccia Fratadocchi, M. A., R. Savoia, F. Minto and A. Breccia. 1972. Non-destructive analysis of fungus pigments on works of graphic art by spectroscopic technique. *Abstract. ICOM Committee for Conservation, Madrid*, ICOM report, 2317211.

Burnett, J.H. 1976. *Fundamentals in Mycology*. 2nd edition, Edwrad Arnold (Publishers) Ltd, London.

Burnett, J.H. and A.P.J. Trinci. 1979. *Fungal Walls and Hyphal Growth.* Cambridge University Press, London.

Cain, C.E. 1993. Foxing caused by inorganic factors. *Biodeterioration of Cultural Property, Proceedings of the 2nd International Conference, Yokohama, Japan, October 5–8*, pp278–291.

Cain, C.E. and B.A. Miller. 1982. Photographic spectral and chromatographic searches into the nature of foxing. *American Institute of Conservation*, Preprint (May), pp26–30.

Cain, C. and B.A. Miller. 1984. Proposed classification of foxing. *American Institute for Conservation, Book and Paper Group, 10th Annual Meeting*, Postprints, pp29–30.

Daniel, V.1988. The discoloration of paper on aging. *The Paper Conservator*, 12:93–100.

Edmond, P. and D. Horten-James. 1991. Enzymatic breakdown and decolorisation of black fungus embedded in acrylic paint: a progress report. *AICCM Bulletin*, 17(4):53–61.

Eusman, E. 1995. Tideline formation in paper objects: cellulose degradation at the wet–dry boundary. In *Conservation Research.* University Press of New England, pp11–27.

Florian, M-L.E. 1996a. The role of the conidia of fungi in fox spots. *Studies in Conservation*, 41(20):65–75.

Florian, M-L.E. 1996b. Characterization of foxing and other spots in archival books and the fungal role in foxing. *American Institute of Conservation, 24th Annual Meeting, Norfolk, June 10–16*, abstracts.

Florian, M.-L. and C. Preston, 1997. Analyses for melanoidins in fungal fox spots. (unpublished).

Florian, M.-L. and N. Purinton. 1995. Determination of location of stains in fungal spots and enzymatic removal of pigmented hyphae in paper. *3rd International Conference on Biodeterioration of Cultural Property, Bangkok, Thailand, July 4–7*, Preprints, pp255–266.

Florian, M.-L.E. and D. Dudley. 1976. The inherent fungicidal features of some paper conservation processes. *American Institute of Conservation, 4th Annual Meeting, Dearborn, Mich., May 20--June 1*, Preprint, pp41–47.

Fourest, E. and J. Roux. 1992. Heavy metal biosorption by fungal mycelium by-products: mechanisms and influence of pH. *Applied Microbiology and Biotechnology*, 37:399–403.

Gadd, G.M., D.J. Gray and P.J. Newby. 1990. Role of melanin in fungal biosorption of tributyltin chloride. *Applied Microbiology and Biotechnology*, 34:116–121.

Gallo, F. and G. Pasquariello. 1989. Foxing: ipotesi sull'origine bologica. *Bollettino de l'Instituto Centrale per la Patologia del Libro*, 43:139–176.

Gallo, F. and M. Hey. 1986. Foxing – a new approach. *The Paper Conservator*, 12:101–102.

Gooday, G.W. 1981. Biogenesis of sporopollen in fungal spore walls. In *The Fungal Spore*, Eds G. Turian and H.R. Hohl. Academic Press, London, pp487–505.

Griffin, D.H. 1981. *Fungal Physiology*. Wiley-Interscience publication.

Hawks, C. and W.F. Rowe. 1988. Deterioration of hair by airborne microorganisms: implications for museum biological collections. *Biodeterioration 7: Seventh International Biodeterioration Symposium, Cambridge, UK, September 6–11*, pp461–465.

Hayashi, T. and M. Namiki. 1986. Role of sugar fragmentation in an early stage browning of amino-carbonyl reaction of sugar with amino acid. *Agricultural Biology and Chemistry*, 8:1965–1970.

Hocking, A.D. 1986. Effects of water activity and cultural age on the glycerol accumulation of five fungi. *Journal of General Microbiology*, 132:269–275.

Hughes, M.N. and R.K. Poole. 1989. *Metals and Micro-organisms*. Chapman and Hall, London.

Karel, M. 1978. Stability of low and intermediate moisture foods. In *Water Activity: Influences on Food Quality*, Eds L.B. Rockland and G.F. Stewart, Academic Press, New York, pp643–674.

Kowalik, R., I. Sadurska and E. Czerwinska. 1962. Microbiological deterioration of old books and manuscripts – remedies. *Bolletino de l'Instituto Centrale perla Patologia del Libro*, Rome, 21(3-4):116–151.

Korytowski, W. and T. Sarna. 1990. Bleaching melanin pigments. *Journal of Biological Chemistry*, 265(21):12410–12416.

Kost, H. 1989. *CRC Handbook of Chromatography. Plant Pigments. Vol. 1, Fat-Soluble Pigments*. CRC Press Inc., Boca Raton, Florida.

Kuo, M.J. and M. Alexander. 1967. Inhibition of the lysis of fungi by melanins. *Journal of Bacteriology*, 94(3):624–629.

Lee, M.W. 1988. *Prevention and Treatment of Mould in Library Collections With an Emphasis on Tropical Climates*. UNESCO, PG1-88/WS/9, Paris.

Linterink, F., H.J. Parek and W. Smit. 1991. Foxing stains and discoloration of leaf margins and paper surrounding printing ink: elements of a complex phenomenon in books. *The Paper Conservator; Journal of the Institute of Paper Conservation*, 15:45–52.

Luef, E., T. Prey and C.P. Kubicek. 1991. Biosorption of zinc by fungal mycelial wastes. *Applied Microbiology and Biotechnology*, 34:688–692.

Makes, F. 1984. Damage to old bookbinding in the Skokloster Library. In *Skokloster Studies, Skokloster Castle No. 17. Nordisk tidskrift for bok – och biblioteksvasen* 71:33–57.

Meynell, G.G. and R.J. Newsam. 1978. Foxing, a fungal infection of paper. *Nature*, 274(5670): 466–468.

Muzzarelli, R.A.A. 1977. *Chitin*. Peragon Press.

Neil A.P. 1987. Synthesis of natural fungal pigments. Dissertation, University of Nottingham, UK. (*Diss. abstr. Int. B*. 1988, 49(5), 1529 avail Univ. microfilms Int., order no. BRD-81679, 190pp).

Nobre, M.F. and M.S. Da Costa. 1985. The accumulation of polyols by the yeast *Debaryomyces hansenii* in response to water stress. *Canadian Journal of Microbiology*, 31:1061–1064.

Nygam, N. 1995. Hair perforation leading to its deterioration by some keratinophilic fungi in Indian Museums. *3rd International Conference on Biodeterioration of Cultural Property, Bangkok, Thailand, July 4–7*, Preprints pp33–36.

Nyuksha, Y.P. 1960. A microscopic study of paper pigmented by the fungus *Gymnoascus setosus*. *Mikrobiologiya*, 29(1):133–136.

Potgieter, H.J. and M. Alexander. 1966. Susceptibility and resistance of several fungi to microbial lysis. *Journal of Bacteriology*, 91(4):1526–1532.

Rast, D.M., H. Stussi, H. Hegnauer, and L.E. Nyhlen. 1981. Melanins. In *Fungal Spore: Morphogenetic Controls*, Eds G. Turian and H.R. Hohl, Academic Press, pp508–527.

Schmit, J.C. and S. Brody. 1976. Biochemical genetics of *Neurospora crassa* conidial germination. *Bacteriology Review*, 40(1):1–41

Sharpely, J.M. and M.E. King. 1972. Laboratory analysis of problems in papermakers' felts. In *Biodeterioration of Materials*, Vol. 2, Eds A. H. Walters and E.H. Hueck-van Der Plas. Wiley, New York, pp1161–1167.

Sirianuntapiboon, S., P. Somchai, P. Sihanonth, P. Atthasampunna and S. Ohmomo. 1988. Microbial decolorization of molasses waste water by mycelia sterilia D90. *Agricultural Biology and Chemistry*, 52(2):393–398.

Strzelczyk, A., and M. Pronobis-Bobowska. 1993. Characteristics of foxing stains on paper historic objects. In *Scientific Bases of Conservation and Restoration of Works of Art and Cultural Property Items*. Uniwersytet Mikolaja Kopernika w Toruniu, Torun, Poland, pp327–333.

Szczepanowska, H. 1986. Biodeterioration of art objects on paper. *The Paper Conservator*, 10:31--39.

Szczepanowska, H. and C.M. Lovett. 1992. A study of the removal and prevention of fungal stains on paper. *Journal of the American Institute of Conservation*, 31(2):147–160.

Tang, L. 1978. Determination of iron and copper content in 18th and 19th century books by flameless atomic adsorption spectroscopy. *Journal of American Institute for Conservation*, 17(2):19–32.

Valentin, N. 1986. Biodeterioration of library materials disinfection methods and new alternatives. *The Paper Conservator*, 10:40--45.

Wales, D.S. and B.F. Sagar. 1990. Recovery of metal ions by microfungal filters. *Journal of Chemical Technology and Biotechnology*, 49:345–355.

Weete, J.D. 1980. *Lipid Biochemistry of Fungi and Other Organisms*. Plenum Press, New York.

Willetts, H.J. and S. Bullock. 1992. Developmental biology of sclerotia. *Mycological Research*, 96(10):801–816.

Wojtczak, M. 1990. Proby usuwania zaplamien grzybowych z papieru zabytkowego. *Acta Universitatis Nicolai Copernici*. 15:114--126. English abstract BCIN Number 160769.

Zikakis, J.P. 1984. *Chitin, Chitosan and Related Enzymes*. Academic Press, Inc.,Orlando.

Zomer, E., A.B. Saada, D. Klein, A. Todar and Z. Er-el. 1985. Enzymatic degradation of fungal cell walls with respect to polysaccharide composition. In *Chitin in Nature and Technology*, Eds. R. Muzzarelli, C. Jeuniaux and G.W. Gooday. Plenum Press, New York, pp249–251.

19

Eradication and Control of Fungal Activity

The introduction to the biology of fungi suggests that there may be methods to kill hydrated conidia and growing hyphae, such as freezing and heat treatment, chemicals, altered atmospheric gases and radiation. But it is emphasized that the best approach is prevention, by protecting surfaces from becoming contaminated, controlling moisture in materials and relative humidity (RH) to prevent growth and avoiding treatments which may activate conidia. However, disasters do happen, especially those involving water.

19.1 FREEZING WATER-SOAKED MATERIALS FOR MICRO-ORGANISM CONTROL

19.1.1 Effects of storage at freezing temperatures used to control micro-organism growth on water-soaked organic materials

19.1.1.1 Introduction

Water-soaked materials are vulnerable to micro-organism activity. Conidia of fungi are airborne and fall on all surfaces. When the surface is wet or damp they may germinate and growth can occur within 48 hours at optimum temperatures. Growth can occur over a wide range of temperatures, from 30°C to −4°C (see fungal growth section 17.2). Bacteria and yeast readily grow in free water. The purpose of freezing water-soaked objects is for temporary storage, to prevent biological and chemical deterioration until the objects can be dried. What is the effect of sub-zero temperatures on micro-organisms and the water-soaked materials?

When disasters have occurred and library and museum collections have had extensive water damage from floods, storms and fire extinguishing, commonly, because of the enormity of the problem, the collections have been removed from the site and stored under freezing conditions until methods have been devised and money found for treatment.

We assume that storage under freezing temperatures prevents fungal growth and chemical deterioration until the materials can be treated and dried. But is this in fact the case? Poulsen and Lindelv (1978) have discussed accelerated chemical reactions in frozen food, and report that at below 0°C, besides oxidation and auto-oxidation, enzymatic reactions may continue and fungal and bacterial activity may occur as well. Does this also happen in water-soaked organic materials during storage at freezing temperatures?

Freezing water-soaked heritage objects is necessary in preparation for freeze-drying. In freeze-drying, the wet materials must be frozen first. Then the ice is removed by sublimation and the frozen materials become dry. What is the effect of ice crystals in the organic materials of heritage objects?

Before going into these subjects in detail, a description of the water-soaked material and the effects of the freezing process on it is essential.

19.1.1.2 The nature of water-soaked organic material

The structural components of plants and animals are commonly used as materials because of their structural strength. These include skin, parchment, leather, bone, wool, wood and wood fibres, and plant leaves, roots and fibres.

These tissues, when alive, have a moisture content of up to 80% dry weight, and approximately 70% of this is free water. When the tissue, for example skin, is made into leather and dried, it looses all the free water; only the multi-layer and bound water remains. This remaining water, on average, is between 5 and 12% equilibrium moisture content (EMC) of the dry weight of the leather. The amount of this water will depend on the kind of leather, changes due to fabrication and treatments, deterioration, and the environment.

In the initial drying process the cells and fibres have collapsed and shrunk, and inherent and added chemicals have become concentrated and precipitated. What happens when this dry material becomes water soaked?

19.1.1.2.1 Water-soaked leather

Leather is similar to a felted material except that the protein (collagen) fibres are endless, giving it great wet strength. If by accident leather becomes wet, it will readily adsorb water. The water will cause the protein (collagen) fibres to swell and this is the first stage of solubilization. Water will separate the fibres by attaching to their hydrophilic surfaces and will dissolve the soluble, inherent and added, chemicals. The hydrated protein fibres become vulnerable to bacterial digestion and chemical reactions.

Dry skin, leather and parchment, all composed of collagen fibres, imbibe large amounts of water and swell in all directions because of their fibrous structure. Leathers, because of the cross-linkage effect of the tanning process on the protein molecules, will adsorb less water than skin and parchment. Depending on the state of deterioration, some hydrated protein may dissolve into the solution and some may shrink at room temperature. The water solution in the water-soaked leather will contain water-soluble protein, tannage, salts, acids, etc. This protein solution may support micro-organism growth. Fungal conidia commonly contaminate all surfaces and easily germinate on wet or damp leather surfaces. Water-soaked skin, leather and parchment heritage objects are often frozen, prior to drying treatment, to prevent this growth.

19.1.1.2.2 Water-soaked textiles

Some water-soaked woven textiles, made of natural and adsorbent synthetic fibres, adsorb large amounts of water because of the large amount of hydrophilic surfaces of the fibres. Deteriorated, fragile textiles can tear with the weight of water or stretch dramatically. The fibres of natural textiles differ in their structure and chemicals, for example wool, mainly keratin protein, is a cellular structure, whereas cellulose cotton fibres are individual cells.

Textiles are notorious for collecting dust on their surface. In the dust are a multitude of conidia which can germinate on and in the damp textile. Many fungi associated with textiles produce black spots which are almost impossible to remove, therefore prevention of fungal growth is imperative. Water-soaked textiles are commonly stored frozen, prior to drying treatment, to prevent biodeterioration.

19.1.1.2.3 Water-soaked paper

Paper, because of its felted fibre structure, has a large amount of hydrophilic surfaces which can adsorb large amounts of water. During paper making, the paper is dried under pressure, burnished or carded to compact the surface fibres. When the paper becomes wet, water is attracted to the surfaces of all the fibres. This causes separation and swelling of the compacted fibres, thus the paper loses its compactness, even after drying. The water solution will contain soluble chemicals used in paper making or treatments. These may act as nutrients or activators for fungi and also may cause problems, such as gluing pages together, on drying. Paper-like textiles are covered with conidia which can germinate and produce fungal growth, often in a variety of colours. Yeasts and bacteria can also develop in free water in paper. Only a few of the micro-organism are capable of damaging the cellulose fibres. In disasters, because of the large volume of material, papers are commonly stored frozen, prior to the drying treatment, to prevent micro-organism development.

19.1.1.2.4 Water-soaked wood

Dry wood, especially with varnished or coated surfaces, is not a readily adsorbent material and will not become water-soaked by surface water unless exposed for a long period of time. Thin veneer or carved wood that has become wet requires immediate special drying treatment. Dry wood can adsorb up to 28% of its dry weight from water vapour in the air, anything above this comes from wetting, i.e. free water. Some wood species have very porous wood which becomes wet more easily than non-porous, dense wood. Surface fungi may develop only if the surface remains wet for over 48 hours.

It takes years for wood to become water-logged. The cell walls become swollen and there is free water in the cell lumen. Water-logged wood is often treated by freeze-drying because this method prevents collapse and distortion during the drying process.

19.1.1.2.5 Water-soaked plant parts

Plant tissue, such as leaves and stems that are used, for example, in basketry, textiles and paper, is flattened or dried under stress when fabricated for weaving. If water-soaked, the porous tissue adsorbs the water readily, which releases the stress and flattening. Unfortunately, when it dries it has no 'memory' of how it was before wetting and does not regain its original flattened surface.

Water-soaked objects made from these materials are usually treated immediately to prevent as much of this distortion as possible. Conidia on surfaces and in the crevices of the weave can germinate, but because the materials are thin they can be rapidly dried at room temperature. The drying will prevent subsequent fungal growth. Freezing of water-soaked objects made from plant parts is not recommended.

19.1.1.3 Does ice form in water-soaked materials stored under freezing temperatures?

The storage temperature will determine if ice is formed. It is surprising that at 0 to –4°C very little water in materials actually freezes. If ice forms there may still be water present and this unfrozen water can support micro-organism activity even down to –7°C. In frozen beef at –30°C, only 85% of the water is frozen. In bread crumbs with a larger surface area and lower moisture content, only 65% of the water is frozen (Poulsen and Lindelv, 1978). In fresh collagen samples with 45–60% water, the water did not freeze at temperatures as low as –50°C (Dehl, 1970). There are two reason for this: free water in fine capillaries below 30mm in diameter does not freeze (Horne 1969), and the unfrozen water has a solute concentrate prevents freezing, similar to antifreeze. The water in the capillaries is physically altered and is similar to molecularly bound water which cannot freeze. In organic materials some of the compact tissue organization is changed by fabrication methods, and there will be more and bigger spaces between fibres or cells for ice formation. There is no conservation research that reports if ice is formed when water-soaked organic materials of heritage objects are subjected to freezing. We assume that in fine capillaries in the organic materials the water may not freeze, but that in large spaces the free water will freeze. Some water may not freeze at all. The temperatures of the freezing storage unit may range from about –4 to –20°C.

19.1.1.4 Do ice crystals cause damage?

Ice is extremely strong due to the double hydrogen bonds in the ice crystal structure. We are all familiar with water freezing in glass bottles and causing them to break, the force of the frost front lifting cement or the frost splitting of trees. The amount of expansion of water upon freezing is given as approximately 8.5%. These same forces are present during the freezing of wet organic materials.

When ice does form during frozen storage or freeze-drying, the large hexagonal crystals are formed. As was discussed under lethal effects on cells (section 12.1.12), these crystals can pierce cell membranes and organelles. Even if small crystals are formed they will, over time, change to large hexagonal forms. Ice crystallization is a time-dependent phenomenon.

The food we freeze in our chest freezers can be damaged by expansion, as well as ice spears, which can make holes of up to 30mμ in diameter in cells. This causes cells to leak when thawing. In the food processing industry and in cryobiology specific methods of freezing, using cryoprotectors (adding glycerol or sorbitol solutions) and flash freezing (using liquid nitrogen), have been designed to prevent ice crystal and expansion damage as well as the concentration effects. Unfortunately, cryoprotectors and flash freezing cannot be used with water-soaked heritage materials. The blast-freezer – simply a rapid cooling chamber and used in the food industry to obtain a freezing core temperature of food rapidly in order to reduce micro-organism growth and the size of the ice crystals – could be applied to freezing water-soaked heritage materials, but research is necessary.

19.1.1.5 Do chemical reactions occur in frozen materials?

We rarely think about chemical deterioration of water-soaked materials. Our main concern is usually what we can see, the fungal activity. The aqueous solution in the water-soaked material may contain inherent proteins, carbohydrates and chemicals used in fabrication, such as tannins, alkalines or acids. Water can increase the rates of chemical reactions.

Freezing is more than just lowering the temperature. As a result of the removal of water during freezing, the increased concentration of solutes and the possible shift in the pH may increase some reactions (Potthast *et al.*, 1975; Poulsen and Lindelv, 1978). Certainly, some chemical reaction rates are reduced by lowering the temperature, but freezing may also increase some rates.

Lipid oxidation is a powerful chemical reaction which produces very destructive peroxides. Lipid oxidation occurs when materials are frozen and increases with decrease in temperature (Golblith *et al.*, 1975, 1975, 1980) and decrease in water activity. Poulsen and Lindelv (1978) reported that the rate of reaction was greater at –20°C than at 0°C and almost equal to that at 20°C. Even at extremely low temperatures around –130°C, auto-oxidation of lipids occurs, which releases high-energy radicals that deteriorate proteins (Karel and Young, 1978).

19.1.1.6 Summary

The purpose of this section is to describe what happens in wet materials when they are frozen for the purpose of limiting micro-organism growth, not to examine suitability of this treatment in reference to conservation treatment standards. There are many other issues that have to be investigated such as the method of drying after freezing, i.e. air-drying, freeze-drying (with and without vacuum) and heat drying. For example, in frozen water-soaked paper there will be the loss of the smooth carded or pressure treated surface, as well as the expansion of freezing and ice crystals separating the fibres. If this material is freeze-dried the expanded size will remain and require more space for storage than was originally needed. It is possible to dry frozen material by sublimation without vacuum. Unfortunately, it is beyond the scope of this book to discuss these treatments.

Evaluating the whole process on heritage object material is complex. There is some pertinent literature which can help. Dawley (1993) investigated the conservation freezing treatments of clean, new, wet and dry wool. The evaluation includes scanning electron microscopy, tensile strength, extension at break, regain ability, solubility and morphology. She reported no change, in both wet and dry new wool, after cyclic and continuous freezing at –25°C for up to 60 days. Flyate and Grunin (1974) reported that frozen cellulose, when thawed, produced a paper which has low mechanical strength and increased adsorbancy as a result of ice damage.

The information on freezing water-soaked materials is presented, also, to clarify the differences between: freezing dry materials, (see 12.1.2), and freeze-drying frozen materials.

19.1.2 Freeze-drying water-soaked materials of heritage objects for micro-organism control

19.1.2.1 The basic steps in the freeze-drying process

Freeze-drying is a method of drying wet materials to prevent evaporative stress and internal differential drying rates which result in shrinkage, crinkling, collapse, warping and other distortions. Parker (1989) and Waters (1979) discussed its use with water-damaged library materials. Florian (1990) and Hower (1979) discussed its influence on natural history specimens.

The procedures of freeze-drying may vary in parameters but the following basic steps are involved. The initial step is to freeze the material. The frozen material is placed in a vacuum chamber at a temperature which will retain the frozen state. The material is usually associated with a heat source to supply heat for sublimation. Somewhere in the system there is a condensing surface that is held at a lower temperature than the frozen material. The vapour pressure of the ice in the material is greater than that on the colder condenser surface, thus the sublimed water vapour will diffuse from the material to the condenser surface. The ice is removed from the condenser surface by some means of thawing. This diffusion process is slow and can be increased in speed by using a vacuum, which allows freer water molecule movement. Fry (1984), Smith (1984) and Schmidt (1985) described equipment used for freeze-drying artifact materials.

In preparation for freeze-drying, the usual method of placing the materials in a freezer will not prevent the damaging hexagonal ice crystals from forming. In freeze-drying by direct sublimation drying, ice crystals which connect with each other on the free surface of the material are required. When the frozen object is in the functioning chamber the sublimation front moves from the outside of the material inward. This means that the outer layer of the material is continually being dried. The disadvantage of this is that bound water will be lost in the outer material. Even if materials are removed before they are completely dry, this outer surface may still have lost bound water and the inner material will hold its original water content.

Sublimation allows water to be removed without the effects of evaporative forces which can cause collapse of structures and distortion; however, the loss of bound water is a damaging process. In thick materials, sometimes this front becomes impermeable or case-hardened, and the centre does not dry or takes an inordinately long time to dry.

19.1.2.2 Physical changes in material due to freeze-drying

Materials are unnaturally porous after freeze-drying. The pores are the spaces that were occupied by ice crystals (Meryman, 1966). The material has an increased surface area and the wetting ability of the material is decreased. These changes are reflected in the change in regain ability of the materials.

Wolf *et al.* (1972) showed that the hysteresis curve (difference in adsorption and desorption) is altered after freeze-drying to different degrees for specific food types (apple, pork, rice). They also showed that with increased storage time there was a decrease in sorption ability. Kapsalis (1978 and Regier and Tappel, 1956) showed a decrease in moisture content of freeze-dried foods after storage.

In assessment of the physical characteristics of freeze-dried food products (Kapsalis *et al.* 1970), archaeological wood and biological specimens, brittleness is always mentioned. Freeze-dried meat, besides being porous, is light in weight and brittle, similar to balsawood. These changes are a result of ice damage, as well as freeze-drying, which cause the loss of bound water. It is bound water that gives the plasticity to organic polymers, such as cellulose, collagen and myosin.

Colloidal materials (adhesives, gelatine films) may be disrupted because of loss of bound water (Blanchard, 1940; Lea and Hawke, 1952). Tests on freeze-drying wet photographic materials showed that the best method of drying wet photographic films was to air-dry without freezing (Hendriks and Lesser, 1983). Films that had been freeze-dried showed loss of density and loss of gloss which can be explained by loss of bound water and colloidal disruption. On the other hand, freeze–thaw cycling of dry, motion picture film did not cause any changes (Kopper and Bard,1985).

19.1.3 The effect of sub-zero temperatures on the growth of the micro-organisms

19.1.3.1 The effects of storage at sub-zero temperatures

Even below 0°C micro-organisms will grow (see 17.2.3.2). Experimentation on frozen food showed that growth of some bacteria did occur at −5°C on unfrozen media but it took several months to show visible increases. Also, some fungi were reported to grow at −7°C as long as the substrate was not frozen (Haines, 1934).

The limiting factor for growth is the water activity (a_w). This is calculated as the ratio of the vapour pressure of the water in the material to that of pure water under the same conditions, thus the range of a_w is 1.0 to 0.0. Vapour pressure is influenced by temperature, solute concentration and the physical state of the water as described below.

The water activity of the three physical states of water varies. Wolf *et al.* (1972) reported the following: a_w of 0.3 for water bound in a monomolecular site, a_w of 0.3–0.7 for water in a multi-layer region, and a_w above 0.7 for free water. The water activity is important in that it governs moisture hysteresis (adsorption and desorption rate and amount), chemical activity and micro-organism growth.

Only water in the free or condensed state above approximately 0.75 a_w, will support growth (Poulsen and Lindelv, 1978).

Lowering the temperature lowers the water vapour and the water activity and thus limits growth. Also, ice formation withdraws free water and increases the solute concentration, which lowers the water activity and limits growth.

Free water in materials at just below 0°C may not be frozen because it may be held in capillaries in the condensed state, or because the solutes present will lower the freezing point of the solution.

The significance of this in reference to micro-organism growth is if wet materials are stored at below 0°C for a prolonged period, the temperature must be low enough to stop or prevent growth. Certainly, the rate of growth and metabolic activity is reduced by low temperature, and maybe this is all we have been striving for in the past, but the goal should be to limit or stop growth. Growth can be stopped in storage at −20°C, which is a common storage temperature for frozen foods; but at this temperature, ice damage of the water-soaked materials probably occurs.

19.1.3.2 The effects of freeze-drying on micro-organisms

It has been reported (Mazur, 1968) that freeze-drying is more injurious to fungi than freeze-thawing because of the loss of bound water. Also, the fluctuation of temperature on heating the material during freeze-drying increases the lethal effect. Vegetative yeast cells and fungal hyphae are both vulnerable to the freezing of water and few survive freeze-drying. This process will greatly reduce the population size, but some cells may survive.

There is nothing in the literature about a decreased vulnerability of freeze-dried food to insect attack. In the author's experience, psocids have been observed to live on the legs of freeze-dried taxidermy, bird specimens and sea otters on exhibit.

19.1.4 Summary

Often very little water is frozen in water-soaked organic materials at temperatures just below 0°C. A temperature of −4°C will support micro-organism growth if the water in the materials is not frozen. When the water is frozen, the growth of the micro-organisms is limited. At temperatures close to −20°C the freezing and thawing conditions normally used will kill the actively growing hyphae and some hydrated spores. This will reduce the micro-organism population but will not eradicate it. Dry spores are resistant to freezing.

The freezing of water-soaked organic materials causes expansion and damage from ice crystals. Chemical reactions may occur in unfrozen supercooled water.

Freeze-drying is a method of drying frozen, water-soaked materials which prevents evaporative stress and differential drying rates that cause crinkling, collapse, warping and other distortions. However, this method causes loss of bound water and morphological and physical changes, such as brittleness, increase in size and porosity and low regain. Micro-organisms rarely survive freeze-drying.

The vacuum, or decrease in pressure, does not cause any effects on materials, but the rapid removal (boiling) of water and gases may cause physical damage to the materials.

The loss of bound water cannot be prevented during sublimation of frozen materials and causes brittleness of material.

The materials, after freeze-drying, maintain the same morphology as the frozen state, but are 8.5% larger in volume than the original. The areas where the ice was present remain as voids and make the material more porous, with increased surface area and decreased regain ability.

Freeze-drying causes physical strength changes, such as brittleness, moisture regain changes and colloids (adhesives, photographic films) may be disrupted as a result of loss of bound water.

The literature on freezing of fungi suggests that initial freezing will cause death to a large percentage of a population and subsequent freeze-drying will cause further death. If materials are heavily infested by fungi this process will decrease the size of the population, but some cells may still survive.

This review is not intended to give specific advice. Relevant information is presented for each specific situation, which will assist in making logical decisions.

19.2 ADVANTAGES AND DISADVANTAGES OF REFRIGERATION AT APPROXIMATELY 4°C

Placing wet materials in refrigeration at above 0°C is done for temporary storage of the wet materials until their dehydration and cleanup can be arranged. The only advantage is that it reduces the rate of growth of fungi. Fungi will grow slowly under refrigeration and often because they are under stress they produce black pigmented hyphae as well as coloured metabolic products in the material. The black hypae are very difficult if not impossible to remove from textiles and paper.

19.3 DEHYDRATION AT ROOM TEMPERATURE OR HIGHER

This is probably the best way to stop fungal activity. Dehydration stops and prevents growth of mycelia, germinating conidia and many hydrated conidia. Temperatures above 40°C are lethal to most hydrated states of fungi.

The aspect of dehydration that presents problems is the dimensional changes that occur with rapid dehydration; slow drying is usually recommended with delicate fragile objects. One approach to overcome this problem is drying under constraint. For example, in drying a water-logged wood fish hook, the hook was bound by thread to ridged polyethylene, cardboard mimicking its shape, and this in turn was attached to a piece of wood. On air drying, the delicate hook retained its water-logged orientation. There was some shrinkage of the wood but no distortion of shape. Another example is with water-soaked books. The hydrated books were left on the shelves. They had increased in volume because of the water soaking and were tightly shelved. Rapid dehydration of the room resulted in dehydration of the books *in situ* and under constraint, preventing fungal activity, and warping and cockling of the book and its paper. A further example is water-soaked garments from a leaky roof. The wet garments were laid on new sheets of white blotting paper. The blotters were removed as soon as they were soaked. The garments dried rapidly without conservation problems.

It would be inappropriate to give advice on what can or cannot be dried in this manner. Each object must be assessed according to its conservation needs. However, dehydration should be carried out as soon as possible if it is the eradication method of choice.

19.3.1 Advantages and disadvantage of in situ dehydration at room temperature and higher without prior freezing or refrigeration

The advantages are that: dehydration stops growth and germination; temperatures between 30 and 40°C will kill most hydrated conidia and hyphae; it is a one-step method with no follow-up; and it eliminates moving the objects.

The disadvantage is that some objects may distort during the drying process, but these can be separated for special treatment.

19.4 ERADICATION BY FUNGICIDE TREATMENT: IS IT REALLY NEEDED, IS IT EFFECTIVE?

Chemical fungicides are still widely used, but with our understanding of the interaction of these chemicals with the materials of the artifacts and our concern for health issues we should always look for an alternative. Often treatments are applied without knowing if they are really needed. The following review related to leather reveals these problems.

There are many questions that need to be answered when considering chemical treatment: Is there a need for treatment? Is there a health hazard? What is its effect on the material of the object? Is it effective against conidia and vegetative growth? Is it a fungicide that kills or is it a fungistat that only stops growth? Some of these questions are answered below.

19.4.1 Advantages and disadvantages of the use of fungicidal chemicals and fumigants

There are many reports which suggest the use of fungicides for mould control on leather and parchment. Calan (1985) lists 30 fungicides used in conservation, reported in 34 reference papers covering the years 1945–1983. He also reported on tests of the effectiveness of 36 commercial fungicides used on wet chrome-tanned or vegetable-tanned commercial leather in storage.

Calan (1985) cautioned conservators that the fungicides used must be inert to the object and not interfere with subsequent treatment or research analysis, be safe to use and must be extractable; but this information is not available.

Another problem with using commercial products is the change in formulations over the years. One example is the use of the commercial spray called 'Lysol'. It was recommended by Florian in 1976 because at that time it contained orthophenol phenol and ethyl alcohol, but today 'Lysol' does not contain these same chemicals. The use of trade name products is also misleading; again with 'Lysol', the word lysol is a synonym for carbolic acid which was not present in the commercial product. Today we realize that the value of such commercial products may be in the clean-up of contaminated storage shelves and floors but not on artifacts. Even then, when they are used, if they are registered legally (by COSHH-UK [Control of Substances Hazardous to Health] in the UK, by EPA [Environmental Protection Agency] in the USA and by PCPA[Pest Control Products Act] in Canada) they must be used only according to label directions.

Another problem with the use of toxic chemicals is the health hazard to people using the chemicals, and subsequent use of the objects. The problems of past insecticides such as arsenic and *p*-dichlorobenzene (PDB) in dry skin preparations for natural history, and the DDT or lindane (as well as other residual chemicals) on objects, present a health hazard in the use of these collections today. Because of the large size of such collections, at the Royal British Columbia Museum all bird skins are alert-labelled according to WHMIS (Workplace Hazardous Materials Information System). The use of a fungicide makes the handling and cleaning of objects a health hazard.

Under selection of fungicides, Calan (1985) stated that the simplest way to prevent fungal attack is environmental control and that fungicidal protection is only needed when leather is to remain wet or at a high relative humidity for more than a few weeks. The above information on the numbers of fungicides and lack of information on material interaction and safety issues makes it obvious that controlling the moisture in the materials is the easiest approach.

19.4.2 The reason for using a fungicide or toxic chemical must be clear and there must not be an alternative method of treatment

Fungicides that are residual will kill organisms present on the material and protect it from re-contamination as long as the fungicide remains active. How long it remains active is difficult to determine. Most fungicides do not have a residual effect and do not protect the material from reinfestation after the initial treatment.

The reason for treatment is usually to stop micro-organism activity, but this can be done simply by the reduction of the moisture content of the materials. If the materials have to be exposed to repeated high moisture increases in the future that will support micro-organism growth, a method of storage in a microenvironment should be investigated. A microenvironment may be as simple as storage with buffering materials, or as complex as storage in a container that is impermeable to water vapour.

Even with materials which have become wet and present an urgent need to prevent fungal growth, a fungicide is not the best treatment. The first thing that must be done is to decrease the moisture content of the material. Temperature extremes may assist in increasing the rate of drying or reducing the rate of growth and may even be lethal. The effect of the temperature extremes must be assessed as to their effect on the materials.

From the above it is clear that the best approach is to reduce the moisture in materials at ambient temperatures and as quickly as possible. Only if this cannot be done should alternative approaches be considered.

19.5 ERADICATION BY HIGH-ENERGY IRRADIATION

An excellent review of the use of gamma irradiation in the control of biodeterioration in artifact materials is presented by Wellheiser (1992). The description of the historical use, methods and procedures and results are reviewed. She reported that gamma radiation is effective in killing biodeteriorating organisms (insects, bacterial spores, fungal spores or conidia), but the doses required for kill cause physical changes in adhesives, cotton, leather, paper, parchment, pigments, plastics and wood. If the damage by the organisms will be greater than that of the treatment, it may be a last resort treatment. Again, it must be remembered that immediately after treatment the materials can be reinfested, thus prevention is the key to success. When materials are wet they are vulnerable to contamination by airborne conidia.

Gamma irradiation has been tested for killing fungal conidia on papers. After irradiation the paper was not more prone to reinfection, but there were some physical changes such as reduced resistance to breaking as a result of the irradiation levels required for complete disinfestation.

19.6 ERADICATION BY LOW OXYGEN ENVIRONMENTS

New approaches involving altered atmospheric gases have been suggested and widely used in the food industry. They commonly use gas- and water-impermeable plastic bags with the addition of an oxygen chelator. They are successful in extending the shelf-life of some high-moisture foods. If this technique was used with heritage objects it would be in a preventive role. By putting the object in its own microenvironment for storage it is possible to prevent potential conidial contamination and germination in environments in which fungal activity cannot be controlled (see also 17.2.4).

Its application to conservation still needs research. The anoxic environment influence on materials of objects is still unknown. The initial temperature increase from the chelator exothermic adsorption of oxygen must be guarded against. Water-vapour impermeable bags cannot be used with wet objects, also there is the inevitable problem of leaky bags. Thorough reviews of these methods are given by Brokerhof (1989), Craig (1986) and Wellheiser (1992),

REFERENCES

Blanchard, K.C. 1940. Water, free and bound. *Cold Spring Harbour Symposium on Quantitative Biology*, 8:1–8.

Brokerhof, A.W. 1989. *Control of Fungi and Insects in Objects and Collections of Cultural Value: 'State of the Art'.* Central Research Laboratory for Objects of Art and Science, Amsterdam.

Calan, C.N. 1985. *Fungicides Used on Leather.* The Leather Conservation Centre, Northampton.

Craig, R. 1986. Alternative approaches to the treatment of mould biodeterioration – an international problem. *The Paper Conservator*, 10:27–30.

Dawley, C.A. 1993. The Effect of Conservation Freezing Treatments on Selected Properties of Wool. MA Thesis, University of Alberta, Department of Human Ecology, Edmonton, Alberta, Canada.

Dehl, R.E. 1970. Collagen: mobile water content on frozen fibres. *Science*, 170 (3959):738–739.

Florian, M.-L.E. 1976. Fungicide treatment of eskimo skin and fur artifacts. *Journal of the International Institute of Conservation*, 2(1):10–17

Florian, M.-L.E. 1990. The effects of freezing and freeze-drying on materials of natural history specimens. *Collection Forum*, 6(2):45–52.

Flyate, D.M. and Y.B. Grunin. 1974. Influence of freezing on the state of bound water in cellulose fibres. *Zhurnal Prikladnoi Khimii*, 47(12):2739–2741.

Fry, M.F. 1984. An economy vacuum freeze-dryer for archaeological organic materials. *Vacuum*, 34(5):555–558.

Goldblith, S.A., L. Rey and W.W. Rothmayr. 1975. *Freeze Drying and Advanced Food Technology*. Academic Press, New York.

Haines, R.B. 1934. The minimum temperature of growth of some bacteria. *Biological Applications of Freeze-drying*, 34:277–282.

Hendriks, K.B. and B. Lesser. 1983. Disaster preparedness and recovery: photographic materials. *American Archivist*, 46(1):52–68.

Horne, R.A. 1969. *Marine Chemistry*. Wiley-Interscience, New York, pp.364.

Hower, R.O. 1979. *Freeze-drying Biological Specimens. A Laboratory Manual*. Smithsonian Institution Press, Washington, DC.

Kapsalis, J.G. 1978. Moisture sorption hysteresis. In *Water Activity: Influences on Food Quality*, Eds L.B. Rockland and G.K. Stewart. Academic Press, New York, pp 144–177.

Kapsalis, J.G., B. Drake and B. Johansson. 1970. Textural properties of dehydrated foods. Relationships with the thermodynamics of water vapor sorption. *Journal of Texture Studies*, 1(3):285–308.

Karel, M. 1975. Stability of low and intermediate moisture foods. In *Freeze Drying and Advanced Food Technology*, Eds S.A. Goldblith, L. Rey and W.W. Rothmayr. Academic Press, New York, pp651–663.

Karel, M. 1980. Lipid oxidation, secondary reactions, and water activity of foods. In *Autoxidation in Biological Systems*, Eds M.G. Simic and M. Karel. Plenum Press, New York pp191–193.

Karel, M. and S. Young. 1978. Auto-oxidation initiated reaction in food. In *Water Activity: Influences on Food Quality*, Eds L.B. Rockland and G.K. Stewart. Academic Press, New York, pp511–520.

Kopper, D.F. and C.C. Bard. 1985. Freeze/thaw cycling of motion-picture films. *Society of Motion Picture and Television Engineers Journal*, 94(8):826–827.

Lea, C.H. and J.C. Hawke. 1952. The influence of water on the stability of lipovitellin and the effects of freezing and of drying. *Biochemistry Journal*, 52:105–114.

Mazur, P. 1968. Survival of fungi after freezing and desiccation. In *The Fungi an Advanced Treatise, Vol. III. Fungal Populations*, Ed. G.C. Ainsworth. Academic Press, New York, pp325–394.

Meryman, H.T. 1966. Review of biological freezing. In *Cryobiology*, Ed. H.T. Meryman. Academic Press, London : New York, pp2–114.

Parker, A.E. 1989. The freeze-drying process. Some conclusions. *Library Conservation News*, 23:4–6,8.

Potthast, K., R. Ham and L. Acker. 1975. Enzyme reactions. In *Freeze Drying and Advanced Food Technology*, Eds S.A. Goldblith, L. Rey, and W.W. Rothmayr. Academic Press, New York, pp375–370.

Poulsen, P.K. and F. Lindelov. 1978. Acceleration of chemical reactions due to freezing. In *Water Activity Influences on Food Quality*, Eds L.B. Rockland and G.F. Stewart. Academic Press, New York, pp650–678.

Regier, L.W. and A.L. Tappel. 1956. Freeze-dried meat. IV. Factors affecting the rate of deterioration. *Journal of Food Research*, 21:640–649.

Schmidt, J.D. 1985. Freeze drying of historical cultural properties. *Technology and Conservation*, Spring:20–26.

Smith, R.D. 1984. Fumigation dilemma: more overkill or common sense? *The New Library Scene*, 3(6):1–3.

Waters, P. 1979. *Procedures for Salvage of Water-damaged Library Materials*. Library of Congress, Washington.

Wellheiser, J.G. 1992. *Nonchemical Treatment Processes for Disinfestation of Insects and Fungi in Library Collections*. K.G. Saur, Munich.

Wolf, M., J.E. Walker and J.G. Kapsalis. 1972. Water vapor sorption hysteresis in dehydrated food. *Journal of Agriculture and Food Chemistry*, 20(5):1073–1077.

20

Summary of Fungal Activity Prevention, Collection Recovery, Preparedness and some Disasters

20.1 PREVENTION

Prevention includes protecting the heritage objects from contamination by conidia and controlling the environment to prevent development of conidia which may be on or in the material. Any treatment must be assessed as to its influence on the fragility of an object and executed according to conservation standards. It is beyond the scope of this book to discuss this in detail. Refer to the code of ethics of conservation professional organizations and manuals on conservation standards.

When undertaking an aqueous treatment, effort should be made to keep the work area, solutions and tools sterile, and the wet surfaces protected from contamination after treatment (i.e. aseptic technique). It is impossible and unreasonable to try to eliminate contamination completely, but the goal is to prevent excessive and unnecessary contamination. The commonest types of infestation have been caused by contamination from dust, washing with contaminated solutions and association with mouldy materials.

The following list gives a few examples of preventive activities. It is certainly not complete, but it is a start and gives an awareness of the problems. It will also help in designing your personal manual on procedures for collection recovery and disaster planning.

20.1.1 Eliminate airborne conidia from surfaces of heritage objects – prevent contamination

1. Use protective dust covers for heritage objects in storage, when being moved and during use, i.e. for documentation, research, conservation, exhibit, etc. Clean dust covers regularly.
   For further information on dust deposition see Nazaroff and Cass (1991) and Nazaroff *et al.* (1990).
   The air quality, in reference to airborne viable conidia, is usually considered in regard to health hazards, but it also influences heritage objects. This subject is beyond the scope of this book, but a few significant works are listed in the references (Broder, 1994; Buttner and Stetzenbach, 1993; Clark, 1985; Kozak *et al.* 1980; Smid *et al.* 1989; Solomon, 1975; US Department of Labour, 1994; Wanner *et al.* 1993; World Health Organization, 1988).
2. Inexpensive positive-pressure equipment can be installed in display cases to prevent dust contamination (Byers and Thorp, 1990).
3. Eliminate surface conidia by vacuuming or dusting surfaces according to conservation standards. If a fan is used for drying it must be directed away from the wet surface not onto it.
4. Undertake regular maintenance of storage areas:
   - Keep shelves, cabinet tops, etc. free from dust
   - Use electrostatic cloths or damp rags which are disposed of after use
   - Vacuum floors; use built-in central vacuum system or normal vacuum with an extension tube from vacuum machine to exhaust outside the storage area. Use hepa filters in vacuum
5. Eliminate sources of conidia such as food and plants from storage or work area.
6. When possible separate offices and registration activities from storage areas.

20.1.2 Eliminate conidia in solutions and ancillary materials used in, on or adjacent to artifacts – prevent contamination

1. Use sterile aqueous solutions for cleaning and treatment. Many solutions can be made sterile by using a pressure cooker or by just boiling. Solutions can be sterilized by biological, medical or microbiological facilities in universities or research centres.
2. Sterilize organic compounds, e.g. starch, protein, adhesive grounds or adhesives. Don't use pastes that have been stored in the refrigerator for longer than a week. If they are mouldy keep them covered and dispose of them in closed containers.
3. Test commercially prepared dry powders or solutions for excessive fungal contamination before use. Many supplies may have this information. Commercially available dip sticks or swab test kits can be used. These are available from medical, biological and food technology supply companies. The commonest airborne contaminates, *Penicillium* and *Aspergillus*, would be the target species. Get advice on the appropriate test kit from the suppliers.
4. Test ancillary materials that will be used for backings or repairs for fungal contamination or dry-heat sterilize before use.

20.1.3 Prevent activation of conidia

1. Assess solutions used for treatments in regard to their activation ability; for example, any detergent is a conidial activator, are there alternatives?
   Chemicals reported in the literature (see section 16.5) to activate conidia are dilute solutions of alcohols, glycerol, surfactants, detergents and humectants, as well as heating for drying or curing.
2. Remove remnants of detergents or surfactants used for cleaning or washing.

20.1.4 Prevent germination of conidia

1. Prevent hydration of conidia: do not keep materials wet for a long period of time, i.e. 24 hours at room temperature, 48 hours under refrigeration.
2. Do not use aqueous solutions unless absolutely necessary.
3. Prevent high humidity and look out for microenvironments: assess humidification methods in regard to germination of conidia.
4. Use ancillary materials (storage boxes, paper, cloth) with low regain adjacent to artifacts.
5. Keep artifact surfaces free of organic nutrients, e.g. sugars, proteins.

20.1.5 Prevent vegetative growth

1. Control moisture in air and materials: use dehumidifier when needed; assess conservation treatments that use humectants (glycerol, PEG) or hydrophilic salts.
2. Eliminate nutrients and ions which stimulate growth, e.g. proline.
3. Keep in mind the influence of temperature on optimum growth and on moisture in materials.
4. Avoid microenvironments such as cold windows and humid sink areas.

20.2 COLLECTION RECOVERY – WET AND MOULDY OBJECTS, ARTIFACTS AND ARCHIVAL MATERIALS

When everything is covered with mould – what do you do?

20.2.1 Consider all health protection measures for staff

When an extensive infestation is located, the first thing to consider is the health hazard for the staff and to ensure that protective measures are used (see references listed under 20.1.1.)

Suggested procedures for staff are:

- First and foremost, persons with an allergic history or those who are asthmatic should not be involved with the project
- Protective particulate masks must be worn and, in extreme cases, disposable clothes and gloves should be used during any activity relating to the infestation
- Positive-pressure fume hoods are recommended for clean-up procedures
- Movement of uncovered contaminated materials must be prevented, cover with ramie or a water-permeable material.

20.2.2 Interpretation of the situation is required

- Is there a health hazard?
- Is the fungus still viable?
- Why is it there – environmental, treatment or other reason?

20.2.3 Document everything:

- The environmental parameters
- Eradication treatments used
- Fungal identification, if undertaken. When is identification needed (see section 15.4 and 15.6)?
- Detailed records of location and movement of objects.

20.2.4 Treatment/eradication methods: advantages and disadvantages

20.2.4.1 ADVANTAGES AND DISADVANTAGES OF REFRIGERATION

Advantages:
- Rates of growth and germination reduced
- Bid time for follow-up treatment; only temporary storage
- Some germinating conidia killed.

Disadvantages:
- Moisture in materials remains high, hydrates conidia
- Fungi under stress but viable, may produce heavy pigmentation
- Limited growth continues.

20.2.4.2 ADVANTAGES AND DISADVANTAGES OF FREEZING

Advantages:
- Growth stops
- Hydrated conidia, germinating conidia and vegetative growth killed
- Bid time for follow-up drying treatment; only temporary storage.

Disadvantages:
- Ice crystals may damage some object materials
- Moisture in materials remains high
- Dry conidia may be activated
- Material, after freezing, may increase in porosity and thickness

For further information, see section 19.1, freezing water-soaked materials for micro-organism control.

20.2.4.3 ADVANTAGES AND DISADVANTAGES OF IN SITU *DEHYDRATION AT ROOM TEMPERATURE AND HIGHER WITHOUT PRIOR FREEZING OR REFRIGERATION*

Advantages:
- Dehydration stops growth and germination
- Temperatures between 30 and 40°C will kill most hydrated conidia and hyphae
- One step, no follow-up drying treatment. Eliminates moving of objects.

Disadvantages:

- Some objects may distort during the drying process, but these can be separated for special treatment

For further information, see Brokerhof (1989), Craige (1986) and Wellheiser (1992).

20.2.4.4 ADVANTAGES AND DISADVANTAGES OF FREEZE DRYING

Advantages:

- Kills all stages of fungi
- One step, dehydrates wet materials
- Eliminates some movement of wet materials.

Disadvantages:

- Causes loss of bound water and normal regain of materials
- Ice crystals may cause structural damage to some materials
- Materials after treatment will increase in porosity and thickness
- Cleanup of dead fungal structures is still required after drying.

20.2.4.5 COMPARISON OF THE DIFFERENT PROCESSES OF COLLECTION RECOVERY

The following chart shows the comparison of different treatments of wet organic materials in the process of collection recovery.

The treatments are:

1 Immediate dehydrate at room temperature or up to 30° in situ:
2. Temporary storage in a refrigerator (4°C);
3. Temporary storage in freezer (below −10°C);
4. Freezing-drying;
5. Dehydrating above 40°C.

+ = Positive - = Negative feature +/- Not clear

Treatments	1	2	3	4	5
One step: no follow up drying	+	-	-	+	+
Eliminates moving of materials	+	-	-	-	-
Effect of treatment on fungus					
Kills dormant or activated conidia	-		+/-	+	+/-
Kills germinating conidia	+	+/-	+	+	+
Kills hyphae	+	-	+	+	+
Reduces rate of growth	+	+	+	+	+
Effect of treatment on material					
No dimensional change	-	-	-	-	-
No ice damage	+	+	-	-	+
No loss of bound water	+	+	+	-	+/-
Prevents coated papers sticking together	-	-	-	+	-

20.2.5 The aftermath – the clean-up

Once the objects are dry, vacuuming the surface to remove conidia and hyphae is usually recommended (Lee, 1988). The objects cleaned should be covered to protect them from recontamination. Waste materials and disposable garments used during drying or the clean-up should be contained in plastic bags and incinerated.

Surfaces of working areas should be wet-wiped to remove conidia. If possible, surface sterilize with 70% ethyl alcohol or household bleach (use according to label, about 0.5 % solution). If the infestation was extensive it is recommended that a person from the health profession should advise on clean-up procedures.

Research is needed to determine if, for example, metabolic products associated with growth should be removed.

20.3 PREPAREDNESS

The literature on preparedness for disasters is extensive, as is shown in the Shure (1992) bibliography on this topic. It is essential to design a plan to cope with a disaster and collection recovery before such an event. A small manual with essential procedures is a must. The following is a list of a few additional steps which can be taken in order to be prepared for a disaster:

- designate staff responsibilities
- emergency supplies should be prepared, e.g. masks, gloves, paper, cloths
- containers to move the objects should be ready, or a potential loan arranged
- consider leaving the objects *in situ* and proceeding with cleaning treatments *in situ*. The more the contaminated objects are moved, the greater the chance of contaminating clean areas and clean objects
- arrange for an alternative work area and familiarize the staff with the alternative space
- have portable vacuum equipment available, or arrange a potential loan
- prepare to keep full records of treatment, movement and location of objects.

20.4 SOME DISASTERS

We can always learn from the experiences of others.

The literature on disasters and subsequent collection recovery of wet materials is extensive, as is shown in the Shure (1992) bibliography on this topic. The purpose of reviewing someone else's experiences is to look at them in reference to the biology of the fungus and determine what is relevant in terms of collection recovery.

In personal discussions (Buchanan, 1994; Primanis, 1994) on collection recovery procedures after fire and subsequent water damage, a number of interesting observations surfaced which have reference to the biology of the fungi.

In the case of wet book and paper materials taken from the fire site and air-dried in another facility, fungal growth developed within 2 days after removal from the site, whereas those remaining on the site did not develop fungal growth after 2 weeks (Primanis, 1994).

In another disaster, books that were left unopened to dry did not develop fungi inside, but those that were fanned to dry supported fungal growth on the exposed pages (Primanis, 1994). This may be caused from contamination by viable airborne conidia.

With the Los Angeles Public Library fire (Buchanin, 1993), the extreme heat evolved in the fire was distributed throughout the library. The damp books that remained on site for up to 10 days did not develop mould. The damp materials were moved directly from the fire site to freezing facilities in closed boxes and were not opened until they were freeze-dried. During the time before moving the materials to freezing facilities, the building was aired by local San Anna winds with moderately high temperatures and extremely low humidity. Air quality tests of these winds show extremely low allergen levels, which suggest low conidia counts. This experience shows that the heat of the fire and/or the hot, dry, sterile air prevented fungal activity.

In a more recent disaster where winter ambient temperatures were extremely low and the wet materials were always cold, mould did not develop. However, in the Leningrad library fire, high heats were not present in many areas where books became wet, and mould developed on the materials in the library in a few days (16.8.2).

20.4.1 Summary

There are a number of features of these examples that will help us to deal with similar situations in the future. It will also make us think about every action taken and its consequence on the object, the staff and the fungus:

- It is suggested that heat-evolved toxic fumes, or oxygen depletion caused by fires may kill fungal conidia, and the books (etc.) are sterile but subsequently become contaminated during moving. Ideally, if drying could occur *in situ*, subsequent mould development may be prevented.
- It is shown that sterile, wet materials will develop mould if exposed to airborne, viable conidia, and the need to protect materials during moving to another facility for drying is suggested.
- It is suggested that the drying environment's temperature and relative humidity should be such as to immediately prevent germination and growth of conidia. This can be accomplished by reduced temperatures or rapid (within 48 hours) dehydration.
- Handling and moving the wet materials increases the chance of contamination by airborne conidia and is labour intensive and expensive, thus minimum handling must be the goal. Packing materials in suitable containers which prevent contamination and handling must be considered.
- Materials that are to be dried must be dried rapidly and must be protected from contamination of airborne conidia during the drying process. Sterile ramie and blotting paper are items which could be included in the disaster preparedness supplies.

REFERENCES

Broder, I. 1994. *Primer on Airborne Fungi and Other Microorganisms for Safety Officers of Human Resources Development, Labour Component.* Final report to Technical Services Division, Occupational Safety and Health Branch, Labour Component, Human Resources Development, Government of Canada, 29 March (1994), Contract: 1993, File YR82893-049.

Brokerhof, A.W. 1989. *Control of Fungi and Insects in Objects and Collections of Cultural Value: 'State of the Art'.* Central Research Laboratory for Objects of Art and Science, Amsterdam.

Buchanan, S.A. 1994. Personal communication. Associate Professor, University of Pittsburgh, Dept. of Library Science, Pittsburgh, USA.

Buttner, M.P. and L.D. Stetzenbach. 1993. Monitoring airborne fungal spores in an experimental indoor environment to evaluate sampling methods and the effects of human activity on air sampling. *Applied and Environmental Microbiology*, 59(1):219–226.

Byers, R. and V. Thorp. 1990. Positive pressurized display cases. *International Institute for Conservation- Canadian Group 16th Annual Conference*, Quebec City, May 25–27, Preprints, pp.34.

Clark, S. 1985. Every breath you take: indoor air quality in the library. *Canadian Library Journal*, 42(6):327–334.

Craig, R. 1986. Alternative approaches to the treatment of mould biodeterioration – an international problem. *The Paper Conservator*, 10:27–30.

Kozak, P.P., J. Gallup, L.H. Commins and S.A. Gillman. 1980. Currently available methods for home mould surveys. II. Examples of problem homes surveyed. *Annuals of Allergy*, 45(3):167–176.

Lee, M. 1988. *Prevention and Treatment of Mold in Library Collections with an Emphasis on Tropical Climates.* UNESCO, PG1-88/WS/9, Paris.

Nazaroff, W.W. and G.R. Cass. 1991. Protecting museum collections from soiling due to the deposition of airborne particles. *Atmospheric Environment*, Part A, General Topics, 25A(5–6):841–852.

Nazaroff, W.W., L.G. Salmon and G.R. Cass. 1990. Concentration and fate of airborne particles in museums. *Environmental Science Technology*, 25(1):66–77.

Primanis, O. 1994. Personal communication. Senior Administrative Conservator, Harry Ransom Humanities Research Centre, The University of Texas, Austin, Texas, USA.

Shure, S.E. 1992. *Disaster Prevention, Response, and Recovery: A Selected Bibliography.* The Technology Organization Inc., Boston Mass. USA.

Smid, T., E. Schokkin, J.S. Boleij and D. Heederik. 1989. Enumeration of viable fungi in occupational environments: a comparison of samplers and media. *American Industrial Hygiene Association Journal*, 50(5):235–239.

Solomon, W.R. 1975. Assessing fungus prevalence in domestic interiors. *Journal of Allergy and Clinical Immunology*, 56(3):235–242.

US Department of Labour, Occupational Safety and Health Administration. 1994. *OSHA Indoor Air Quality – Proposed Rule.* 29 CFR Parts 1910, 1915, 1926, and 1928, April 5, Washington DC, pp.15968.

Wanner, H.-U., A.P. Verhoeff, A. Colombi, B. Flannigan, S. Gravesen, A. Mouilleseaux, A. Nevalainen, J. Papadakis and K. Seidel. 1993. *Indoor Air Quality and its Impact on Man. Report No. 12. Biological Particles in Indoor Environments.* Commission of the European Communities, Brussels.

Wellheiser, J.G. 1992. *Nonchemical Treatment Processes for Disinfestation of Insects and Fungi in Library Collections.* K.G.Saur, Munich.

World Health Organization, Regional Office for Europe. 1988. *Indoor Air Quality: Biological Contaminants.* WHO Regional Publications, European Series No. 31, Copenhagen.

Index